The Economics of Ignorance and Coordination

NEW THINKING IN POLITICAL ECONOMY

Series Editor: Peter J. Boettke, *George Mason University, USA*

New Thinking in Political Economy aims to encourage scholarship in the intersection of the disciplines of politics, philosophy and economics. It has the ambitious purpose of reinvigorating political economy as a progressive force for understanding social and economic change.

The series is an important forum for the publication of new work analysing the social world from a multidisciplinary perspective. With increased specialization (and professionalization) within universities, interdisciplinary work has become increasingly uncommon. Indeed, during the 20th century, the process of disciplinary specialization reduced the intersection between economics, philosophy and politics and impoverished our understanding of society. Modern economics in particular has become increasingly mathematical and largely ignores the role of institutions and the contribution of moral philosophy and politics.

New Thinking in Political Economy will stimulate new work that combines technical knowledge provided by the 'dismal science' and the wisdom gleaned from the serious study of the 'worldly philosophy'. The series will reinvigorate our understanding of the social world by encouraging a multidisciplinary approach to the challenges confronting society in the new century.

Recent titles in the series include:

Anarchy, State and Public Choice
Edited by Edward Stringham

Humane Economics
Essays in Honor of Don Lavoie
Edited by Jack High

Public Choice and the Challenges of Democracy
Edited by José Casas Pardo and Pedro Schwartz

Fiscal Sociology and the Theory of Public Finance
An Exploratory Essay
Richard E. Wagner

Institutional Competition
Edited by Andreas Bergh and Rolf Höijer

Political Failure by Agreement
Learning Liberalism and the Welfare State
Gerhard Wegner

The Neoliberal Revolution in Eastern Europe
Economic Ideas in the Transition from Communism
Paul Dragos Aligica and Anthony J. Evans

Employees and Entrepreneurship
Co-ordination and Spontaneity in Non-hierarchical Business Organizations
Ivan Pongracic, Jr.

Media, Development and Institutional Change
Christopher J. Coyne and Peter T. Leeson

The Economics of Ignorance and Coordination

Subjectivism and the Austrian School of Economics

Thierry Aimar
Assistant Professor of Economics, Sciences Po Paris, University of Nancy 2 and Paris 1 Panthéon-Sorbonne, France and ESSEC Business School, France

NEW THINKING IN POLITICAL ECONOMY

Edward Elgar
Cheltenham, UK • Northampton, MA, USA

Published by
Edward Elgar Publishing Limited
The Lypiatts
15 Lansdown Road
Cheltenham
Glos GL50 2JA
UK

Edward Elgar Publishing, Inc.
William Pratt House
9 Dewey Court
Northampton
Massachusetts 01060
USA

A catalogue record for this book
is available from the British Library

Library of Congress Control Number: 2009930873

FSC Mixed Sources
Product group from well-managed forests and other controlled sources
www.fsc.org Cert no. SA-COC-1565
© 1996 Forest Stewardship Council

ISBN 978 1 84844 104 0

Typeset by MMM Typesetting
Printed and bound by MPG Books Group, UK

Contents

‘If Austrian economists are to be able to work constructively in the rough and tumble of the intellectual market place, anything approaching rhetorical brawling must once and for all be rejected’ (Kirzner, ‘Reflections on the Misesian Legacy in Economics’, 1996a, p.148).

General Introduction

Does economic theory satisfactorily treat the problem of coordination?

It may seem odd to see this question here, as it has been asked so much in the history of economic thought, first emerging out of late 18th century political and moral philosophy. It comes to us through, among others: the classical tradition; Marx; the beginnings of marginalism and Keynes. Many authors would answer 'yes', if asked in the context of the 'efficient markets' or 'rational expectations' theories. According to the efficient markets analyses, actors form expectations using information from current prices; for the rational expectations theorists, individuals form their predictions out of their knowledge of the theoretical model and relevant past and present economic variables. The cognitive hypotheses supporting these two theories seem, however, to be too unfounded to justify the general conclusion, which is: in the absence of technological shocks,[1] the markets' equilibrium is automatically guaranteed by price flexibility.

This observation on the limits of the best known theories suggests that any reflection on the problem of coordination should be based on the fact of economic actors' ignorance. The theme of the institutions could be seen as one solution to the problem. Viewing the discipline from these twin points of view, we consider an all too often neglected current, the Austrian economic tradition.

Few economics students know of this tradition, founded by Carl Menger (1840-1921) although it has never quite disappeared off the historians' radar. It has always hovered on the edges of the discipline. However, this 'Austrian School' has inspired many a first rate vocation and, often without users being aware of it, is the source of numerous widely used concepts in contemporary theory.

Carl Menger's two main disciples, Friedrich von Wieser and Eugen Böhm-Bawerk have in turn familiarised generations of students with their mentor's theses. Thus in Austria between the wars, the school developed mainly through the work of Ludwig von Mises and Friedrich Hayek, the only Nobel Prize winning Austrian economist. Many authors, variously leaving their mark on history, were formed by the school at this period: Ludwig Lachmann, Paul Rosenstein-Rodan, Oskar Morgenstern, Richard Strigl, Fritz Machlup, Gottfried Haberler and more.

These authors' often forced emigration during the 1930s did not extinguish the tradition, far from it. Hayek's and Mises' arrival in the USA gave birth after World War 2 to a whole new generation of economists inspired by the Austrian analysis, Murray Rothbard and Israel Kirzner in particular contributing to the tradition. Their influence explains that most of the major representatives of the Austrian tradition are today American: Garrison, Rizzo, Boettke, Salerno, Selgin, Koppl, White, Caldwell and more. They today use Austrian tools to contribute in many important fields of study such as money, expectations, evolutionism and cycles. In Europe, some often isolated individuals have also made important contributions to the advancement and renewal of the tradition, such as Foss and Witt.

So although the Austrian school is today intellectually lively, many students are still as unaware of its existence as much as the public, in spite of a growing body of literature over the last 25 years.[2] Out of the many reasons for this renewal of interest; two outstanding points can probably be agreed on.

Firstly, that this new interest in this long ignored current has had an unexpected effect on its image: the theoretical unity of the tradition is now being questioned. Thus, in contrast to Shand's analysis (*Subjectivist Economics, The New Austrian School*, 1981) and especially O'Driscoll and Rizzo (*The Economics of Time and Ignorance*, 1985), the thesis of the school's heterogeneity has gained in strength to the point of dominating the horizon. Commentators habitually remark on various analytical and doctrinal divergences between its various members. They note the fact that the Austrians share the same fundamental principles of methodological individualism, subjectivism and the market as process. They do not, however, attribute to them the same characteristics or even the same meaning. This seems to have become a habit, which has given the Austrian tradition the image of a scattered jigsaw puzzle with some of its pieces missing. The confusion caused by this has led some authors to wonder where this school's analytical boundaries lie. Thus, many works have spread the image of a tradition which has steadily become absorbed into the mainstream of economic thought.

The second point is that along with this 'renewal' of the Austrian tradition has most regrettably come its abuse for partisan purposes. Certain Austrian authors' militant support for the free market added to an otherwise fortunate democratization of Hayek's and Mises' ideas has unhappily led to the crystallization of anti free market critiques and the condemnation of the school by commentators hostile to any form of illumination of free market economy mechanisms, leading to the institutional sidelining of the Austrian school. This rich, complex tradition is a valuable tool to shed light on one's own convictions, as long as its integrity is respected by responsible attitudes to its use. If this is not the case, then economic analysis is impoverished.

The aim of this book is to clarify the specific nature of the Austrian problematic. Reacting to the image of a school instrumentalized on the political front and analytically swamped with competing 'trends' and 'trans-currents', this book seeks to restore the unity and open-mindedness of it as a whole. Our intention is not to offer a collection of different or parallel ideas, but rather to retrace, from a pedagogical and positive viewpoint, the various stages of the building of a proper theoretical edifice.

There are, of course, fractures within the Austrian tradition, which in fact would appear to be less due to the differences between contemporaries than to the generations. There would thus seem to be a clear distinction between the first Austrian tradition, founded by Carl Menger, Wieser and Böhm-Bawerk and a 'neo'-Austrian tradition organised around the works of Mises and developed by colleagues and successors such as Hayek, Lachmann, Kirzner and Rothbard.

Most commentators seem to agree with this distinction. Hutchison (*The Politics and Philosophy of Economics: Marxists, Keynesians and Austrians*, 1981); Shand (*The Capitalist Alternative, an Introduction to Neo-Austrian Economics*, 1984) and also Ioannides (*The Market, Competition and Democracy*, 1992), explicitly support the idea of a 'neo-Austrian' school based around Mises' and/or Hayek's works. Yet such a division has not been analytically founded. The question is: can this be justified?

The idea developed in this present work is the following: the two families seem to have the same preoccupation, which is to found the idea of economic theory, yet their epistemologies and analyses are far enough apart to warrant separate studies. So our objective is to concentrate on the neo-Austrians to see what possibilities there are of transferring from a neo-Austrian tradition to a neo-Austrian economy. In other words, would it be possible to create an analytical identity from what would at first seem to be a splintered group of concepts? To answer this, we have developed a three-part argument.

Firstly, we discuss the way Mises' epistemological analyses shaped a general reflection founded on the principles of human action, which would appear to form the basis of the neo-Austrian tradition. For it was Mises who initially rearticulated the teaching of the first Austrian generation then, directly or indirectly, determined his successors' own analytical trajectories. Whether the problematic they developed has been to complete, redefine or simply extend his own thinking, they have never challenged its legitimacy (Part 1).

The second part of our reflection concerns the way Mises' ideas formed an economic problematic of ignorance. Examining the various facets of this integral part of human action allowed the neo-Austrian authors to define the consequences of ignorance in the organisation of social activities. The market economy (catallaxy), may be envisaged in this frame as a form of answer to this ignorance. We study the analytical problems in the logic of market formation to reveal its functioning principles, then we determine the implications of the neo-Austrian analysis concerning the success of individual plans (Part 2).

The third and last stage develops the various applications of Austrian ideas on economic systems and policy. The Austrian argument has often been structured during controversies and debates in that field. Much has been exchanged and developed concerning the analyses of the functioning principles of collectivism, cycle mechanisms or welfare economics. We note these controversies and the way in which they reveal the nature of the Austrian problematic of ignorance (Part 3).

ACKNOWLEDGEMENTS

My wholehearted thanks go to the various people and institutions which helped me in this work: the delegates from section 37 of the CNRS national committee; the University of Nancy II and its faculty of law and economics; Professor Daniel Datkine, the PHARE director, to whom I am infinitely grateful for having accorded me so much freedom in my work organisation; Professors André Lapidus and Jack Birner who from the start supported my work. I would also like to express my gratitude to Professors Pierre Garrouste and Francis Bismans, not only for reading certain parts of the book but also for their unflagging friendship and support through thick and thin. I would additionally like to express all my gratitude to my various economics teachers, from Grenoble to Paris, in high school and university, who developed in me a taste for ideas and also gave me the freedom to choose my own.

I would particularly like to thank the Forum Culturel Autrichien (Paris, France) and its Director, Ms Christa Sauer, as well as the Austrian Ministry of Foreign and European Affairs for having so generously assisted in the financing of this English language version.

My thanks also go to Pr Peter Boettke, for adding the present work to the Series 'New Thinking in Political Economy' and the anonymous referees. Thanks are also due to Emma Griffiths, Permissions Administrator of Taylor and Francis Books (UK) for permission to use the four graphs from *Prices and Production* used in Chapter 8.

Lastly I would like to thank Mark Manners, translator, whose invaluable intercultural insight, professional skill and tireless patience has constantly informed the development of this work.

The usual disclaimer applies.

forum culturel autrichien[par]

NOTES

1. See the 'New Classical Economics' Real Business Cycle (RBC) theory.
2. In fact it was in the 1970's that a first set of works revealed the Austrian anew (Hicks and Weber (eds), *Carl Menger and the Austrian School of Economics*, 1973; Machlup, *Essays on Hayek*, 1976; Dolan (ed), *The Foundations of Modern Austrian Economics*, 1976; Moss (ed), *The Economics of Ludwig von Mises,* 1976; Loasby, *Choice, Complexity and Ignorance*, 1976; Spadero (ed), *New Directions in Austrian Economics*, 1978; Rizzo (ed), 1979; *Time, Uncertainty and Disequilibrium, Exploration of Austrian Themes*, 1979; White, *The Methodology of the Austrian School of Economics*, 1977, and so on). This literature only really started to develop in the 1980s, however. Most of the contributions appeared in post-conference collections, giving various points of view around a particular theme. Unfortunately this type of publication never offers a complete overview of the Austrian tradition, so grasping the whole tradition from them is difficult.

PART 1

Foundations

Introduction

Mises' epistemological analysis is central, forming the foundation of two important areas: not only his own theories but more especially the entire neo-Austrian tradition. He produced it as a reaction to social thinking dominated by ideas of inductivism and historicism developed in late 19th century Austria and Germany which aimed to apply empirical approaches of the natural sciences to the social sphere. Mises emphatically rejected these methods (Chapter 1).

Both Mises' and Menger's epistemological projects were intended to found an economics theory. But Mises opposed a deductive approach to Menger's inductivism, claiming that the founding of universal theoretical laws must spring from theorems, in turn based on a series of axioms defined in an *a priori* way, independently of any empirical reference. Mises' insistence on the social field's needs for a specific approach resulted in Praxeology being formed as the defining science of human action, studying its characteristics, conditions and consequences. We shall see how economic theory is grounded in Praxeology (Chapter 2).

Praxeological theorems were accepted as valid by all the neo-Austrian authors but their ability to fully account for the whole of social interaction were not. Hayek in particular felt the need for subsidiary hypotheses to analyse the field of interpersonal exchange. We consider a reflection on these as crucial; it is by their formulation that cognitive and epistemological foundations of the market will be made (Chapter 3).

1. Mises and the Austrian Tradition[1]

Mises started his theoretical works studying monetary analysis (*The Theory of Money and Credit*, 1912[2]), rapidly widening his investigations after World War 1 to the organisation of economic systems and planned economies. Ensuing controversies about collectivism ('Economic Calculation in a Collectivist Regime', 1920; *Socialism*, 1922) ensured Mises' academic fame throughout Europe.

To study Mises, one should start with his later epistemological contributions, although they admittedly come after these publications. Originally appearing as articles, most were then published in book form (*Epistemological Problems of Economics*, 1933, *Theory and History*, 1957, and *The Ultimate Foundations of Economic Science*, 1962a),[3] his major work, *Human Action* (last living edition 1966),[4] being the great summing up of the various aspects of his work.

Mises' epistemological approach may be analysed on three levels: opposition, rehabilitation and departure. Opposition corresponds to the refusal of an inductive approach to social phenomena, Mises rejecting the Vienna circle's theses (Carnap, Wittgenstein, Neurath, Schlick, and so on), dominated by logical positivism (1). Rehabilitation is the theoretical approach, rejected by the historicists, who denied its relevance in social matters. However, for Mises, rehabilitation does not question the historical approach's legitimacy but serves to define the respective roles of theory and history in both human sciences and social matters (2). The last level corresponds to a departure from the first Austrian school (Menger, Böhm-Bawerk, Wieser). Mises' hostility towards an inductive approach in social practices is behind a number of departures from his predecessors, which all Austrian authors after Mises have maintained; 'Misesian' epistemology may thus be considered as founding a neo-Austrian tradition (3).

1. POSITIVISM AND HISTORICISM: SPECIFICITY OF THE SOCIAL FIELD

Mises devoted a large part of his work to denouncing the positivist theses defended by the Vienna circle. His criticisms were shared and pursued by all his successors in the Austrian tradition (Hayek, Rothbard, Kirzner, Lachmann, and so on). Positivism, through its two main branches (panphysicalism and behaviourism), is the expression of scientism, namely the application of methods used in natural science for theorizing in the social domain. According to Mises, positivism necessarily fails because it ignores social phenomena's specificity (1.1). However, recognising this specificity should not lead the economist into historicism and oblige him to dismiss the possibility of theorizing on social matters (1.2).

1.1 The Vienna Circle and the Positivist Theories: A Critical View

In the 1920s and 1930s, the Vienna circle brought a group of researchers together around a single idea: to rid social science of any metaphysical reference. The group's epistemological manifesto, 'The scientific conception of the world', expressed its attachment to the principles of 'logical positivism'. Social science was to be built upon the experimental method, like Newton's physics. Scientific laws were to be formulated and checked by confrontation with facts, without the human mind's interference with its mental categories, so the immediate direct experience of phenomena was to constitute the ultimate criterion of scientific knowledge. The facts would speak for themselves and justify this inductive approach so as Mises nearly quotes John Locke: 'The mind is a sheet of white paper upon which the external world writes its own story' (Mises, *The Ultimate Foundations of Economic Science*, 1962a, p. 12).

For Mises, this 'neopositivism' was simply a modern formulation of classical empiricism (Locke, Berkeley, Hume, Stuart Mill) or of Comte's theses. But it was to dominate the academic stage between the wars as it legitimized practices that were current in research. It encouraged the use of statistical methods, endorsing the cult of quantitativism and measurement in economics. According to this 'epistemological scientism', the rules describing the way social mechanisms functioned were to be determined *a posteriori* from experience. So social studies would justifiably become experiments, comparable with those in the physical sciences, with emphasis on data collection. From this viewpoint, history would be viewed as a field of experiment enabling the researcher to formulate 'social physics', that is, a sociology expressing the complete set of social and political laws. There would be no methodological dualism separating the domains of natural and social phenomena.

Mises was fiercely opposed to establishing a 'unified science' (1962a, p. 124) around the positivist method. In his view, two major obstacles stood in the way of establishing physical laws about society through observation: firstly, the inductive approach requires regularity, quite alien to the domain of human relations; and secondly, social experimentation deals with complex phenomena, unlike laboratory experiments carried out in the natural sciences.

On the first point, any inductive approach implicitly requires stability in the field of study or at least the existence of certain empirical constants. But for Mises, the specificity of the social domain meant the absence of any such constants, which explained why 'the methods of the natural sciences cannot be applied to human behaviour because this behaviour … lacks the peculiarity that characterizes events in the field of the natural sciences, viz., regularity' (ibid., p. 39). The discovery of such empirical regularities would not be possible in the social domain since human behaviour is governed by categories such as volition and purpose. Unlike animals, man is not subject to his instinctive desires; his freewill and conscience constantly act on his internal and external environment, preventing the organisation of stable empirical relations.

The behaviourists claimed to be able to reduce human decisions to external factors, potentially identifiable by experimental research. True, in Mises' view, causal relations governed the formation and the dynamics of ideas. But the behaviourist study of behaviour provides no key to understanding individual reactions to changes of environment: 'The problem is precisely this, that we do not know anything about the physiological phenomena constituting the process that produces poems, theories and plans' (*Theory and History*, 1957, p. 95) and so:

> It is a gratuitous pastime to apply to the description of the behaviour of man to the behaviour of mice or of iron. The same external events produce on different men and in the same men at different times different reactions. The natural sciences are helpless in the face of this 'irregularity'. Their methods can deal only with events that are governed by a regular pattern (1962a, p. 37).

So in the current state of research there is no satisfactory explanation for the emergence of individual value judgements: 'From the epistemological point of view it must be emphasized that Marxian philosophy does not accomplish what a materialist philosophy claims to do. It does not explain how definite thoughts and judgments of value originate in the human mind' (Mises, 1957, p. 158). Ideas are therefore to be considered as the ultimate data of analysis, their contents heterogeneous, each individual assigning different, evolving meanings to their environments. As opposed to the natural sciences' method of regularity, a teleological approach is needed, characteristic of human behaviour.[5]

The absence of constant relations also explains why using mathematical equations to describe the social universe is as unscientific as it is impractical; mathematical formalism essentially requires static equilibrium, absent in human actions and therefore cannot deal with them:

> The formulation of the equation has practical importance because the constant relations which it includes are experimentally established and because it is possible to introduce specific known values in the function to determine those unknown. [Thus] The physicist has to deal with magnitudes and numerical relations, as he is entitled to believe there exist certain invariable relations between the properties. Experiment provides him with the associated numerical value … But in economics, where there are no constant relations between magnitudes, the equations are void of practical application … In human behaviour there are no such constant relations, there is no

> standard which could establish uniformities of this type (Mises, *Social Science and Natural Sciences*, 1942, p. 6).

The notion of function cannot be established in the social field, which is why econometrics has no place in economic theories. This is the reason, Mises believed, that the form the Austrian school adopted was incomparably superior to that of the Lausanne school (see *Epistemological Problems of Economics*, 1933, p. 165).[6]

The second reason for Mises' opposition to epistemological scientism was that it ignored the complex nature of social experience. In natural science, the various elements of a phenomenon are isolated in laboratory experiments. Studying phenomena under artificial conditions legitimizes inductive knowledge. However, social sciences 'never enjoy the advantage of observing the consequences of a change in one element only, other conditions being equal' (Mises, 1942, p. 5). So dealing with them requires abstraction to provide the observed phenomena with meaning. Experiments in the social domain '… do not provide us with facts which could be used in the manner in which the natural sciences use the results of their experiments for the forecast of future events. They cannot be used as building materials for the construction of theories' (Mises, 'The Treatment of Irrationality in the Social Sciences', 1944a, p. 18).[7]

A theoretical and practical misunderstanding in statistical economics stemmed directly from two elements: the impossibility of carrying out experiments using natural science methods, causal relations between the observed phenomena not being isolatable in statistics' mass of social elements. The cognitive value of such research therefore is not in drawing lessons in the form of theoretical propositions. The other element is the need to deal with constant change:

> We never find fixed relations that are open to numerical calculation. The long cherished assumption that a proportional relationship, which could be expressed in a equation, exists between prices and the quantity of money has proved fallacious; and as a result the doctrine that knowledge of human action can be formulated in quantitative terms has lost its only support (Mises, 1933, p. 10).

The experimental method is not applicable to the social domain. Universal statements do not, in the end, emerge from any observation of reality. Since the ultimate reference is not empiricism, an inductive approach cannot be employed; it has no universal validity. Accordingly 'For the social sciences, statistics constitutes a method of historical research' (Mises, 1942, p. 6).[8] The positivist approach to the social domain is the product of intellectual error, which is the basic reason for the failure of scientism.[9] Clearly, for Mises, this epistemological monism is the logical consequence of an inability to account for the specificity of social matters. Mises then condemned the use of biological and mechanistic metaphors to describe social phenomena, since they necessarily lead to failure. The historicists erroneously deduced that it is impossible to theorize about and to define social laws. Mises fully agreed with Windelband, Ricker and above all Max Weber on the impossibility of applying the methods of physics and the natural sciences to the social field. But all these authors committed the error of believing that it was impossible to derive human and social matter from universally valid laws.

1.2 The Refusal of Epistemological Relativism: Opposition to Historicism

Well before Mises, many authors had observed the limits of the positivist approach in social matters, emphasising the absence of constants in the domain of human relations. The development of historicist thought is the result of this view, its contents changing with time. But according to Mises, as an epistemological doctrine, some of its essential features led to erroneous conclusions, since its representatives claimed the impossibility of discovering universal and timeless social laws:[10]

> The fundamental thesis of historicism is the proposition that apart from the natural sciences, mathematics and logic, there is no knowledge but that provided by history. There is no regularity in the concatenation and sequence of phenomena and events in the sphere of human action. Consequently the attempts to develop a science of economics and to discover economic laws are vain (Mises, 1957, p. 199).

Historicists like Knies and Max Weber claimed only the inductive approach could be used in the social domain as no other usable method existed. But they did note its limits; the only observable regularities were always contextual and dated, rendering inoperable the ascribing of universal validity to economic propositions. For these advocates of 'epistemological relativism', social science had to be restricted to propositions established by the historical method with all its limitations.

According to Mises, the radical empiricism of these first historicists missed its target, since any confrontation with experience, even 'dated' required a process of abstraction to give significance to a necessarily complex social reality. Yet no understanding of social phenomena can be formulated without the use of general and universal propositions.

For Mises, it is not all about simply condemning polylogism, the idea that 'each social class, nation, race or period of history is endowed with a logic which differs from the logic of other classes, nations, races or eras' (1957, p. 31). It is essentially about the logical impossibility of having no logic. Some late developments in historicist thought confirm this principle: Mises observed in several of Sombart's writings, one of the most eminent historicists, a near explicit acknowledgement of certain economic laws' universal nature, even if their validity was limited to a narrow field of little practical use. Aside from this point, this approach opposed Sombart to Knies, who was against the 'absolutism of theory', that is its 'pretension to set forth propositions in the scientific treatment of political economy that are unconditional and equally valid for all times, countries and nationalities' (Knies, quoted by Mises, 1933, p. 6-7). For Mises, any refusal to accept scientism, or underlining its constraints in the social field, does not imply being trapped in this epistemological pseudo-nihilism erected as dogma. There is indeed something that 'is absolutely valid for all human action, irrespective of era, geography and the racial, national or cultural characteristics of the actors' (Mises, 1962b, p.49). This is precisely the objective of theorization.

2. ANALYSIS OF THE SOCIAL FIELD: THEORY AND HISTORY

Any criticism of scientism should not be considered as an expression of the problem of imperfect induction. True, for Mises it was impossible to positively establish a general proposition on the basis of a finite series of singular statements.[11] No 'confirmation' or 'verification' can be established since no ultimate sources of knowledge derive from induction. But for neo-Austrian authors, the natural sciences are rightly based on experimentation, since the inductive method is the only one applicable in this field, the intrinsic characteristics of which mean there can be no introspective knowledge. Its phenomena must therefore be studied from the outside.

The situation is completely different in the social field. Induction is totally impractical here, due to the complexity of the facts observed and the absence of empirical constants. Analysis is free of the natural sciences' constraints, for it is possible to understand phenomena from the inside: 'Because we are human beings, we are in a position to grasp the significance of human action, i.e. the significance that the actor ascribes to his action. It is this comprehension of significance that makes us capable of formulating general principles by which we explain the phenomena of action' (Mises, 1933, p. 130).

The social sciences must therefore base their method of investigation on the idea of 'comprehension' of the phenomena. This operates at two levels: conception and understanding. Conception corresponds to the logical structure of the human mind and an *a priori* form of knowledge arising from the exercise of mental categories, so it corresponds to theory (2.1). Understanding delivers some meaning to human choice: it corresponds to history (2.2). These two approaches are clearly complementary, but there is a principle of subordination at an epistemological level: firstly, understanding cannot come into conflict with the teaching of the aprioristic sciences; and secondly, this work of understanding is necessarily (logically and chronologically) preceded by the exercise of conception (2.3).

2.1 Apriorism, the Foundation of Theory

According to Mises, the formulation of statements and universal laws in human matters is not only possible but well-founded on an epistemological level. However, this undertaking necessarily escapes the rules of induction, which is substituted by an aprioristic approach. This epistemological apriorism expresses 'a knowledge unconditionally valid for all beings endowed with the logical structure of the human mind [and] the fact that man does not have the creative power to imagine categories at variance with the fundamental logical relations and with the principles of causality and teleology' (Mises, 1966, p. 40; 62). Based on the work of deduction, the *a priori* method is a series of theorems stemming from a series of apodictic axioms. It is why *a priori* teachings are valid outside of place, time, nationality or race. However, claiming an *a priori* base for economic and social analysis does not mean negating the idea of reality. On the contrary, the human mind's mental categories take account of the organisation of the real and therefore investigate it. From this viewpoint, 'they are not arbitrarily made, but imposed upon us by the world in which we live and act and which we want to study. They are not empty, not meaningless, and not merely verbal. They are – for man – the most general laws of the universe, and without them no knowledge would be accessible to man' (Mises, 1962a, p. 14). But at the same time this corpus of laws 'is not derived from experience; it is prior to experience. It is, as it were, the logic of action and deed' (Mises, 1933, p. 12-13).

More exactly, the relationship of epistemological apriorism with reality was considered in two different ways. The *a priori* approach permits knowledge of an internal reality through introspection, knowledge which 'is not dependent upon experience, unless one wishes to call aprioristic cognition inner experience' (ibid, p.19). Whereas, external reality is part and parcel of the human mind because it imposes itself daily, with the resistances and obstacles it offers human intentions 'by the fact that man is not omnipotent. There is in the world something that offers resistance to the realisation of his wishes and desires .... We may define the external world as the totality of all those things and events that determine the feasibility or unfeasibility, the success of failure, of human action' (Mises, 1962a, p. 6).

This inclusion of *a priori* categories in an effective reality enabled Mises to claim a Kantian heritage. Not only did Kant oppose empiricism and historicism, but his epistemology aimed at defending synthetic *a priori* categories.[12] Indeed, if

> new experience can force us to discard or modify inferences we have drawn from previous experience … no kind of experience can ever force us to discard or modify *a priori* theorems. They are not derived from experience: they are logically prior to it and cannot be either proved by corroborative experience or disproved by experience to the contrary. We can comprehend action only by means of *a priori* theorems (Mises, 1933, p. 27-28).

So while scientific laws in social matters are manifested in experience, referring us to internal experience of our own categories of causality, they do not require the support of external experience to demonstrate their ultimate validity. Reason, governed by the actor's mental equipment, can deliver necessary universal knowledge, established in an *a priori* fashion. As any reasoning presupposes *a priori* categories, neither its proof nor disproof is required: 'The positivistic principle of verifiability as rectified by Popper is unassailable as an epistemological principle of the natural sciences. But it is meaningless when applied to anything about which the natural sciences cannot supply any information' (Mises, 1962a, p. 120). *A priori* categories cannot be tested because the tests themselves would imply the existence and use of these *a priori* categories. Fundamentally, Mises viewed the idea of having to justify social knowledge with positive reasons as a derivative of scientism.

2.2 History, Field of Understanding

By definition, the *a priori* deals with what is universal and explains it using the rational. History intrinsically deals with individuality and that which escapes deductive reasoning, that is, the ultimate datum represented by ideas and value judgements. History begins at the point where, in terms of cognition, the *a priori* method has exhausted all its resources.

In considering social phenomena, the theoretician necessarily runs into epistemological obstacles. Human ideas and value judgements cannot be deduced; the researcher cannot refer them back to something from which they were derived. The inability to define the causal link between an outside event and the actor's decision expresses the individual (or singular) character of phenomena:

> There is no answer to the question why Frederick II invaded Silesia except because he was Frederick II. It is customary, although not very expedient, to call the mental process by means of which a datum is traced back to other data rational. Then an ultimate datum is called irrational. No historical research can be thought of that would not ultimately meet such irrational facts (Mises, 1957, p. 183-184).

The ultimate datum signifies the end of the area of competence of the theorician. But it opens up the field of study of the historian.

The natural sciences are also faced with the ultimate data, the final limit of analysis, where the physician and the biologist come up against irreducible features. The researcher in the social sphere is unfettered however, the specific nature of this field authorising further investigation. Individual behaviour may be subject to interpretation; the researcher is able to attempt to define actors' objectives and value judgements and so give meaning to their actions, since 'although it is impossible to reduce them to their causes – they would not be ultimate data, if such a reduction were possible – the observer can understand them because he is himself a human being' (Mises, 1944a, p. 27).

Treating the individuality of phenomena is history's domain, whose task it is to 'establish what content the value judgments of the action individuals had' (Mises, 1957, p. 21). It therefore requires a thymological approach (Mises prefers the term thymology to that of literary psychology), its function being to deal with the mental activities of individuals that determine their actions.[13] But this interpretative approach is above all described by Mises as an exercise in Verstehen.[14] It:

> establishes the fact that an individual or a group of individuals have engaged in a definite action emanating from definite value judgments and choices and aiming at definite ends … It furthermore tries to appreciate the effects and the intensity of the effects brought about by an action; it tries to assign to every action its relevance, i.e., its bearing upon the course of events (Mises, 1966, p. 55).

Consequently, for Mises, analysis of the social field was not limited to the aprioristic method: 'Both theory and history are equally legitimate, and both are equally indispensable. The logical contrast between them is in no sense an opposition' (1933, p. XXIII). Moreover, Mises did not confine himself to theoretical considerations in his research; he also took a lively interest in history, writing especially on institutional and political history.[15] At a cursory glance, some might see an ideological streak in his works; more objectively, however, they are the practical expression of his particular interest in historical method alongside his interest in theory. This said, while Mises claimed complementarities of theory and history, he was at pains to strictly differentiate between the two and explain the nature of their relationship, thus defending his thesis of the epistemological subordination of history to theory.

2.3 Practical Complementarity, Epistemological Subordination

For Weber and all the historicist authors (Rickert, Windelbrand, Croce, and so on), the distinction between theory and history was more a matter of degree than of substance. As they saw it, no explanation of social phenomena, reliant on induction and history, can achieve the degree of generality required to lay claim to absolute universalism. Various interpretations might to a greater or lesser degree approach but not reach this inaccessible criterion and would be more or less 'general'. Thus the greater the degree of generality, the more the interpretation could be described as theoretical. For Mises, such statements were a matter of epistemological misunderstanding. The work of certain historicists, like Weber, certainly brought home the specific nature of the logic of historical study compared with methods in the natural sciences. But these authors failed to consider the specific character of theory compared with history. Theory cannot constitute a general form of historical events, since by definition 'science is universally human, and not limited by nationality, bound to a particular time, or contingent upon any social class' (Mises, 1933, p. 152).

History, by its very nature, possesses no generic validity; no theoretical corpus can be derived from a review of facts.

This does not deny history's legitimate place alongside the aprioristic method. Any reality, internal or external, can only be grasped with the aid of *a priori* categories. But no situation, internal or external, can escape individuality. The practical apprehension of human and social reality requires both the exercise of an aprioristic, generic and abstract tool, firstly, to appreciate that reality's structure, and secondly to carry out the historical, interpretive work needed for the study of both the individual and the concrete. These two complementary approaches' sole purpose is to help individuals make decisions and plan action. Theoretical and historical planning are the two tools required for human decision-making.

So history is not solely concerned with the past. Quite the contrary: 'Its most important use is to be seen in the service it renders to the anticipation of future conditions and to the designing of action that necessarily always aims at affecting future conditions' (Mises, 1957, p. 306-307). Its purpose is to define action strategies for the future, so it is obvious that this method of defining historical research is not reserved for the scientist, any more than the aprioristic method. Any actor necessarily deploys an interpretative method, for 'no action can be planned and executed without understanding of the future. Even an action of an isolated individual is guided by definite assumptions about the actor's future value judgments and is so far determined by the actor's image of his own character' (Mises, 1962a, p. 50).

Consequently, in practice, history is complementary to but not equated with theory.[16] Of course, 'The concept of theory, in contradiction to the concept of history, is, and always and universally has been, understood as involving a regularity valid for the future as well as the past' (Mises, 1933, p. XX). But history also aims to foresee the future, although within certain limits, because of the irregularity of human decisions.

The character of history's epistemological subordination to theory should, however, be stressed. History's teachings obviously cannot contradict what we learn from logic, defined *a priori*. But the fundamental point is that theory is 'logically prior to all historical and descriptive research' (ibid., p. 152) since it governs the logical processing of experience. As history is always a complex of events, the historian needs theory to interpret the events and identify relations between cause and effect.

> The truth is that the experience of a complex phenomenon – and there is no other experience in the realm of human action – always be interpreted on the ground of various antithetic theories. Whether the interpretation is considered satisfactory depends on the appreciation of the theories in question established beforehand on the ground of aprioristic reasoning. History cannot teach us any general rule, principle or law. There is no means to abstract from a historical experience *a posteriori* any theories or theorems concerning human conduct and policies (Mises, 1966, p. 41).

It is impossible to apprehend human reality without aprioristic categories. The historian needs theory, for he interprets by using abstract categories. If they are correct, the interpretation may be correct; if they are wrong, the interpretation must be wrong.

The domains of economic theory and economic history are often confused due to not taking into account this subordination. The economic historian accumulates and examines data, in appearance like the researcher of natural sciences. But history and its methods are epistemologically very different from natural science. The economist behaves differently from the economic historian, not accumulating facts but basing his affirmations on aprioristic reasoning, on the development of theoretical thought.

History nonetheless remains, for Mises, a necessary branch of social study and a complementary tool to theoretical approach. It occupies a legitimate place alongside the *a priori* tool: 'History must rest on theory, not to alienate itself from its proper tasks, but on the contrary, in order more than ever to discharge them in the true sense of history. And Bagehot's words should never be forgotten: "Rightly conceived, the historical method is no rival to the abstract method rightly conceived"' (1933, p. 124). Aprioristic theory and history are inescapably the two branches of human and social phenomena.

3. MISES AND HIS PREDECESSORS: CONTENTIONS AND CONTINUITIES

Within neo-Austrian literature there are recurring questions on the relation between Mises' work and that of his predecessors (Menger, Wieser, Böhm-Bawerk). In particular, the theme of the relationship with Menger was controversial. Some, like Selgin see Mises as a simple follower of Menger, since his apriorism 'does not fundamentally differ from the Aristotelian essentialism of Menger' (*Praxeology and Understanding: An Analysis of the Controversy in Austrian Economics*, 1982, p. 133). Others, however, see a real break with Menger in his analyses. Langlois had no doubt: 'Proceeding from a Neo-Kantian rather than an Aristotelian philosophy, Mises argues against Menger' (Langlois, 'Knowledge and Rationality in the Austrian School: An Analytical Survey', 1985, p. 316). However, these two extreme positions do not reflect the much more complex reality of Mises' relation with Menger.

Mises always showed enormous respect for the thought and work of Carl Menger, frequently emphasising his quality and creativity. More specifically, Mises remained faithful to Menger's methodology of social science, agreeing with his analysis of the individualist dimension of social phenomena and his refusal of the mathematical method (3.1).

But at the same time his own criticism of scientism forced Mises to distance himself from other aspects of Menger's thinking, causing a fundamental epistemological shift. Mises' judgement is bleak: 'The inadequacy of empiricist logic hampered the endeavours of Carl Menger still more seriously than those of the English thinkers. His brilliant "Investigations into the Method in Social Sciences" is even less satisfactory today than, for example, Cairnes' book on methodology' (Mises, 1933, p. XVII-III)[17] (3.2).

3.1 Fidelity to a Methodological Approach

A traditional reading of Menger (Stigler, 1937, Schumpeter, 1952 and 1954), presents him as one of the founders of the neoclassical corpus. As noted by Kirzner in a text entitled 'Entrepreneurial Discovery and the Competitive Market Process': 'The early work of the Austrian School until the 1930s was correctly perceived as simply one variant of the dominant early twentieth century mainstream approach to economic understanding (often loosely referred to as "neoclassical")' (Kirzner, 1997, p. 61). But some authors find both original and specific questionings in Menger's work (such as the insistence on the role of dynamic time and the refusal of the mathematical formalism adopted by his marginalist contemporaries.[18] As Vaughn remarked (*Austrian Economics in America: The Migration of a Tradition*, 1994), Menger was certainly all of this at once. When he wrote *Principles of Economics* (*Grundsätze der Wirtschaftslehre*, 1871), he expressed most of the fundamentals of the marginalist analysis developed by Walras and Jevons (marginal utility, exchange theory, determination of prices, and so on).[19] But he was also the author of *Investigations into the Method in Social Sciences, with Special Reference to Economics* (*Untersuchungen über die Methode der Sozialwirtschaften und der politischen Ökonomie insbesondere*, 1883), on epistemology and method, where his analyses of institutional economic matters bear no comparison with the writings of his marginalist contemporaries.

Investigations was a response to the indifference shown in Germany and Austria on the publication of *Principles*. The German intelligentsia, then dominated by the historical school,[20] rejected the possibility of universal laws in the social domain. Its representatives (Roscher, Schmöller) opposed the theoretical approach in economics to their historical description and interpretation. Since *Principles* affirmed the legitimacy of theoretical research in economics, Menger was ostracised by the proponents of the German Historical School.[21] The divide was widened by the rehabilitation of the validity of universal laws in the social sphere being accompanied by Menger's refusal of positivism, whose undivided reign, he proclaimed, 'has led to most serious methodological errors, and to idle play with external analogies between the phenomena of economics and those of nature' (Menger, 1871, p. 47). The researcher cannot be content with the historical approach, consisting of poring over singular, concrete and dated phenomena.

Menger claimed, furthermore, in *Principles of Economics* that theoretical analysis required the individual to be central, explaining that the development of a theory of price needed to refer to individual behaviour. With *Investigations*, he asserted once again the need for an individualistic basis to analyse social phenomena and in particular, institutions. In his comment on Mengerian methodology, Milford explains that 'while Menger tried to show that the principle that individuals try to achieve their aims in the best possible manner is vital for the explanation of changing price structures, he also showed that the same principle can be applied to the explanation of the origin of certain other institutions' (Milford, 'Menger's Methodology', 1990, p. 218). Holism is incapable of explaining the origin of social structures or their evolution. Menger's ambition, through the 'analytic-compositive' method (Menger, 1883), is to reconstruct the way in which complex institutions are formed on the basis of individual strategies and behaviour. It will be seen in the next chapter that in his desire to accentuate the individualistic requirement for apprehending the social, Mises simply repeats a series of fundamentals already established in Menger's work.

Menger, as Mises was to after him, questioned the use of mathematical methods in analysing the social sphere. The absence of mathematical theory in his work has received many well-known comments. Schumpeter (see 1954, p. 110) claims this absence was the only difference between Menger and the two other representatives of the marginalist revolution, Jevons and Walras, due in fact only to Menger's level of mathematical knowledge. Carl Menger's son, Karl, seems to substantiate this argument. He stressed the poor teaching of mathematics in Austria in the first half of the 19th century and noted his father's weaknesses in the subject (see Karl Menger, 'Austrian Marginalism and Mathematical Economics', 1973, p. 44-45).

A closer look at C. Menger's text shows a very different story, however. Commentators such as Antonelli ('Leon Walras and Carl Menger's correspondence', 1953) take a keen interest in the now famous correspondence between Walras and Menger, 1883-1884, the period the publication of 'Investigations'. Garrouste ('Leon Walras and Carl Menger à propos de l'utilisation des mathématiques en économie politique', 1994) claims this correspondence strongly suggests Menger's firm rejection of mathematics for substantial rather than formalistic reasons. Although Menger is obviously sympathetic to Walras' development of the marginalist approach, he does explain, during a discussion of the 'Théorie mathématique de la richesse sociale' (Walras) his reluctance to accept mathematical methods, their application in the social sciences being only 'method of exposition and demonstration, not of research' (Menger, letter, 1883, p. 271). As it is only a 'science subsidiary to economics' (ibid., p. 272), it cannot penetrate to the essence of a discipline which researches the causes of phenomena and defines their structure rather than studying how they are presented.

It is clear then that the economist's work is not to show magnitudes but to explain the origins and characteristics of economic events. The mathematical tool is of no use here whatsoever.

So there seems no doubt that Menger and Mises' methodologies are identical. They are however different in their epistemologies and a major rift emerged within the Austrian tradition as a consequence.

3.2 An Epistemological Rift

The main aim of *Investigations* is to show that a theory of the economy is possible, that is, a 'general' approach of economic events that permits knowledge, forecast and control. This objective led Menger to seek 'strict laws of phenomena, of regularities in the succession of phenomena which do not present themselves to us as absolute, but which in respect to the approaches to cognition by which we attain to them simply bear within themselves the guarantee of absoluteness' (Menger, 1883, p. 59). The human mind discovers these absolute regularities which appear as obvious, through forming epistemological laws, the aim of which is to express strict relations and strict types, or 'exact' laws between the various economic events. These 'exact laws' are not only without exception, but in accordance with our laws of thought are not conceivable other than without exception' (ibid. p. 61).

Menger claims however that the 'exact' approach is not the only one which permits 'general' knowledge of economic events. The 'empirical-realistic' approach can be successfully added. Empirical-realist economic theory is designed to record regularities observable 'in the sequence and co-existence of the real phenomena of the human economy' (Menger, 1883, p. 57). As contrasted with the 'exact' approach, it includes all types of economic subjects' attitudes and behaviour, doing which considerably increases its field of operations. But there is another side to the coin. Empirical-realist laws can and generally do suffer exceptions that result in a less rigorous definition of economic regularities. The issue is all the more important in that these exceptions may be located 'even within a defined nation and often express on each market a specific dimension of the facts dealt with, which as far as the measurement of the effects of demand on prices is concerned can only be determined subsequently' (ibid., p. 72).

Nevertheless, the empirical-realist method retains its legitimacy and its value alongside the exact approach. For Menger, these two lines represent two different, autonomous ways of addressing the problem of establishing a theoretical science of economics (see Menger, 1883, p. 67). They are at the same time alternative and complementary in practice, corresponding to two ways of knowing, predicting and controlling.

Examining these elements gives us the opportunity of comparing a number of Mises' oppositions to Menger's epistemological views. The biggest point is obviously the importance of induction. As Milford ('Menger's Methodology', 1990) and Maki ('Mengerian Economics in Realist Perspective', 1990) consider, the combative tone of *Investigations* should not hide the fact that Menger's reproach to the German school was not in using an inductive method but of using a naïve version of it.[22] The empirical-realistic method has by definition a clear relation to external reality as it is by observing economic reality that regularity in a variable chain is discovered. Although Mises did not explicitly treat the empirical-realistic method, we can guess the strength of his feelings with his remark on the 'The inadequate character of [Menger's] empirist logic', his rejection of which is the result of his total refusal to allow the slightest room for use of induction in the social sciences.

It might be thought that Mises would look on the 'exact' method with kinder eyes, as it consists of an abstraction, isolating various elements in phenomena and their relations, outside time and space; however Mises heavily criticized it.

In Menger's view, universal statements must emanate from an experience of reality and not from any conceptualising of it.[23] So the exact method is based on an inductive approach, the construction of 'exact' types being preceded that of by 'real' types, by which the most elementary phenomena are defined. The difference between the 'exact' and 'empirical-realistic' laws is finally a question of contrast between, firstly, research into an Aristotlean-essential structure of phenomena and secondly, their full complexity, rather than the conceptual on one side and the real on the other. Statements and universal laws in the social field must be made in the same way as in the natural sciences. Menger defends here an epistemological monism.

Now, as Milford summarized, 'since the "exact orientation of theoretical research" cannot clarify the possibility of a theoretical science claiming to be strictly universal and empirical, it has to be rejected not only for logical but for epistemological reasons as well' (Milford, 1990, p. 234). Induction is incapable of providing epistemological legitimacy for the notion of economic theory: 'Concepts are never and nowhere to be found in reality' (Mises, 1933, p. 78).

Mises interprets these errors as the result of the limitations of epistemological thinking in Menger's time and the 'pernicious' influence of Stuart Mill on its development. According to Mises, Stuart Mill believed that the axioms underlying economic theory rely on experience and thus derive from an inductive conception. Mises claims Menger was misled by this approach, which resulted in him making actual epistemological mistakes (see Mises, 1933, p. 23), which were unfortunately propagated by his successors, Böhm-Bawerk and Wieser. Thus, for the latter, the function of economic theory was 'to explain scientifically and to develop the content of common economic experience' (Wieser, 1914, quoted by Mises, 1933, p. 21). Yet this idea of individuals' common character reflects no more than an introspective approach that Wieser himself defines as psychological. Mises deplores the fact that the latter remains governed by the 'Millian' idea inherited from Menger, that is, that these axioms of thought must ultimately find an inductive expression.

Thus Mises clearly rejected Menger's epistemology, and that of the Austrian 'first tradition'[24] in general, with his denial of the legitimacy of an inductive approach in social sciences. Nevertheless, even if its characteristics differ, Mises' epistemological viewpoint remains clearly identical in its purpose to Menger's: the foundation of an economic theory. But according to Mises, the universally valid character of economic laws cannot be defended and legitimized other than as the statement of theorems springing from a series of axioms defined *a priori*, denying any inductivist reference. The desire to found economic theory on this basis resulted in the development of praxeology, defined as the *a priori* science of human action (see Mises, 1957, p. 309), or 'general theory of human action' (Mises, 1966, p. 4). While post-Misesian authors like Hayek would try to add to or build on the lessons of praxeology with 'subsidiary' propositions, none would question its findings and the need to observe the framework of formal propositions it establishes. It is from this point of view that praxeology, conceived as an architecture for the human sciences, remains a consensual feature of the neo-Austrian tradition and constitutes its epistemological foundation.

NOTES

1. For literature on Mises, see Moss (*The Economics of Ludwig von Mises, Toward a Critical Appraisal*, 1976); Butler (*Ludwig von Mises: Fountainhead of the Modern Microeconomics Revolution*, 1988); Gordon (*Ludwig von Mises: An Annotated Bibiography*, 1988; *The Philosophical Contributions of Ludwig von Mises*'), 1994); Herbener ('Ludwig von Mises and the Austrian School of Economics', 1991; *The Meaning of Ludwig von Mises*, 1993); Kirzner (*Ludwig von Mises, The Man and his Economics*, 2001); Hülsmann (*Mises, The Last Knight of Liberalism*, 2007).
2. The second German edition of the work was published in 1924. The various English-language versions (1942, 1934, 1953, 1981) correspond to this edition.
3. The collection of articles *Money, Method and Market Process* (1990), published posthumously may be added to the list. The first part brings together three of Mises' epistemological articles: 'Social Science and Natural Sciences' (1942); 'The Treatment of Irrationality in the Social Sciences' (1944a); 'Epistemological Relativism in the Sciences of Human Nature' (1962b).
4. Literature often considered that a work published by Mises in German under the title *Nationalökonomie* is a preliminary version of *Human Action*, 1940, but the first 'official' version published directly in English is dated 1949. Authors generally refer to the third and last edition published in the author's lifetime, 1966. The fourth edition was published posthumously in 1996 with revisions by Bettina B. Greaves. In 1998 the Ludwig von Mises Institute brought back the first edition as the 'Scholars Edition'.
5. 'The reason for the natural sciences' neglect of final causes and their exclusive preoccupation with causality research is that this method works. The contrivances designed according to the scientific theories run the way the theories predicted and thus provide a pragmatic verification for their correctness. On the other hand the magic devices did not come up to expectations and do not bear witness to the magic world view … But the same pragmatic proof that can be advanced in favour of the exclusive use of teleological methods in the field of human action. It works, while the idea of dealing with men as if they were stones or mice does not work. It works not only in the search for knowledge, but no less in daily practice' (Mises, *Theory and History*, 1957, p. 248).
6. For a more finely-drawn neo-Austrian opinion on the role of mathematics in social science, see Hayek ('Coping With Ignorance'): '… it is a an erroneous belief, characteristic of bad mathematicians, that mathematics is essentially quantitative and that, therefore, to build on the great achievements of the founders of mathematical economics, men like Jevons, Walras and Pareto, one has to introduce quantitative data obtained by measurements. That was certainly not the intention of founders of mathematical economics. They understood much better than their successors that algebraic mathematical formulae are the pre-eminent

methods for describing abstract patterns without assuming or possessing particular information about the specific magnitudes involved. One great mathematician has indeed described a mathematician as a maker of patterns. In this sense, mathematics can be very helpful to us' (1978a, p. 4). Hayek challenges mathematical quantification much more than mathematics itself to deal with social phenomena. See also Rizzo, 'Praxeology and Econometrics: A Critique of Positivist Economics' (1978).

7. In certain natural sciences, when it is impossible to single out the elements of complex phenomena observed, research always implies beforehand the construction of a hypothesis which 'is already an intellectual elaboration of experience' (Mises, 1933, p. 9). This being the case, it is thus impossible to derive the theory of the observation of natural phenomena for the nature of this 'observation' is itself governed by a grid of theoretical analysis. Interpretation, clearly open to discussion, is needed from the scholar. In 'The Facts of the Social Sciences', Hayek reproduces this kind of analysis when dealing with the complex dimension of social phenomena, the structure of which 'is not "given" to our observation but which we can only laboriously "reconstruct"' (Hayek, 1942, p. 71).

8. All the neo-Austrians share this opinion of the irrelevant and inflated role of statistics, for example, Lachmann: 'Statistics, as Mises has often explained, merely record what happened over a certain record of time. They cannot tell us what might have happened had circumstances been different' (Lachmann, 'Ludwig von Mises and the Market Process', 1971b, p. 182). Similarly, Hayek discussed the subject several times, for example in 'The Counter-Revolution of Science': 'Most of the economic statistics which we ordinarily met, such as trade statistics, figures about price changes, and most 'time series' or statistics of the 'national income', are not data to which the technique appropriate to the investigation of mass phenomena can be applied … If they refer to significant phenomena they may be very interesting as information about the conditions existing at a particular moment. But unlike statistics proper, which may indeed help us to discover important regularities in the social world (though regularities of an entirely different order from those with which the theoretical sciences of society deals), there is no reason to expect that these measurements will ever reveal anything to us which is of significance beyond the particular place and time at which they have been made' (Hayek, 1952b, p. 62-63). Thirty years later he defends the same view: 'What has done much damage to microeconomics is striving for a pseudo-exactness by imitating methods of the physical sciences which have to deal with what are fundamentally much more simple phenomena … the model which is followed is provided by the physical sciences which, where they have to deal with true mass phenomena such as the movement of millions of molecules with which thermodynamics has to deal, where we admittedly know nothing about the movement of any individual molecule, the law of large numbers enables us to discover statistical regularities or probabilities which indeed, in this way provide an adequate foundation for reliable predictions. The trouble is, unfortunately, that in the disciplines which endeavour to explain the structure of society, we do not have to deal with true mass phenomena. The events which we must take into account in any attempt to predict the outcome of particular social processes are never so numerous as to enable us to substitute ascertained probabilities for information about the individual events … both in the biological and in the social sciences frequently we cannot rely on probabilities, or the law of large numbers, because unlike the positions which exist in the physical sciences, where statistical evidence of probabilities can be substituted for information on particular facts, we have to deal with what he calls organized complexity, where we cannot expect to find permanent constant relations between aggregates or averages. Indeed this intermediate field between the simple phenomena of the physical sciences, where everything can be explained by theoretical formulae which contain no more than two or three unknowns, and the instances where a large enough number of events to be able to deal with true mass phenomena to rely on probability is our subject. In the social sciences we have to deal with something which Warren Weaver called organized complexity, phenomena which are not made up of sufficiently large numbers of similar events to enable us to ascertain the probabilities for their occurrence' (Hayek, 1978b, p. 5).

9. Mises' judgement of scientism was supported and pursued by all the neo-Austrian authors. Rothbard, for example, in 'The Mantle of Science' sees in scientism '...the profoundly unscientific attempt to transfer uncritically the methodology of the physical sciences to the study of human action' (Rothbard, 1960, p. 3). Hayek very early systematically dismisses this 'slavish imitation of the method and language of Sciences' (Hayek, 1952b, p. 15) which explains why literature often associates the condemnation of the scientism with his name with it more than Mises'.
10. Mises clearly distinguished the historicist viewpoint from the empirical one: 'The thesis of those who affirm the possibility of deriving empirical laws from historical data we shall call empiricism. Historicism and empiricism are, consequently, not the same thing' (Mises, 1933, p. 8-9). Boettke and Koppl ('Introduction to the Special Issue on Alfred Schütz' Centennial') highlight nonetheless: 'Mises' 1960 introduction to the English translation of *Epistemological Problems of Economics* shows that he thought the arguments he used against historicism worked on positivism too' (Boettke, Koppl, September 2001, p. 112).
11. 'Natural sciences deal with past events. Obviously, each experience is the experience of something past: there is no experience of future phenomena' (Mises, 1944a, p. 18).
12. Commentators spent much time wondering whether Mises' position is Kantian or neo-Kantian. Thus, for White (*The Methodology of the Austrian School of Economics*, 1977), Mises' position was Kantian inasmuch as Kant's propositions were solely '*a priori*'. However, other commentators (Smith, 'Aristotle, Menger, Mises: An Essay on the Metaphysics of Economics', 1994) maintain that while Kant rejected the idea that all knowledge springs from experience, he would not reject the idea that there is no relation between knowledge and experience: hence the term of synthetic *a priori* judgements, as opposed to analytic judgements (complete break) and synthetic judgements (purely empiricist knowledge). Whether this reading of Kant is correct or not, Mises hardly wavered from it.
13. 'Thymological experience is what we know about human value judgments, the actions determined by them, and the responses these actions arouse in other people' (Mises, 1957, p. 312).
14. In Mises' mind the idea of 'Verstehen', generally associated with the work of Max Weber, originates in the philosophy of Bergson. 'The mental act for dealing with such historical facts is, in the philosophy of Bergson, "une intuition" [in French in the text] namely "la sympathie par laquelle on se transporte à l'intérieur d'un objet pour coïncider avec ce qu'il a d'unique, et par conséquent d'inexprimable" (Bergson, La pensée et le mouvant, 1934 – 4ème édition). German epistemology calls the act "das spezifische Verstehen der Geistesswissenschften," or simply "Verstehen". I suggest it be translated into English as "specific understanding" or simply as "understanding"' (Mises, 1944a, p. 26).
15. See, among others, *Nation, State and Economy* (1919), *Liberalism in the Classical Tradition* (1927), *Omnipotent Government: the Rise of the Total State and Total War* (1944b), *Bureaucracy* (1946); Rothbard, rehabilitates this dimension of Mises' work: 'The Laissez-Faire Radical: A Quest for the Historical Mises' (1981).
16. 'The specific understanding of history can try to interpret the why of such changes effected in the past and to anticipate changes likely to happen in the future' (Mises, 1957, p. 85). But 'It is obvious that this knowledge which provides a man with the ability to anticipate to some degree other people's future attitudes is not *a priori* knowledge (ibid. p. 311).
17. Thirty-six years later in *The Historical Setting of the Austrian School* (1969), Mises continued to deplore the perverse effects of Carl Menger's empiricist trends on the coherence of the latter's own reasoning. He thus noted in a comment on the Methodstreit that 'Menger was too much under the sway of John Stuart Mill's empiricism to carry his own point of view to its full logical consequences' (Mises, 1969, p. 27-28).
18. Despite several premonitory articles (particularly Kauder 'The Retarded Acceptance of Marginal Utility Theory', 1953), the very first instance of this understanding of Menger can be found in the collective work *Carl Menger and the Austrian School of Economics*, published under Hicks and Weber. Streissler's contribution: 'To What Extent was the Austrian School Marginalist?', 1973, should also be cited. The main stages in the development of this literature were: the much discussed article by Jaffé, 'Menger, Jevons and Walras de-

Homogenized', 1976; a special issue of the *Atlantic Monthly* (September 1978), 'Carl Menger and Austrian Economics'; *The Economics of Time and Ignorance* (O'Driscoll and Rizzo 1985); a collection of articles *Carl Menger and his Legacy in Economics* (ed. Caldwell, 1990); *Carl Menger and the Origins of Austrian Economics* (Alter, 1990); finally, another collective work, instigated by Mark Blaug, simply called *Carl Menger* (1992).

19. Along the same lines as these authors, Menger stated in the preface of *The Principles of Economics* (1871) that the origins of his thinking involved the desire to reconstruct the theory of value on bases other than those established by classical analysis, so as to provide a more satisfactory explanation of price formation. More broadly speaking, the ambition of *Principles* was to take the general theory of prices out of the rut in which the classical school had left it and to structure it around a general principle. Mises himself considered that the differences between the Austrian tradition and the Lausanne School lay 'only in their way of expression of the same fundamental idea' and that they 'differ only in their mode of expressing the same fundamental idea and they are divided more by their terminology and by peculiarities of presentation than by the substance of their teachings' (1933), p. 214). In his later writings, he continued to defend the same argument: '… after some years all the essential ideas of the Austrian school were by and large accepted as an integral part of economic theory. About the time of Menger's demise in 1921, there was no longer any distinction between an Austrian School and other economics. The appellation 'Austrian School' became the name given to an important chapter of the history of economic thought; it was no longer the name of a specific sect with doctrines different from those held by other economists' (Mises, 1969, p. 41).
20. For a summary of the intellectual atmosphere in Austria at the time, see Seager ('Economics at Berlin and Vienna', 1893), Johnston (*The Viennese Mind, an Intellectual and Social History 1848-1938*, 1972) and Craver (*The Immigration of the Austrian Economics*, 1986).
21. In the preface to *Investigations*, Menger stated that he wished to combat the 'erroneous methodological principles' (Menger, 1883, p. 27) adopted in Germany under the influence of the German Historical School. The work's publication ignited the famous 'battle of methods' (Methodenstreit), opposing Menger and Böhm-Bawerk on the one hand and the proponents of the German Historical School, under Schmöller's leadership, on the other. This controversy proved to be completely sterile, since they were arguing at cross-purposes. Schumpeter summing it up perfectly, described it as a 'history of wasted energies' (1954, p. 814), while Bostaph: 'The Methodological Debate between Carl Menger and the German Historicists', 1978, took a less clear-cut position.
22. Menger's method for acquiring knowledge of the world of phenomena is based on an inductive approach. But since it is not a naïve form of inductivism, this should be described, according to Birner's expression ('A Roundabout Solution to a Fundamental Problem in Menger's Methodology and Beyond', 1990), as a 'justificationist-inductivist' position.
23. He is, in this regard, remarkably explicit: 'The phenomena, or certain aspects of them, and not their linguistic image, the concepts, are the object of theoretical research in the field of economy. The analysis of the concepts may in an individual case have a certain significance for the presentation of the theoretical knowledge of economy, but the goal of research in the field of theoretical economics can only be the determination of the general nature and the general connection of economic phenomena. It is a sign of the slight understanding, which individual representatives of the historical school in particular have for the aims of theoretical research, when they see only analyses of concepts in investigations into the nature of the commodity, into the nature of economy, the nature of value, of price and similar things, and when they see "the setting up of a system of concepts and judgments" in the striving for an exact theory of economic phenomena ... A number of French economists fall into a similar error when, with an erroneous view of the concepts "theory" and "system", they understand by these terms nothing more than theorems obtained deductively from *a priori* axioms …' (Menger, 1883, p. 37).
24. With the notable exception of Rothbard, who had the peculiar virtue of being at the same time a staunch defender of the Aristotelian variety of Mengerian realism and a fierce supporter of Mises' theses, this distant relationship with Menger's epistemology is a constant

in neo-Austrian literature. Accordingly, while Kirzner seems not to be offended by Menger's essentialism, he still considers his general conception of the economic system 'prevents him appreciating later steps taken in the development of subjectivist economics' (Kirzner, *The Meaning of Market Process: Essays in the Development of Modern Austrian Economics*, 1992a, p. 71).

2. Praxeology, Axiomatic System of Economics

Mises' thought was that deductive reasoning in the social spheres leads back to the concept of action. It being the first link in the chain of knowledge, action is the very axiom which supports the entire construction of economic theory. Praxeology is the definition of a grammar of human action;[1] it must supply us with apodictic knowledge of the structuring elements of human action. Praxeology 'is not concerned with the changing content of acting, but with its pure form and its categorial structure' (Mises, 1966, p. 47).

> It does not deal in vague terms with human action in general, but with concrete action which a definite man has performed at a definite date and at a definite place. But of course, it does not concern itself with the accidental and environmental features of this action and with what distinguishes it from all other actions, but only with what is necessary and universal in its performance (ibid., p. 44).

This knowledge is acquired in an *a priori* way, built out of introspection. 'Like logic and mathematics, praxeological knowledge is in us; it does not come from without' (ibid., p. 64). From this perspective, praxeology's teachings 'are not subject to verification or falsification on the ground of experience and facts. They are both logically and temporally antecedent to any comprehension of historical facts' and also 'Its statements and propositions are not derived from experience' (ibid., p. 32).

Praxeology in fact expresses the ultimate given: action; and also forms theorems growing from the axiomatic status of action. Mises devoted to it much of his epistemological writings (1). The implications of his studies led him to promote the idea of subjectivism (2) and also to clearly draw the lines between praxeology and psychology (3).

1. THE PRAXEOLOGICAL MODEL'S STRUCTURE

All of Mises' epistemological works (1933, 1957, 1962a, and so on) show his constant wish to define the various components of the whole discipline of praxeology. These different elements are finally brought together in a systemised form in the various editions of *Human Action* under a general study of the characters (1.1), the conditions (1.2) and the implications (1.3) of action.

1.1 Characters

One of the defining and foremost principles of praxeology is that of a methodological individualism. As '... only individuals think and act' (Mises, 1957, p. 190), 'praxeology begins its investigations from the individual action ... The Ego is the unity of the acting being. It is unquestionably given and cannot be dissolved or conjured away by any reasoning or quibbling' (1966, p. 44). This individualism is echoed in the criticism of 'hypostatization', that is to say the tendency 'to ascribe substance or real existence to mental constructs or concepts' (1962a, p. 78). In Mises' opinion a collective has no praxeological reality. It is itself the result of a pattern of actions, springing from the group's constituent individuals' strategies and behaviours, the only ones able to be scientifically examined. 'Thus the way to a cognition of collective wholes is through an analysis of the individuals' actions' (1966, p. 42). This praxeological Ego cannot be ignored by the social sciences. Mises, in all logic, is drawn to a critique of the method of macro-economics. In the whole of economics, there is no common movement but multitudes of individual actions, each directed towards subjective ends. The 'macro-economic concept of national income' takes no account of the individual activity which goes to make it up. So it is nothing more than 'a mere political slogan devoid of any cognitive value' (1962a, p. 87).

Action's second characteristic is that of direct cost, as scarce resources are inevitably used up. According to the types of action, various resources are at play; two at least, those of mental faculties and time, always being needed. Time, in particular is a 'praxeological factor' (1966, p. 99).

The third corollary of the action axiom is that of choice. Action supposes a consideration of the alternatives available to the actor. 'What counts for praxeology is only the fact that acting man chooses between alternatives' (ibid., p. 127). Action always requires accepting and rejecting, as one can never take all the opportunities available. This reflects the idea of scarcity which frames any individual's activity. Choice also supposes the existence of an infra-individual asymmetry of values, because choosing, by definition implies the concept of preference: 'All conscious conduct on the part of men involves preferring an A to B' (Mises, 1933, p. 149).

Action's final characteristic is of its purpose: 'Action means conscious behaviour or purposive activity. It differs as such from the biological, physiological, and instinctive processes going on within human beings' (Mises, 1944a, p. 19. So the final objective of any action is to replace a certain situation with another more satisfactory one. Of course, individuals define their own aims. These are born of individual mental states and value judgements which will determine the set of choices underlying action.

Human beings are not passive in their social and physical environment; they are capable of influencing events and to a certain extent, of redirecting them.

It is from this point of view that Mises says man has a free will, with its own powers of decision which express the deliberate, conscious character of action.

> There is a sphere within which man can choose between alternatives. He is not, like other animals, inevitably and irremediably subject to the operation of blind fate. He can, within definite narrow limits, divert events from the course they would take it left alone. He is an acting being. In this consists his superiority to mice and microbes, plants and stones (1957, p. 179).

Asserting that man is a free agent does not mean to deny any form of determinism, the particularities and workings of which are mostly inaccessible to the conscious mind, making realisation impossible. So 'The sciences of human action start from the fact that man purposefully aims at ends he has chosen. It is precisely this that all brands of positivism, behaviourism and panphysicalism want either to deny altogether or to pass over in silence' (ibid., p. 3).

So action is by itself purposeful: 'Individuals act in order to bring about definite results' (ibid., p. 195). The intention of an act is to obtain results and nothing else. Even following a routine is a deliberate strategy, obeying the conscious will. Letting events take their natural course instead of modifying them is also the result of a conscious decision and should be seen as action in itself. According to Mises, Max Weber's distinctions between emotional and intentional action are invalid from a theoretical point of view, as these distinctions come from historical categories. So as any behaviour stems from an individual's desire to consciously obtain results, 'the "seeking to attain" and the "striving after a goal" cannot be eliminated from the concept of action' (Mises, 1933, p. 33-34).

1.2 Conditions

Praxeology's heuristic contents clearly show us what the three conditions of action are. Firstly, action must aim to eliminate uneasiness, identifiable as an idea of disequilibrium: 'An acting being is discontended … if he were contended, he would not act' (Mises, 1966, p. 69).

Secondly, the idea of uneasiness must immediately summon up the image of a more desirable situation: 'Acting man is eager to substitute a more satisfactory state of affairs for a less satisfactory. His mind imagines conditions which suit him better, and his action aims at bringing about this desired state' (ibid., p. 13).

Finally, any action supposes the idea of a belief in action's successful outcome, which obviously does not exclude the notion of one making mistakes. The reason for the belief that action will succeed is the knowledge of a relation of cause and effect. If there is intention in an action, so reflecting a teleological dimension, its description and its acting out 'presupposes the category of cause and effect' (Mises, 1957, p. 93). Action expressing the use of means to reach goals is inextricably bound by relations of cause and effect, and so requires the use of reason. Reason informs man which resources are best-suited to reach his goals and also which of these goals are incompatible.[2]

Establishing a causal relation does not necessarily mean staying within the bounds of logic in its generally accepted meaning; superstitions and other beliefs in their various forms can often form the basis of such a relation.

> A peasant eager to get a rich crop may – according to the content of his ideas – choose various methods. He may perform some magical rites, he may embark upon a pilgrimage, he may offer a candle to the image of his patron saint, or he may employ more and better fertilizer. But whatever he does, it is always action, i.e., the employment of means for the attainment of ends. Magic is in a broader sense a variety of technology. Exorcism is a deliberate purposeful action based on a world view which most of our contemporaries condemn as superstitious and therefore as inappropriate. But the concept of action does not imply that the action is guided by a correct theory and a technology promising success and that it attains the end aimed at. It only implies that the performer of the action believes that the means applied will produce the desired effect (Mises, 1966, p. 37).[3]

1.3 Implications

Praxeology's last teaching here provides an analysis of the implications of action. Mises tells us there are two linked consequences to action, the idea of an infra-individual exchange and of uncertainty as to the results of action.

Action's characteristic of choice means it expresses an infra-individual exchange, from the individual's point of view. Action necessitates 'both taking and renunciation' (1966, p. 12), so imposes an opportunity cost on and is always involved in the idea of 'the renunciation of something to which a lower value is assigned in order to attain or to preserve something to which a higher value is assigned' (1957, p. 24).

Action corresponds to a will of transforming the unsatisfactory nature of a state to a more satisfactory one; this infra-individual exchange means also exchanging a present state for a future one. 'The concepts of change and of time are inseparably linked together. Action aims at change and is therefore in the temporal order. Human reason is even incapable of conceiving the ideas of timeless existence and of timeless action' (1966, p. 99). The temporal character of action (exchanging the present for a future) means the result will be uncertain, as: 'One of the fundamental conditions of man's existence and action is the fact that he does not know what will happen in the future'

(1957, p. 180). If we knew the future, it could never be separated conceptually from the present.[4] So, for Mises, 'action necessarily always aims at future and therefore uncertain conditions and thus is always speculation. Acting man looks, as it were, with the eyes of a historian into the future' (1966, p. 58). Uncertainty of the future is a praxeological given.

This aspect of time needed for human action gives an added dimension to the analysis of the use of mathematics in the social sciences. Mises holds that action's necessarily temporal aspect does not allow a mathematical representation, as 'the relations and implications of their [mathematical] system are coexistent and interdependent. We may say as well that they are synchronous or that they are out of time'. Mathematics and the praxeological system share the same *a priori*, deductive character. On the contrary, however, to mathematics, 'change is one of its [praxeology's] elements. The notions of sooner and later and of cause and effect are among its constituents. Anteriority and consequence are essential concepts of praxeological reasoning' (Mises, 1966, p. 99). Some will object that change and causality are very much elements of the natural sciences, within which mathematics operate with such effect. But the specific element to the social field is the total absence of empirical constants; in the final analysis, it is from this view that mathematics cannot fit praxeological logic (Figure 2.1).

2. PRAXEOLOGICAL SUBJECTIVISM

The praxeological model represents an analytical whole, characteristic of the neo Austrian economy. Its structure allows for a certain number of developments, the first of which is the idea of Wertfreiheit. This means the absence of any value judgement from praxeological thought (2.1); the second concerns the status of rationality in human action (2.2).

2.1 The Reign of Wertfreiheit

In Mises' eyes, the praxeological model is characterised by the idea of Wertfreiheit. In his epistemological works, this term seems to have acquired a double meaning.

Firstly, the praxeological model is Wertfrei in that the validity of what it teaches us is not dependent on the goals and knowledge of its actors.

> Everything that we say about action is independent of the motives that cause it and of goals toward which it strives in the individual case. It makes no difference whether action springs from altruistic or from egoistic motives, from a noble or from a base disposition; whether it is directed toward the attainment of materialistic or idealistic end (1933, p. 34).

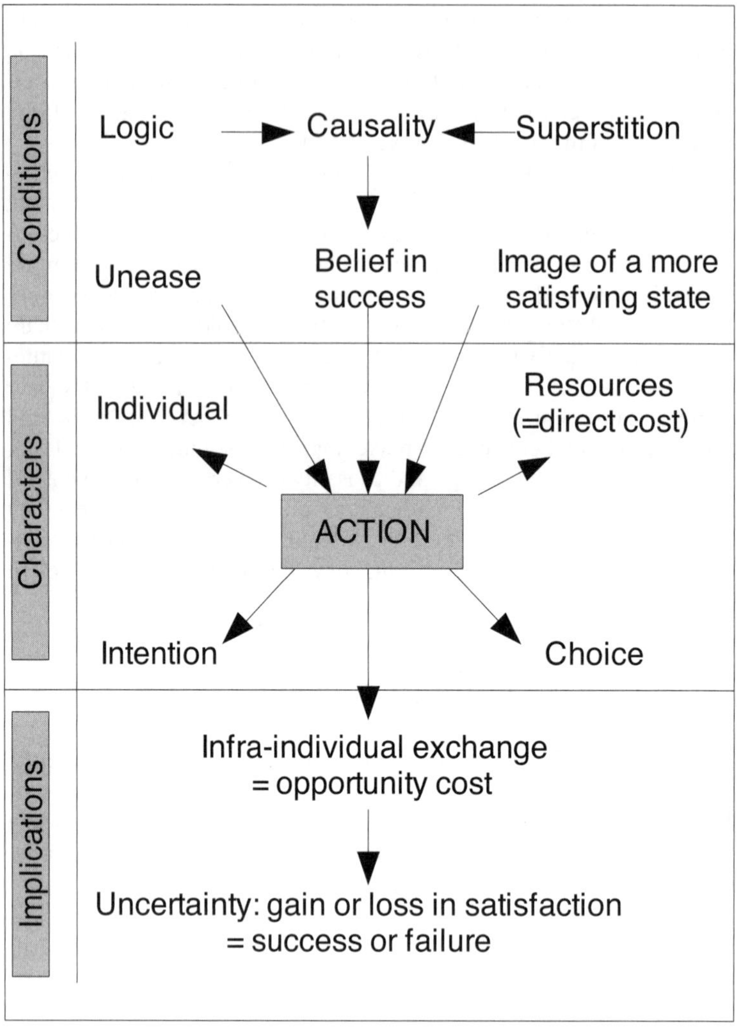

Figure 2.1 The Praxeological System

For Mises, the logic of human action is identical whatever its goals. Its value is apodictic: no human desire, no personal strategies, no result of human action can escape this. A praxeological analysis must take no account of particular aspects of an actor's behaviour, so praxeological laws are clearly set apart from Menger's 'exact laws', which depend on actors' knowledge and also their driving motivations.

Secondly, the praxeological model is Wertfrei because it must suppose the theorist's moral neutrality. In Mises' view, anyone recognising praxeology's validity cannot bring any value judgement to bear on an actor's objectives. Each individual takes opportunities useful to him as an individual, so improving his satisfaction,

> Since satisfaction and dissatisfaction depend only on the subjective view of the individual, there is no room for argument on this question in a science that does not presume to establish a scale of values or to make judgments of value. Its conception of an end, in the strict sense, is more deductive than empirical: ends are determined by the wishes and the desires of the individual. Whenever reference is made to the greater or lesser appropriateness of means, this can only be from the point of view of the acting individual (1933, p. 32-33).

2.2 The Rationality of Human Action

This amoralism has far reaching consequences. As actions can only come about to improve an individual's situation, from a praxeological point of view, each action reveals the agent's preferences. A scale of values is built out of behaviour[5] and so: 'However one twists things, one will never succeed in formulating the notion of "irrational" action whose "irrationality" is not founded upon an arbitrary judgment of value' (Mises, 1966, p. 104). From this standpoint, Mises opposes Max Weber's distinction between rational action and irrational action:

> Action is, by definition, always rational. One is unwarranted in calling goals of action irrational simply because they are not worth striving for from the point of view of one's own valuations. Such a mode of expression leads to gross misunderstandings. Instead of saying that irrationality plays a role in action, one should accustom oneself to saying merely: There are people who aim at different ends from those that I aim at, and people who employ different means from those I would employ in their situation (Mises, 1933, p. 35).

Action is always rational, where the goal of action is to obtain the desired end. In Mises' view it is legitimate, through the notion of causality, to praxeologically associate the notion of action to that of rationality.[6]

3. PRAXEOLOGY AND PSYCHOLOGY

The epistemological basis of the notion of action comes from its axiomatic characteristic. The human mind and knowledge of human matters cannot escape the concept of action; thought is action, and all action brings us in a circular fashion back to the concept of thought. The completion of the praxeological circle is thus demonstrated. However, its logic shows additional heuristic elements, bringing up important issues in the field of economic analysis. It firstly clarifies the indifference/preference relation within the neo-Austrian tradition (3.1); secondly, it shows up the relation between the analysis of human action and psychology (3.2); and lastly it gives us one praxeological definition of the notion of tendency towards equilibrium (3.3).

3.1 Preference and Indifference

The figure above clearly shows the position of preference in the praxeological model. The idea of choice implies an infra-individual asymmetry of values: 'If an individual prefers A to B, we say that, at the moment of the act of choice, A appeared more important to him (more valuable, more desirable) than B' (Mises 1933, p. 149). To put it another way, the actor ascribes more value to a future situation than to a present one. As it is impossible to conceive action without associating it to the notion of preference, the epistemological value of the latter is established, in the same way as it finds its correct position in the praxeological scheme.

So what about indifference? Rothbard ('Toward a Reconstruction of a Theory of Utility and Welfare Economics') rightly notes: 'Indifference can never be demonstrated by action. Quite the contrary. Every action necessarily signifies a choice, and every choice signifies a definite preference. Action specifically implies the contrary of indifference' (Rothbard, 1956, p. 237).

So we have established that no person can conceive perfect indifference, without coming up against a logical contradiction. The very fact of imagining this situation implies thought, therefore action, so an expression of preference is obligatory. Rightly, Mises often speaks of the conceptual impossibility of expressing or thinking the perfect being, that is, being Perfectly Indifferent. Even if Absolute Indifference is unthinkable, we have to say that someone would be able to conceive a situation to which he would be indifferent. Mises recognises this: 'It may happen that the judging individual considers both things or conditions envisaged as equal. He is not concerned whether there is A or B. Then, his judgment of value expresses indifference' (1957, p. 24). Each actor is able to mentally represent himself as being indifferent in his comparison of goods or bundles thereof. His actions, however, will always express a preference.

We can also look at this from a different angle, through the odd idea of Absolute Preference. This is not just semantically absurd, but it is also a praxeological impossibility: prefer everything to everything would be to deny the idea of Action, as the act (thought) must mean you change one situation for another. The idea of Absolute Preference is praxeologically unfounded, as is Absolute Indifference. In the same way, as particular preference is allowed, because identified to action, we must also allow particular indifference as being epistemologically valid. These concepts of preference and indifference are in fact two sides of the same coin. Deny the first and you must deny the second; allow one and you are obliged to allow the other.

3.2 Action, Creator of Preference

The traditional position of the Austrian authors (Mises, Rothbard, Kirzner) is to make a clear separation between the world of praxeology and of psychology, given here as the study of the formation and transformation of preferences. For Mises, what is important is not to explore what action's motivations, as they are not accessible to the observer, but to simply define a grammar of action.

> Psychology, in turning to the individual, found the right stating point. However, its path necessarily leads in another direction than that of the science of human action. The subject matter of the latter is action and what follows from action, whereas the subject matter of psychology is the psychic events that result in action. Economics begins at the point at which psychology leaves off (1933, p. 3).[7]

Mises' view determined the official position of all the neo-Austrian tradition's representatives,[8] yet some recent studies question its value. A number of commentators, such as Birner ('The Surprising Place of Cognitive Psychology in the Work of FA Hayek', 1999), have noticed Hayek's interest in theoretical psychology (*The Sensory Order*, 1952a) and have rightly brought up questions about the whole neo-Austrian view, given this new light.

Yet at this stage of our study, our concern is to examine the coherence of Mises' reasoning, so we can consider the proper place of psychology in the analysis of human action and avoid misunderstandings. Mises' refusal of psychology does not mean the praxeological model is incomplete. Human action's axiomatic and circular dimensions mean that an action has to lead to another action and so on. In other words, any action is initiated by unease and any action must lead to other unease. This would be easy to understand if action always led to failure but nothing in the praxeological model implies this.

Action may also succeed and put the agent in the best position of any of those he envisaged; equilibrium is thus achieved and action leads to no other action. The circular reasoning is then broken and the praxeological model's completion called into question. The only way out of this problem is to assume that the satisfaction of a need leads to another need appearing. So any success must logically lead to the forming of a preference. This puts Rothbard's comment in a different light: 'All we can say is that an action, at a specific point of time, reveals part of a man's preference scale at that time. There is no warrant for assuming that it remains constant from one point of time to another' (1957, p. 228-229).

We can therefore see two major theoretical implications here: firstly that equilibrium and disequilibrium are correlated ideas; each time an individual attains his objective (that is a certain level of satisfaction), he conceives other goals (he seeks gains in satisfaction). There is no stable equilibrium possible as it brings disequilibrium.[9] Secondly, if, as Mises states 'life implies an endless sequence of acts of choosing' (1957, p. 12), then existence may be defined as an endless quest for gains in satisfaction. It eternally seeks a 'state of perfect happiness and contentment at which all human activity aims without ever wholly attaining it' (ibid., p. 15). The feeling of happiness cannot then come from some fictitious state of equilibrium. It comes from taking opportunities and trajectories, therefore not from results or final endowments. Whether action succeeds or not, the unease is perpetual as is the will to gain in satisfaction.[10]

So life can be described as process of gaining in satisfaction, action being the means of creating it.

> In colloquial speech we call a man 'happy' who has succeeded in attaining his ends. A more adequate description of his state would be that he is happier than he was before. There is however no valid objection to a usage that defines human action as the striving for happiness (Mises, 1966, p. 14).

3.3 The Tendency Towards Equilibrium: A Praxeological Definition

All we have discussed indicates a praxeological view of the notion of a tendency towards equilibrium.[11] On the one hand, action comes before the desired goal, so by definition tends towards a goal. Action is the process between being in a state of disequilibrium and moving towards a state of equilibrium, so action's characteristic is one of tending towards equilibrium. On the other hand, on closer examination of the last point, we see that attaining equilibrium creates disequilibrium. The actor cannot escape the perpetual movement in and out of unease. Action can only tend towards equilibrium, but can never reach it. 'Our science shows that aiming at ends is necessary to existence' (Mises, 1933, p. 40). As an individual imagines another framework for action, that is, another goal and other means, he initiates a new sequence of action. This imagination and construction of a praxeological framework is part of the continual creation of the individual self. This permanent unease, from the impossibility of contentment with current endowment and the desire to continually gain in satisfaction (explaining the unease of stasis) leads the individual to entrepreneurship. So here there is a praxeological dimension to entrepreneurship, which thus completes the cycle of human action.

The actor as entrepreneur

Seen from the praxeological viewpoint, this entrepreneurship is essentially a incessant search by its actors for gains in satisfaction. It is this feeling of unease which propels actors forward to seek new sources of satisfaction. The entrepreneur-actor discovers goals, chooses the means and structures his own action, to afterwards arrive at new plans. This is why Kirzner, in *The Economic Point of View* (1960), generically defines entrepreneurship as the search for more satisfaction. As his commentators have rightly pointed out, 'its exercise must be considered a general feature of human existence' (Ioannides, *The Market, Competition and Democracy: a Critique of Neo-Austrian Economics*, 1992, p. 65).

At the praxeological level, entrepreneurship can be defined as the task of identifying aims and possible means and also of structuring action. We could say that the entrepreneurial human being is a goal-seeker, the idea of the goal being a concretisation of an individual's will to gain in satisfaction, that is to have more tomorrow than today. Entrepreneurship could also include, as Kirzner strenuously underlines in his works (*Competition and Entrepreneurship*, 1973; *Perception, Opportunities and Profits*, 1979, and so on) the idea that each actor ceaselessly seeks out errors. The goals chosen might possibly be inconsistent with the desire to gain in satisfaction, or other goals may reveal themselves to be more efficient. By the same token, the choice of the means is incessantly re-evaluated as to their quality but also their definition. The individual constantly scans the horizon to identify better means, the value of which cannot, in his eyes, be pre-established:

> The notion of given ends and means may be useful for certain purposes, but it does serious violence to the full reality of choice. The acting person never approaches the moment of decision already equipped with a clear, given picture of the relevant ends and means. It is only at the moment of decision itself that man is compelled to bring to some kind of focus to all his doubts and conjectures concerning what goals are worth pursuing and what resources and technologies are available (Kirzner, 1979, p. 227).

So the evolution of taste, preference, goals and means can all legitimately be considered as the results of exercising entrepreneurship. These changes do not fit with some traditional ideas of rationality but express others, of an adaptive nature. It is not a question of allocating finite resources to fixed goals, it more fundamentally means defining a structure of action which gives the most possible satisfaction.

There is an interesting comparison to be made between Mises' viewpoint and Lionel Robbins' concept of economics (*An Essay on the Nature and Significance of Economic Science*, 1932). In his well-known definition: 'Economics is the science which studies human behaviour as a relationship between ends and scarce means which have alternative uses' (Robbins,1932, p. 15, note 1). To the best of our knowledge, Mises did not feel the need to take position with Robbins on this point.[12] There are, however, extensive writings on this subject.

Mises and Robbins

We could consider Addleson's article ('Robbins' Essay in Retrospect: On Subjectivism and an Economics of Choice', 1984) as the first to study the relationship between Robbins and the neo-Austrian tradition. Following this, Wiseman ('Lionel Robbins, The Austrian School and the LSE Tradition', 1985) then O'Brien ('Lionel Robbins and the Austrian Tradition', 1990),[13] wrote overviews of the neo-Austrian and especially Mises' and Mayer's influence on Robbins' ideas, clarifying a certain number of historical and analytical lineages. Boettke and Koppl (2001) join them in remarking that when Robbins proposed his famous definition of the economy, he added a footnote mentioning that he considered himself as following authors such as 'Menger, "Grundsätze der Volkswirtschaftslehere", 1te Aufl., pp. 51-70; Mises, "Die Gemeinwirtschaft", pp. 98 *seq*.; Fetter, "Economic Principles", ch.i; Strigl, "Die ökonomischen Kategorien und die Organisation der Wirtschaft, passim"; Mayer, *op.cit*' (Robbins, 1932, p. 16).[14]

Kirzner helps us to further understand the analytical relationship between Mises and Robbins. He carefully shows throughout his works all the common points between the two authors; more interestingly he also points out areas of often sharp contrast.

In Kirzner's first work, *The Economic Point of View*, 1960, which he states was influenced by Mises (see p. XIV), Kirzner sees a very important step in Robbins' conception towards a proper definition of economics, which he likens to Mises': a general principle of human activity rather than a particular field of it. He also contentedly points out Robbins' total indifference to the particular content of ends and means. Whether or not the ends are material and the means are financial is unimportant, as

> Robbins' own formulation ... is analytical. It 'does not attempt to pick out certain kinds of behaviour, but focuses attention on a particular aspect of behaviour, the form imposed by the influence of scarcity' (Robbins, 1932) ... An act pertains to economic science in so far as it reveals the consequences of a compulsion to allocate scarce resources among conflicting ends. Robbins' formulation thus differs from others perhaps less in its choice of a criterion for definition than in its radi-

cally different conception of the kind of idea that is to be defined (Kirzner, 1960, p. 118).

So like Mises, Robbins clearly defines the economy as a principle of human activity, rather than just a component part, just as he states his analytical neutrality on the nature of the ends and the means.

Whatever similarities may exist between Mises and Robbins, it would be a mistake to confuse them. Kirzner, right from the beginning was keen to show the difference between Robbins' 'economizing man' and Mises' 'acting man' (*homo agens*): 'Economizing consists in the allocation of scarce resources among competing ends. Acting, in the praxeological sense, consists in selecting a pattern of behaviour designed to further the actor's purpose' (Kirzner, 1960, p. 161). So Mises' human action has a wider scope than Robbins' 'economizing' behaviour, being more global and more fundamental. Analyzing behaviour in terms of allocative decisions leaves the question of the pursuit of individual action unanswered. So we must consider Robbins' conception as a limited application of praxeology and many 'of its apparent inadequacies are seen to disappear when it is related explicitly to the broader concepts of a general theory of human action' (Kirzner, 1960, p. 148).

Robbins' individual operates inside a given framework of 'means-ends', its structure being data for analysis: the ends exist before action, ready prioritised; the means are seen as objective elements to attain the ends. However interesting this approach may be, it does not represent the whole praxeological logic. It particularly leaves aside the question of how the actor comes by the means and it does not give any clue as to how an individual moves from a means-ends structure to another. It does not explain the flow from one action to another and does not allow the completion of the praxeological cycle.

Kirzner continued to point out Mises' and Robbins' differences throughout his works with the same care as he did their similarities. The praxeological approach does not mean that an individual is obliged to act within a rigid, objective means-end framework that he cannot modify, like a straightjacket. On the contrary, decision processes 'reflect not merely the manipulation of given ends to correspond faithfully with the hierarchy of given ends, but also the *very perception of the ends-mean framework* within which allocation and economizing is to take place' (Kirzner, 1973, p. 33). Robbins no doubt concentrated a little too much on this allocative dimension of human action, which should not obscure the more fundamental, creative dimension of the deciding individual. A close reading of Mises' epistemological works strongly indicates that the actor permanently constructs his own internal environment, to be able to exploit every possible gain in satisfaction.

Of course, allocation is an economic act, as 'In a formal sense it is even possible to consider all human action as consisting in such allocation; but this involves the kind of artificiality in the conception of ends and means with which Professor Robbins' definition was charged' (Kirzner, 1960, p. 184).

Praxeologically speaking, establishing means to attain a chosen end defines the economic act, or any other. Yet, importantly, if the ends and means chosen by the actors are a given for the observer, they are not for the actors; they are chosen by the actors in a creative and continually corrective act: 'While the Robbinsian framework does not preclude a later discovery that the given ends-means framework is incorrect and must be replaced, this process of the discovery of error itself occurs, somehow, outside the Robbinsian human laboratory' (Kirzner, 1979, p. 166). We can sum up the difference between Robbins' 'economic' approach and Mises' 'praxeological' view in the two following points.

Firstly, in all of Robbins' approaches, it is as if 'economizing man' establishes a list of ends and means available and then allocates one to the other. Here, this allocation defines the economic characteristic of the individual. But 'acting' man does not make a means-end list; he fixes an objective and looks for the best way to reach it. Ends and means are correlated in the actor's mind, not segmented or even sequential (where the actor first makes a list of ends, then means and finally allocates means to ends). The means only becomes such for the actor when it enables him to reach an objective, which in turn only comes into being where he pursues it. Ends and means are not given to him, he actively searches out and selects both, 'that deliberation being essentially creative' (Kirzner, *Discovery and the Capitalist Process*, 1985, p. 48). So this means-ends duality is rather reductive. The individual's choice from a whole set of possible action is un-predetermined.

Secondly, Robbins' approach is undeniably subjective (that is an individual will always take his own decisions and consciously allocates a means to an end); yet it is still a rigid, static individual who chooses. Thus Kirzner rightly criticizes Robbins' structure as excluding real, or dynamic subjectivism: 'A fully subjectivist treatment of choice must grapple with the way the decision-maker, with all his spontaneous creativity in the face of a radically uncertain world, chooses which of the infinite possible pictures of the future he adopts as the basis for the alternatives scenarios among which he undertakes the path he is to pursue' (Kirzner, *The Meaning of Market Process: Essays in the Development of Modern Austrian Economics*, 1992a, p. 126). Robbins' allocative scheme excludes the shifting of choice, means and ends and therefore cannot explain action as a succession of decisions.

NOTES

1. In his first epistemological writings, Mises called this science of human action 'sociology' in order to differentiate it more precisely from history. He noted in the preface of the 1962

English edition of *Epistemelogical Problems of Economics*: 'When, in 1929, I first published the second essay of this collection, I still believed that it was unnecessary to introduce a new term to signify the general theoretical science of human action as distinguished from the historical studies dealing with human action performed in the past. I thought that it would be possible to employ for this purpose the term sociology, which in the opinion of some authors was designed to signify such a general theoretical science. Only later did I realize that this was not expedient and adopted the term praxeology' (1933 p. XV). However, in the works' very first editions, this 'sociology' was already clearly defined as 'a theoretical science of human action, i.e., a science that aims at the ascertainment of universally valid laws of human conduct. All that this science owes to August Comte is its name' (ibid., p. 68). The first time Mises ever published the word 'praxeology' was in *Nationalökonomie*, 1940. He had discovered it in an article by Espinas dated 1890; 'The origins of technology' (see Mises, 1966, p. 4; 1944, p.18). Prendergast ('A. Schütz and the Austrian School of Economics'), distinguishing general sociology from a descriptive sociology, which he considered a 'historical' discipline, says 'The Austrians always believed that economics was a branch of general sociology, understood as a universal science of social phenomena as such' (Prendergast, 1986, p. 23).

2. 'The philosophical, epistemological, and metaphysical problems of causality and of imperfect induction are beyond the scope of praxeology. We must simply establish the fact that in order to act, man must know the causal relationship between events, processes, or states of affairs. And only as far as he knows this relationship, can his action attain the ends sought. We are fully aware that in asserting this we are moving in a circle. For the evidence that we have correctly perceived a causal relation is provided only by the fact that action guided by this knowledge results in the expected outcome. But we cannot avoid this vicious circular evidence precisely because causality is a category of action. And because it is such a category, praxeology can not help bestowing some attention on this fundamental problem of philosophy' (Mises, 1966, p. 23).
3. Only logic or superstition will allow us to establish a causal relationship. We know experience cannot speak of itself, as attaching significance to facts must be preceded by theoretical investigation. Tradition, one of Hayek's much used concepts (see Part 2, Chapters 1 and 3) can be viewed at this stage as a way of escaping this categorisation, situated 'between instinct and reason' (see Hayek, *The Fatal Conceit*, 1988).
4 'The present *qua* duration is the continuation of the conditions and opportunities given for acting' (Mises, 1966, p. 101).
5. '... the scale of values or wants manifests itself only in the reality of action. These scales have non independent existence apart from the actual behaviour of individuals. The only source from which our knowledge concerning these scales is derived is the observation of a man's actions. Every action is always in perfect agreement with the scale of values or wants because these scales are nothing but an instrument for the interpretation of a man's acting' (Mises, 1966, p. 95)
6. Of course, Mises' assertion of the necessarily rational aspect of action does not exclude actors making mistakes or being led up the wrong path to failure. 'To make mistakes in pursuing one's ends is a widespread human weakness. Some err less often than others, but no mortal man is omniscient and infallible. Error, inefficiency and failure must not be confused with irrationality' (Mises, 1957, p. 268).
7. Mises' position never varied throughout his work. So in *Human Action*, he says again: 'The field of our science is human action, not the psychological events which result in an action. It is precisely this which distinguishes the general theory of human action, praxeology, from psychology ... The theme of psychology is the internal events that result or can result in a definite action. The theme of praxeology is action as such ... Psychoanalysis ... does not investigate action but the forces and factors that impel a man toward a definite action' (Mises, 1966, p. 11-12).

8. So '… desires exist by virtue of the concept of human action and of the existence of action' (Rothbard, 1956, p. 228), '... utility is a praxeological, rather than a directly psychologic concept' (ibid, p. 241).
9. 'The assumption it makes, viz., that all other conditions remain perfectly unchanged, is an indispensable fiction for reasoning and science. In life everything is continually in flux but for thought we must construct an imaginary state of rest' (Mises, 1933, p. 108).
10. '[Human action] can never bring full satisfaction; it merely gives for an evanescent instant a partial removal of uneasiness. As soon as one want is satisfied, new wants spring up and ask for satisfaction' (Mises, 1966, p. 881).
11. Most neo-Austrian authors accept this notion. However, there are several interpretations possible of its meaning and bearing. There are many internal debates on this subject and some little disagreement, explored further in Chapter 3.
12. Mises alludes to Robbins twice (*Human Action*, p. 109 and p. 558), in two footnotes yet does not mention the question of the definition of the economic sciences. Before this, in *Epistemological Problems of Economics* (1933), on the theme of rationality, Mises briefly refers to Robbins' work in a bibliographical note (p 35, note 7). In his other epistemological works (*Theory and History*, 1957; *The Ultimate Foundations of Economic Science*, 1962), as well as the relevant part of *Money, Method and the Market Process*, 1990, there is no mention at all of Robbins. However, without directly quoting him, Mises defines the economy in the introduction to *Human Action* as 'a science of the means to be applied for the attainment of ends chosen' (Mises, 1966, p. 10).
13. See Blaug's very useful commentary (1990) on O'Brien's article.
14. In the preface to the work's first edition, Robbins expressed his 'special indebtedness to the works of Professor Ludwig von Mises' (Robbins, 1932, p. XV-XVI).

3. Action and Interpersonal Exchange: The Limits of the *A Priori* Approach

From Mises' point of view, the praxeological scheme of things is the basis of economics. All the economic categories appear there, for example: value (all action moves towards an ultimate objective of gain in satisfaction), cost (using scarce resources) and preference (choice involving an asymmetry of values).

We also know that notions of action and exchange are inseparable. Action is always an infra-individual[1] exchange, whether theoretically or empirically viewed. Distinct exchange categories, however, should be noted, taking two practical forms: isolated and social (involving several individuals). In the case of isolated action, the only exchange is infra-individual. Mises describes it as an 'autistic exchange' (Mises, 1966, p. 206). Social action additionally involves interpersonal exchange which 'weaves the bond which unites men into society' (ibid, p. 206).

Mises' disciples define some particular epistemological aspects out of this exchange taxinomy. Establishing two distinct categories means that neither can be individually a theorem of action.[2] They are contingent, impossible to approach in an *a priori* or introspective mode (1). Particularly, moving from a formal analysis of action to the study of social action requires 'subsidiary' (Hayek 'Economics and Knowledge', 1937a) hypotheses to the praxeological structure. In other words, certain particular conditions must be present for interpersonal exchange to not only take place but be conceptually analysed. This question was to become crucial in the monetary field, leading Hayek to question the epistemological foundations of market theories (2).

1. VARYING FORMS OF INTERPERSONAL EXCHANGE: FROM BARTER TO MONEY

Social or interpersonal exchange (involving several individuals) can be divided into two empirical categories: direct exchange, which expresses a barter economy (1.1) and indirect exchange, resulting from self-generating processes (1.2).

1.1 Barter, a Product of Theory and History

Barter is direct or bilateral exchange of real goods or services. Quite apart from actors' anticipated gains in satisfaction being validated or not – examined in Chapter 6 – barter shows a photograph of its participants subjective appreciation of the quantity of goods exchanged, at the moment of transaction. This intersubjective information is a side effect rather than a goal of the exchange, a positive externality. This is important information as it reduces the constraint of ignorance.

The phenomenon of ignorance is a given of praxeological reasoning. It expresses the basic fact that an actor cannot have *a priori* knowledge of another actor's preferences, knowledge or strategies; so every actor is in fundamental ignorance of other actors' evaluations of goods and services. It is therefore impossible to base economic analysis on perfect knowledge about other actors. It is also impossible for the external observer to use technical knowledge to evaluate actors' preferences concerning available goods.

This ignorance is a real hindrance to organising economies, as

> the practical man, eager to improve human conditions by removing uneasiness as far as possible, must know whether, under given conditions, what he is planning is the best method, or even a method, to make people less uneasy. He must know whether what he wants to achieve will be an improvement when compared with the present state of affairs and with the advantages to be expected from the execution of other technically realizable projects which cannot be put into execution if the project he has in mind absorbs the available means (Mises, 1966, p. 208).

This problem finds its roots, of course in the issue of subjectivism. The particularity of individual values makes it impossible to superimpose one's own preferences on another agent. So fitting production with actors' consumption wants comes up against a problem of division of knowledge, which has to be solved to be able to rationally allocate resources. The constraints that subjectivity imposes would be reduced if factors were specific, able to produce only one type of goods. In this case, all factors could be allocated in a predetermined way. But this is often far from being the case, as a resource such as labour can have many differing uses, expressing the factors' non-specific character. So what is needed is a procedure to reveal agents' preferences in order to adjust production to their needs. We can thus clearly understand the advantages of interpersonal exchange.

Passing from autistic to interpersonal exchange offers the observer information on actors' value judgements and enables him to put a figure on their choices. A transaction, bringing out an exchange rate, means progressing from an ordinal calculation (choice of A or B) to a cardinal type (how much of A will be exchanged against how much of B). It is only in these terms that we can make an economic calculation; a producer thus has an indicator which he uses to base decisions on and allocate resources.

Bartering requires three conditions: the presence of at least two individuals, the double coincidence of wants and of a mode of communication between the partners.[3] It is worth taking a closer look at this third element, seeing its importance and the type of mechanisms it sets into motion.

When two potentially exchanging partners meet, both actors are mutually ignorant of the other's preference structure. All they have is *a priori* information (Mises has it as theoretical) which comes from the laws of human action: a rising demand-curve on the part of the buyer and a falling offer-curve on the part of the seller. One actor's curve shape is totally unknown to the other at the moment of meeting.

The process of bargaining or of negotiation has precisely the objective of acquiring this knowledge. The actors learn the others' preferences, by an exchange of propositions, adjusted continually in reaction to the other actor. By proposition (a quantity of X for a quantity of Y) and counter-proposition, each potential exchanger formulates, through trial and error, a map of the others' interests. Using his theoretical knowledge and his growing concrete information acquired from the bargaining process, each individual interprets the other's interest structure and tries to fit his own strategies with his partner's. By this gradual discovery of each other's subjectivity, each agent is able to adjust his offer to reach exchange, if their interests allow it.[4]

So although the process starts from a theory standpoint, it takes an 'understanding' approach (or as Mises says, historic), necessary to reach the common point which will seal an exchange, the terms of which will reveal the agent's preferences.

Barter, however, has marked limitations. It is especially governed by the double coincidence of wants, the chance-based character of which limits exchange possibilities. If preferences towards the goods were similar, there would be no opportunity of exchange at all. Individuals would have to make do with their initial endowments, making no gains in satisfaction. However, this frustrating state of affairs is not the crucial point. Non-exchange makes information production on actors' preferences impossible and thus the creation of any criterion of rational resource allocation. Introducing an intermediary into the exchange, to transform barter into indirect exchange gets rid of this limitation. This problem directed the neo-Austrian authors' attention particularly to the question of monetary price.

1.2 Indirect Exchange, The Money Price Generator

Indirect (or monetary) exchange is the other form of interpersonal exchange. Introducing the intermediary of money to carry out transactions widens the scope of exchange opportunities, therefore of gains in satisfaction. The Austrian authors saw in fact that where the double coincidence of wants is missing; the role of money becomes essential in producing otherwise hidden information. It is the 'more saleable' (Carl Menger, 1871, 1883) good which can be exchanged for any other goods in the economy. It is the intermediary by which other goods' subjective values are expressed even when they are not being directly exchanged. Monetary calculation unites individual costs and profits into the same good. A whole set of relative prices appears, guiding production. This information produced by the money-price structure encourages a level of division of labour and of productivity impossible in its absence. As Rothbard sums up, 'The establishment of a money on the market enormously increases the scope for specialization and division of labor, immensely widens the market for every product, and makes possible a society on a civilized productive level' (*Man, Economy and State: a Treatise on Economic Principles*, 1962, vol. 1, p. 165).

Money is the only instrument of widespread communication of knowledge available to a community of division of labour in the context of division of needed information for the coordination of various individual actions. As Mises says, it becomes 'the vehicle of economic calculation' (Mises, 1966, p. 208). So, 'Fundamentally, in a system in which the knowledge of the relevant facts is dispersed among many people, prices can act to co-ordinate the separate actions of different people.' (Hayek, 'The Use of Knowledge in Society', 1945 p. 85). The market, that is the whole of indirect interpersonal exchange, gives access to information. Answering the problem of division of knowledge, it is an element of appreciation for guiding production and inputs.

In *Human Action*, Mises distinguishes praxeology, the economic field in its widest sense, from catallaxy, the economy in its narrower sense: 'The field of catallactics or of economics in the narrower sense is... the analysis of those actions which are conducted on the basis of monetary calculation' (1966, p. 234). So catallaxy is the sphere of indirect exchange, or in other words it is the place 'of the determination of money prices of goods and services exchanged on the market' (ibid., p. 234).[5] Catallaxy, the definition of which came to be adopted by all the neo-Austrian authors, is the product of an auto-generated order.

The Austrians were especially interested in market forces' origins. For Mises, catallaxy is neither the creation of a higher will nor of any contract. It is simply the expression of individuals' social cooperation.

> It was not first planned as an utopian scheme and then put to work. Spontaneous actions of individuals, aiming at nothing else than at the improvement of their own state of satisfaction, undermined the prestige of their coercive status system step by step. Then only, when the superior efficiency of economic freedom could no longer be questioned, social philosophy entered the scene and demolished the ideology of the status system (1962a, p. 109).

Catallaxy is the result of individuals' interacting strategies which participate in interpersonal exchange.

Hayek's analysis from this perspective was that institutions were the spontaneous results of individual actions. One of the social sciences' main foci is 'to explain the unintended or undesigned results of the action of many men' (1952b, p. 25). He bases himself on a Mengerian social overview, which projects collective wholes out of individual attitudes, seeing how 'the independent action of many men can produce coherent wholes, persistent structures of relationships which serve important human purposes without having been designed for that end' (ibid. p. 80). These undesigned social processes promote in turn individuals' interests, producing positive externalities in the same way as Menger's organic phenomena or Smith's invisible hand, so the various economic agents can thus widen their scope of consumption opportunities.

Hayek expounds at length on the subject:

> I have deliberately used the word 'marvel' to shock the reader out of the complacency with which we often take the working of this mechanism for granted. I am convinced that if it were the result of deliberate human design … this mechanism would have been acclaimed as one of the greatest triumphs of the human mind. Its misfortune is the double one that it is not the product of human design and that the people guided by it usually do not know why they are made to do what they do. But those who clamor for 'conscious direction' and who cannot believe that anything which has evolved without design (and even without our understanding it) should solve problems which we should not be able to solve consciously – should remember this: The problem lies precisely in how to extend the span of our utilization of resources beyond the span of the control of any one mind (1945, p. 87-88).

The importance of money accorded by all the Austrian authors explains their keen interest in its nature and origins. Carl Menger very early studied the problem in *Principles*, appendix J, contesting the tradition that money was some sort of a state invention. It was not the fruit of some carefully worded agreement by 'economic individuals' nor the product of 'legislative acts' but 'a natural product of human economy' (Menger, 1871, p. 262).[6]

Menger gives money as the typical example of a non planned, organic (as opposed to pragmatic) institution which Hayek was to treat at such length much later. It is the result of evolution brought about by agents ever seeking wider opportunities of exchange. Custom and imitation play large parts in this process which results in selecting goods 'acceptable to everyone in trade, and thus capable of being given in exchange for any other commodity. These goods were called "Geld" by our ancestors, a term derived from "gelten" which means to compensate or pay. Hence the term "Geld" in our language designates the means of payment as such' (Menger, 1871, p. 260).[7]

This approach provokes discussion even today[8] but all Menger's successors followed this view of money as the most saleable good, all its other functions being necessarily linked to this most basic principle.[9]

As with any goods, subjective value of money is linked to the utility of the latest unit to be possessed, a reflection of the use value of the goods that it buys. Money also has an objective value of exchange, expressing its relative price to other goods and thus its buying power in the economy. There is a theoretical problem with this analysis however: the marginalist analysis tells us that a good's price expresses a match of subjective appreciations. Money's only use is in fact its exchange value; it does not possess a use value in itself, unlike other goods in the marketplace. Its only utility is indirect, through the goods it can buy on the market.

Mises solves this problem by an explanation of the value of money's history, based on 'the regression theorem'. In *The Theory of Money and Credit* (1912), he shows how the use value of goods is the basis for their money function. Because of its many possible uses, many individuals are prepared to accept it in exchanges, so it becomes more liquid than other goods. As its monetary function develops, there is a separation between the good's initial usage and its being valued for ease of circulation. So there is increasing distance between money's objective value and the use value of the object constituting it. In Mises' view, the present subjective value of money results from its objective value in the immediate past, depending on estimations of its subjective value in the immediate past, and so on. If we carry the process of regression back in time to its logical conclusion, we arrive at the point where money's purchase power depends on the match of individuals' estimations of its use value or industrial value. So money's objective value originates in individuals' subjective appreciations of its constituent goods' value.[10]

2. EPISTEMOLOGICAL PROBLEMS WITH MARKET EXCHANGE

Mises' analyses show us the way we acquire the necessary knowledge to form a barter exchange. But it would appear that market exchange, implying money, runs into cognitive limitations which Mises appears not to have mentioned (2.1). The need to add hypotheses to the praxeological model led Hayek to question the very foundations of market theory (2.2).

2.1 The Question of Subsidiary Hypotheses: The Constraints of Ignorance

In Mises' terms, the subject of barter throws up a body of work of theorisation and history, or in other words, it takes both a deductive and interpretive approach. We see that mutual learning and discovery of preference is made with the bargaining process. Then the moment of actual exchange confirms the compatibility of each partners' interests.

Indirect exchange, however, poses some particular analytical problems. It represents the acquisition of goods not for their usage but for their exchange value. Therefore, the acquirer is aware of a demand for the goods before he acquires them. If a direct exchange of these goods, with its accompanying bargaining has not already taken place, then how does the acquirer know the precise character of the demand? How does an agent form a representation of another agent's interests with no prior direct contact by negotiation?

Throughout his writings, Mises puts reason before all else in the social process. This process is expressed in two ways: the law of association, based on the Ricardian principle of comparative advantage and the division of labour: 'The fundamental facts that brought about cooperation, society, and civilisation and transformed the animal man into a human being are the facts that work performed under the division of labor is more productive than isolated work and that man's reason is capable of recognizing this truth. But for these facts men would have forever remained deadly foes of one another, irreconcilable rivals in their endeavors to secure a portion of the scarce supply of means of sustenance provided by nature.' So, 'The fundamental social phenomenon is the division of labor and its counterpart human cooperation … The factor that brought about primitive society and daily works toward its progressive intensification is human action that is animated by the insight into the higher productivity of labor achieved under the division of labor' (Mises, 1966, p. 157; 160).

From that perspective, all that is needed is that agents realise the advantages of the division of labour to be able to set up the division of labour. The reign of reason is sufficient and is the condition to constitute a social order with all its rules of property, laws and so on. Society is seen as the result of teleological laws, its individual actors consciously and deliberately choosing its structure. 'Human society is an intellectual and spiritual phenomenon. It is the outcome of a purposeful utilization of a universal law determining cosmic becoming, viz., the higher productivity of the division of labor' (ibid., p. 153).

The problem with this vision of the formation of 'Oecumene', Mises' society founded on the division of labour, is that it presupposes the following element: the agents must know that they can sell their merchandise. This requires the access to information about qualitative and quantitative demand for their products before they organise the division of labour. So Mises' approach implies cognitive capacities that escape reason alone.

Of course it could be said that this knowledge is gleaned by the various actors during past exchanges. But this idea would only work if there was a continuum between past and present and nothing in the praxeological framework allows for a future reproduction of a past condition. Quite the opposite, in fact, this model shows perpetual and unpredictable change in action's particularities because of the entrepreneurship in each agent's mind.

So the problem of indirect exchange is different from that of direct barter. There is nothing in Mises' world that indicates 'representative agents', whose common traits would reduce ignorance of the other, quite the opposite; agents are shown as subjective, heterogeneous beings, their choices and knowledge praxeologically indeterminate. Anonymity thus becomes a hindrance to understanding the way the market is formed and it raises questions that are not answered by negotiation during direct exchange. How do agents gain access to constantly changing and dispersed information, which cannot be acquired by introspection or by a learning process during barter? Coordinating individual strategies faces two aspects of ignorance: division of knowledge and future conditions. At this point, it is impossible to explain how this coordination might work.

Hayek was the first to point out the theoretical difficulties in the concept of a market economy in 'Economics and Knowledge' (1937a): forming monetary prices supposes particular cognitive conditions. This landmark article, both in Hayek's work and in the neo-Austrian tradition, shows some of the distance that he had taken from the formal economy and of the 'pure logic of choice' tautologies. Certain writers were talking of a 'U-turn', (Hutchinson in *The Politics and Philosophy of Economics: Marxists, Keynesians and Austrians*, 1981), mentions a Hayek I and a Hayek II) or else of a 'transformation' (Caldwell, 'Hayek's Transformation', 1988).[11] 'Economics and Knowledge' is built around the claim that it is impossible to analyse the market without introducing specific learning mechanisms, which Mises never explained. For Hayek, before asking questions about knowledge of present prices or expectation of future prices, we should be asking more basically 'how the different commodities can be obtained and used, and under what conditions they are actually obtained and used, that is, the general question of why the subjective data to the different persons correspond to the objective facts' (Hayek, 1937a, p. 51-52).

The relevant question is not to know if the equilibrium price shows the right information; it does, by definition, so the argument is circular and does not shed light on the basic question, which is to know how the information carried in the market prices can be accessed. In other words, through which cognitive processes are market prices formed?

The nature and definition of economic representations, from a equilibrium point of view, would require all market actors' behaviour and expectations to be perfectly coordinated, which would in turn require both common and perfect knowledge. The problem is that the sum total of knowledge in an economy '... never exists in concentrated or integrated form but solely as the dispersed bits of incomplete and frequently contradictory knowledge which all the separate individuals possess' (Hayek, 'The Use of Knowledge in Society', 1945, p. 77).

So it is impossible to agree with the neoclassicals on a definition of the conditions of equilibrium, unless we examine how these conditions may come about; the idea, as found in Arrow's 'Towards a History of Price Adjustment' (1959) or Hicks's *Value and Capital*, 1939, that these conditions are automatically present, by timeless adjustments, is unacceptable. Even the models of dynamic equilibrium (for example Samuelson, *Foundations of Economic Analysis*, 1947) possess this artificial, unreal characteristic.

Walras' view of how equilibrium is reached may be recalled: it is based around a 'tatonnement' involving an 'auctioneer'; subjective agents can only know the prices with the auctioneer's announcements. But the overriding question here is: In the auctioneer's absence, how are the markets organised from a cognitive point of view?

2.2 What Theoretical Bases for Market Economics?

Hayek, studying the field of monetary exchange, found the need to widen Austrian epistemological horizons, which many saw as a radical break with Mises' original message. Hayek partly nourished this opinion. In 'Coping with Ignorance' (the text of a memorial conference for Mises), he remembers his intellectual rapport with Mises:

> Though I learned that he usually was right in his conclusions, I wasn't always satisfied by his arguments, and retained to the end a certain critical attitude which sometimes forced me to build different constructions.... I do not know whether my making our incurable ignorance of most of the particular circumstances which determine the course of this great society the central point of the scientific approach would have Mises' approval (Hayek, 1978a, p. 2).

Similarly, in the book of interviews *Hayek on Hayek, an Autobiographical Dialogue* (1994), he illuminates with hindsight the questions raised in 'Economics and Knowledge':

> What I see only now clearly is the problem of my relation to Mises, which began with my 1937 article on the economics of knowledge, which was an attempt to persuade Mises himself that when he asserted that the market theory was *a priori*, he was wrong; that what was *a priori* was only the logic of individual action, but the moment that you passed from this to the interaction of many people, you entered into the empirical field (Kresge and Wenar, 1994, p. 72).

Kirzner echoes this sentiment but far more radically:

> There can be no doubt that, on key elements in the Misesian system, Hayek is not Misesist at all. For Mises the possibility of economic understanding rests entirely on insights achieved *a priori*; his praxeological view of economic science expresses this apriorism in consistent and unqualified fashion. Yet early on in his career as an economist, Hayek made it clear at a pivotal moment that he was unable to follow his mentor in this matter. For Hayek the possibility of economic regularities capable of being comprehended by science rest squarely on an empirical basis. Unaided human logic, for Hayek, is able to generate no systematic truths concerning economic processes (Kirzner, 1992a, p. 120).

Aside from all these opinions, further reading of the various texts involved suggests a more subtle approach. Hayek never means that an analysis of the social processes contradicts praxeology's deepest teachings or challenges the legitimacy of its findings. He does maintain that these teachings, although certainly necessary for analysis of social interaction, are not enough. More precisely, in 'Economics and Knowledge', the subject of market exchange is impossible to deal with unless one adds subsidiary hypotheses to the pure logic of choice; logic, incidentally not just in Mises' work but in all standard neoclassical theories. So it should be said that Hayek's work, rather than being contradictory to Mises', is complementary to praxeology.

We could say that in this case Hayek is simply taking Mises' work further. The idea of needing 'subsidiary hypotheses' added to the analysis of human action was not new to Mises. In *Epistemological Problems of Economics*, he noted that, beyond the general conditions of action, 'other categorial conditions of action are independent of the basic concept: they are not necessary prerequisites of concrete action. Whether or not they are present in a particular case can be shown by experience' (Mises, 1933, p. 24). He also notes, in *Human Action*, 'Having shown what conditions are required by any action, one must go further and define – of course, in a categorial and formal sense – the less general conditions required for special modes of acting' (Mises, 1966, p. 64).

However, the question here is, rather than whether or not we need to introduce subsidiary hypotheses to studies of social interaction and praxeology, what are those hypotheses and what epistemological foundations exist for them?

More especially, if studies of market exchanges were not exclusively made of *a priori* categories, how could a market theory legitimately exist? 'Economics and Knowledge' seems to have been mainly written around the objective of establishing the epistemological bases of a market theory. Although Hayek used new tools to reach this objective, he did not manage at the time to illustrate them clearly enough for a full understanding of their role.

It would appear however, that Karl Popper's work in fact played an important role from this period, work which Hayek refers to in reference to the empirical character of any subsidiary hypotheses to praxeology. He asserts, in reference to *The Logic of Scientific Discovery* (1934),

> In short, I shall contend that the empirical element in economic theory – the only part which is concerned not merely with implications but with causes and effects and which leads therefore to conclusions which, at any rate in principle, are capable of verification – (or rather falsification, see K. R. Popper, 'Logik der Forschung', Vienna, 1935, *passim*) – consists of propositions about the acquisition of knowledge (Hayek, 1937a, p. 33).

He adds further on: 'The significant point here is that it is these apparently subsidiary hypotheses or assumptions that people do learn from experience, and about how they acquire knowledge, which constitute the empirical content of our propositions about what happens in the real world' (Hayek, 1937a, p. 46).

The Hayek-Popper relationship is a very controversial one among commentators. No one denies their friendship, but it is the nature of their analytical relationship that ignites debate. Some writers (Barry, *Hayek's Social and Economic Philosophy*, 1979), Blaug, *The Methodology of Economics: or 'How Economists Explain*', 1990), talk of parallel arguments and even of inspiration (especially visible in Hayek's later work). Other commentators refuse to see Hayek's affiliation to Popper as legitimate, claiming that Hayek's references to Popper's epistemology is a simple semantic misunderstanding.

There seems to be no ready-made answer to this endless debate. In fact, relations between Popper and Hayek are uneven and many commentators such as Birner 'Human Knowledge and Social Institutions: Popper and Hayek on Evolution' (1997), rightly point out the coexisting similarities and differences between the two. Whether Hayek is right to refer to Popper in 'Economics and Knowledge' is not something we need attend to here, but rather we can attempt an interpretation of what he may have meant. The two significant factors would seem to be firstly that Hayek openly recognises Popper's epistemological influence on his development; and secondly that this confers a certain significance on 'Economics and Knowledge' and explains, as we will see in the next part, some later developments.

How does Popper's work, from Hayek's point of view, contribute to an epistemological base of market theories, the study of which necessarily escapes the *a priori* dimension? Popper's epistemological approach ('critical rationalism') is well-known enough not to have to present it at length here. In Popper's works and articles (*The Logic of Scientific Discovery*, 1934, *Conjectures and Refutations*, 1963, *Objective Knowledge*, 1972 and so on) his 'critical rationalism' rejects the inductive approach at the same time as rehabilitating an empirical approach founded on falsifiability. Popper maintains that a scientific theory must be subject to empirical tests allowing its 'corroboration' or 'refutation' by facts. In the first case, the theory attains a 'verisimilitude', which is constantly tested by pitting the proposed explanation against the phenomena being studied, and also by confronting it constantly with other theories, tested in their turn.

In Popperian analysis, one forms hypotheses and conjectures, without needing them to attain an axiomatic status, so which do not express *a priori* truths. But this process's scientific value (the principle of 'demarcation') is subject to a condition: any deductions formed must be testable against facts. If a lesson is taken from an external reality, its conclusions must be falsifiable.

Hayek's interest in Popper's epistemological approach is appreciable, as according to him, propositions concerning social learning processes cannot be approached by an '*a priori* method'. So complementary, rather than alternative epistemological approaches must be found. Popper's work shows that this is possible but only on condition of finding a relation between an 'explanatory pronouncement' (an explanation of principle) and an 'empirical reference', through which testing of any theories would be made. From Hayek's writings, tendency towards equilibrium seems to define it as designating them to play the role of this empirical reference. However, the principle of coordinating individual activities seems to be beyond the reach of 'Economics and Knowledge', Hayek at the time admitting his inability to find the necessary mechanisms of knowledge in the formation of the market and its activities.

NOTES

1. Action always means an infra-individual exchange, as it means any one individual abandoning a present for a future situation, sacrificing an initial endowment for one expected to be more satisfying. Infra-individual exchange is therefore a theorem coming from the axiom of action.
2. The isolated and interpersonal expressions of exchange are not theorems of action, as neither necessarily develops from the idea of action. The laws of action do not imply that it is obliged to take the form of interpersonal exchange, any more than they indicate that any act must be only infra-individual exchange.
3. To these conditions should be added the existence of all and any institution which instils individuals' rights and duties in the exchange.
4. The late and much missed Michel Rosier gave us a remarkable account of bargaining mechanisms in an article ('On Smith's Bargaining Process: Learning by Talking', 2003), illustrating both Smith's and Hayek's contribution on this subject. We have plentifully referred to his arguments here.
5. This definition of catallaxy as a sub-set of praxeology has logical consequences. Everything that is true for praxeology is true for catallaxy and the latter's laws cannot contradict the former's. 'Catallactics does not ask whether or not the consumers are right, noble, generous, wise, moral, patriotic, or church-going. It is concerned not with why they act, but only with how they act.' The task is 'to explain the formation of the exchange ratios of economic goods that are actually observed in the market, and not those which would come about if all men were to act in a way that some critic regards as rational' (Mises, 1933, p. 94; 171). Therefore catallactic subjectivity is necessarily drawn from praxeological subjectivism. Catallaxy is foreign to all normative aspects and 'the term "value", whose meaning for catallactics must not be confused with the "absolute" values of ethics' (ibid., p. 170). The economist must be morally neutral whenever he analyses exchanging individuals' motivations.
6. The state can improve the monetary characteristics of spontaneous money's constituent good by imposing particular means of payment, but it can never be its source.
7. Menger, describing the spontaneous character of monetary phenomena using the compositive method, stresses the importance of notions of custom and imitation. Only a small minority of the population will grasp the advantages of using more liquid goods at the same time, aware of 'the economic gains that can be derived from exploitation of existing exchange opportunities' (Menger, 1871, p. 257). Custom and imitation will be responsible for its spread to the rest of the population, which will need to observe the material advantages and disadvantages of this kind of behaviour before it decides on adopting these

attitudes on concluding on its virtues. The 'compositive' method, defined by Menger in 'Investigations' aims to show how complex social patterns can come out of individual behaviour. In particular, it shows how the apparent paradox is solved of a good or group of goods becomes money throughout the community without any of its members having had that intention (for certain developments, see Jones 'The Origin and Development Media of Exchange', 1976, O'Driscoll; 'Money: Menger's Evolutionary Theory', 1986; Aimar, 'Money and Uncertainty in the Economic Thought of Carl Menger', 1996, etc).

8. For contemporary views on these controversies, see the very useful Klein and Selgin ('Menger's Theory of Money: Some Experimental Evidence', 2000); Schmitz ('Carl Menger's 'Money' and the Current Neoclassical Models of Money', 2002); Stenkula ('Carl Menger and the NetWork Theory of Money' 2003).
9. 'Money can take various forms, only two conditions being required: universal acceptation and its ability to circulate' (Wieser, 1927).
10. '... an object cannot be used as money unless, at the moment when its use as money begins, it already possesses an objective exchange value based on some other use' (Mises, 1912, p. 131). He reproduced this reasoning in *Human Action*: 'If we trace the purchasing power of money back step by step, we finally arrive at the point at which the service of the good concerned as a medium of exchange begins. At this point yesterday's exchange value is exclusively determined by the nonmonetary – industrial – demand which is displayed only by those who want to use this good for other employments than that of a medium of exchange' (Mises, 1966, p. 409). In the same way, Rothbard says 'To function as a money, an entity must have emerged on the free market out of barter, as a particularly marketable commodity selected on the market as a medium for virtually all exchanges. Nothing can be originally adopted as money by government fiat, or by some sort of social contract. Nothing can be adopted as a money, as a medium of exchange, unless it had a pre-existing purchasing-power as a non-monetary good' (Rothbard 'The Present State of Austrian Economics', 1995, p. 74).
11. Commentators (Hutchison, *The Politics and Philosophy of Economics. Marxists, Keynesians and Austrians* (1981); Langlois, 'Knowledge and Rationality in the Austrian School' 1985; Caldwell, 'Hayek's Transformation', 1988; Foss, 'More on "Hayek's Transformation"', 1994c; Vaughn, 'Hayek's Implicit Economics: Rules and the Problem Order, 1999b) and French writers too (Aréna, 'Hayek et l'équilibre économique: une autre interpretation', 1999; Schmidt and Versailles 'Une théorie hayekienne de la connaissance économique?', 1999) have been examining the very particular issues in 'Economics and Knowledge'. These have all shed new light on the whole of Hayek's work in some detail.

PART 2

Catallaxy, a Response to Ignorance

Introduction

Mises' epistemological analysis showed that ignorance has two facets: division of knowledge and uncertainty of the future. Firstly, if we presume the idea of each social actor's singularity, no individual can *a priori* know what values, ends or strategies exist in others' minds until these are translated into action. The knowledge needed to coordinate individual plans is divided throughout society.

Secondly, entrepreneurship as exercised through the praxeological model prevents the future being a simple extension of the present or the past, opportunities changing unpredictably, leaving actors in ignorance of future circumstances.

Recognising the existence of knowledge division brings up the question of conceptualizing the necessary cognitive mechanisms to enable market exchange. The problem is in fact that on one hand exchange presupposes actors' mutual knowledge, while on the other the Austrians view actors as *a priori* anonymous; certain efforts were made to solve this apparent paradox by reflecting on elements of intersubjectivity in society. Hayek, in particular, referred to evolutionary biology and theoretical psychology to produce an explanation of the way agents form intersubjective representations; he thus sheds light on elements of market formation, which we examine in Chapter 4.

The central problem of division of knowledge was to bring the Austrian authors to develop an interpretation of market mechanisms as a way of changing information into knowledge. Which structures may be developed to transmit singular knowledge from one actor to another becomes an important issue. Distinguishing the body of information in society from the knowledge which each actor holds gave the neo-Austrians the opportunity to free themselves from the neoclassical model of equilibrium. They thus underline the importance of entrepreneurship, profit and competition to understand the functioning of the market, which can then be seen as a whole 'World of Discovery' (Chapter 5).

The second Austrian source of ignorance, uncertainty of the future, comes from a realisation of the temporal aspect of action. Necessary knowledge for action is fragmented between not only individuals but also between present and future. So the question of prediction arises, also highlighting a second constraint of coordination: a principle of the formation and success of individual expectations. Present prices reflect present-type information but do not bring any knowledge of the future, the basis of any success of plans. So they do not explain plan-making and certainly in no way guarantee success of expectations. Moving from a concept of coordination by price in response to knowledge division, to a coordination of plans in reaction to uncertainty of the future provoked a whole series of reflections in the neo-Austrian analysis of catallaxy, which we examine in Chapter 6.

4. Market Formation

> … though at one time a very pure and narrow economic theorist, I was led from technical economics into all kinds of questions usually regarded as philosophical. When I look back, it seems to have all begun, nearly thirty years ago, with an essay on 'Economics and Knowledge' in which I examined what seemed to me some of the central difficulties of pure economic theory. Its main conclusion was that the task of economic theory was to explain how an overall order of economic activity was achieved which utilized a large amount of knowledge which was not concentrated in any one mind but existed only as the separate knowledge of thousands or millions of different individuals. But it was still a long way from this to an adequate insight into the relations between the abstract rules which the individual follows in his actions, and the abstract overall order which is formed, as a result of his responding, within the limits imposed upon him by those abstract rules, to the concrete particular circumstances which he encounters (Hayek, 'Kinds of Rationalism', 1964, p. 92).

It is Hayek himself who contributes to the solution of the problem of market formation. Having expressed his perplexity on this subject in 'Economics and Knowledge',[1] he moves towards an early form of answer in *The Sensory Order* (1952a).

Published in the same year as *The Counter-Revolution of Science* (1952b), this work is quite particular, both in terms of its history and its purpose. Historically speaking, it is the publication of Hayek's personal reflections from the early 1920s, when he took an interest in psychology, inspired by his discovery of Mach's theses (see Hayek, 1967a) and probably Schlick's (see Birner, 1999). In terms of its purpose, the book has an original status: it is in no way a direct economic or social analysis, but corresponds, as stated in the sub-title, to 'An Inquiry into the Foundations of Theoretical Psychology'. However, *The Sensory Order* should not be considered as a mere aside, isolated from Hayek's main preoccupations.[2] On the contrary, its publication must be looked at in the context of the cognitive problems related to the conceptualization of a market economy. Even then, Hayek explains, 'In the end it was concern with the logical character of social theory which forced me to re-examine systematically my ideas on theoretical psychology' (Hayek 1952a: V). He was to reaffirm this idea more than 25 years later, in the last volume of *Law, Legislation and Liberty*:

> My colleagues in the social sciences generally find my study on *The Sensory Order* uninteresting or indigestible. But the work on it has helped me greatly to clear my mind on much that is very relevant to social theory. My conception of evolution, of spontaneous order and of the methods and limits of our endeavours to explain complex phenomenon have been formed largely in the course of the work on that book (1979, p. 229). [3]

The formulation of a theory of the mind is one of Hayek's major preoccupations. *The Sensory Order* is today seen by many as an attempt to found the epistemological base of the notion of subjectivism (1). This is not to obscure another important aspect of the work which would appear to be a form of solution to the cognitive problems posed by subjective, anonymous individuals in the formation of the markets (2). From this point of view, it sheds light retrospectively on previous works of Hayek's at the same time as providing the key to his later theoretical works (3).

1. *THE SENSORY ORDER*: HAYEK'S CONTRIBUTION

The objective of *The Sensory Order* is to find an 'explanation of mental phenomena' (Hayek, 1952a, p. VIII), with the main aim being to solve the problem of the 'relation between the physical and the phenomenal order' (Hayek, 1952a, p. 5). It is therefore mainly an attempt to explain how an actor's interior, or subjective, environment is formed: 'We want to know the kind of process by which a given physical situation is transformed into a certain phenomenal picture' (ibid., p. 7).

Hayek starts with the following observation: the world of the mind – the phenomenal world – or the entire set of mental events present in an individual's mind, may not be equivalent to the order of physical events. The aim of theoretical psychology is precisely to account for this gap, explaining that which

> has no place in our scientific picture of the external world and is no way explained by the sciences dealing with the external world: qualities. Whenever we study qualitative differences between experiences we are studying mental and not physical events, and much that we believe to know about the external world is, in fact, knowledge about ourselves (ibid., p. 6-7).

The order of mental qualities does not necessarily reflect those of external events. Hayek thus studied human physiological structure to measure this difference (1.1), which permitted him to found a psychological theory of subjectivity (1.2).

1.1 The Mind as Classifying Structure

The order of mental qualities is the result of an act of classification of stimuli which is performed by the central nervous system. These stimuli, defined as physical or physiological events that are exterior to the nervous system, generate processes operating across certain neural fibres from the spot where the stimulus takes place to another part of the nervous system. The nervous impulse is the phenomenon produced in and spread through and the nerve fibres: 'It will be the impulses which (as individuals or groups) will be the object of the classificatory process' (Hayek, 1952a, p. 51); and it is these impulses which, to a large extent, are translated in the mind as mental equivalents, or in other words, as sensory qualities.

The classification of impulses is assured by the nervous system itself, which is a neuronal set. The process occurs in each individual through the formation of neuronal maps, which provide the link between the physical world and the sensory world. From these structures, emerge the mind and knowledge. To a final extent, the mind is but a classification structure.[4]

1.2 Psychological Foundations of Subjectivity

This procedure shows that mental qualities are perceived by the mind as elements of classification, external events being classed by their ability to regularly create analogous mental events. In the same way, classes of external events, in interaction with others, are defined by their capacity to produce a particular class of internal events. It is logical therefore that the human mind only perceives complexes:

> The immediate data of consciousness are not in fact built up in mosaic fashion from elementary sensations. We perceive directly such complexes as configurations (gelsats) ... the immediate data of consciousness will therefore be 'abstract' not only in the sense that they never convey to us more than certain generic 'attributes' of the perceived objects, but also in the sense that they will always reflect only some of these generic properties which might be ascribed to the perceived object (ibid., p. 143-144).

As class elements are defined by other elements of the same class and as classes are defined by other classes, the structure of sensory qualities is a relational phenomenon. We can therefore speak of a sensory order. The various sensory qualities express, through nerve impulses, the differences in mental response to physical stimuli: 'Even the so-called elementary sensory qualities are in this sense "abstractions", since they are determined by bundles of relationships which we have learnt to attach to certain stimuli which in a physical sense may or may not possess identical properties' (ibid., p. 143).

Sensory perceptions must therefore be abstract; they are the product of classification, or evaluation or even of discrimination[5] by the central nervous system. Their qualitative differences express differences in mental events.

In physiological terms, nerve impulses are classified by the nerve fibres through which they travel, a process called connectionism. This structure of nervous connections in our organisms is exactly reflected by the structure of our sensory qualities. In other words, our sensory order is the perfect reproduction of the network of nervous fibre connections which makes up our central nervous system.

By this abstraction, which Hayek used physiological notions to construct, mental representations are seen to be not just a mirror of the physical world. In this way, *The Sensory Order*, anticipating, among others, Bertalanffy and Simon's developments in cognitive psychology in the 1970's, contributes a psychological theory of subjectivity to the Austrian tradition which may be considered to complete Mises' work. The scope of *The Sensory Order* is in fact much wider than most literature gives it credit for.

2. MARKET AND SOCIETY

The mental or sensory qualities in individuals' minds are not linked with those of the physical attributes of the stimuli.[6] So it is important to know how the neural system organises the classification of nervous impulses.

The question is: if individual impulses are classed as to their resulting mental events – according to their identity or difference – then what is the relation between one (or a group of) nerve impulse and a mental event? Or: what is the basis of classification? Hayek's answer seems to give us the keys, albeit indirectly, to a market theory. He highlights the role of the pre-sensory experience in the organisation of qualities (2.1) and simultaneously formulates the elements of a social dimension of representations which sheds light on the formation of the market exchange process (2.2).

2.1 The Map and the Model: The Role of Pre-Sensory Experience

Hayek explains that the central nervous system's subjective classification system does not only rely on individual categories and is not disconnected from the physical world, thus giving us a materialist definition of associationist logic. The physical world, on the contrary can be seen as the ultimate reference. Hayek says the connections system tends to reproduce 'at every stage of its development certain relationships existing in the physical environment between the stimuli evoking the impulses' (Hayek 1952a, p. 53). The mind is thus able to partially reproduce the physical order as mental representations.

This learning process can be seen on an individual level but also in terms of a legacy of the 'development of the species' (Hayek, 1952a, p. 53).

In this way, Hayek highlights the idea of pre-sensorial experience – the notion of linkage – which thus creates the classification apparatus. In fact the linkages are a reproduction of the relations between the physical stimuli, as expressed and defined inside the individual's or his social group's environment. They refer therefore to the actor's particular context and social structure. Thus, these relations 'will not necessarily be representative of those existing in the whole of it' (ibid., p. 108). In other words, they are not the whole picture of all physical relations but only of those which the individual and his social group has experienced.

These linkages thus tend to reproduce the structure of external events. In some ways they form a map of the physical world, which produces an 'underlying outline picture of the environment' (ibid., p. 140). This map might be seen as a canal network or of 'the semi-permanent connexions representing not the environment of the moment but the kind of events which the organism has met during its whole past' (ibid., p. 115). It is a memory system, an abstract architecture of physical relations, either individual or socially considered.

Within this map, the individual forms 'a kind of model of the particular environment in which the organism finds itself at the moment and which will enable it to take account of that environment in all its movements' (ibid. p. 114-115). This model, which Hayek defines as an internal structure, reproducing certain relations between external events, is an '… apparatus of orientation. By providing a reproduction of the environment in which the organism moves at the moment, it adjusts the responses to those elements in the environment which are represented in it' (ibid., p. 113).

The map and the model complementarily allow the 'microcosm in the brain' to approach the 'macrocosm of the external world' (ibid., p. 108). This is no accident and it is simply an expression of the need of each living organism to adapt to the physical order. The idea of matching the mental order to the physical is simply an expression of the submission of internal facts to external ones; a process to allow the organism 'to behave in a manner which will assist its continued existence' (ibid., p. 127), that is, to survive.

The map and its incorporated model are not rigid entities however: 'Sensory qualities can be changed by the acquisition of new connexions between sensory impulses' (ibid., p. 152). The map is no more than the recording of past external events and relationships between their corresponding physical stimuli. This is why it is only semi-permanent, changing along with new event experiences, thus changing the model with it.

Analogously and somewhat linked to this last point, neither map nor model must be seen as perfect objective representations of present environments or past events. On the contrary, they are not exempt from errors:

> Learning to discriminate does not necessarily produce a better reproduction of the physical order of the stimuli; it merely means the creation of a new distinction in the phenomenal order which, if it were the result of a non-recurring, accidental or artificial combination of stimuli during a particular period, might indeed prove later not a help but an obstacle to orientation and appropriate behaviour (Hayek, 1952a, p. 158).

However, interaction between the physical world and individuals' behaviour builds agents' maps by trial and error, or negative feedback. The learning process is one of permanent sensory reorganisation, redefining categories to give meaning to stimuli. The mind reclassifies sensations as it continually makes suppositions about its structure, to adapt to the outside world. There is therefore an objective dimension to individual subjectivism.

2.2 Cultural Representations

Hayek uses this idea to go further; *The Sensory Order* is not just about the infra-individual but also the inter-individual experience. He illustrates a number of elements that contribute to reducing agents' anonymity, thus developing the idea of a community of perceptions:

> It would, of course, not be possible to discuss the phenomenal world with other people if they did not perceive this world in terms of the same, or at least of a very similar, order of qualities as we do. This means that the conscious mind of other people classifies stimuli in a manner similar to that which we know. In other words, although the system of sensory qualities is 'subjective' in the sense of belonging to the perceiving subject as distinguished from 'objective' (belonging to the perceived objects) – a distinction which is the same as that between the phenomenal and the physical order – it is yet inter-personal and not (or at least not entirely) peculiar to the individual (Hayek, 1952a, p. 23).

He adds 'we also learn that what appears alike or different to us usually also appears alike or different to other men' (ibid., p. 23). Of course, Hayek refuses any idea of isomorphism: the maps will never be identical, as that would 'presuppose not only an identical history of the different individuals, but also complete identity of their anatomical structure. The mere fact that for each individual the map will be subject to constant changes practically precludes the possibility that at any moment the maps of two individuals should be completely identical' (ibid., p. 110). Actors' subjectivity is always the main point; however, the matrix of classification bears some similarities as some of its factors are shared by individuals.

Hayek crystallises all these elements into the notion of isofunctionality, an important factor in understanding the process of market formation. The problem of agents' anonymity is considerably reduced by an analysis which deals with the idea of abstract culture as the result of individual and collective experience. This culture, as expressing actors' common representations, provides the means for all in the community, in a same socio-temporal context, to share in the structure of interpretation.

Thus the idea of radical singularity of individuals' subjective worlds is reduced as a result of this cultural dimension. When an individual has memories of his community's social past and of agents' values and habits on his map and he makes a model of his own experience and analysis, he is able to form the image of his social environment, reducing the above cognitive problem. Also, as agents' representations have a shared aspect to them, an individual's introspection-based knowledge of his own representation gives him partial knowledge of others of his society. This legacy, whether directly or indirectly gathered, allows agents certain access to other agents' knowledge, *a priori* anonymous and subjective, without direct contact or learning. Direct knowledge of others is thus replaced by accumulated layers of abstract information, allied with a procedure of 'disposition' or 'set' (Hayek, 1952a, p.141) which could also be called an actor's curiosity about or alertness to his surroundings.

A part of actors' individual representations has social origins when participating in the same cognitive environment. Actors' learning comes partially from their laying of social roots and involves an imitation process of positive 'feedback'. This logically means social aspects precede the market, that culture predates money calculations.

The real bearing of *The Sensory Order* is most clearly revealed in this light. Hayek shows which cognitive mechanisms are at work in bringing to actors' minds this type of abstract, common representation. The work gathers and illustrates elements which had been scattered throughout his earlier contributions and also lays important foundations for major themes which he was to develop later.

3. PROLEGOMENA AND PROLONGATIONS

According to Caldwell ('Hayek and Socialism', 1997), *The Sensory Order* represents a central position in Hayek's thinking. In a 1948 letter in which he discusses his work of laying the ground for this subject, Hayek stated that it is 'the most important thing I have yet done' (letter to John Nef, November, 1948). On its publication, theoretical psychologists seized on it as being an important work and it was widely read by them[7] but not by the economists of the time. Closer analysis would suggest, however, that this work is the high point of a whole series of reflections which he started in the 1930s (3.1), with implications and refinements to follow (3.2).

3.1 Ideal Types: Hayek, Schütz and the Austrian Tradition

The arguments contained in *Economics and Knowledge* represent Hayek's fundamental questioning of coordination of action. Without finding an answer as such, he did leave a long footnote to the effect that theoretical analysis of the social processes required reference to ideal types:

> The distinction drawn here may help to solve the old difference between economists and sociologists about the role which 'ideal types' play in the reasoning of economic theory. The sociologists used to emphasize that the usual procedure of economic theory involved the assumption of particular ideal types, while the economics theorist pointed out that his reasoning was of such generality that he need not make use of any 'ideal types'. The truth seems to be that within the field of the Pure Logic of Choice, in which the economist was largely interested, he was right in his assertion but that, as soon as he wanted to use it for the explanation of a social process, he had to use 'ideal types' of one sort or another (Hayek, 1937a, p. 47).

Hayek's reference to ideal types as a theorist's tool may surprise Mises' readers. This concept, as formulated by Max Weber, should be applied contextually, rather than generally: they should be seen as useful practitioner's methods, not conceptual contributions to abstract economic theory. The fundaments of Austrian theory have Weberian ideal types as referring to particular historic events with strong interpretative aspects,[8] so their definition is somewhat approximate. However, Hayek seems to be saying in *Economics and Knowledge* that the conditions, characteristics and implications of social exchange do not obey this approximate dimension, especially where the constraints of acquiring the knowledge necessary for their action are concerned. How are we then to explain Hayek's strange outlook?

One possible explanation comes from Selgin (*Praxeology and Understanding: An Analysis of the Controversy in Austrian Economics*, 1982). He was among the first to underline the importance of the philosopher and sociologist Alfred Schütz, to draw attention to certain paradoxes of Austrian economics.[9] In *The Phenomenology of the Social World* (1932), Alfred Schütz tried to enlarge Mises' theoretical base, by formulating 'economic ideal types'. In doing so, he incorporates the non-*a priori* character of economic relations which Max Weber had already noted. But the definition of these 'economic ideal types' is not approximate. 'Our ideal-type will be defined as having definite and invariant motives, and from these motives we will be able to deduce invariant acts and sequences of acts ... It is this formalization and generalization which gives the ideal-types universal validity' (Schütz, 1932, p. 228; 244).[10]

Since then, Schütz's close ties with the Austrian school[11] has been demonstrated by plentiful literature of which it would seem that Helling was among the first authors ('A. Schütz and F. Kaufmann: Sociology between Science and Interpretation', 1984). Schütz was one of the first members of the Mont-Pelerin Society, founded by Hayek in 1947 and he was also more particularly a regular attendee of Mises' seminar in Vienna. Although there is no reference in 'Economics and Knowledge' to Schütz's work, the whole text seems to be impregnated with his influence. This impression is strengthened by Kurrild-Klitgaard's (2001) analysis, mentioning that Hayek had sent Schütz a first version of the text in 1936. Schütz commented on this in 'Political Economy: Human Conduct in Social Life' (1935),[12] which seemed to meet with Hayek's approval, at least at the time. Like Schütz, Hayek states in 'Economics and Knowledge' that the economy, as a sphere of interpersonal exchange, does possess empirical content but it is structured objectively with strictly defined implications, following Schütz's rules of the economic ideal type.

According to Prendergast ('A. Schütz and the Austrian School of Economics', 1986), both texts that Schütz presented at Mises' Vienna seminar show his appreciation of Austrian ideas. Based around the theme of the subjective importance of social phenomena, they show Schütz's awareness of the coordination problems which individuals' singularity poses; to study cognitive market conditions would require a wider analysis of individuals' knowledge of intersubjectivity. Schütz asks the same questions as Hayek does in 'Economics and Knowledge': how do individuals acquire a picture of other agents' representations without directly contacting them?

Schütz insists on the necessity of constructing a theory of social interaction to answer this question. However, this cannot function in Mises' terms, where social interaction mobilizes historic-type tools, with is antithetical to theory. In Mises' view, history and understanding are in fact not a base for theory. Yet this reasoning appears to condemn the whole Austrian school to closing the door on a real appreciation of the markets. As Prendergast says: 'Marginalism lacked a credible theory of intersubjective understanding; it had no way of showing how economic actors knew the motives of other actors, short of assuming universal motivation discernible by introspection' (Prendergast, 1986, p. 11). The Austrian school is thus faced with the problem of explaining intersubjectivity.

This is precisely where the concept of the ideal type comes into play. The theme of 'typically similar' actions and meaning is at the very centre of Schütz's thinking. It follows Husserl's phenomenological problematic in terms of needing common beliefs and perceptions to progress in society.

> Schütz found an adequate explanation of how subjective experiences are transitioned to objective conception, which is essential to his theory of typification. It is in the process of typification that the social reality is so constructed as to provide meaning to the different individuals as well as the social scientists. It is in the 'everyday life' that the individuals through typifications pursue the meaning and the knowledge that is to be interpreted (Augier, 'Review of Alfred Schütz's Collected Papers', 1999, p. 148).

In Schütz's view, society is filled with structures of intersubjectivity which allow agents who are *a priori* strangers to cooperate and coordinate. It would appear now that Hayek, in 'Economics and Knowledge', felt through Schütz's ideal types the possibility of conceptualizing one form of intersubjectivity, which would have solved the problem of the agents' lack of concrete information about each other. At this period, however, he was not able to fully articulate this concept's characteristics.

Schütz himself later developed an approach strangely similar to Hayek's *The Sensory Order*. He advances the idea that ideal types are a common interpretative scheme, offered to each individual through his social heritage:

> This world existed before our birth, experienced and interpreted by others, our predecessors, as an organised world. Now it is given to our experience and interpretation. All interpretation of this world is based on a stock of previous experiences of it, our own or others handed down to us by parents or teachers; these experiences in the form of 'knowledge at hand' function as a scheme of reference (1953, p. 7).

The classification of social phenomena into ideal types, themselves referring to abstract categories formed in the individual's mind, allows the actor to give roles to others and so infer their behaviour, strategies and also values.

These ideal types represent a sort of 'social distribution of knowledge', significantly anticipating Hayek's arguments. This knowledge comes from a structure of pre-experience, its meaning not being questioned as long as it is efficient. It represents the community's contribution to individual knowledge, and is the phenomenological equivalent to a psychological abstraction process. Individuals' idiosyncratic behaviour comes from differences in their life stories and present situations, making great differences to the information available to them. The imprecise and varied characteristics of the data[13] to be interpreted makes for very 'open horizons'.

3.2 Abstract Rules and Spontaneous Order

In Hayek's collection of articles *Individualism and Economic Order* (1948a), the 1942 essay, 'The Facts on The Social Sciences' frequently refers to the human mind's classification processes. Hayek announces several themes which he develops in *The Sensory Order*. He is already investigating the 'types' of knowledge and questions the idea that a classification process in the human mind would depend on physical attributes,

> because the elements of these classes need not possess common physical attributes, and we do not even consciously or explicitly know which are the various physical properties of which an object would have to possess at least one to be a member of a class. The situation may be described schematically by saying that we know that the objects a, b, c …, which may be physically completely dissimilar and which we

> can never exhaustively enumerate, are objects of the same kind because the attitude of X toward them all is similar. But the fact that X's attitude toward them is similar can again be defined only by saying that he will react toward them by any one of the actions α, β, γ… which again may be physically dissimilar and which we will not be able to enumerate exhaustively, but which we just know to 'mean' the same thing (Hayek 1942, p. 61-62).

Similarly, Hayek insists on the theme of shared characteristics in the human mental structure. He underlines the importance of these intersubjectivities in processes of interaction and articulation of individual expectations: 'We can never be certain whether any particular instance is really a member of the class about we talk … we all agree that in the great majority of cases our cases will be correct' (ibid., p. 63-64).

The Sensory Order can be paired with *The Counter Revolution of Science* (1952b). This is a three-part essay, with anterior publication, the first part appearing from 1942 to 1944 ('Scientism and the Study of Society'), the second in 1941, ('The Counter-Revolution of Science') and the last in 1951 ('Comte and Hegel').[14] Hayek unleashes a systematic criticism of scientism, the blind, mechanical application to the social field of the natural scientific methods. He stresses the necessity of returning to the compositive method so dear to Menger, to understand how social complexes are formed from an individual's actions.

The important point is that this work, especially in its first part, contains reflections on the mind's functioning and the way opinion is formed. Here Hayek is already examining the theme of classification around the idea of regularity. 'We learn to regard as alike or unlike not simply what by itself looks, feels, smells, etc, alike or unlike, but what regularly appears in the same spatial and temporal context' (Hayek, 1952b, p. 19), with the idea that this classification 'is probably based on a pre-conscious learning of these relationships in the external world which are of special relevance for the existence of the human organism in the kind of environment in which his is developed and that it is closely connected with the infinite number of 'conditioned reflexes' which the human species had to acquire in the course of its evolution' (ibid., p. 208).

Hayek also posits the idea of a uniformity of the mind's structure, while of course continuing to assert the subjectivity of values and human beliefs. This is a determining factor in organising social processes: 'People perceive the world and each other through sensations and concepts which are organized in a mental structure common to all of them' (ibid., p. 23).

This approach finds its extension and application in a collection of his writings from over the previous 20 years and dedicated to Popper: *Studies in Philosophy, Politics and Economics* (1967b). Hayek here returns to the need for an intersection of the various branches of knowledge and the economy and develops the theme of 'Rule-guided Action' ('Rule, Perception and Intelligibility', 1963a, p. 43), explaining that advanced economic societies 'must always act on some rules which (the individuals) cannot communicate' (ibid., p. 62). These rules, which Hayek defined as being tacit, influenced by Polyani (*Personal Knowledge: Towards a Post-Critical Philosophy*, 1962), emerge from tradition, custom and habits of behaviour structured by social contact, crystallised in the psyche through cultural inheritance. It is as if each actor catches abstract signals transmitted mostly through action, giving him knowledge on classes of individuals without having had direct contact with them. Through this, each member of a community benefits from more knowledge than that offered by direct relations with others. A part of individuals' cognitive whole is thus the fruit of a social, cultural capital; their ability to make plans in accordance with others' subjective plans stems from their belonging to a community rich in shared traditions and culture, where practice and imitation play a fundamental role.

In 'The Kinds of Rationalism' from the same volume, Hayek refuses to reduce rationality of action to a formal deliberation. Explicating reasons for a particular choice of action and decision-making based on explicit information would reduce cooperation to a very narrow range of possibilities, that is, the face-to-face encounters so characteristic of barter. Referring to traditions and habit is of the greatest help 'to the co-ordination of the actions of many different individuals in concrete circumstances which are known only partially to each individual and become known only as they arise' (Hayek, 1964, p. 91).

Lastly, in the three volumes of *Law, Legislation and Liberty* (1973, 1976a, 1979), as in his final work, *The Fatal Conceit* (1988), Hayek sums up his argument on the importance of abstract rules. By reintroducing themes appearing in a more elaborate form in *New Studies in Philosophy, Politics, Economy and the History of Ideas* (1978b), Hayek contrasts 'consciously constructed' rules with 'spontaneous abstract' rules. Implementing the latter allows the emergence of a complex order, as it gives actors knowledge and adaptive instruments that no conscious process would.

> It is because it was not dependent on organization but grew up as a spontaneous order that the structure of modern society has attained that degree of complexity which it possesses and which far exceeds any that could have been achieved by deliberate organization. In fact, of course, the rules which made the growth of this complex order possible were initially not designed in expectation of that result; but those people who happened to adopt suitable rules developed a complex civilization which then often spread to others (Hayek, *Law, Legislation and Liberty*, 1973, p. 50).

In his last work, *The Fatal Conceit* (1988), Hayek again addresses the mechanisms of 'cultural evolution' and their importance for adapting to the unknown. We will return to these questions in Chapter 6.

NOTES

1. On the subject of 'concrete hypotheses concerning the conditions under which people are supposed to acquire the relevant knowledge', Hayek admits that he was '... getting to a stage where it becomes exceedingly difficult to say what exactly are the assumptions on the basis of which we assert ... that our analysis has an application to the real world' (Hayek, 1937a, p. 48).
2. Hayek himself (*Hayek on Hayek*, 1994 p. 125) points out that *The Sensory Order* manuscript only returned to his attention in 1946. To the best of our knowledge, there was no development between the version first written at the beginning of the 1920s and its final publication date. We can only infer changes, as Hayek mentions himself in the preface that 'the present version of this book has occupied me for several years' (Hayek, 1952a, VIII). In addition to this, his disappointed words in 'Economics and Knowledge' on his inability to find a proper answer to the problem of market formation seems to rule out any absence of evolution of his thoughts on the subject. Apart from a brief reference to Gabriel Tarde (*Psychologie Economique*, 1902), he also makes no mention of any cognitive psychological aspect to any solution.
3. *The Sensory Order* had long been ignored by economists and its treatment in economic literature was relatively late. Without being exhaustive, we can mention the following authors: Yeager (1984); Tuerck (1995); Smith (1997); Birner (1999b); Nadeau (2001); Koppl (2002); Rizzello (2003) and Caldwell (2004). Less directly but just as importantly, McCann, Jr, 'F.A. Hayek: The Liberal as Communitarian' (2002); Caldwell, 'The Emergence of Hayek's Ideas on Cultural Evolution' (2000), Horwitz, 'From The Sensory Order to the Liberal Order: Hayek's Non-Rationalist Liberalism' (2000).
4. According to Smith (1997), Birner (1999) and Nadeau (2001), these theories of Hayek's are very similar to those developed by Wiener (1948a, 1948b) and Hebb (1949), whose works appear in *The Sensory Order*.
5. The concept of discrimination means the differences between the effects on mental phenomena generated by individual or groups of stimuli (see Hayek, 1952a, p 37).
6. Mental processes 'describe all processes which involve a classification of events in terms of a qualitative order, similar to that which we know from our subjective sensory experience, and differing from the physical order of these events' (Hayek, 1952a, p. 132).
7. The book seems to have found a ready audience among philosophers of sciences (Weimer 1982). In particular, it had a profound influence on significant works in neuropsychology and neurosciences in general. It is important to point out here that Edelman (1987, 1988, 1989, 2004) openly admits his indebtedness to Hayek in the formulation of his famous 'Theory of Neuronal Group Selection' (TNGS), based on the ideas of consciousness, topobiology and degenerescence (see bibliography). In the same way, the respective works of Minsky (1986) and Damasio (1999), on the modes of internal communication of the mind and decision making, manifest obvious similarities with Hayek's approach. We can also mention the current initiated by Varela's studies (1991; 1999) on human perception and the emergence of consciousness, which Dupuy (2002) was able to link to the Hayekian theory of self-organisation.
8. In *Human Action*, Mises clearly explains: 'Ideal types are specific notions employed in historical research and in the representations of its results. They are concepts of understanding. As such they are entirely different from praxeological categories and concepts and from the concepts of the natural sciences. An ideal type is not a class concept, because its description does not indicate the marks whose presence definitely and unambiguously determines class membership. An ideal type cannot be defined; it must be characterized by an enumeration of those features whose presence by and large decides whether in a concrete instance we are or are not faced with a specimen belonging to the ideal type in question. It is peculiar to the ideal type that not all its characteristics need to be present in any one example. Whether or not the absence of some characteristics prevents the inclusion of

a concrete specimen in the ideal type in question, depends on a relevance judgment by understanding' (Mises, 1966, p. 59-60).

9. However, Rothbard in his texts from the 1950s and 1960s already referred to Schütz to support his own arguments. Lachmann ('The Legacy of Max Weber', 1971a) referred to Schütz, noting a close relationship. In *Epistemological Problems of Economics* (1933), Mises himself noted Schütz's work: 'Schütz's penetrating investigations, based on Huserl's system, lead to findings whose importance and fruitfulness, both for epistemology and historical science itself, must be valued very highly. However, an evaluation of the concept of the ideal type, as it is newly conceived by Schütz, would exceed the scope of this treatise. I must reserve dealing with his ideas for another work' (Mises, 1933, p.125-126). As Selgin notes (1982), Mises most unfortunately never came back to this question.
10. Boettke and Koppl ('Introduction to the Special Issue', 2001) state that Schütz fully recognises the validity of Mises' criticism of Weber's ideal types. However, they remark (p. 113) that his work was precisely intended to 'cover the concepts and propositions of the theoretical social sciences, included those of pure economics' (Schütz, 1932, p. 244).
11. It is only possible here to mention the most important contributions: Boettke ('Interpretative Reasoning and the Study of Social Life', 1990, 'Rational Choice and Human Agency in Economics and Sociology: Exploring the Weber-Austrian Connection', 1998a); Ebeling ('Toward a Hermeneutical Economics: Expectations, Prices and the Role of Interpretation in a Theory of the Market Process', 1986, 'Cooperation in Anonymity', 1987, 'Austrian Subjectivism and Phenomenological Foundations', 1995; Foss ('Spontaneous Social Order: Economics and Schützian Sociology', 1996a); Koppl ('Alfred Schütz and George Shackle: Two Views of Choice', 1992, 'Lachmann on Schütz and Shackle', 1994; 'Mises and Schütz on Ideal Types', 1997; 'Big Players and the Economic Theory of Expectations', 2002); Kurrild-Klitgaard ('On Rationality, Ideal Types and Economics: Alfred Schütz and the Austrian School', 1997); Prendergast ('A. Schütz and the Austrian School of Economics', 1986, 'Rationality, Optimality and Choice', 1993); Augier ('Some Notes on Alfred Schütz and the Austrian School of Economics: Review of Alfred Schütz' Collected Papers', 1999). A special issue of *The Review of Austrian Economics* (September, 2001), reviewing the Austrian literature devoted to Schütz, demonstrates contemporary Austrian interest in these questions.
12. These commentaries ('Über Wissen und Wirtschaft') were published in English entitled 'Political Economy: Human Conduct in Social Life' in *Alfred Schütz, Collected Papers*, vol. IV (1996) p. 93-105, published by Wagner, Psathas and Kersten.
13. 'All my experiences of the external situation on which I have no influence are data' (Schütz, *Collected Papers*, p. 96).
14. This last article, however 'was prepared from notes collected at the same time as those for the first two essays' (Hayek, preface to *The Counter-Revolution of Science*).

5. A World of Discovery

The analysis of market formation allows certain elements of intersubjectivity to appear, which we can use to explain market exchanges mechanisms. Yet the prices formed from these monetary transactions cannot be seen as a way of removing all ignorance. Even when the market exists, when exchanges have established monetary prices, agents are still incapable of grasping all the available information; they still have to deal with ignorance. Catallaxy here becomes a central point in dealing with this problem, the market mechanisms thus becoming a means not of getting rid of ignorance but of encouraging discovery.

Catallaxy places ignorance in the very centre of the study of economic phenomena, obliging much more specific examination of the themes of disequilibrium and equilibrium (1). The Austrian tradition considers the market as a process and claims the entrepreneur plays an important role in its activities (2). In turn, entrepreneurship in a market economy cannot be analysed independently of the institutional context which structures its activities: competition (3).

1. MARKETS, EQUILIBRIUM AND DISEQUILIBRIUM

The Austrians carefully separate 'information' from 'knowledge' (1.1). From this distinction comes the idea that market prices are disequilibrium prices (1.2). Agents commit errors, governed as they are by the logic of disequilibrium; in trying to correct them, they show the market to be a process (1.3).

1.1 Information is Not the Same as Knowledge

Evidence of agents' *ex ante* ignorance means the market's role can be conceptualised. The latter's function, as we noted in Part 1, is to narrow the sphere of ignorance by transforming hitherto unnoticed opportunities into as-of-now known opportunities. In other words, its essential function is to discover existing exchange possibilities. Market prices, in their formation and their evolution, all contain elements of discovery but their existence is still incapable of completely removing agents' ignorance.

The Austrians argue that the phenomenon of individual ignorance is unavoidable. Notions of knowledge and ignorance are only able to be applied to the individual. Only individuals can know or be ignorant (the market cannot, as it is not a sentient being). Each individual constantly takes decisions and acts on them, inevitably in ignorance of what others are deciding and doing at the same moment. Each exchange is thus locally contextual, involving particular actors and knowledge.

Knowing what is happening 'here' implies ignoring what is happening 'there'. So 'different individuals have different knowledge' (O'Driscoll and Rizzo, 1990, p. 336). Each price only incorporates a part of the available information and is an expression of only a fraction of opportunities. So we can say each price is formed in ignorance of those being formed elsewhere at the same time. This means there is no common knowledge of prices; each agent can only know particular prices.[1] Prices prise cracks apart in the wall of ignorance, but they cannot bring it down.

The opportunities known to each actor will always be fewer compared with existing exploitable opportunities; ignorance is prevalent, despite the discoveries expressed by monetary prices. Each price represents knowledge of a part of reality, but the actor is kept in the dark as to knowledge of other parts of reality. This brings the neo-Austrian economists to defend the idea of an 'open-ended' character of an environment which is open to each actor to discover and explore. In other words, there will always be more information than knowledge. It is indispensible to bear this major constraint in mind when exploring the themes of equilibrium and disequilibrium.

1.2 Disequilibrium Prices

It is easy to understand why the Austrians believed the market could never be in equilibrium, seeing the nature of ignorance. The market can never do away with ignorance; an individual can never know all the existing opportunities in any one moment. In this way, the market can only produce disequilibrium prices.

If we associate equilibrium with the idea of perfect mutual knowledge, the notion of an equilibrium market can no longer exist and defending it can only lead to contradictions. The real markets are marked by agents' inevitable 'dis-knowledge' of the ensemble of available exchange opportunities. The essentials of price theory cannot therefore be linked to equilibrium, as they cannot explain the real world markets' workings: 'The real economic problems in any society arise from the phenomenon of unperceived opportunities. The manner in which a market society grapples with this phenomenon cannot be understood within an exclusively equilibrium theory of the market' (Kirzner, *Perception, Opportunities and Profit*, 1979, p. 12). The idea of disequilibrium can only be understood by accepting a certain degree of agents' ignorance. In 'The Use of Knowledge in Society', Hayek clearly stated the 'fact that the knowledge of the circumstances of which we must make use never exists in concentrated or integrated form but solely as the dispersed bits of incomplete and frequently contradictory knowledge which all the separate individuals possess' (Hayek, 1945, p. 118). Based on this, Kirzner explains that

> at any given moment, opportunities exist for socially significant exchange and production activities. The ingredients for such opportunities consist of pieces of information concerning resources and products which, if brought together in a single mind, could present clearly identifiable opportunities. The problem is that they are not, at the moment in question, present to any single mind (Kirzner, *The Meaning of Market Process: Essays in the Development of Modern Austrian Economics*, 1992a, p. 51-52).

Market prices must therefore be seen not as equilibrium prices but as expressing the discovery of previously unnoticed opportunities. This vision of prices as expression of discoveries is fundamental. Kirzner disapproves of some authors making the leap from Hayek's idea of knowledge division to the erroneous idea that the price system's role was to record all available and existing opportunities, as this is to mistake the market's role. If every available opportunity was known, there would be no more prices and no more markets or exchange, as there would be nothing left to discover. Prices do not bring about equilibrium; they reveal the existence of disequilibrium.

The difference between the range of opportunities known to the individual and the full range of opportunities available is the essence of the Austrian question of ignorance and disequilibrium. This difference does not prevent other forms of disequilibrium also appearing, even within the market; different conceptions and levels of disequilibrium coexist within the Austrian tradition, inviting a confusion of terms between them which often befuddles the minds of various commentators.

A first level of disequilibrium is the buyers' or sellers' 'proposed price'. When a seller suggests a price deemed too high for the product – no one therefore buying it – it is clearly a disequilibrium price. It will have to be lowered in order to be actual, that is accepted, then validated by an exchange. In a symmetrical way, a consumer making too low an offer to obtain the goods he wants is proposing a disequilibrium price. He will have to raise his offer sufficiently to make the exchange; the proposed price is then validated.

A second level of disequilibrium can be found on the actual prices level. Actual prices, that is mutually acceptable for exchange between buyer and seller, might still be disequilibrium prices if at the same moment in other market segments, unknown to either agent, other transactions are being carried out more favourably to one or the other parties. So if the seller has the opportunity to offer his goods on that market at higher prices, his actual transaction price is a disequilibrium price. Similarly, if the consumer has the opportunity of buying the same goods elsewhere, at a lower price, again the actual transaction price is a disequilibrium price. This is the 'different market price for the same product cohabitation', with some agents knowing of or seeing opportunities in certain market segments and others not.

It is the entrepreneur-promoter's job to 'clear' the market, as we will see in a moment.

A third level of disequilibrium exists in a market which has indeed been cleared, where prices are actual and coherent with others. It still does not mean they are equilibrium prices in Austrian terms. Even if the markets are coherent and all exchanges perfectly coherent, prices can never record all the existing information and express all the available opportunities. Any market opportunities seized do not reflect all the opportunities available at that moment; this means that market prices must remain in a state of disequilibrium. Cleared markets (that is equilibrated markets from a neoclassical point of view), may still be suboptimal (see Kirzner, 1992a, p. 174).

We are hence faced with 'utter', 'genuine' or 'sheer' ignorance.

1.3 Ignorance, Errors and Processes

It is only possible to envisage the idea of disequilibrium and disequilibrium prices by accepting the inevitability of agents' ignorance. This is fundamental ignorance, required information being missing to the individual, 'which includes, of course, the possibility of his being altogether ignorant of the very existence of valuable information' (Kirzner, 1992a, p. 189). This is not simply a question of faulty or costly gathering of relevant information, but recognition of a fundamental: an individual cannot know in any one moment everything that is useful for him to know.

This phenomenon has some important implications. It is possible to conceptualize the notion of errors, because of the existence of ignorance and it is because there are errors that the market can be considered as a process.

If the criteria for market success were that the market supplied all its agents with all the necessary knowledge of all available opportunities, the market would fail, ignorance being prevalent; actors commit errors, 'dis-knowing' as they do all the available opportunities. *In Market Theory and the Price System*, Kirzner states the inevitability of errors 'from the fact that these plans may not reflect the opportunities that "really" exist' (Kirzner, 1963, p. 258). From this perspective, 'Disequilibrium conditions emerge as soon as someone perceives the profit possibilities inherent in the situation' (ibid., p. 258).

In his first work, *The Economic Point of View* (1960), Kirzner was already examining the error in economics in order to refute traditional conceptions, particularly the Italian philosopher Croce's. In *Perception, Opportunity and Profit* (1979), returning to the question, he focuses on the notion of 'genuine error'. His view, as opposed to Croce's, which is that error comes from a weakness of will, is that an actor's error comes from failure to perceive objectively offered information about an opportunity: 'I therefore claim justification for a terminology that maintains that, where ignorance consists not in lack of available information but in inexplicably failing to see facts staring one in the face, it represents genuine error and genuine inefficiency' (Kirzner, 1979, p. 131). Information may be available yet not transformed into knowledge as it is not perceived. Making genuine errors consists of not seizing the best opportunities and of taking decisions 'made in unwitting ignorance of pertinent information' (ibid., p. 207).

It is therefore this ignorance that leads the actor to behave in a way corresponding to the notion of error:

> decisions are often made in ignorance of the very need or possibility of acquiring information that might be freely available. It is one thing to know that one is ignorant and to deliberately maintain one's ignorance because of the high cost of gaining knowledge. It is another to be ignorant simply because one has no inkling that one is ignorant, because one has no inkling that information exists, or indeed that any such thing is imaginable, in the relevant context, as information. Surely the latter kind of ignorance is abundantly present; genuine error is alive and well. We cannot rule out the possibility that market decisions have been not out of deliberately accepted ignorance, but out of genuine error (Kirzner, 1979, p. 207).

So we can only explain market disequilibrium by a situation of ignorance, which brings us to the ideas of market errors and of a disequilibrium price. These last two lead logically to a view of the market as a process, disequilibrium being associated with non-stable situations which have to be transformed. Disequilibrium expresses situations where errors are noticed and their correction would be required; as prices are disequilibrium prices, they too would have to be modified.

Equilibrium price theory thus has to be opposed to a theory of market process. All the Austrian authors carefully distinguish the neoclassical models, which analyse the market as a state from their conception of catallaxy as a process. Kirzner sees this distinction's origins in Hayek's 'The Meaning of Competition' (1948b), '... a pioneering and penetrating article', (Kirzner, *Competition and Entrepreneurship*, 1973); this does not stop him from later referring to the argument of Mises', who

> showed how the belief held by theorists that equilibrium states are actually attained led them to misunderstand grossly what markets in fact achieve. For Mises, the essence of a theory of markets must be to explain the forces that generate changes in prices and quantities; the equilibrium concept is useful precisely in its offering, in its utterly hypothetical freedom from change, a contrast to the world of incessant change (Kirzner, 1979, p. 17).

Erroneous or tardily acquired knowledge results in later changes of action, changes which constitute the very essence of the market process. This means it is indeed ignorance that drives the market and Kirzner rightly considers that without the concept of error, analysing market dynamics is impossible. To return to a previous argument, the fact of there even being an economic dynamic shows the existence of individual error and therefore of unperceived opportunities.

2. THE ENTREPRENEUR-PROMOTER

Writings on the entrepreneur and his economic functions have become an important part of contemporary analysis. They are, however one of the most specific features of the Austrian tradition. Menger (*Principles of Economics*, 1871; *Investigations into the Method in Social Sciences*, 1883) and Wieser (*Social Economics*, 1914) takes the first important steps of an Austrian reflection on the entrepreneur. It is Mises, however, who first gives entrepreneurship an autonomous, explicit status in Austrian theory (2.1), by closely involving it in the neo-Austrian market price analysis through the notion of discovery. Kirzner will define the two notions of alertness (2.2) and learning from this perspective (2.3) as the two main characteristics of entrepreneurship. These show up the essential role of the concepts of profit and loss, which could be seen as the frontiers of ignorance and knowledge.

2.1 From the Praxeological Entrepreneur to the Market Promoter

The best way of viewing entrepreneurial activity on an infra-individual or praxeological level is by contrasting Robbins' allocative maximizing type of decision with the creative approach of Mises' *homo agens*. As we noted in Part 1, Robbins' individual acts inside a means-ends framework of data; the ends pre-exist action, they are ready-ranked, the means being objective elements to the ends. Useful though this representation may be, it does not account for the whole of human action; it in particular leaves aside how the actor defines both ends and means. It also does not show how an individual moves from one means-ends structure to another, that is to say, from one action to another and so to close the praxeological cycle.

The completion of the cycle requires that each actor by definition discovers new structures of action; he discovers ends, chooses means, decides on strategy and moves forwards to new plans. This is how any actor can be defined as an entrepreneur, as he is a creator. He actively and continually produces his own internal environment.

We have already seen Mises' feeling of 'uneasiness', which in his vision of human action is the source of the actor's discovery, pushing him from his present situation to seek new sources of gains in satisfaction. Seen from a praxeological point of view, entrepreneurship thus escapes Robbins' narrower 'economizing' vision (Kirzner) and is finally seen as the expression of any actor's desire to gain in satisfaction.

Both praxeology and catallaxy claim for themselves the term of entrepreneur. In *Human Action*, Mises discusses 'the catallactic concept of the entrepreneur' (Mises, 1966, p. 252), linking it with the idea of change being etched into the very nature of action. It is because action aims for an uncertain future that 'In any real and living economy every actor is always an entrepreneur and speculator' (ibid., 52). He adds a little further: 'The term entrepreneur as used by catallactic theory means: acting man exclusively seen from the aspect of the uncertainty inherent in every action' (ibid., p. 253). It is clear from these definitions that any individual in the market is engaged to a greater or lesser extent in entrepreneurial activities. If we see entrepreneurship as a function relative to a state where the results of action are uncertain, then anybody in action is an entrepreneur, so it is impossible to see a difference between the actors.

Mises thus produced the term of promoter, to describe a more specific and narrower form of entrepreneurship. He candidly admits the impossibility of precisely defining this notion, yet he gives it some substance, as understanding catallactic logic is impossible without this role. With this term, Mises names those 'who are especially eager to profit from adjusting production to the expected changes in conditions, those who have more initiative, more venturesomeness, and a quicker eye than the crowd, the pushing and promoting pioneers of economic improvement' (Mises, 1966, p. 255).

Of all the authors after Mises, Kirzner doubtless went the furthest in explaining the role of Mises' promoter, the market entrepreneur. In *Perception, Opportunity and Profit*, Kirzner takes the representation of the market promoter from the motion of praxeological entrepreneurship: '... the phenomenon of market entrepreneurship is not merely parallel to the entrepreneurial element in individual action, but in fact depends on the latter element for its own existence' (Kirzner, 1979, p. 176). For Kirzner, beyond Mises' quite explicit words, 'alertness' and 'learning by discovery' are the two elements that characterise praxeological dimensions of entrepreneurship and obviously apply as such to the market place. These are still fairly controversial elements within the neo-Austrian tradition (see next chapter) yet have been sufficiently dominant and commented on to constitute a solid point of reference.

2.2 Alertness as Ability of Perception

The first of the entrepreneurial elements is the idea of 'alertness'. It describes an agent's aptitude for perceiving previously ignored opportunities and can take many forms.

The entrepreneur may see opportunities which no other actor had perceived, putting them on the market by exploiting them through exchanges and prices.

Another case would be that some actors can make profitable market exchanges whereas others in a similar market exchange and make prices in worse conditions through their own lack of alertness.

Realising these contradictions in prices is an entrepreneurial discovery which will lead alert actors to restructure their activities. Contrary to the neoclassicals, the Austrian promoter is not a 'price-taker'; through his actions he modifies the price and exchange structure. By 'arbitraging', they tend to clear the market and reveal all the opportunities known by at least some of the agents to the others.

In *Market Theory and the Price System* (1963), Kirzner mentions the idea of entrepreneurial superior information, the term alertness still being absent from his vocabulary. But in *Competition and Entrepreneurship* (1973) and subsequently, he uses the explicit term of alertness to mean 'capacity of perception'. The entrepreneur's essential strength does not rest on an 'asymmetric information', as this is available to all actors, but his capacity to transform information into knowledge, to see opportunity in his external environment of gains in satisfaction or of profit.

It is in fact not so much a question here of an information difference as a difference in perception. In *Perception, Opportunity and Profit*, Kirzner once again insists on the need to differentiate alertness and possession of information. One can possess information without using it, if one does not perceive the opportunities within it.

A variation of this analysis is to highlight the entrepreneur's capacity of flushing out information which would lead to profit opportunities. Driven by his natural curiosity, he would here be an agent who, unlike other economic actors, would be permanently on the lookout for any profitable information. Here, the entrepreneur's main quality is not to possess better knowledge of market information than other agents, but know where to find it. Yet further in the work, Kirzner prefers to talk about 'alertness to information, rather than of its possession' (Kirzner, 1973, p. 68). What counts is not possessing information but knowing where and how to find it. 'Entrepreneurial knowledge is a rarefied, abstract type of knowledge – the knowledge of where to obtain information (or other resources) and how to deploy it' (Kirzner, 1979, p. 8). The entrepreneur is the one who captures a signal. Not only is he alert to facts, seeing profit opportunities in them but he is also alert as to the means of finding information. He is the one who unlike the others goes 'around the corner' (ibid., p. 8) to see if there is just one more opportunity somewhere else.

So the entrepreneur is *a priori* just as ignorant as the other agents. However, ignorant of the nature and depth of his ignorance as he is, unlike other actors, he knows he is ignorant. It is his knowledge of his 'dis-knowledge' that explains his curiosity and drive to seize all opportunities to reduce this lack.

Kirzner insists on another point, which is that, praxeologically speaking, all actors are entrepreneurs but they all display different degrees of alertness. Kirzner publicly regretted the frequent generalisations in the analysis of entrepreneurship, as it is so heterogeneous, following the various forms of alertness and ways of discovery. In fact this notion of alertness is in some ways a black hole; behind this concept are some largely unexplained determining factors (Kirzner, 1985, p. 26 calls for an analysis of aspects of the entrepreneur's psychology).

2.3 The Nature of Learning

In the Austrian way of thinking, learning fundamentally means realising error, or realising that one has neglected available opportunities. Whether they were unknown to all or only a few agents does not change the problem; learning for an actor means noticing opportunities.

Learning and discovery are thus two sides of the same coin; discovering is learning and learning is seeing that one has made errors. Realising this, that is to say identifying the nature of the disequilibrium, brings about a disappointment of expectations. This leads agents to a process of revising their beliefs and adjusting their activities.

So behind price formation and evolution there is a process of 'learning by discovery', which represents a realisation of errors.

> During this process each step consists of revised opinions on the part of potential participants concerning the market situation which they face. These revisions consist, as we have seen, either in a rude awakening to the fact that one has been, up until now, over optimistic, or in the realization that one has in fact, until now, overlooked an attractive opportunity that is available. It is these discoveries that are expressed in the continually changing arrays of bids and offers being made in markets (Kirzner, *Discovery, Capitalism and Distributive Justice*, 1989, p. 82).

Learning is not a search: the notion of surprise

Kirzner presented a strict definition of the learning process, carefully distinguishing the Austrian representation of it from other 'search' models – as they are called – being offered. One must not confuse the Austrian 'sheer ignorance' with the notion of imperfect information found in neoclassical models as well as the neo-Keynesians. 'The standard literature has indeed incorporated the economics of search, but not the economics of discovery' (Kirzner, 1989, p. 29). The idea of search assumes the agent knows the nature of his ignorance, whereas discovery obviously implies the opposite.

For a number of years, contemporary mainstream theory has been examining imperfect information, an idea which leaves aside core questions posed by the Austrians:

> Imperfect information refers to known-to-be-available information which it is costly to produce. But for Austrians the focus is upon what has been termed 'previously unthought-of knowledge' (Esteban Thomsen, 1992) … Austrian appreciation for the discovery potential of market processes does not at all imply that 'informational efficiency' for market outcomes which Stiglitz has denied … For Austrians it is unacceptable to claim that, at each and every instant, the configuration of production and consumption decisions currently made, is one which could, in the light of the relevant costs, not possibly have been improved upon. To claim that, at any given instant, all conceivably relevant available opportunities have been instantaneously grasped is to fly in the face of what we know about real world economic systems (Kirzner, 1997, p. 65).

The problem with these models is that acquiring information can only be regarded as a deliberate undertaking. If we think we already know what it is we are looking for, we have insidiously introduced the idea of initial knowledge which is not explained by these models.[2] The Austrian learning representation, on the contrary, shows there is not deliberate search of learning or of information as agents do not know the particular nature of their ignorance. Even if entrepreneurs are cognizant of their ignorance, they do not know where their ignorance lies. It is easy to see how Kirzner came to the opinion that any discovery resulting from the process of learning must be a surprise.

A legitimate distinction can thus be made between discovery and deliberate learning: 'Sheer ignorance differs from imperfect information in that the discovery which reduces sheer ignorance is necessarily accompanied by the element of surprise – one had not hitherto realized one's ignorance' (Kirzner, 1997, p. 62). This is why the Austrians consider it impossible to conceive a market of ignorance: knowing the nature and boundaries of one's own ignorance is impossible, it is therefore equally impossible to transfer ignorance or fix a price on it.

Learning is not production

In the same way, for Kirzner, learning and production should be kept well separate. Production is a deliberate act, whereas discovery is a result of alertness, which is not a choice but an aptitude. We should also not see in this aptitude a resource, that is, a productive factor that we find in the rest of the economy, which we can allocate to various ends at our convenience. 'Entrepreneurial alertness is not an ingredient to be deployed in decision making; it is rather something in which the decision itself is embedded and without which it would be unthinkable' (Kirzner, 1985, p. 22). Viewing alertness as a resource serving production would be to assimilate entrepreneurship to Robbins' economizing view. This would mean that entrepreneurship would be only one means among others used to attain a predetermined goal.

In *The Meaning of Market Process*, Kirzner systematically brings out discovery's distinctive elements to better contrast it with the idea of production. He defines production as a project planned collectively or individually, during which inputs are put to work to reach a consciously defined goal chosen from many.

Discovery is not a conscious cost-profit relationship, where information production costs are minimized to maximize net gains of a product being searched for. These are not Robbins' efficiency rules here, as 'An act of discovery contains no such expression of constrained maximization; it involves no plan, no allocation, merely the grasping of a perceived, available objective' (Kirzner, 1992a, p. 218). It is thus spontaneous.

The final point to be made here is that as alertness cannot be seen as a productive factor, then its result, discovery, cannot be seen as a simple process of transformation of existing knowledge, as it would be for production.

Learning is not a question of chance

So as learning is not the result of planned production, it would be unfortunate to fall into the trap of thinking that it is the result of chance, of a windfall dropping into the lap of just any actor whatever his attitudes and qualities. Of course,

> in the discovery case, alertness was never deliberately deployed to achieve discovery; all on can say is that, because Jones was alert, he noticed the lumber. One can never say that alertness 'ensured' discovery – in the sense that possession of alertness rendered its possessor sure that he would successfully discover that which he later discovers. This is so 1) because the alert agent has as yet no inkling that the item-to-be-discovered is indeed available for discovery and 2) because … alertness is not enough, discovery involves also these elements of sheer good fortune (Kirzner, 1989, p. 24).

So chance is a part of the discovery process, as alertness coupled with entrepreneurship is not in itself a guarantee of discovery; it happens where alertness and chance meet (see Kirzner 1989, p. 24 and p. 29-33). In *Perception, Opportunity and Profit*, Kirzner noted: 'Entrepreneurial vision may not be arrived at deliberately, rationally, but neither is it arrived at purely by chance. In fact… it is an implication of the purposefulness of human action that tends to ensure, in some degree, that opportunities come to be noticed' (Kirzner, 1979, p. 170). Similarly, he observes in *The Meaning of Market Process*:

> An act of discovery, even though it is not an act of deliberate production, is the expression of human motivation and human alertness. That which has been discovered might never have been discovered but for this motivation and alertness; it is

> quite wrong to see the discovery as merely the product of blind chance (Kirzner, 1992a, p. 219-220).

Discovery is thus a mix of luck and alertness.

2.4 From Ignorance to Knowledge: The Role of Profit

Pure profit is a gain in satisfaction, in praxeological terms, which takes many different forms.[3] It is the desire for gains in satisfaction which pushes agents to leave the closed, Robbins type of model for an entrepreneurial mode. 'We know very little about the precise way in which pure, profit opportunities attract entrepreneurial attention. But there can be little doubt about the powerful magnetism which such opportunities exert. To say that pure product opportunities attract attention is not at all to say that awareness of the opportunities is secured by deliberate, costly search on the part of entrepreneurs. Rather it is to recognize that the lure of pure profit is what permits an individual decision maker to transcend the limits of a given, perceived planning framework and to escape, to some extent, the basic knowledge that surrounds all individual decision making' (Kirzner, 1992a, p. 160-161). The idea of pure gain, of profit is thus '... the spark that switches on the entrepreneurial alertness' (Kirzner, 1979, p. 96).

Entrepreneurial profit and alertness

The idea of profit is associated much more with that of pure, rather than net gain, because it is the result of surprise, with no deliberate search and so with no particular investment (Kirzner, 1992a, p. 224). When considering the question of incentives in entrepreneurial activity, it is impossible to analyse cost advantages, as alertness has no cost; it is also impossible to predict gains resulting from the activity. The only thing that can 'be stated with considerable confidence [is] that human beings tend to notice that which it is in their interest to notice. Human beings notice "opportunities" rather than "situations"' (Kirzner, 1985, p. 28). Of course, profit on the markets is monetary. It is simply defined: 'the phenomenon of pure profit corresponds to prices paid for outputs which exceed the sums of prices paid for all necessary inputs. The difference between these sets of prices is grasped by the entrepreneur as pure profit' (ibid., p. 48).

Monetary gain is thus the product of a discovery, according to the praxeological definition of profit, and that monetary gain is the income source and result of entrepreneur-promoter activity.

> Every case of pure profit, we have noted in earlier chapters, constitutes a case of pure discovery. Pure profit is what is grasped as a result of being able to buy and sell in different markets, to buy where the price is low, and to sell, now or in the future, where or when the price is higher ... The nature of pure profits, therefore, is

> such that pure profits can never be won except through an act of pure discovery … The alert entrepreneur has discovered an opportunity to which on one else has hitherto laid claim, an opportunity in fact, of which no one was even aware (otherwise that opportunity would already have been snapped up) (Kirzner, 1989, p. 109; 111).

These profits, once again, must not be thought of as a matter of luck, where the entrepreneur's personal qualities count for nothing. In Kirzner's view, even such a highly penetrating thinker on entrepreneurship as Knight takes analysis in the wrong direction when he sees the promoter as

> the fortunate beneficiary of changes which no one could have foreseen. This is not to assert that Knight is not fully aware of the incentive to entrepreneurial activity that the prospect of profit provides; it is merely to point out that for Knight the realization of a prospect for profit has not very much to do with the entrepreneur's superior ability at noticing such prospects. 'Both profit and loss arise in many cases from circumstances entirely apart from human foresight.' (Knight, *Profit*) (Kirzner, 1989, p. 58-59).

The only necessary elements for discovery are the qualities of alertness and learning. They are thus at the very centre of a promoter's gain and even if luck does intervene, it is not specific to his activity and cannot be considered as central. Analysis does not therefore require that chance be taken into account of an explanation of monetary profit.

Profit does not come from possessing capital

It has been seen earlier that pure profit has to be viewed as a generic idea, a result of discovery of gains in satisfaction. Being a praxeological category, it is obvious it is not analytically linked to the notion of capital.

However, even when seen from a monetary point of view, the idea of profit cannot be intrinsically linked to a notion of productivity or capital. Mises had already noted that '… it is not the capital employed that creates profits and losses' (Mises, *Planning for Freedom*, 1962c, p.120). In Kirzner's eyes: 'Pure profit, by its very definition, is not to be attributed to inputs. Its source is not to be identified with anything possessed by the entrepreneur; it is, as were, uncaused. It has simply been discovered … pure profits cannot be explained ("justified") as reward for services rendered' (Kirzner, 1989, p. 49). Or again, 'pure speculative profit is an example of a discovered gain, a kind of gain to which "productivity" justifications are essentially irrelevant' (Kirzner, 1989, p. 50).

Profit is linked to the notion of discovery but is independent of the ideas of capital endowment or property. Kirzner regrets (1985, p. 1) that in spite of precursors such as Cantillon or Jean-Baptiste Say,[4] most economists commenting on entrepreneurship did not separate it sufficiently from capital ownership. It was Mises who first came up with the distinction:

> Entrepreneurial profits, in this [Mises's] view are not captured by owners, in their capacity of owners, at all. They are captured, instead by men who exercise pure entrepreneurship, for which ownership is never a condition. The Misesian theory of entrepreneurial profit can be described as an 'arbitrage' theory of profit: 'What makes profit emerge is the fact that the entrepreneur who judges the future prices of the products more correctly than other people do buys some or all of the factors of production at prices which, seen from the point of view of the future state of the market, are too low' (Mises, *Planning for Freedom*, 1962, p. 109) (Kirzner, 1979, p. 94-95).

Every individual capitalist is always an entrepreneur, because each actor is a speculator, but promoters are not at all necessarily capitalists.

Of course in practice we see situations where known opportunities are being exploited in coexistence with new opportunities being discovered. Kirzner (1989, p. 174-177) explains that when a promoter is also a capitalist, his revenues come in varying proportions from entrepreneurial discovery and production. These two revenues should not be confused however, as discovery consists of seizing as yet unknown opportunities and production of exploiting know opportunities.

So from the capitalist-entrepreneur's point of view it can be said that in the short term the pure production elements dominate, surprise not playing a major role. But in the medium and long term, the more opportunities are able to be modified, the more the unknown elements will weigh on the situation and discovery in the end dominates as a source of monetary gain. As a general rule, in periods of high technological innovation, the unknown elements dominate and the promoter's role becomes more important than the producer's.

Profit, loss and errors

So there is an analytical relation between the notions of alertness and pure profit; there exists a similar relation between the ideas of pure profit and discovery. But as profit is linked to discovery, it is also linked to the notion of ignorance: 'The phenomenon of pure profit … cannot be imagined to occur except as a result of sheer ignorance' (Kirzner, 1989, p. 110).

Pure profit could be said to pierce ignorance in a brief, limited victory, it being the reward for having changed ignorance to knowledge.

More precisely, this profit can be seen on several levels: it can be the motivation and reward for discovering opportunities that no other market participant had seen, for example a new use for factors, the entrepreneur creating a new structure of exchange. It can also be the reward for having cleared the market, in the case of errors in price.

But whatever view is taken, the important thing to remember is that pure monetary profit stems from an actor's discovery of opportunities previously ignored by the others, meaning that an entrepreneur's profits may exist only because others have erred. Kirzner is very clear on this point:

> The market transactions which result in the winning of pure economic profit must in retrospect be judged to have been made, in part, as a result of 'sheer error' on the part of one or other of the relevant participants ... Such profit could hardly arise unless those from whom the entrepreneur buys have been aware of the sum of the prices accepted by those from whom the entrepreneur bought (Kirzner, 1992, p. 215).[5]

Wave after wave, discovery throws entrepreneurs onto the shores of the market and changes them into promoters; ignorance sucks promoters less alert than others back off the market beach. This ebb and flow reflects the integration and dis-integration of the marketing of entrepreneurial knowledge.

The idea of errors can also be seen on several levels: total ignorance of all the opportunities on the markets; entrepreneurs' failure to seize opportunities already seen by certain of their number on the market; and a failure to forecast the events properly, as we will see in the next chapter.

Different types of loss correspond to the different levels of error: it comes either from the cost of not seizing existing opportunity or from breaking off activities as others discover different, more favourable opportunities. Profit is a reward yet it also activates a principle of selection, a point which brings us to the subject of competition.

3. THE INSTITUTIONAL DIMENSION OF ENTREPRENEURSHIP

We have already seen the relation between the entrepreneur-promoter and prices. The entrepreneur rolls back the limits of ignorance and highlights existing opportunities, pushing them into the field of known, exploitable knowledge through developing exchange and forming prices. The entrepreneur ceaselessly questions the information found in the pricing system through his own particular brand of alertness.

The entrepreneur is continually faced with ignorance, as his job is essentially to reduce it; it is by this light that the notion of competition, intimately linked to the market's functioning, should be examined.

Mises and his successors saw the idea of competition in the context of a cognitive analysis. In *Human Action*, Mises contrasts biological type-competition with social-type competition, which is nothing but 'the striving of individuals to attain the most favourable position in the system of social cooperation' (Mises, 1966, p. 273). The two types certainly are ruled by scarcity but the first one ends with the physical elimination of the other competitor, whereas the second is a proportional relation between individuals' economic efficiency and their social position. Catallactic competition more precisely gives the consumer the final choice: 'To assign to everybody his proper place in society' (ibid., p. 275).

However, the Austrians left most of the explanations of the cognitive basics of competition to Hayek, who sees it as a 'procedure of discovery' (3.1) and Kirzner, who completes Hayek's analysis by defining competition as 'free entry' (3.2). For both authors, competition is at once the possibility and incentive of discovering available opportunities. From it, they defend the idea of the 'increment of freedom' (Kirzner); Hayek's analysis of catallaxy's workings will lead him also to condemn the myth and the dangers of social justice (3.4).

3.1 Competition as a Discovery Process

Hayek's cognitive conception of economic structures is woven into his work in patterns by which he reflected systematically on the institutions framing price formations and shaping market efficiency. In a series of major writings ('The Use of Knowledge in Society', 1945; 'The Meaning of Competition', 1948; 'Competition as a Discovery Procedure', 1968; *Law, Legislation and Liberty*, 1973, 1976a, 1979), he argues that discovering and exploiting opportunities, or in other terms entrepreneurs reducing ignorance, is a process which agents can only operate if they are allowed to do so. Only by leaving agents the liberty to exercise their activities can the transfer of knowledge and the piercing of ignorance take place: 'I propose to consider competition as a procedure for the discovery of such facts as, without resort to it, would not be known to anyone, or at least would not be utilised' (Hayek, 1968, p. 179) ... 'in which people acquire and communicate knowledge' (Hayek, 1979a, p. 68). Revealing previously neglected exploitable opportunities is dependant on there existing a competition process, which is:

> essentially a process of the formation of opinion: by spreading information, it creates that unity and coherence of the economic system which we presuppose when we think of it as one market. It creates the views people have about what is best and cheapest, and it is because of it that people know at least as much about possibilities and opportunities as they in fact do (Hayek, 1948, p. 106).

So competition offers the structure to transform existing information into socially transmitted information. Competition is thus 'a discovery procedure' (Hayek, 1968).

However, this process will only be possible if individuals are able and motivated to react to the changes in it. Entrepreneurial discoveries can only be conveyed into a price system if the actors are free to react to their discoveries by forming strategies and acting them out. By leaving each individual free to use his particular entrepreneurial talents, we arrive at the above process of socialization of agents' particular knowledge.

Ignorance of relevant data is not an accident or a technical glitch that the economist or actor hopes to resolve at some future moment. It more fundamentally reveals the existence of tacit, local knowledge deep in actors' minds, that they would not know how to express other than by their actions. Thus:

> combinations of individual knowledge and skills, which the market enables them to use, will not merely, or even in the first instance, be such knowledge of fact as they could list and communicate if some authority asked them to do so. The knowledge of which I speak consists rather of a capacity to find out particular circumstances, which becomes effective only if possessors of this knowledge are informed by the market which kind of things or services are wanted, and how urgently they are wanted. This must suffice to indicate what kind of knowledge I am referring to when I call competition a discovery procedure (Hayek, 1968, p. 182).

Along with the idea of competition as possibility of making profits, the idea of incentive expresses the requirement for each individual in the market to be entrepreneurial. No market actor can afford to be static. Competition forces people to discovery or else it will eject them from the market. Most individuals confuse known opportunities with existing opportunities, which leads them to think of any discovery or new development with suspicion, as if this discovery was just some senseless fantasy and should not exist in reality. Hayek explains

> ... it is one of the chief reasons for the dislike of competition that it not only shows how things can be done more effectively, but also confronts those who depend for their incomes on the market with the alternative of imitating the more successful or losing some or all of their income. Competition produces in this way a kind of impersonal compulsion which makes it necessary for numerous individuals to adjust their way of life in a manner that no deliberate instructions or commands could bring about (ibid., p. 189).

The cost of adapting and of the forced abandonment of comfortable certainties explain the reticence expressed by a large part of the population to these processes of discovery.

This argument is Hayek's clearest explanation for the distance between himself and the neoclassical theories. In 'The Meaning of Competition' (1948b), he already expresses his difference from the critiques aimed by the imperfect competition theorists at the standard model, meanwhile discussing some elements not examined by the neoclassicals, such as product differentiation and advertising. Twenty years later, in 'Competition as a Discovery Procedure' he brings up the 'absurdity of the usual procedure of starting the analysis with a situation in which all the facts are supposed to be known. This is a state of affairs which economic theory curiously calls 'perfect competition', which is presumed to have already done its task' (Hayek, 1968, p. 182).

Hayek claims the problem, when perfect competition theories are dominant in ideas concerning the institutions of competition, 'is largely due to mistakenly treating the order which the market produces as an "economy" in the strict sense of the word, and judging results of the market process by criteria which are appropriate only to such a single organised community serving a given hierarchy of ends' (Hayek, 1968, p. 182). Competition answers the satisfaction of *a priori* desires, unknown to agents generally and deciders in particular.[6]

Any misunderstanding must be avoided at this point. The virtue of competition is not its capacity to mirror models of pure and perfect competition, as this would miss the function of discovery at the heart of the competitive processes.

> … the modern theory of competition deals almost exclusively with a state of what is called 'competitive equilibrium' in which it is assumed that the data for the different individuals are fully adjusted to each other, while the problem which requires explanation is the nature of the process by which the data are thus adjusted (Hayek, 1948b, p. 94).

Hayek is here discussing inappropriate use of the tautological method to analyse social problems, which he already showed the limits of in 'Economics and Knowledge'.

He explains further: 'If anyone really knew all about what economic theory call the data, competition would indeed be a very wasteful method of securing adjustment to these facts … it is on the ground that we do not know in advance the facts that determine the actions of competitors' (Hayek, 1968, p. 179). In fact: 'the knowledge they (the consumers) are supposed to possess in a state of competitive equilibrium cannot be legitimately assumed to be at their command before the process of competition starts' (Hayek, 1948b, p. 96).

So the real efficiency in competition is not in striving to imitate a model of pure and perfect competition, which would be absurd. Competition is of course imperfect in a mainstream sense which is why the markets have a role to play.

Models of pure and perfect competition do not explain the markets any more than models of imperfect competition do, as in the end they are built on the same logic; the latter retains the formers' faults while discarding their qualities. In fact, the two views both exclude in the same way the entrepreneur from their universe. The hypothetical case of general economic equilibrium, corresponding to a 'decentralised planned economy' leaves no room by definition for entrepreneurship, as agents would know all the existing opportunities.

3.2 Free Entry Competition

In the preface to *Competition and Entrepreneurship*, Kirzner presents his argument as a critique of the modern analysis of price or, as he similarly puts it, the assertion of a theory of the entrepreneur and competition. In fact, his project of reconsidering price analysis is based on the idea that competition, the entrepreneur and prices are all related (see Kirzner, 1973, p. X). To understand the market workings, it is necessary to introduce the terms of entrepreneur and competition: '... a useful understanding of the market process requires a notion of competition that is analytically inseparable from the exercise of entrepreneurship' (ibid., p. 9). The entrepreneur and competition are parallel notions: 'two sides of the same coin' (ibid. p. 16).

To succeed, each buyer or seller must at all times offer more favourable opportunities than the others; profit opportunities appear to one actor only because they have been neglected by the others. Every actor must be an entrepreneur and a more efficient one than the others. This is why Kirzner claims the market is naturally competitive and that entrepreneurial activity happens only in a competitive world. Competition in the market motivates individuals to discover opportunities, in fact obliges them to, as they will be ejected if they do not.

In the light of all this, equilibrium situations of neoclassical pure and perfect competition are in fact not competitive. In contrast to the unrealistic and contradictory hypotheses of this model, only one condition is required for effective competition: 'guaranteeing free entrepreneurial entry into any market where profit opportunities may be perceived to exist' (Kirzner, 1997, p. 74).

The principle of free entry does not mean however, actual entry. Freedom to discover and exploit existing opportunities does not always mean that they exist or will be discovered. If not, then the market stays still. Besides this, if discovering certain opportunities means sacrificing others of a higher value, then they will of course not be exploited, as the opportunity cost would be too high. In this way, technological progress could coincide with economic regression.[7]

Similarly, the idea of monopoly should not be taken as a failure of competition. Kirzner certainly thought a market would be a monopoly in the case of one producer being the only source of a product or a service. But as long as there is liberty to sell and buy, the market is always competitive. The amount of sellers or buyers is not a criterion of market competitiveness.

Here, Kirzner turns to *Human Action*, in which Mises explains that the market and catallactic competition can in fact produce monopoly prices:

> It would be a serious blunder to deduce from the antithesis between monopoly price and competitive price that the monopoly price is the outgrowth of the absence of competition. There is always catallactic competition on the market. Catallactic competition is no less a factor in the determination of monopoly prices that it is in

> the determination of competitive prices. The shape of the demand curve that makes the appearance of monopoly prices possible and directs the monopolists' conduct is determined by the competition of all other commodities competing for the buyers' dollars. The higher the monopolist fixes the price at which he is ready to sell, the more potential buyers turn their dollars toward other vendible goods. On the market every commodity competes with all other commodities (Mises, 1966, p. 278[8]).

So: 'Freedom of entry, for the Austrian approach, refers to the freedom of potential competitors to discover and to move to exploit existing opportunities for pure profit' (Kirzner, 1985, p. 142). If the free market principle requires only one condition, that is the idea of market openness, then state or centrally regulated prices cannot truly be seen as a hindrance to the competitive process. Interference in the free forming of prices certainly does form obstacles to entrepreneurial discovery and exploitation of opportunity, but if the free entry principle is upheld, a mixed economy can still be called competitive. 'Administered' prices would still be market prices (see Kirzner, 1985, p. 36).

3.3 The 'Increment of Freedom'

The central theme in all the questions surrounding competition is of course freedom, that is freedom to discover existing opportunities and exploit those already discovered. Hayek uses the theme of freedom to explain differences in development between countries:

> From all I have seen of the world the proportion of private persons who are prepared to try new possibilities, if they appear to them to promise better conditions, and if they are not prevented by the pressure of their fellows, is much the same everywhere. The much lamented absence of a spirit of enterprise in many of the new countries is not an unalterable characteristic of the individual inhabitants, but the consequence of restraints which existing customs and institutions place upon them (Hayek, 1968, p. 189-190).

This is a highly damaging situation for certain countries' growth perspectives. In *The Constitution of Liberty*, Hayek had already noticed that if 'the necessary condition for a free evolution – the spirit of individual initiative – is lacking, then surely without that spirit no viable civilization can grow anywhere. So far as it is really lacking, the first task must be to waken it' (Hayek, 1960, p. 2-3). Hayek's argument shows the concept of development as a coefficient of discovery of opportunities. Apart from the fact that competition and mobilizing tacit knowledge are powerful vectors of innovation and technological progress,

> possibilities of growth are likely to be greater the more extensive are a country's yet unused opportunities. Strange though this may seem at first sight, a high rate of

> growth is more often than not evidence that opportunities have been neglected in the past. Thus, a high rate of growth can sometimes testify to bad policies of the past rather than good policies of the present (Hayek, 1968, p. 189-190).

With stocks of ignored opportunities being higher in this type of country, freedom of discovering and exploiting them leads to higher levels of development. Imposing institutional rigidities will have a correspondingly greater negative impact on potential growth. Hayek logically underlines the following:

> Apart from the fact that there is in such countries so much more to be discovered, there is still another reason why the greatest freedom of competition seems to be even more important there than in more advanced countries. This is that required changes in habits and customs will be brought about only if the few willing and able to experiment with new methods can make it necessary for the many to follow them, and at the same time to show them the way. The required discovery process will be impeded or prevented, if the many are able to keep the few to the traditional ways (ibid., p. 189).[9]

Kirzner emphasizes several times to the institutional aspects of entrepreneurial activity particularly in *Discovery and the Capitalist Process* (see especially chapters 2, 5, 6 and 7): 'The central question then looms even more significantly than ever: what institutional frameworks are best suited to tap the reservoir of entrepreneurial alertness which is certainly present in potentially inexhaustible supply – among the members of society?' (Kirzner, 1985, p. 25).

In *The Meaning of the Market Process*, he proposes a way 'of evaluating the institutional environment in terms of its potential to inspire genuine discovery (of opportunities previously overlooked as a result of utter ignorance' (Kirzner, 1992, p. 191).

By developing the theme of the 'increment of freedom' (Kirzner, 1979, p. 234), Kirzner is led to the promoter, that great structuring force of the market economy. Increasing freedom means increasing perception of opportunity as, if it is impossible to exploit these then it is an obvious waste of time to look for them. 'The entrepreneurial view of freedom permits us to see how freedom to choose may inspire the discovery of opportunities that may be invisible to those to whom this freedom is denied' (ibid., p. 234). Built around a procedural conception of freedom, which in the end joins Hayek's, Kirzner successfully defends the system of competition, laissez-faire and private property.

Kirzner himself recognises that the generic character of entrepreneurship means it can be used in all types of institutions: 'it may be argued that in the broad sense of the term the concept of entrepreneurship is not necessarily confined to capitalism; after all, central planners may exercise entrepreneurial imagination, creativity and discovery for the benefit of the socialized society'

(Kirzner, 1985, p. 167). Three elements of his argument still, however, support free market principles.

Firstly, the extreme decentralisation of decision making, characteristic of the market economy, means many more possibilities for entrepreneurial action. When interventionism places obstacles in the path of free entry, it slows entrepreneurial activity (see Kirzner 1985, p. 141-144). Aside from this, rigidities of certain prices, associated with interventionist systems, mean it is impossible for the entrepreneur to modify them after discovering errors. In the long term this discourages alertness in seeking out errors and clearing the market, which becomes steadily less harmonised. If certain transactions are forbidden or prevented, an entrepreneur has no reason to exercise his alertness to try to solve equilibrium problems through new forms or conditions of exchange.

Another element is that if the functioning of an economic system is somewhat disconnected from the idea of monetary profit, agents' revenues will, to a greater or lesser extent be independent from their capacities of discovery; there will simply be weaker forces constraining agents to take an entrepreneurial attitude as well as less encouragement. Not only this, but the absence of monetary sanction in 'public entrepreneurship' prevents a natural selection process, which would allow their replacement in case of failure. Without monetary profit or loss, how do we know if the entrepreneur is efficient and if his discovery is real or pretended?

The third element that Kirzner established is that economic interventionism will modify the structure of entrepreneurial activity compared with that of a market economy, as it will favour a different set of opportunities of monetary gains. In this way, entrepreneurial gain, in an administered economy can come from the discovery of opportunities for rent-seeking, protection or 'corruption' (see Kirzner, 1985, p. 145) by the interventionist authorities rather than discoveries of improvement of the consumers' lot. But the important point does not seem to be to compare well-being of different sets of categories of individuals. It is much more that this new situation will not allow economic activity to reflect to the same degree as in a market economy structure of existing exchange opportunities. In other words it will not allow the same extent of conversion of information into knowledge.[10]

3.4 The Myth of Social Justice

Literature has widely commented on Hayek's conception of social justice,[11] the logical consequence of his analysis of competition. Social (distributive) Justice, in contrast to Procedural (commutative) Justice, emphasises the results of social action, rather than its methods; Hayek claims it is first and foremost the result of an intellectual error. His main objective, however, is to show the dangers of social justice for the efficiency and even existence of self-organised structures.

Social justice: intellectual error

Hayek's claim is that justice can only refer to individual will or action,[12] as it is irrevocably wedded to the notion of responsibility. Illness, epidemics and natural catastrophes cannot be called unjust as human responsibility is not involved.[13] The idea of social justice means giving society the responsibility for individual situations, which is scientifically unacceptable. The social order is the unconscious product of each individual's acts, controlled by nobody. It is like some game, where talent and merit exist along with notions of chance. This being so 'the particular results of the social process cannot be just or unjust' (Hayek, 1976a). It is the same thing for him concerning revenue distribution: 'if it is not the intended or foreseen result of somebody's action that A should have much and B little, this cannot be called just or unjust' (ibid., p. 33).

Contemporary society's eagerness to grasp the idea of social justice, in Hayek's eyes manifests atavistic tribal behaviour. In primitive societies, individuals worked together to survive in a conflictual world. Subordination of individual needs to group conservation meant that every individual's interest was to submit to the community. The community with relatively few members at that time held conscious objectives and knew very well each member's contributions to their society's common goals in ways that modern society does not. Even with the evolution of social rules, these instincts have survived in individuals' subconscious. Hayek claims these themes have been taken up, modernised and legitimised by the socialists to make them an instrument of their action.

Another element is industrial society, seeing a growing number of people working in often large organisations with explicit and conscious rules: 'An ever increasing part of the population of the Western World grow up as members of large organizations and thus as strangers to those rules of the market which have made the great open society possible. To them the market economy is largely incomprehensible' (Hayek, 1979, p. 165). So in their everyday lives, individuals find it increasingly difficult to see the existence of meta-rules in society and consider the absence of explicit rules as a problem of society, rather than a condition of its existence.

Social justice destroying the social order

Beyond the intellectual or sociological considerations shown in the previous section, Hayek's claim is that social justice represents a danger for the economic order, as applying it disturbs general activities. It is precisely because individuals submitted to general rules that a social order was able to emerge and develop to such a high degree.

Applying social justice poses a practical problem, which is deciding on the scale of revenue sharing; outside of market dynamics, finding objective criteria is impossible. 'When we ask what ought to be the relative remunerations of a nurse and a butcher... the appeal to 'social justice' does not give us the slightest help in deciding' (Hayek, 1976a, p. 77-78). Any attempt to solve this problem is totally arbitrary if it happens outside a free market mechanism. Government price fixing in this authoritarian way leaves it open to all sorts of corporatist claims;[14] today, social justice has become a pretext for pressure groups to obtain privilege in their own interest.

The main disadvantage with this process is that it interferes with economic activity. Hayek speaks in cognitive terms of income inequality, in which incomes are prices and so express discoveries about consumer desires concerning resource allocation. If government fixes salary and other revenue levels, resources would no longer be freely fixed by consumer wants. This would represent an erroneous placing of factors (malinvestment) and waste of resources.

The most important point, however, is that disturbances caused by interventionist policies lead to ever increasing central intervention. This idea was already present in *The Road to Serfdom* (1944), where he follows Mises' ideas exposed in *A Critique of Interventionism* (1929) and other of his writings, rejecting the idea of a Third Way and of its reforming ideals developed in the West after World War 2:

> … most people still believe that it must be possible to find some middle way between 'atomistic' competition and central direction. (Yet) although competition can bear some admixture of regulation, it cannot be combined with planning to any extent we like without ceasing to operate as an effective guide to production. Nor is 'planning' a medicine which, taken in small doses, can produce the effects for which one might hope from its thoroughgoing application. Both competition and central direction become poor and inefficient tools if they are incomplete; they are alternative principles used to solve the same problem, and a mixture of the two means that neither will really work and that the result will be worse than if either system had been consistently relied upon (Hayek, 1944, p. 89-90).

Little by little the network of rules spontaneously thrown up, framing social and economic activity, is broken down by state intervention in revenue allocation. The pretext of social justice legitimizes arbitrary economic decision making, dislocating the resource-allocating structure and disturbing the discovery system of the market economy. The state intervenes with explicit rules, replacing aspects of the spontaneous order as they are progressively broken down and destabilised. It performs worse and worse, the abstract rules governing it losing in effectiveness so even more state intervention is required. In the end, the whole social order is replaced by consciously regulated institutions.

The perversion of democracy: the coming of the political market[15]

The Rule of Law expresses the political superstructure of competition and the spontaneous order. In reaction to deficiencies in modern western institutions,

Hayek suggests a bicameral system, 'demarchy' which has drawn a number of criticisms due to its rather singular approach.

> The object of policy in a free society, according to Hayek, should not be to redistribute incomes on some rather arbitrary notion of "social justice" therefore, but to help the total product to grow as large and as rapidly as possible, so that the size of the share of any individual, taken at random is maximised (Butler, 1983, p. 97).

The problem in Hayek's eyes is that this ideal cannot work in the face of our political institutions. Democracy has for a number of years been perverted from its original role, which was to resist arbitrariness, whether or not from the majority. This comes from defective structural logic in our institutions, which is the confusion of the legislative and executive. This situation extends state powers, encourages arbitrary behaviour and erodes market systems.

In modern society, parliamentary majorities name governments and so make laws. There is no limiting principle behind any of these, as they are deemed to be the expression of the will of the people. This double effect encourages what could be called a political market, where horse-trading and clientism is rife. Members of Parliament and other governing figures only get elected following the satisfaction of various interest groups, which are themselves in competition with each other for the aid and protection of the powers that be, resulting in a constant bargaining process: 'majority government does not produce what the majority wants but what each of the groups making up their majority must concede to the others to get their support for what it wants itself' (Hayek, 1979, p. 11).

This has several dramatic consequences. The first one is that the party political programmes have become a catch-all trying to satisfy the largest selection of interests possible, while papering over the inevitable cracks that occur in their platforms between the widely differing objectives.

The second problem is that government treats the various pressure groups according to their electoral influence rather than any notion of the justice of their claims.

This situation has given society ever-increasing state control of the economy. To reply to the various lobbies' demands, the state increases monetary expansion and various taxes, redistributing wealth from the less organised groups to the more influential in a growing vicious circle: the more one group is protected from competition, the harder it is for other social categories to exist in the market. They, in turn, demand protection from the cold winds of competition in order to survive; this is how an interventionist logic develops.[16]

This process totally discredits politics. The government's role becomes that of coercing one category of citizens into feeding other categories of citizens, rather than obliging them to respect the general rules, which is a denial of democracy; all of which is deeply disturbing to the spontaneous order. It was in this light that Hayek proposed his rather particular vision of political renewal, 'demarchy'.

Hayek's bicameral system sharply separates the two regulating functions of legislative justice and executive organisation, or the Legislative Assembly and the Governmental Assembly. They would operate under a constitution, the spirit of which would be defined by a 'Basic Clause' which would underpin and guarantee the Rule of Law and protect the social institutions necessary for catallaxy to function.

The Legislative Assembly would be the instrument for 'law' to pass into legislation. Close to British common law in spirit, its objective would be to define the 'rules of just conduct (nomos)', to convert them into legislation and define 'all enforceable rules of conduct' (Hayek, 1979, p. 114). Its members would have to be of the highest calibre to be able to formulate these laws. So in Hayek's mind, only the wisest of men would be suitable to express the ruling opinions about justice. This group of 'nomothetae' would be aged between 45 and 60 and be small in number for greater efficiency. Their electors, to ensure their own wisdom, would also be a minimum of 45 years old.

The 'nomothetae' would be elected for a non-renewable 15-year period in order to relieve them of all exterior pressure and would be the past or present members of no political party. After their tenure, they would benefit from a high paying pension and an honorary position, thus ensuring absolute integrity during their long period of service.

They would, however, submit to the authority of a disciplinary committee of present and past nomothetae, which would also be responsible for naming judges. This would make the entire judiciary an indirect emanation of the Legislative Assembly.

The Legislative Assembly's second task would be to define the general rules of dividing individual levels of tax among the population. Hayek disassociates this task from that of defining the volume and allocation of fiscal income which would be the Governmental Assembly's job.

The Governmental Assembly fixes finalized rules (thesis), within a framework of the rules of just conduct. Its Executive Committee, the Government, would organise and regulate the civil service. The Governmental Assembly's job would be to decide on public spending. It would be elected by universal suffrage, excluding all state employees as benefitting directly from public spending.[17]

The Basic Clause would preface the new constitution, stating the fact that 'In normal times, and apart from certain clearly defined emergency situations, men could be restrained from doing what they wished, or coerced to do particular things, only in accordance with the recognized rules of just conduct designed to define and protect the individual domain of each' (Hayek, 1979, p. 109).[18] The Constitutional Court would arbitrate conflicts of interest between the two Houses, made up of serving judges and ex-Members of both

Houses. It thus ensures the Rule of Law is upheld by ensuring each measure conforms to the spirit of the Basic Clause.

However the rules of just conduct could be suspended in the case of extreme situations, defined by whether citizens are prevented from going about their legitimate personal business. The recovery of this liberty being the common objective, the political institutions would be qualified to impose finalised rules on the population. To prevent abusive use of emergency measures, they constitutionally would not be declared by the House which exercised the resulting special powers.

Demarchy's general role is to enforce the laws ensuring peace, liberty and justice, the three great negative values, as without them individual activity would be impossible. As Nemo states, 'Politicians who understand that their highest ambition must be to protect the freedom of their fellow citizens from interior strife and exterior enemies are not only the real libertarians but also the creators of modern politics, creating a whole new rhythm to the progress of civilisation' (*La société de droit selon F.A. Hayek*, 1988, p. 361, our translation). Through the idea of demarchy, Hayek promotes the idea of the state as the final guarantor of self-organised systems' efficient functioning, which is why the state must hold the monopoly of coercive techniques.

NOTES

1. By definition, no actor can know all the prices present, he can only know past prices up to the present moment, at best. Aside from this, in a complex economy, individual actors, being limited in their capacities of information acquisition and treatment, cannot mentally grasp all of these past prices.
2. See the article 'Knowing about Knowledge' (Kirzner, 1979) on the difference between search models and the Austrian approach.
3. 'The original praxeological categories of profit and loss are psychic qualities and not reducible to any interpersonal description in quantitative terms. They are intensive magnitudes. The difference between the value of the end attained and that of the means applied for its attainment is profit if it is positive and loss if it is negative' (Mises, *Planning for Freedom*, 1962c, p. 125-126).
4. 'the classical economists (with some notable exceptions such as J-B Say, who continued the French tradition begun by Cantillon) did not recognize an entrepreneurial function distinct from that of the capitalist' (Kirzner, 1985, p. 1).
5. Boettke also concisely notes that 'A profit opportunity that is known to all will be realized by nobody' ('Information and Knowledge: Austrian Economics in Search of its Uniqueness', 2002, p. 269).
6. In this relationship with ignorance, Hayek's distinction between economy and catallaxy is now explained. The economy is consciously regulated activity with explicit and deliberately chosen ends, following the Robbins model ('An economy in the strict sense of the word, is an organisation or arrangement in which someone deliberately allocates resources to a unitary order of ends', Hayek, 1968, p. 183). Conversely, catallaxy analyses a domain where many means serve many often tacit ends. It 'describes the order brought about by

the mutual adjustment of many individual economies in a market' (Hayek, 1976a, p. 109). Similarly, this famous passage could be quoted from 'The Use of Knowledge in Society': 'The economic problem of society is thus not merely a problem of how to allocate 'given' resources ... It is rather a problem of how to secure the best use of resources known to any of the members of society, for ends whose relative importance only these individuals know. Or, to put it briefly, it is a problem of the utilization of knowledge which is not given to anyone in its totality' (Hayek, 1945, p. 77-78). Also see see Littlechild, 'Equilibrium and the Market Process' (1982); Addleson, 'Competition' (1994) and Thomsen, *Prices and Knowledge* (1992).

7. Mises (1966) already examined this question in the chapter 'Action in the Passing of Time', where he refuses to identify technological progress with economic progress, claiming that these two terms were not necessarily symmetric.
8. Mises and the Austrians, let us remember, considered monopoly prices in a market expressing a well-known situation from the manuals, where the seller can maximize his profits when he is selling in lower quantities or at a higher price than in the virtual market situations (see, for example Mises, 1966, p. 294). On the idea of monopoly in the Austrian theories, see also O'Driscoll, 'Monopoly in Theory and Practice' (1982).
9. Hayek deduces from this idea that 'it is unreasonable to expect in already highly developed countries as high a rate of growth as can for some time be achieved in countries where effective utilisation of resources was previously long prevented by legal and institutional obstacles (1968, p. 189).
10. First Littlechild (*The Fallacy of Mixed Economy: An Austrian Critique of Economic Thinking and Policy*, 1978) then Ikeda (*Dynamics of the Mixed Economy: Toward a Theory of Interventionism*, 1997) attempted to define a general Austrian analysis of interventionism. Harper, in 'Institutional Conditions for Entrepreneurship', 1998, develops a long piece on the institutional determinants of entrepreneurship.
11. This analysis which was already started in *The Road to Serfdom* (1944), was to be developed in *The Constitution of Liberty* (1960) and finished in volume two of *Law, Legislation and Liberty* (The Mirage of Social Justice, 1976a).
12. 'Strictly speaking, only human conduct can be called just or unjust' (Hayek, 1976a).
13. Nemo (*La société de droit selon F.A. Hayek*) notes the anthropomorphological aspect of seeing a will in nature (see p. 182).
14. As Butler sums up in 'Hayek: His Contribution to the Political and Economic Thought of our Time', 'Incomes, therefore, will come to be decided not on the worth which a supplier or an industry has to its customers, but on the ability of different groups to persuade the government of the merits of their case' (Butler, 1983, p. 96).
15. Hayek's political reflection was divided into three major parts. Already in the *Road to Serfdom* (1944) and 'The Economic Conditions of Interstate Federalism' (1939), he had formulated several ideas of an international classical liberal order; in *The Constitution of Liberty* (1960) his analysis was more elaborate but was still fairly traditional. It was not until the third volume of *Law, Legislation and Liberty* (The Politics of a Free People, 1979) which recorded progress of interventionism, that his thoughts would take much more radical and original forms. For more details of his political analysis, see particularly Bay (1971); Baumgarth, 'Hayek and Political Order: The Rule of Law' (1978); Manin, 'Le libéralisme radical de Friedrich-August Hayek' (1983); Gray, *Hayek and Liberty* (1984); Hamowy (1978, 1982); Barry, *On Classical Liberalism and Libertarianism* (1987).
16. A whole range of resources and a lot of energy is diverted from production to political endgames, in the end to the consumer and taxpayer's cost: 'to have political pull becomes much more rewarding than adding to the means of satisfying the needs of one's fellows. As everything tends to become a political issue for which the interference of the coercive powers of government can be invoked, an ever larger part of human activity is diverted from productive into political efforts' (Hayek, 1979, p. 138).

17. 'That civil servants, old age pensioners, the unemployed, etc should have a vote on how they should be paid out of the pocket of the rest, and their vote be solicited by a promise of a rise in their pays, is hardly a reasonable arrangement' (Hayek, 1979, p. 120).
18. An additional clause must also mention the individual freedom to choose one's currency: 'Parliament shall make no law abridging the right of anybody to hold, buy, sell or lend, make and enforce contracts, calculate and keep their accounts in any kind of money they choose' (Hayek, 1979, p. 148). On monetary competition and free banking, see Chapter 8.

6. Tendency Towards Equilibrium

> Most human aims can be achieved only by a chain of connected actions, decided upon as a coherent whole and based on the assumption that the facts will be what they are expected to be. It is because, and insofar as, we can predict events, or that we can achieve anything (Hayek, 1960, p. 134).

Having examined the formation of catallaxy and then analysed its workings, it is now time to look at market dénouement. Because of what is at stake, the question of how individual's expectations are formed takes a very special place in the Austrian world as it indirectly governs market institutions' capacities to formulate and ensure the principle of success of agents' plans.

In Chapter 5, ignorance was examined in the light of the social division of knowledge; however, this is not all that conditions Austrian ignorance, as it also stems from the passage of 'real' time.[1] Ignorance is all the more inevitable as individuals' knowledge, preferences, material and cognitive situations shift constantly. Dynamics here is the issue, what is appropriate today becoming outmoded tomorrow. Decisions which today seem relevant to present circumstances will soon appear out of date, as other actors' knowledge, preferences and material situations will have changed in the interval. This is not just an accident, this is the way all human action works. As Lachmann argues in *The Market as Economic Process* (1986a), any individual's act is a new experience with his environment, whether internal or external, which will modify his knowledge of it and the way he interprets it. Action always transforms the actor and his choices too, in his entrepreneurial search for gains in satisfaction. Dynamics, of course subjectively viewed by individuals, adds one more facet to the Austrian phenomenon of ignorance.

After examination of several concepts, the definition of which determine the terms of the problem (1), the approach that the neo-Austrian economists took to the formation of agent's expectations will be discussed (2). Their reflection gave rise to a search for a principle of success in individuals' plans which produced different views in each author involved. Some lively arguments ensued but on closer analysis these varying viewpoints turn out to be more complementary than otherwise (3).

1. ANALYTICAL FRAMEWORK

In the last 20 years a number of debates have developed within the Austrian tradition on the subject of success of plans. In order to understand the intricacies of these debates, three analytical levels should be defined before examining them: the difference between 'statics' and 'dynamics' (1.1); the question of exogenous or external change (1.2) and the relationship between equilibration and success in plans.

1.1 Statics and Dynamics

The Austrians often use these ideas of statics and dynamics, but their analysis is somewhat obscured as the notion of periods is not always well-defined.

One way of conceptualizing the difference between statics and dynamics is by the notion of available opportunities of exchange. Ignorance, which must be taken on an individual level, is defined as the inevitable difference between known and available opportunities. However, ignorance may still exist even without a change in the available opportunities. It can very well survive in a static world, which is to say with no change in these available opportunities. So we can define 'statics' as being the – fictitious – period where the structure of opportunities available to society remains the same.

By contrast, a 'dynamics' universe is one where existing opportunities change as a logical result of human entrepreneurial action. In the final analysis, entrepreneurship is a discovery and a reconstruction of the self, which transforms its own knowledge and preferences. This means the opportunities existing in society change over time. It is the entrepreneurial dimension of action, taken on an infra-individual level, which is the basis of the transformation from statics to dynamics.

1.2 'Exogenous Changes' and Entrepreneurship

In addition to the theme of statics/dynamics, it is also important to discuss the definition of exogenous change.

Kirzner defines the market as 'a sequential, systematic process of continual adjustment, incessantly buffeted and redirected by exogenous changes' (Kirzner, 1985, p. 156). Later he states:

> We can conceive this process to run out of steam, in the absence of exogenous changes, only in the utterly imaginary state of affairs in which mutual awareness on the part of market participants has attained completeness – that is, when all opportunities for mutually gainful exchange are being exploited, so that no scope for further market discovery remains (Kirzner, 1989, p. 84).

By these two passages, Kirzner meant that there is a natural – or rather, praxeological – tendency to want to discover all the available opportunities. At the 'end' (that is the fictitious point where all the opportunities would be known to each actor) of the static period, market prices would exhaust ignorance. However, there would be nothing left to discover and the market would simply die of its own accord. The logical explanation of this reasoning is that the market continues to be driven on because available opportunities evolve through time. This means the market can only subsist in a dynamic framework.

In Kirzner's view, catallaxy is simply the direct or indirect response to changes in existing yet external opportunities operating outside the market sphere.

This does not mean to say that what happens inside a market does not influence exogenous data. Changes in price and quantity will determine changes in the structure of activities, bringing changes in action, knowledge and preference. Then markets will retroactively act on the structure of existing opportunities, feeding ignorance and disequilibrium. This reasoning simply implies the following: it is not possible to conceive dynamics in existing opportunities with no consequences on market activity, any more than it is not necessary to introduce market activities to explain the transformation in opportunities of exchange.

Kirzner thus claims that change and therefore disequilibrium does not necessarily rely on the market's existence. On the contrary, all market activity is always equilibrating, as the market only reacts directly or indirectly to exogenous changes, that is, changes in opportunities not necessarily produced by the market. The term exogenous should not, however be interpreted as describing elements outside action or actors. Change can not take place outside action.[2]

Kirzner therefore quite logically does not see the promoter as an agent of disequilibrium, as he reacts to underlying, exogenous disequilibrium. The promoter is not the first link in the chain but the second; he only responds to disequilibrium which existed before his actions, or which may exist independently of his existence. Disequilibrium does not stem from the markets and the promoter, rather, their activities are the result of disequilibrium. So the situation is potentially discoordinated before market processes start.

1.3 'Equilibration' and Periods

One of the constantly recurring neo-Austrian themes was the tendency towards equilibrium or 'equilibration'. All the Austrians referred to it in many different forms, it being defined in many different ways and levels. This has lead to much debate.

A first level of analysis, examined in the first part of this chapter, is on a praxeological, infra-individual level and results in two conclusions: that all action aims at equilibrium and that each time an end is met, the actor places himself in disequilibrium by setting a another one; in doing so he is striving to reach new (unattainable) equilibrium.

A second level of analysis is at market level, meaning a catallactic tendency towards equilibrium. What meaning can we give to this idea? A first dimension would be the market tendency to convert existing opportunities into known opportunities: actors are ignorant of existing opportunities but they tend to discover them. Another dimension, compatible with the first, would be the idea of tendency towards equilibrium as the market's tendency to clear itself, that is to exploit every opportunity in it. The last dimension, treated in this chapter, is of the success of actors' plans. Tendency towards equilibrium would mean here that in a catallactic universe, individuals' expectations would tend to be validated by facts.

Is there any foundation for this idea of tendency to success of agents' plans? Any answer will differ according to whether the period of reference is static or dynamic; they must here be carefully distinguished from each other.

In a statics universe, it would seem there is no difficulty at all to found this idea of plan success. If we think in terms of single periods (with no change in available opportunities), then agents adjust their expectations to existing opportunities through trial and error. All available opportunity ends up by being discovered, any market errors being smoked out and corrected by the promoters. In the end all available opportunities, initially 'dis-known', become known and exploited on the market. In this fictional static situation, equilibration is the final equilibrium, agents' plans having succeeded.

Formulating the problem in a dynamics (or multiperiod) universe completely changes the solution. Simply referring to a praxeological dimension of tendency towards equilibrium, however, shows that the search for gains in satisfaction must produce a dynamics of opportunity.

As already stated, having several periods introduces the idea of there being changes in existing opportunities, which in turn implies the passing of real time.

Entrepreneurial forces allow disequilibrium to be found and eliminated. In a static world this would lead to final equilibrium, but it is in fact never found in the dynamic world. Forces that Kirzner described as exogenous, as they are not especially brought into play by market activity, appear, bringing disequilibrium and profit opportunities, thereby provoking another sequence.

The given references to the consequences of dynamics-type economics provide a new dimension to the notion of tendency towards equilibrium. The question now is, in this multiperiod context, to apply some meaningful content to the idea of tendency to success of agents' plans. In contrast to a statics-type reasoning, a dynamics tendency towards equilibrium has no *a priori* reason to be linked with the validation of expectations. It cannot simply express a 'time limit' for agents' acquisition of the knowledge required for their enterprises' success, as this time limit is no longer the only factor in the success of plans; continual changes in price due to ceaseless changes in opportunities mean this becomes in fact impossible to attain. Incessant evolution requires incessant modifications to agents' plans, making it impossible to define a principle of validation of expectations. So as far as success of plans is concerned, the meaning of tendency towards equilibrium must change.

Kirzner's arguments, from certain points of view, clearly show this conceptual difference. His view is that market efficiency in the real dynamic universe is not dependent on its capacity to achieve a general coordination of plans but to discover disequilibrium and correct it as quickly as possible. In other words, coordination cannot be seen as a state of affairs but a process.

> We must distinguish carefully between a) a possible norm of coordination in the sense of a co-ordinated state of affairs and b) a possible norm of co-ordination in the sense of the ability to detect and to move towards correcting situations in which activities have until now been discoordinated ... The distinction between these two possibilities corresponds to the two different meanings of the word 'co-ordination': it may refer to the activities being carried out when these activities are indeed dovetailing with one another; alternatively it may refer to the process through which initially clashing, discoordinated activities are somehow being hammered out in a manner such as to approach a more smoothly dovetailing pattern of activities (Kirzner, 1992a, p. 190-191).

This reasoning is largely reflected by most neo-Austrian literature. It has, however, both a negative side and major implications, as it means the disconnection of the principle of tendency towards equilibrium from that of success of individual plans. This would not be in itself a difficulty if one could define a principle of formation of individual actors' plans without having to at the same time formulate the principle of success of those plans. This is not, unfortunately, the case. How can an actor start any social activity without an individual or social mechanism allowing him a modicum of belief in his plans chances of success? So the problem is to find on what basis an individual forms an idea of his chances of succeeding in his plans. This translates as explaining the formation of actors' plans in a dynamic universe.

2. FORMING EXPECTATIONS

Neo-Austrian literature is far from ignoring the mystery of the formation of actors' plans. This question has on the contrary increasingly contributed to its development. Mises, as his work continued, was increasingly explicit about the role of speculation and of interpretation in the process of forming actors' expectations (2.1). Hayek's additional work on cognitive psychology contributed to and refined the notion of ideal types and the way mental activity structures actors' plans (2.2). It is however Lachmann, with the dynamic aspects of subjectivism in expectations, who tips Austrian thinking into another dimension. By extending the subjectivist paradigm to the domain of predictions, Lachmann questioned the markets' capacity to guarantee the success of agents' plans (2.3).

2.1 Speculation and Understanding

Praxeology teaches us that action is linked to the idea of uncertainty of the future.

> Action must needs be affected by every change in the data. As action necessarily is directed toward influencing a future state of affairs, even if sometimes only the immediate future of the next instant, it is affected by every incorrectly anticipated change in the data occurring in the period of time between its beginning and the end of the period for which it aimed to provide (period of provision). Thus the outcome of action is always uncertain (Mises, 1966, p. 252).

This characteristic of action must have implications for the process of the emergence of a market, whose characteristics, in Mises' view, cannot contradict praxeology's general and apodictic laws. But if agents do not know the future, how can they act?

There are two possible answers to that question. The first one would be that all agents are ignorant of the uncertain character of the future, so they would take decisions simply on the basis of present data, anticipating no possible change. This unlikely hypothesis would suppose an actors' knowledge of praxeological laws to be less than the theorist's; there is simply nothing in praxeological reasoning to support this idea.

The second possibility is the much more likely idea of agents being fully conscious of their own uncertainty of the future and therefore on the speculative characteristics of their actions. This uncertainty, for praxeological reasons, concerns every individual, as it affects each of their actions. This is why 'In any real and living economy every actor is always an entrepreneur and speculator' (Mises, 1966, p. 252). If the term entrepreneur is taken to mean any actor whose results are uncertain, then any person engaged in any activity can be called entrepreneur. But we can further explore the relationship between speculation and human action: in contrast to ordinary humans who try to hide from this uncertainty, some seek it out deliberately, to use it for their own purposes. For these people, uncertainty of the future is not a handicap, threatening their revenue but a liberating opportunity of increasing their income. They consider, rightly or wrongly, that they will be able to gain more from the uncertainty than they would if they tried to protect themselves from it. Mises called these the 'promoters' or the market entrepreneurs. They use uncertainty of the future as a chance of enrichment.

The catallactic profile of the promoter is, for Mises, the will to benefit from speculation surrounding human action, which he amply illustrates, for example: 'The planning businessman cannot help employing data concerning the unknown future; he deals with future prices and future costs of production' (Mises, 1966, p. 224); but the entrepreneur does not care about 'the possible adverse effects of the uncertainty of future' (ibid., p. 256), as his revenue is measured as a function of his acceptance of facing higher or lower uncertainty.[3]

The Mises promoter is thus the agent who plays with the future, betting on it. He knows the outcome is uncertain, that he can just as well win as lose, but he accepts and seeks out results which contain an element of chance. In this configuration, entrepreneurial action is a simple bet, pure speculation.[4]

Other Mises utterances, however, are less radical about this speculative, totally chance-driven dimension to the entrepreneur, who does in fact possess other qualities: 'An entrepreneur can make a profit only if he anticipates future conditions more correctly than other entrepreneurs' (ibid., p. 293). The entrepreneur:

> sees the past and the present as other people do; but he judges the future in a different way ... What distinguishes the successful entrepreneur and promoter from other people is precisely the fact that he does not let himself be guided by what was and is, but arranges his affairs on the ground of his opinion about the future (ibid., p. 585).

He also stated

> In the living, perpetually changing market society there are always profits to be earned by efficient entrepreneurs ... A prospective entrepreneur does not consult the calculus of probability which is of no avail in the field of understanding. He trusts his own ability to understand future market conditions better than his less gifted fellow men (ibid., p. 299).

Thus he suggests that it is the qualities of anticipation and imagination which set promoters apart from the ordinary masses, in the dark as the latter are regarding future exchange opportunities. Entrepreneur-promoters see the future in a way which is not simply a reproduction of the present. Only the entrepreneur is capable of this kind of speculation; other individuals are incapable of imagining and anticipating. In *Planning for Freedom* (1962c), Mises comments that 'the average man lacks the imagination to realize that the conditions of life and action are in a continual flux ... His world view is static and stationary' (Mises, 1962c, p. 146) and in *Human Action* similarly notes the 'mental inertia' of 'average man' (Mises, 1966, p. 699).

Entrepreneurs' imaginative qualities seem to spring in turn from a capacity of interpretation. Their ability to anticipate springs from their abilities to interpret a series of phenomena constituting the context of any action. They identify past and present elements which indicate not what will be but what might be. Interpretation is here a faculty of generating a future vision based on the past and present. This superior vision, judged by Mises to be associated with the promoter, illustrates some of his remarks on their 'competence' or 'talent'.[5] Rothbard would seem to agree, declaring on entrepreneurs' expectations: 'These forecasts must also be guided by insight, by Verstehen, into present and future conditions ands into the values, preferences, and changing habits of other human actors' (Rothbard, 1995, p. 52).

This conforms to Mises' view. We know the interpretative or historical approach (see Chapter 1) is the practical man's tool. Mises refuses to use the ideal type to define an economic theory but they are the condition for forming expectations in practice: 'The main epistemological problem of the specific understanding is: How can a man have any knowledge of the future value judgments and actions of other people?' (Mises, 1957, p. 311). In fact:

> the task with which acting man, that is, everybody, is faced in all relations with his fellow does not refer to the past; it refers to the future. To know the future reactions of other people is the first task of acting man. Knowledge of their past value judgments and actions, although indispensable, is only a means to this end. It is obvious that this knowledge which provides a man with the ability to anticipate to some degree other people's future attitudes is not an a priori knowledge. The a priori discipline of human action, praxeology, does not deal with the fact that men value and then act according to their valuations (ibid., p. 311).

Basing himself on Bergson and Weber's approach, Mises therefore states

> What we know about the actual content of judgments of value can be derived only from experience ... For lack of any better tool, we must take recourse to thymology if we want to anticipate other people's future attitudes and actions. Out of our thymological experience, acquired either directly from observing our fellow men and transacting business with them or indirectly from reading and from hearsay, as well as out of our special experience acquired in previous contacts with the individuals or groups concerned, we try to form an opinion about their future conduct (ibid., p. 311; 313).

Finally, entrepreneurship would seem to be a mix of pure speculation, firmly rooted in a gambling type logic and of interpretation based on qualities of empathy, insight, appreciation, significance and above all imagination. A capacity of interpreting present-day data and dealing with uncertainty of the future represents two facets that illustrate a more particular form of entrepreneurship.

2.2 The Contribution of Cognitive Psychology

Hayek's arguments on market formation are easily extended to the reflection on the formation of plans as the two themes are bound together. The analytical tools used to answer cognitive questions on market formation can also be used for those of market dénouement. Representations and expectations coming from the same source, Hayek again takes up the theme found in 'the formation of opinion' ('The Meaning of Competition', Hayek, 1948, p. 106) to be able to conceptualize the birth and rise of expectations.

Formation of opinions: psychology at the service of expectations

The importance for Hayek of the notions of 'map' and 'model' in individuals' mental architecture of representations has already been seen in Chapter 1. The model is the compass for the map, so it must be associated with a dimension of expectations which allows the individual to interpret future events: 'The pattern of impulses formed within the structure of connexions will thus function as an apparatus of orientation by representing both the actual state of the environment and the changes to be expected in that environment' (Hayek, 1952a, p. 118). So the model acts as an experience-based filter to interpret any new event (classed singularly or severally). Representation and prediction cannot therefore be separated: 'The reaction to a stimulus thus frequently implies an anticipation of the consequences to be expected from it' (ibid., p. 121), all operating on a protocol of 'trying out' (ibid., p. 121), no doubt a trial and error process.

The map is the product of either an individual's or his community's past experience; it is the general framework within which impulses generated at any moment are evaluated. It supplies actors with a theory of the world's workings.

The model allows the individual to adapt to present circumstances, but also to weigh up the future, for which he makes plans.

In Hayek's mind, forging opinions and beliefs is a learning process stemming not from prices but from culture, whose rules define the configuration of the pre-sensory map. Indeed: 'only in so far as we can find out what the knowledge and beliefs of the people concerned are in the relevant respects shall we be in a position to predict in what manner a change in the price of the product will affect the prices of the factors' (Hayek, 1952b, p. 33). Also,

> The apparatus by means of which we learn about the external world is itself the product of a kind of experience. It is shaped by the conditions prevailing in the environment in which we live, and it represents a kind of generic reproduction of the relations between the elements of this environment which we have experienced in the past; and we interpret any new event in the environment in the light of that experience (Hayek, 1952a, p. 165).

It is the interaction between the physical world and individual behaviour which draws agents' representations, through a process of trial and error, not only of their past and present environment but of their future too.

This dialectic between map and model is what gives us the ideal types, which are formed as a result of a classification by the human mind. Their roots may be plunged deep in the pre-sensory experience, yet the model's adaptive capacities permit them to evolve according to individual experiences, the whole process creating relationships between past, the present environment and what is forecast.

Evolutionism

The system here fits naturally into an evolutionary logic. Individuals' expectations change; Hayek's arguments on the sensory order are centred on evolutionary biology, which forms the nervous system over time. Interpretations come from experience-based knowledge crystallised in the map, which can also be modified after contact with objective facts. If they do not conform to agents' expectations, then the model successively adjusts representations to lead individuals to a more suitable adaptation of physical reality. The evolutionism which runs through all Hayek's thoughts on social structure describes, using the terms of cognitive psychology, a process of reclassification of the nervous impulses.

So it is a reclassification process which allows agents to give meaning to their experiences and to allow a vision of the future too. In 'Economics and Knowledge', Hayek already noted 'all knowledge is capacity to predict' (Hayek, 1937a, note 17, p. 51). Hayek's approach here is an uncanny reminder of Schütz's, who tries to formulate a phenomenological psychology, as he sees in a typification a response to the question of agents' prediction-forming capacities.

Koppl (*Big Players and the Economic Theory of Expectations*, 2002) accurately notes that Hayek's and Schütz's approaches are not based on the same domaines (respectively theoretical and phenomenological psychology), but the two have many parallels and come to analogous conclusions which prove the existence of pre-incorporated knowledge in modes of cognition and of interaction with the environment.

In Hayek's writings, Schütz's ideal types become classes of equivalence, the result of an interpretative, supra-conscious classification in the human, its rules being defined by pre-experience and cultural inheritance, often incorporated into language and practices by imitation. Mental activity is nothing more than an ordering process of the nervous impulses into ideal types. For Hayek, knowledge is necessarily a classification; for Schütz, it is type-based; the 'common sense' is both the classification procedure and type-matching of agents belonging to the same social environment. Both authors express meaning and expectation as an abstract sensory classification, its structure defined by indirectly or directly acquired experience. A selection process defines a body of rules of brain responses to external stimuli.

So the same cognitive framework determines the mode of reception and treatment of information and prediction forming capacities. The psychological reasoning which Hayek uses to describe agents' intersubjective representations, explaining market formation, also explains the way agents' representations of the future, or expectations, can be formed. By constructing an exchange theory, Hayek constructs an expectations theory. This retrospectively sheds light on Mises' approach to understanding, at the same time widening its base.

2.3 The Subjectivism of Expectations

Lachmann, out of all the Austrians, went the furthest into the logical consequences of the subjectivist aspects of Menger's thinking, as they appeared to Lachmann in the 1920's. He always referred to himself as a 'radical subjectivist'.

As Prychitko points out, 'Ludwig Lachmann and the Farther Reaches of Austrian Economics',

> For decades Lachmann has indefatigably called for the profession to take notice of the role that subjectivity and expectations play in economic phenomena. His emphatic plea has not only created debate among neoclassical economists, but initially, following his arrival at NYU over a decade ago, brought sharp disagreement among Austrian economists themselves (1987, p. 65).

Lachmann's work concentrates above all on the temporal aspects of ignorance, through the notion of the plan; individuals' plans running into the problem of their uncertainty of the future. He innovates with his reformulation of the relation between time and knowledge and underlines the difficulties of forming expectations and thus the limits to forecasting.[6]

Obstacles to prediction

For Lachmann, the question of expectations is central: 'the theory of expectations represents the second wave of subjectivist economics after Menger's breakthrough in the theory of value' (Grinder, 'In Pursuit of the Subjective Paradigm', 1977, p. 11). In the pioneering article 'The Role of Expectations in Economics as a Social Science' (1943), Lachmann formalises the question, expressing his regret at the question's neglect by the Austrians up to that point. In 'The Science of Human Action' (1951), Lachmann admits that Mises implicitly bases the problem of expectations on the theme of interpretation, but he later somewhat unfairly continues to reproach both Mises and Hayek for their relatively weak interest in the formation of plans: 'Mises hardly ever mentions expectations, though entrepreneurs and speculators often enough turn up in his pages' (Lachmann, 'From Mises to Shackle', 1976b, p. 236). Above all, he considers that Mises did not complete his reasoning as he did not extend subjectivism to expectations.

Subjectivism is a heterogeneous notion

Lachmann identifies three main types of subjectivism: 'subjectivism of utility', revealing agents' diversity of values; 'subjectivism of interpretation', expressing the idea of individuals' heterogeneous perceptions, its characteristics directly linked with the third type: 'subjectivism of expectations';[7] the idea of the diversity of individuals' predictions about their future environment.

In the same way as there is a diversity of subjective interpretations, there must also be differentiations in individuals' expectations: 'In reality expectations almost always diverge between agents, and the same agent's expectations will vary over time under the influence of the daily stream of news' (Lachmann, *The Market as an Economic Process*, 1986a, p. 140). This means expectations are different in each agent and they may diversely interpret and analyse the same facts.

Lachmann considers that the observer or the actor can only analyse concrete action by indirect procedures based on ideal or real types, that is to say by an abstraction process able to group and follow the evolution of elements of reality.

> In economic analysis, as in all generalizing thought, we build in our minds 'models' of reality by deducing necessary consequences from hypotheses arbitrarily chosen. Of course we are all aware that the more 'realistic' our assumptions are, the closer to reality we may hope our conclusions to be. But since it is always impossible to include the whole of reality in our set of assumptions, the selection of the components of this set cannot but be arbitrary (Lachmann, 1967, p. 289).

Faced with the limitations of the heterogeneous character of individual interpretations, the praxeological model, obviously brought into use in the cognitive approach of action's processes, is of no help for prediction. The only certainties it offers are conceptual. As action builds up over time, the praxeological model's practical limits become more obvious. This is where the question is played out:

> ... our network of means and ends, precisely by virtue of the logical necessity inherent in it, is impotent to engender empirical generalizations. Its truth is purely abstract and formal truth. The means and ends it connects are abstract entities. In the real world the concrete means used and ends sought are ever changing as knowledge changes and what seemed worthwhile yesterday no longer seems so today (Lachmann, 1986a, p. 31).

Time by definition changes knowledge as opportunities change:

> Time and Knowledge belong together. The creative acts of the mind need not be reflected in changing preferences,[8] but they cannot but be reflected in acts grasping experience and constituting objects of knowledge and plans of action. All such acts bear the stamp of the individuality of the actor (Lachmann, 1959, p. 85).

Lachmann is illustrating here the dynamic implications of interpretative subjectivism. However, it is not so much subjective appreciations of past, present and future situations, as their inevitable changes in time which poses such problems for prediction.

There are no convergence of expectations mechanisms

Introducing real time must modify individuals' interpretations. Time cannot pass without actors' interpretations changing unpredictably and this poses the question of convergence of interpretation for if there is none and there is no particular *a priori* reason for there to be, most actors will not be able to carry out their plans.[9]

When the future is unknown, it is probable that expectations will fail; disequilibrium will always lead to non-convergence of individuals' plans, which shows that expectations have not succeeded. The market being a process, time creating unexpected change and singular discoveries, the hope of any convergence of expectations is impossible. Lachmann refuses to associate the Austrian notion of tendency towards equilibrium with a principle of plan success; economics is only a succession of continual maladjustments, which is the essential market dynamics.

Lachmann claims that damage to the Austrian tradition is caused by the fact that Mises' and Hayek's conclusions on tendency towards equilibrium are only relevant in a static framework, which paradoxically brings their analysis back to a neoclassical approach:

> Professor Hayek and Mises both espouse the market process, but do not ignore equilibrium as its final stage. The former, whose early work was clearly under the influence of the general equilibrium model, at one time appeared to regard a strong tendency towards general equilibrium as a real phenomenon of the market economy' (Lachmann, 'From Mises to Shackle: An Essay on Austrian Economy and the Kaleidic Society', 1976b, p. 239).

Grinder, commenting Lachmann's argument thus explains

> The strength of the forces of convergence depends almost entirely on the activities of entrepreneurs. If entrepreneurs take advantage of the price-cost discrepancies attending changing circumstances, the entrepreneurial function of using resources in search of profit (the process of innovation and imitation) will, as most Austrian economists agree, lead to a convergence of the plans of individuals in markets. However, because change is ever present and unpredictable, individuals have different expectations about the character and extent of change … The forces for the

> divergence of plans are likely to be stronger than those for their convergence (Grinder, 'In Pursuit of the Subjective Paradigm', 1977, p. 19).

Viewing the same problem from another angle, any effort to converge individuals' plans will rupture existing plans:

> To be able to speak at all of 'the system having an inherent tendency towards equilibrium' we should therefore have to assume that the velocity with which the other elements adjust themselves to changes in tastes is always so high that no new change will occur before a full adjustment to the previous change has taken place. It is difficult to imagine such circumstances (Lachmann, 1969, p. 156).

In this case, it is probably better to adopt the idea of an inherent tendency towards disequilibrium. Converging individuals' plans then becomes an ever changing process and economics a world of continual basic change. Constant restructuring of the stock of information brings about a dynamic universe of successive disequilibria which makes economies' futures impossible to determine.

Having said this, the role of the institutions must also be taken into account. Lachmann (*The Legacy of Carl Menger*) explains that they play a role which: 'enables [the actors] to co-ordinate their actions by means of orientation to a common signpost' (Lachmann, 1971a, p. 49-50). However it would be a mistake to give these institutions too much importance: the 'knowledge of society they do provide in highly condensed form may not all be relevant to the achievement of our immediate purposes' (ibid., p. 50). As it happens, institutions' efficiency is limited by the need to balance the formidably difficult contradictory mix of complementarity, permanence and flexibility, with always such uncertain results when it comes to practical action.

Kaleidic worlds: Lachmann, Shackle and the Austrians

Lachmann, in the light of the above, examines the idea of a common root in the Austrians' and in Shackle's work. In 'From Mises to Shackle: An Essay on Austrian Economics and the Kaleidic Society', he states that 'Mises and Shackle share a common look on the foundations of our discipline' (1976b, p. 230). He goes into a lengthy comparison of the two authors' methodologies and analyses of action: 'In all essentials the views on the nature of human action, the character of world in which it takes place and the methods appropriate to its study, which we find in the work of Mises and Shackle are virtually identical' (ibid., p. 233). There are particular similarities in their conception of time and their rejection of objective probabilities.

Certainly, Lachmann disagrees with Shackle over his conclusion that a science of human action is illegitimate; he clearly 'is going too far when for discontinuity, which is a property merely of our ends, he wrongly claims the status of a universal category of human action' (Lachmann, 'Professor

Shackle and the Economic Significance of Time', 1959, p. 85). Uncertainty of the future in no way invalidates the apodictic character of the ends-means relationship. Lachmann also does not agree with Shackle on the idea that it is the evolution of value scales that gives rise to difficulties in prediction, Shackle claiming that the stability of value scales in time would result in the disappearance of disequilibrium. It seems clear that such a problematic would not exclude economic uncertainty, as

> even in such a world Professor Shackle's general thesis about the creative power of the mind and our inability to predict its acts would still hold, because men would still be interpreting experiences, acquiring knowledge, planning and revising plans. We are able to imagine a world in which tastes do not change but unable to imagine one in which knowledge does not spread from some minds to others. Even continuity of ends does not entail an invariant means-end pattern (ibid., p. 85).

But Shackle was right when he stated that the science of economics was no more capable of reading the future than any social discipline, and in so doing he pushes Mises' reasoning to its logical extremes:

> Our conclusion that economists must confine their generalizations to the knowable past will be deplored by all those who see the main task of economics in the making and testing of predictions. Our answer has to be that the social world, unlike the solar system, is impelled by forces as mutable as thoughts and that no Newtonian model fits it: 'Predicted man is less than human, predicting man is more than human. I conclude, in an expression of mere personal conviction, that man in his true humanity can neither predict nor be predicted' (Shackle, 1958, p. 105) (Lachmann, 1986a, p. 32).

To claim the opposite would be to deny the fundamentally open-ended characteristic of our social structures.

This approach allows Lachmann to share Shackles' conclusions on uncertainty, seen through the prism of dynamic subjectivism.[10] Finally, however, this uncertainty is only due to absence of data on the future: '... while a perfect forward market can provide information and bring production plans into consistency with each other and with the plans of consumers, it cannot predict the future' ('Professor Shackle on Significance of Time', 1959, p. 88). In this way Shackle's approach is correct, accentuating as it does the problems that subjectivism poses in a social economy. However, the academic route he takes between the notion of subjectivism and the emergence of the phenomenon of uncertainty inherent to the social sphere is wrong.

3. SUCCEEDING IN EXPECTATIONS

Lachmann's focus on the idea of total indeterminism of individuals' plans gave rise to a series of controversies in the neo-Austrian tradition, giving it a divided image, with various Austrians responding in different ways to him: Kirzner took what was called the middle ground (3.1), which has been extended with more recent developments on the subject of the Austrian economy of the firm (3.2); Hayek takes a point of view based on the idea of rules (3.3) and Rothbard and his disciples adopted their own position (3.4).

3.1 The Entrepreneur as Creator of the Future

In Kirzner's view, the market entrepreneur is obviously not a factor of disequilibrium; on the contrary, he essentially intervenes in reaction to underlying discoordination. However, while it is one thing to show that the entrepreneur is not a source of disequilibrium, it is quite another to explain how entrepreneurs' expectations are successful in a dynamic universe. In this field, some of Kirzner's writings show that Lachmann's theory found a sympathetic audience.

In 'Entrepreneurial Discovery and the Competitive Market Process', Kirzner approaches the subject of entrepreneurial mistakes in the following way:

> Entrepreneurial decisions may be entirely mistaken; they may in fact be more mistaken than those other entrepreneurial judgments they are replacing. So that, instead of correcting the earlier misallocations of resources, the entering entrepreneurs may be making matters even worse. And such errors may generate still more errors. Moreover, even if one imagined that, in a world of stable resources, availabilities and consumer preferences, entrepreneurial judgments tend to avoid new errors, the possibility of volatile changes in resource supply and consumer demand conditions must inevitably prevent the entrepreneurial discovery process from proceeding very far toward complete mutual awareness by market participants (1997, p. 81-82).

The notion of tendency towards equilibrium, in this particular version and in a dynamic form, is purely abstract. It describes simply an incentive process for entrepreneurs to correct errors that they notice, but with no guarantee of success. In Kirzner's view, it is only in this abstract sense that entrepreneurial errors are not systematic but simply possibilities. Even so, these abstract tendencies would not imply any concrete success of plans.

However, other parts of his work clearly show his will to define a mechanism of plans for success.

Uncertainty of the future is not inevitable

One of the first types of Kirzner's reactions to Lachmann's questioning is a logical one. If there was extreme uncertainty of the future, it would be impossible to make any choices and to consider *ex ante* one action's effectiveness over another. The absence of any principle as to success of expectations would prevent agents from making *a priori* judgements as to the best courses of action; there would be no action rationale. On this basis, Kirzner defends the idea of a limited, rather than unlimited uncertainty of the future:

> If the uncertainty of the future has made it impossible to discriminate between more or less advisable courses of action, the choice has been reduced to emptiness ... The very idea of 'bounded uncertainty' must mean that the prospective chooser feels entitled to conclude, in spite of the uncertainties he faces, that one course of action appears more likely to be successful than another (1992a, p. 25).

This idea appears to have a limited effect. Nothing would prevent the idea of permanent tension between agents, praxeologically obliged to make plans and the social and economic environment which would constantly frustrate their expectations.

A second type of Kirznerian reaction would be the empirical argument. He legitimises his view by paradoxically basing himself on the fact of the market functioning:

> economic science, from its beginnings, has been moored in the empirical circumstance of markets that do display a certain order. The scientific knowledge challenge has been, not to predict an orderliness that has not yet been observed, but to account for the counter-intuitive circumstance of observed market order in the absence of centralized control (ibid., p. 50).

The tendency towards equilibrium is not just an abstract law but can be concretely applied to reality.

This type of argument, similar to that which Hayek uses in 'Economics and Knowledge' (1937a), where he links the idea of tendency towards equilibrium with empirical evidence, is obviously threatened by any analysis which requires an objective and empirical definition of what an order is. How would we define its concrete characteristics? How would we know whether we are living in a world of order or disorder? What criteria would there be to empirically differentiate between situations of coordination and discoordination? Kirzner does not even begin to answer these questions. Bitterness, frustration, misery and failure could all be thought of as empirical manifestations of the real world, just as much as success and coordination of agents' plans. Dangerously relative, the term tendency towards equilibrium floats in the theoretical mid-air, with no tangible horizon or reference to give it any concrete meaning.

So Kirzner seems to have headed towards another type of analysis, basing himself on the work of another Austrian school economist. Garrison ('Austrian Economics as the Middle Ground: Comment on Loasby', 1982) takes the middle ground between the extremist positions of the mainstream final equilibrium economics and Shackle and the post-Keynesians' kaleidic position.[11] In *Discovery and The Capitalist Process* (1985), Kirzner was already referring to this question, but the best explanation of the relation of this theory to Garrison's is in Chapter 1 of *The Meaning of the Market Process* (1992a), called 'Market Process Theory: In Defence of the Austrian Middle Ground'. Kirzner condemns both the ideas of the neoclassical perfect knowledge and the post-Keynesian radical uncertainty which seems to have influenced Lachmann so much. Expressed in other terms, Austrian theory is perched between data's perfect constancy and its total volatility.

The theme of the entrepreneur is once again visited here. In Kirzner's view, the entrepreneur has the power to create his own future environment. It is not just a question of accepting to be 'confronted' with uncertainty; it is also a question of 'overcoming' it (see Kirzner, 1985, p. 65). So not only can one fight uncertainty of the future but one can beat it: uncertainty is not invincible.

The flexibility of alertness

As we saw in the last chapter, in Kirzner's view the notion of entrepreneurial alertness comes in various forms and fields; it can also be expressed over various periods due to the elasticity of the concept.

To briefly review the differences between statics and dynamics, the concept of statics describes a sphere of unchanging opportunities, the market only being an expression of their discovery. The dynamic universe is one of continual change in opportunities with the passing of real time, the market not only being an expression of the discovery of present opportunities but anticipating the appearance of such opportunities in the future.

In *Competition and Entrepreneurship* (1973), Kirzner's primary aim was to discuss the essential entrepreneurial functions in a market economy. To simplify analysis, he couched this discussion in a static framework, or into one period. This reduction, although excluding the theme of uncertainty of the future, stays within the bounds of proper analysis; according to Kirzner, entrepreneurship is not in its essence linked to uncertainty of the future as the latter is not the only possible cause of ignorance.

Of course Kirzner knows that human reality, coming from praxeological laws as it does, is dynamic: every human action modifies opportunities. The market entrepreneur has a fundamental link with this uncertainty of the future. However the essential point, according to him, is that if a fictitious world with no uncertainty of the future could ever exist, there would certainly be room and need for entrepreneurship's distinctive sign, the attitude of alertness. It is not essentially that because information changes constantly that the entrepreneur has a role to play in society but because at any moment in time there is an inevitable difference between the sphere of available opportunities and that of opportunities known to every man. The entrepreneur's task is to steadily reduce this difference, which if the institutions will allow it, can only completely disappear at the 'termination' of a static period. So, for Kirzner, there is no need to introduce real time with its unexpected changes, for the promoter to exist.

His neglect, so to speak, of real time was rapidly criticized by certain Austrian authors,[12] disapproving of the absence of reference to a 'dynamic' concept of the economy. In their eyes it meant there could be none of the imaginative dimension related to uncertainty of the future in entrepreneurship; this absence would reduce the entrepreneur simply to an explorer of the present, an arbitrageur between pre-existing opportunities.

For all these authors, entrepreneurship with no conception of real time is inconceivable, the two being irrevocably linked through the common theme of uncertainty of the future. From this point of view, the idea of alertness to present opportunities is no longer essential to entrepreneurship. Only the future can be relevant and can define success or failure.

Kirzner seems to have quickly included this type of critique in his arguments. In his later work he clarifies his ideas, developing the dynamic aspects of his analysis. In this way, in *Perception, Profit and Opportunities* (1979), he advances an argument the origin of which could already be seen in *The Market and the Price System* (1963), a work sadly neglected by literature. He distinguishes between single period and multiperiod time, the latter including the concept of uncertainty of the future. He states that in this configuration, the entrepreneur does not simply react to present opportunities but anticipates and prepares to meet those possibly exploitable of the future.

Kirzner claims that this apparently new task is not at all contradictory with his existing definition of alertness. In the article 'Uncertainty, Discovery and Human Action: A Study of the Entrepreneurial Profile in the Misesian System' (1982b),[13] he stresses that his depiction of the entrepreneur's 'stylised' approach to present opportunities allows the inclusion of the role of ignorance in its temporal mode. The role of arbitrageur can exist just as well in a present/present as a present/future mode. In Dosi and Fagiolo's terms ('Explaining the Unknown on Entrepreneurship, Coordination and Innovation Driven Growth', 1997), the promoter can just as well make 'ordinary discoveries' – that is of present opportunities – as 'extraordinary discoveries' – expectations of future opportunities. He feels out opportunities in the present and also in the future environment. So we can just as well see the entrepreneur's arbitraging function in an a-temporal as in an inter-temporal way.

Kirzner defends the idea here of a flexibility of alertness great enough to include all the various entrepreneurial roles, depending on the time period being referred to. He paradoxically uses Lachmann's arguments (the future is unknowable, though not unimaginable) to show that following either the

present or future time phase, forms of alertness are expressed differently. Kirzner (1985, p. 116), distinguishes three levels: the level of pure arbitrage, the level of pure speculation and the level of productive creativity.
He allows the idea that entrepreneurial qualities involved in each of these levels would to a certain extent be different, but he does remark that:

> Alertness is a concept sufficiently elastic to cover not only the perception of existing arbitrage opportunities, but also the perception of intertemporal speculative opportunities that can be definitely realized only after the lapse of time, and even also the perception of intertemporal opportunities that call for creative and imaginative innovation (1985, p. 85-86).

The future can be created

So for Kirzner, the concept of alertness is a wide one and can be understood in terms of both statics and dynamics. The interesting point he makes is that dynamic alertness is a way for acting man to create his own future environment, his intelligence, creativity and determination acting hand in hand to combat the uncertainty naturally found there. So man is not a passive participant in his environment, nor is he condemned to entirely submit to it. Kirzner thus solves the apparent and according to him, artificial dilemma between alertness and uncertainty of the future:

> Viewed from this perspective, the tension between the uncertainty environment in which actions occurs, on the one hand, and the discovery-of-error aspect of action, on the other, can be seen to dissolve at a glance. These two aspects of action can be seen immediately as merely two sides of the same entrepreneurial coin … entrepreneurial individual actions, and the systematic market forces set in motion by freedom for entrepreneurial discovery and innovation, harness the human imagination to achieve no less a result than the liberation of mankind from the chaos of complete mutual ignorance (Kirzner, 1985, p. 57; 67).

The entrepreneur defines his own future by his own 'creative' action; he then has to make sure the actual future is the one that he imagined. It means pulling a particular present towards an imagined future, as it were, to make his own future.

Finally, uncertainty of the future means 'The essential freedom with which the envisaged future may diverge from the realized future. Entrepreneurial alertness means the ability to impose constraints on that freedom, so that the entrepreneur's vision of the future may indeed overlap, to some significant extent, with that future he is attempting to see' (1985, p. 66). Of course, in doing this, entrepreneurs may make mistakes. The actual future may be different from the imagined future; the entrepreneur may fail to overcome his environment and be forced into error. In any case, if no entrepreneur made mistakes, no other entrepreneur would be able to make any profits, so the idea of perfect compatibility of plans, or general equilibrium, is impossible:

> For Austrians, however, mutual knowledge is indeed full of gaps at any given time, yet the market process is understood to provide a systemic set of forces, set in motion by entrepreneurial alertness, which tend to reduce the extent of mutual ignorance necessarily invincible. Equilibrium is indeed never attained, yet the market does exhibit powerful tendencies towards it. Market co-ordination is not to be smuggled into economics by assumption; but neither is it to be peremptorily ruled out simply by referring to the uncertainty of the future (Kirzner, 1992a, p. 5).

So the heart of the question separating Kirzner and Lachmann is that the latter believes that future events cannot be predicted because they are non-present whereas Kirzner claims that this it only correct until the promoter is involved. In a dynamics mode, he says, the promoter's role is to make the actual future submit to the imagined future and to actively create the conditions for this. The degree of success in doing this will decide the degree of success of entrepreneurs' plans.

Now, the question is whether Kirzner's thinking is tenable in the structural and interactive relations of the market. In other words, this type of analysis is justified in autarky but will it hold together in the social and interdependent environment, with entrepreneurs' constant efforts to construct their future being continually beaten down by other entrepreneurs as they strive to build their own futures? This question leads us directly to examine the development of the Austrian economy of the firm.

3.2 Austrian Economics of the Firm

Standard theory left to one side for many years that economic organisation, the firm. The neoclassicals considered it to be unimportant as the market was supposed to be optimal in coordinating activities. Most theorists at the time agreed with this outlook.

After Knight's first analyses (*Risk, Uncertainty and Profit*, 1921), there was a long wait for the next step in viewing the firm as an element of efficiency and coordination; this eventually took the form of Coase's transaction-cost approach (Coase, 'The Nature of the Firm', 1937; Alchian and Demsetz, 'Production, Information Costs and Economic Organisation', 1972; Williamson, *Markets and Hierarchies*, 1975; 'The Modern Corporation: Origins, Evolution and Attributes', 1981; '*The Economic Institutions of Capitalism*', 1985, and so on) has spread since its beginning and is now defined in varying degrees in several different branches.

Parallel viewpoints to that of the contractualistic, define the firm as a structure of competencies (Penrose, *The Theory of the Growth of the Firm*, 1959; Richardson, 'The Organization of Industry', 1972; Nelson and Winter, *An Evolutionary Theory of Economic Change*, 1982). These authors' arguments take the firm as being a gathering of competencies and knowledge, shared and defined by its past and present constituting human factors. The firm's objective is then to mobilize and coordinate the particular and heterogeneous knowledge often tacitly possessed by its employees.

A reflection on an Austrian economy of the firm was started in response to O'Driscoll and Rizzo's (*The Economics of Time and Ignorance*, 1985, p. 122-125) call for Austrians to concentrate more specifically on the field. A few years later came a stream of original and varied works from mainly Foss, Garrouste, Ioannides, Langlois and Witt.[14]

Organisation and capital: previous developments

There is one question that should be asked before going any further, however: was it really necessary to create an Austrian theory of the firm? Or rather, more exactly, was this analysis not already implicit in previous developments, notably in the theory of capital and even of entrepreneurship? The answer to this has in fact several layers.

One dimension of the problem is Hayek's argument on the organisation is to be found in several places in his works (for example: *The Pure Theory of Capital*, 1941; *The Road to Serfdom*, 1944; *The Constitution of Liberty*, 1960; *Law, Legislation and Liberty*, 1973). Hayek particularly provided a cognitive explanation of the relation between the organisation and the market, claiming that the organisation in general represents a form of centrally planned conscious knowledge management. Departments centrally organise activities along contractual lines, coordination being ensured not by market prices but by hierarchical control. This type of organisation is efficient as long as gain in control and planning of activities is not greater than the cost of the sacrifice of another type of more abstract knowledge provided by market prices. Small scale structures will obviously have a cost-to-advantage ratio in their favour. Larger, more complex many-layered structures will require more flexible and spontaneous forms of access to knowledge that put market prices at the centre of coordination.

A second level of the argument is the observation that many contemporary analyses of the firm, now considered as classics, are in fact of Austrian origin. Foss ('The Theory of the Firm: The Austrians as Precursors and Critics of Contemporary Theory', 1994a) explains that a modern industrial economy widely refers to the phenomena of specificity and complementarity of capital assets which the Austrian theory of capital and business cycles explicated. We will remark in the next chapter, on collectivism, that the analysis of property rights and the now well known difference between the 'principal' and the 'agent' are strong elements of Hayek's and Mises' argument. Richard Arena ('A propos de l'origine autrichienne de l'economie des coûts de transaction', 1997) sees an Austrian origin in the notion of transaction costs and Klein ('Entrepreneurship and Corporate Governance', 1999) in a similar way expresses his appreciation of Coase's approach).

The main question which today agitates the Austrian firm theorists is still open, however: it is the nature of intertemporal coordinating mechanisms which work through a production process. When analysing in the field of uncertainty of the future, the problem is to know if an entrepreneur wishing to succeed in his plans can afford to renounce ownership of the means of production and still ensure that the imagined future and the real future correspond. In other words, can the success of plans be achieved only through market processes or does it not, on the contrary, also require the use of organisational forms?

An entrepreneurial conception of the firm

This question is what moved contemporary Austrians to theorize an economy of the firm. They did so taking care to differentiate themselves not only from mainstream theories on the firm but also with the old Austrian analyses of production and capital, without however neglecting to incorporate the best aspects of the two currents.

The various contributions which have emerged in the past few years all have their own identities yet share at least one characteristic: they all place the entrepreneur at the centre of the explanation of the firm. It is obviously impossible to understand the capitalist enterprise without the notion of entrepreneur. Yet Böhm-Bawerk completely leaves out the notion of the entrepreneur in his theory of capital, as do all the traditional theories of the firm, with Knight's notable exception.[15]

Contemporary Austrians analysing the firm have naturally gravitated to Kirzner's work in their quest to refer to the concept of the entrepreneur, extending some of his analyses. Ioannides (1999) and Sautet (2000) see the constitution of an Austrian economy of the firm as broadening Kirzner's research on the entrepreneur.

The Austrian theory of the firm is faced with the same problem as that of the entrepreneur. Kirzner claims the entrepreneur is a creator, a notion which supposes that individuals can influence their environment. As Dulbecco and Garrouste say, the individual is 'able to reduce uncertainty by setting up institutions that render the constraints, represented by the behaviour of others, more predictable' (1999, p. 52). So the problem is one of validating expectations; the question is to influence one's environment, to make the imagined and real futures fit.

Some may be surprised at this reference to Kirzner; we observed in the last chapter that the function of promoter does not necessarily require either ownership or usage of productive factors. However, considering on this basis that the Austrian economy of the firm and entrepreneurship are independent would be to forget the teachings of the difference between statics and dynamics.

We know that in Kirzner's view, the conceptualization of the entrepreneur's role in the market economy does not need to include real time or uncertainty of the future. Kirzner rightly says that entrepreneurship at a catallactic level does not require the use or availability of capital, when conceptualizing entrepreneurship in a static world.

Yet in the dynamic, real-world market, constrained not only by division of knowledge but also by uncertainty of the future, things look very different. The institution of the firm is much more at home in this world. In the real economy, the firm meets the entrepreneur's need of being able to influence at least a part of his environment to be able to bring his plans to fruition and validate his initial expectations.[16]

The firm as power

The entrepreneur and his human production factors are linked contractually, the firm being structured internally around long-term employment contracts.

By controlling contract structure the entrepreneur becomes the catallactic agent able to impose his mode of representation on other agents, directing their individual behaviour, his representations hierarchically outclassing and influencing theirs. Not only is the capitalist entrepreneur's cognitive representation the leader among the group's, he must also hold formal power to concretely influence his employees' activities. In the wider social process, an individual may spontaneously assume the role of leader due to certain personal qualities; in the long term, however, leadership requires formal institutions and structures to maintain it; otherwise authority itself is called into question, whatever its nature and source. Authority ensures employees' submission by shaping their standard of living through the contract. As Dulbecco and Garrouste say, the firm corresponds to an *ex ante* definition of certain aspects of coordination. It 'submits autonomous plans of action to a centralized conception' (1999, p. 53).

In Witt's opinion ('Do Entrepreneurs Need Firms? A Contribution to a Missing Chapter in Austrian Economics', 1999), the firm can be seen as a way of creating a common cognitive structure: 'The entrepreneur's venture serves the purpose of jointly realizing a conception that s(he) is unable to realize by her/himself alone' (1999, p. 104). He sees the entrepreneur as a cognitive leader with the capacity of bringing others to adhere to a common cognitive conception; his role is to install a shared social model, or enterprise culture.

Witt starts from the idea that the entrepreneur with a project must formulate it to create his firm and persuade agents to participate in it. The opposite view, however, would seem to be more appropriate; the entrepreneur's problem is to integrate agents into his project rather than to transmit his subjective view which in any case, is hardly possible as it is based on tacit, non transmittable beliefs and knowledge. So the entrepreneur would seem to oblige agents to behave in a certain way through the ownership of factors and the establishment of contracts, without having to completely formulate his project. Ownership and contracts also constitute a barrier to other individuals who might wish to exploit his project for their own ends. The employee prefers to abandon any monetary gains expected from their own representations of entrepreneurship to benefit from secure levels of income offered by the capitalist through the contract. Witt develops the idea that the differentiations and evolutions in wages are a common way of maintaining individuals in the employ of the firm, keeping them from the temptation of establishing their own firm in competition with it.

So underpinning the notion of the contract is the ownership of factors which encourages the actors to follow the capitalist entrepreneur's imagination and adhere to his vision of the future by their behaviour, a future that he does not need to explicitly formulate in its entirety. This type of analysis is in the spirit of Hayek's own argument, when he discusses the organisations' rules: '… the rules each individual must obey depend on the place which have been indicated for him by the commanding authority' (1973, p. 49).

In a dynamic world, creation supposes not only entrepreneurship but also power. This can be defined as the capacity to manage other agents over time and to control them as production factors (see Ioannides, 'Towards an Austrian Perspective on the Firm', 1999, p. 93-94). Creation supposes power, the exercise of which in a monetary market economy implies ownership and the contract.

The firm's existence can thus be explained as the will to combine opportunities of technological and organisational complementarity, under the watchful eye of the entrepreneur who himself possesses knowledge concerning the two types of complementarity. The technical and intertemporal complementarity of factors together with the notion of production enables the firm, through the organisation of contracts, to capture time. So production has to be seen not so much as a final objective as a way of guaranteeing the control of individual behaviour which influence the success of the plan that the entrepreneur has concocted.

In this type of explanation, discovery is implicitly anterior to the firm's creation. However, it must be asked if it possible for an existing firm to encourage discovery. By this question is in fact meant the firm's maintenance and growth after the end of the exploitation of the profit opportunities which led to the firm's initial creation. It is here that Penrose and Richardson's theory of capabilities is brought into action by certain Austrians such as Langlois and Foss, but on a somewhat different basis. The idea is that these 'capabilities', that is a *savoir faire* more or less embedded in the firm's activity, are in fact tacit knowledge, in Polyani's and Hayek's meaning of the word. They above all nourish and develop capacities of discovery, especially when in the context of team cooperation. So an initial entrepreneur who founds a firm in order to better influence his environment would find it in his interest to later keep it, as he benefits from the capacities and talents of his team that he would not be able to on his own or if he were to dismantle it.

It is possible to view the question of firm size in the light of this last question and also of Ioannides's distinction (1999) between the 'outward' and 'inward' entrepreneur, based on management theory. The first is turned outwards to the market and its possible discoveries; the second is turned inwards, concentrating on relationships within his enterprise; the entrepreneur must balance both facets of his activity to ensure the success of his plans. Thus the firm's boundaries are determined by the balance between the development of discovery possibilities and the increase of internal difficulties of control, stemming from the rising number of contracts. The size of the enterprise expresses an arbitrage between the two variables.

In a dynamic world, the firm and the market must be seen as complementary structures. Entrepreneurs' plans can only succeed under constraint of temporal variations in activities and knowledge. The firm's existence enables the entrepreneur to control some of those constraints; production, when he has intertemporal control of factors, provides the entrepreneur with the opportunity to control a part of that ignorance through a structure of appropriate contracts. The Austrian production process allows him to capture time in a nearly automatic suite of events.

This analysis may not be appropriate for all the terms of uncertainty of the future. Dulbecco and Garrouste rightly note 'The enterprises' expectations regarding the future, do not always prove to be accurate, insofar as the production plans implemented by the enterprises take the form of a sequence of actions over time' (1999, p. 47). Temporal complementarities of the production factors, via contracts, certainly permits time to be controlled but these complementarities does produce an additional degree of vulnerability as to changes in demand. Mechanical time needed for production is here faced with shifting, subjective consumer time. The question then is how to determine what possible symmetries can be found between the two worlds. Answering this puts Hayek's studies in an unusual light.

3.3 The Hayekian View: Spontaneous Orders as Pattern Predictions

In *The Counter-Revolution of Science*, Hayek examines 'the problem of the compatibility of intentions and expectations of different people, of the division of knowledge between them, and the process by which the relevant knowledge is acquired and expectations formed' (1952b, p. 33).

Before this, in 'Economics and Knowledge', he had established that:

> under certain conditions, the knowledge and intentions of the different members of society are supposed to come more and more into agreement, or, to put the same thing in less general terms and less exact but more correct terms, that the expectations of the people and particularly of the entrepreneurs will become more and more correct (Hayek, 1937a, p. 45).

The question is: what are these conditions?

In a static world, adjusting expectations and carrying out plans is done as a logical succession. But in a dynamic world, the analysis is different. In a changing world, there would seem to be no learning process allowing agents to move towards success of expectations, as at all times each actor takes decisions in total ignorance of what others are doing. This is seen from a different angle in *Law, Legislation and Liberty*:

> The correspondence of expectations that makes it possible for all parties to achieve what they are striving for is in fact brought about by a process of learning by trial and error which must involve a constant disappointment of some expectations. The process of adaptation operates, as do the adjustments of any self-organizing system, by what cybernetics has taught us to call negative feedback: responses to the differences between the expected and the actual results of actions so that these differences will be reduced. This will produce an increased correspondence of expectations of the different persons so long as current prices provide some indications of what future prices will be, that is, so long as, in a fairly constant framework of known facts, always only a few of them change (Hayek, 1976a, p. 124-125).

Absolutely nothing in fact shows that present prices indicate future prices or that only a small amount of data would be modified.

Coordination of agents' subjective expectations needs some kind of constancy or at least a predictability of objective data. At the time of 'Economics and Knowledge', Hayek had given no clue as to this predictability's source and nature. Only much later, with his concept of rules of just conduct, did he offer an explanation on the principle of plan coordination in texts such as *Studies*; *Law, Legislation and Liberty* and *New Studies*. Completing the market mechanisms, the rules of just conduct stabilise individuals' preferences and put boundaries on their behaviour. They thus facilitate prediction and allow agents to form expectations.

As far as market dénouement and success of plans goes, the problem is one of standardisation of beliefs. It has already been seen how the formation of ideal types is a condition of the attribution of meaning to social reality, based on individuals' common mental structure. Social reality takes on its meaning through this 'typicality'. If individuals' mental structure really is held in common (isofunctionality), as Hayek claims in *The Sensory Order*, it is logical for individuals to use the same procedure, or types, to interpret social reality. Seen from this angle, ideal types allow individuals' interpretations to converge.[17]

Success by the rules

For Hayek, the rules defining the sensory order are abstract knowledge. They are expressed not only by action but also by values, modes of thinking, of interpretation and of perception. They are cognitive frameworks determining information reception and treatment, or in other words they determine data interpretation. Knowledge can in this way be seen as coming from the exercise of rules, assisted and modified by other rules indicating the equivalence or indeed the difference between combinations of stimuli.

Also, rules are a focal point allowing representations to be selected and conciliated; embodying common, shared, collective knowledge, they transform singular individuals into socialized actors. These rules' existence characterize a community of interpretations: individuals understand each other as they share the same rule culture. So it is the conjunction of knowledge of the praxeological laws of human action, of empirical circumstance and the sharing of common culture, often publicised by imitation and practice which explain the formation of agent's plans in conjunction with other agents who are *a priori* perfectly anonymous. Individuals may not know other individuals' situations and concrete knowledge but they do know the type of situations and culture in which they are. In other words, they know their beliefs, the general rules governing their mental activity. In this way, individuals' modes of categorisations are similar, although they would not be able to put words to them as the modes are expressed tacitly. Respecting the rules of behaviour, traditions, habit and conventions increases the likelihood of agents' success in their plans. The rule is a sum of knowledge of the environment.

The rule also economizes information, as it sums up the fabulous amount of information it represents into a synthesized form. The knowledge contained in it is abstract as

> it is the characteristic possessed by all the processes which determine action long before they appear in conscious thought or are expressed in language … abstract concepts are a means to cope with the complexity of the concrete which our mind is not capable of fully mastering' and constitutes 'the basis of man's capacity to move successfully in a world very imperfectly known to him, an adaptation to his ignorance of most of the particular facts of his surroundings (Hayek, 1973, p. 29; 30).[18]

So this synthesization of knowledge is a transformation process of many disparate individual items of concrete knowledge into a series of general rules, incorporating all of the cognitive contents of individual experience and giving the whole a general significance.

Finally and above all, the rules of just conduct are an answer to the problem of uncertainty of the future. They offer a range of tools for adaptations to various possible situations of the future, because of the abstract character of expressed knowledge. Actors can react to unpredictable situations through them, raising their chances of success of their plans. But respecting these rules also reduces ignorance as they also express constancy in agents' reaction to their environment. By the general character of their application, these rules demonstrate in various contexts or types of context a collection of attitudes that will spread to whole groups of individuals. They allow regularity and so a certain capacity of prediction in the social sphere. They therefore stabilize the social environment, which would otherwise be a Kaleidic world, in Shackle and Lachmann's meaning of the word, in an indeterminate configuration.

It is rules which allow the construction of 'types' of agents and to standardize their representations. This convergence leads to the notion of 'common sense', emerging from a process of objectivization of individual representations.

The spontaneous order as a rule structure

In Hayek's view, this complex of rules making up an architecture of social cooperation is a 'spontaneous order'. This theory is doubtless the most commented on and argued over facet of his work, the sheer volume of the literature making it unfeasible to comment on it here.[19] Hayek describes the spontaneous order as:

> a general method of indirectly creating an order in situations where the phenomena are far too complex to allow us the creation of an order by separately putting each element in its appropriate place. It is a sort of order over the particular manifestation of which we have little control, because the rules which determine it determine only its abstract character, while the detail depends on the particular circumstances known only to its individual members ('Kinds of Rationalism', 1965, p. 92).

Social coordination, through its various manifestations (markets, rules, institutions) is a network of ordered activities that the human mind cannot control and that it cannot *ex ante* rationalise either. The 'constructivist' conceit, originating in Descartes, Rousseau and other French Enlightenment philosophers, of improving the whole body of existing rules consciously and deliberately is thus impossible:

> Since our whole life consists in facing ever new and unforeseeable circumstances, we cannot make it orderly by deciding in advance all the particular actions we shall take. The only manner in which we can in fact give our lives some order is to adopt certain abstract rules or principles for guidance, and then strictly adhere to the rules we have adopted in our dealing with the new situations as they arise (ibid., p. 90).

There is a certain symmetry between the spontaneous orders and the abstract rules. The correspondence between the abstract rules of just conduct and the 'pattern predictions' that come from their application explain that 'there must be some discernible regularity in the world which makes it possible to predict events correctly' (Hayek, 1937a, p. 49).

These predictions are certainly not quantitative and do not concern particular events. They are primarily qualitative and often express the impossibility of certain situations rather than the anticipation of predetermined events.[20] Applying these rules certainly does not entirely solve the problem of uncertainty of the future but these rules' predictive capacity is often practical, especially concerning classes or types of events which take the form of structures of regularities.

The models' total variability of data prevents any kind of concrete prediction as there can be no discernable regularity in practical situations. The possibility of predicting is totally dependent on transforming these variables into constants. Hayek's originality is that he allows the possibility of theorizing the formation of these constants, through the rules of just conduct. It goes without saying that these constants are very general; they are also associated with a great number of variables, which can combine in a great variety of ways. Degrees of prediction expressing the presence of regularities in the social structures are conceivable, but impossibly perfect, particular, quantified predictions are not. [21] The rules of just conduct constitute both an answer to and a reduction of ignorance, doubly allowing the emergence of a social order.[22]

This order is nothing more than a structured coherent network of the rules of just conduct; by their regularity, they are the very expression of the spontaneous orders.[23]

Using Adam Ferguson's formula, Hayek defines these orders as 'The results of human action but not of human design' (Hayek, 1967a). They are as much the condition as the result of the regularity of human activities; the only way to understand the forming of these structures is as the result of an evolution. As time progresses, rules are selected by experience, changing with circumstance to progressively ensure better adjusted individuals' plans. However, the spontaneous character of the institutions must be well understood here; spontaneity being the process of their construction and is not associated with their contents.[24] Also, the spontaneous order is not just made up of individuals but of organisations such as family, firm and government, which are all managed with conscious objectives and plans. The important point here is not that the spontaneous order is partly made up of organisations but that the links between them be established through spontaneous rules which are the only ones able to mobilize all knowledge and reduce uncertainty of the future.

Cosmos versus taxis

So clearly, the spontaneous order versus constructed order debate centres around management of uncertainty of the future. It is obvious that precise, concrete knowledge of complex social environments in the spontaneous orders is impossible. But whole classes of individuals, responding to classes of phenomena, do so following a certain class of rules to produce a class of events. The spontaneous orders are characterized by growth in abstract knowledge but applying the general character of the rules of just conduct will inexorably reduce knowledge and mastery of concrete circumstances. However these rules represent qualitative progress, as they allow activities to be coordinated in ever increasing amounts of collectives as well as giving individuals the opportunity to discover and attain more ends than in the constructed orders. So there is an exclusive character to the relationship between the extension of abstract and concrete knowledge. The more one tries to apprehend, inspect and master concrete knowledge, the more one must give up any widening of the abstract knowledge offered by the general rules, which provide a multitude of individuals with a multiplicity of information to attain a multitude of ends.

So the constructed orders, or 'taxis', can be defined as highly regular structures but with few elements. The spontaneous orders, or 'cosmos', are structures with many elements but relations between them are much looser because of their number and the abstract character of the knowledge they transmit. In a constructed order, quantitatively, only a fairly low amount of predictions is possible because of the small number of elements, but they will be qualitatively very reliable. The spontaneous orders have a much higher amount of elements and therefore generate much vaster knowledge and information, but this will be less precise than that produced by the fabricated orders.

The rules of just conduct are in fact nothing more than a way of uniformizing individuals' reactions to an environment that they experience and perceive subjectively;[25] thanks to these rules entrepreneurs no longer face total uncertainty. This does not imply that ignorance is obliterated from their individual activities; applying the rules of just conduct simply narrows its scope. It is these abstract rules which allow most individuals to correctly anticipate.

The idea of contrast between the complex and the simple orders moves into a wider realm when Hayek picks up on Popper's distinction between closed and open societies. As far as our arguments are concerned here, closed society's complexity is so low that the data necessary for coordinating individual plans are accessible to individual minds, so such a society can be consciously organised and managed. On the other hand, an open society displays a much too high level of complexity to be grasped by any authority and its development is a function of man's capacity to communicate abstract thought.

3.4 Plans and Prices

Rothbard and his followers such as Salerno, Hoppe and Herbener[26] claim theirs to be the only true expression of the master Mises' teachings, which their aim is to faithfully reproduce. They accordingly denounce other currents of thought as heretics:

> the correct Austrian paradigm is and can only be the Misesian, *i.e.*, the paradigm of Misesian praxeology- … the competing Austrian paradigms, in particular the fundamentally 'evolved rules', 'knowledge', 'plans', and 'spontaneous order' para-

digm of Hayek; and the more extreme 'ultra-subjectivist' or nihilist paradigm of Lachmann, have both been fallacious and pernicious (Rothbard, 'The Present State of Austrian Economics', 1995, p. 48).

The reflections of this circle can be examined on different levels.

Prices without plans

One of the Rothbardians' first analytical levels on the success of plans can be examined from the viewpoint of the role of psychology in the construction of economic theory. The notion of the plan is praxeological, but knowledge of its concrete contents and of actor's expectations comes from individuals' internal psychological categories, which the observer and the theorist cannot *a priori* know. Action will express interiors, but there is no way of knowing from the exterior if the results of those acts correspond to actors' actual expectations based on a subjective plan. It is therefore a theoretical mistake to associate the theme of coordination with the idea of plan success; moreover it is an approach Mises never contemplated.

Salerno writes of Mises' coordinative aspects of the market:

> This means that the structure of realized (disequilibrium) prices, which continually emerges in the course of the market process and whose elements are employed for monetary calculation, performs the indispensable function of clearing all markets and, in the process, coordinating the productive employments and of all resources with one another and with the anticipated preferences of consumers. Such price coordination, by insuring that scarce resources are secured by the entrepreneurs bidding the highest prices, also insures that at each instant Bohm-Bawerk's Law of Cost prevails, that is, that the constellation of resources prices that emerges on a market unhampered by legal restrictions always reflects the circumstance that existing resources are devoted to their most valuable uses as determined by entrepreneurial appraisements of future of put prices (Salerno, 'Mises and Hayek Dehomogenized', 1993, p. 124).

So for the economist, tendency towards equilibrium can only legitimately mean this: resource allocation operated by entrepreneur-promoters is carried out according to their expectations about future consumer choice. But this 'equilibration' does not necessarily mean that their expectations are correct and that their plans succeed. The existence of a relative price structure may well guarantee market adjustments (through supply and demand) but it does not guarantee success of plans. It can indeed express entrepreneurial success but just as well failure to correctly perceive the future. These respectively explain the phenomena of profit and loss.[27]

In following this logic, Rothbard is anxious to distinguish between: firstly, coordination by pricing, which would simply express the market's existence, according to him conforming to Mises' work both in the spirit and the letter; and secondly, coordination by plans, as a situation of entire success of expectations, corresponding to an unattainable static equilibrium, totally removed from the reality of economic life:

> coordination occurs effectively, and every day, through the price system … not in the Never-Never land of final equilibrium, but every day in markets, in day-to-day equilibrium, the price system coordinates prices, including wages rates and the prices of other productive factors, so that there is never any shortage or unsold surplus. From day-to-day, then, there may, for various reasons, be misallocations of resources, but never shortages and surpluses, so long as prices are free to move (Rothbard, 'The Present State of Austrian Economics', 1995, p. 60).

From this viewpoint, it is easily seen that for the authors of the Rothbardian branch, there is no criterion on the market to measure success of plans and to compare them with each other. Price freedom allows markets to be cleared, but even if there is such equilibrium among all these market situations, it is impossible to indicate any superiority between them in terms of their capacity to provide plan coordination.

By ignoring the problem of validation of expectations in the name of praxeological laws, the Rothbardians deny the existence of a theoretical economic problem of success of achieving plans. This can at first appear a valid approach. Nonetheless, the epistemological impossibility of externally determining if observed agents have succeeded in their plans does not completely prevent an economist from examining this issue. Mises himself says that to exercise catallaxy requires the use of exterior categories to the *a priori* analysis, which is only a base of economic thinking and is not its whole. This happily does not stop the Austrians in general from taking a deep interest in the catallactic sphere. By basing themselves on Mises' writings, the Rothbardians appear to have done the same thing.

From radical to moderate uncertainty

Salerno tells us that Mises thinks that the market economy generates a proc ess which tends to minimise entrepreneurial errors.

> This is what Mises calls the 'selective process' which is continuously and actually operating in calendar time via monetary profits and losses to weed out from the market the relatively unastute and inefficient entrepreneurs while transferring the power to choose the best uses and technical combinations of productive resources to the more farsighted and technically proficient entrepreneurs (Salerno, 1993, p. 131-132).

Rothbard, in the same way adds: 'Over time, entrepreneurs who are successful in bearing risks and forecasting their particular future will earn profits and expand their operations, while poor risk-bearers and forecasters will suffer losses and necessarily shrink their field of activity' (1995, p. 51).

Uncertainty of the future inevitably influences profit and loss making and thus individual entrepreneurs' futures: 'on the market a process of selection is in continual operation. There prevails an unceasing tendency to weed out the less efficient entrepreneurs, that is, those who fail in their endeavors to anticipate correctly the future demands of the consumers' (Mises, 1966, p. 582).[28]

However, errors happily cannot be general to the economy: 'Entrepreneurial errors result in losses for the inefficient entrepreneurs which are counterbalanced by the profits of the efficient entrepreneurs. They make business bad for some groups of industries and good for other groups. They do not bring about a general depression of trade' (ibid., p. 302). So, whoever fails will probably make a loss, which will mean profits for others; 'negative surprises' for some will mean 'positive surprises' for others. It is not so much the whole of monetary profits which is in question here, as their sharing between promoters.

In a free market left to its own devices, when promoters make errors of expectations about consumers' future demand, it is because it has moved to other sectors to benefit other entrepreneurs. Thus, uncertainty of the future operates at an individual level rather than collective and cannot mean a generalised loss for promoters; the free market cannot lead to general crises.

This said, Salerno or Rothbard analyse this in a way which brings the problem to a more individual level:

> Man always acts by using reason to improve his lot; so that his action is always 'rational' that is, his actions are always beneficial, always necessarily equilibrating *ex ante*. And the market mechanism is also such that forecasts tend, in general, to pan out as true, so that *ex ante* decisions become validated *ex post* (Rothbard, 1995, p. 59).

We can also see: 'entrepreneurs will tend to be kept on their toes and be successful in most of their forecasts' (ibid, p. 51).

In fact, Rothbard and his followers seem to be saying that for Mises, uncertainty of the future is not so complete as all that. Rothbard firmly opposes the idea of an unavoidable, radical uncertainty, claiming that if the future is completely impossible to predict, then the laws of causality no longer can exist: 'Since there are no laws of cause and effect in human action, Lachmannian Man would not be able to take the first step in figuring out what is happening, or likely to happen, with prices' (Rothbard, 1995, p. 52). For him, Mises's uncertainty is in fact a 'moderate uncertainty', which Rothbard contrasts with Lachmann's radical uncertainty. The present supplies enough clues for the alert individual to feel confident enough to deliberately face uncertainty.

The Rothbardians leave, however, a few holes. There is hardly any mention of a mechanism that would reduce uncertainty of the future in order to encourage success of expectations.

On this evidence, the spontaneous order and the rules of just conduct can never be a sufficient explanation for these authors. For Rothbard, here following Hoppe ('FA Hayek on Government and Social Evolution: A Critique', 1994):

> Hayek's emphasis on unconscious habit or rule following thus leaves out critical parts of the answer such as (a) how do these rules or institutions get adopted in the first place; and (b) how do they ever change, often suddenly. To fall back, as Hayek does, on 'evolution' as the sole answer to the fist question not only misapplies the very concept of 'evolution' which requires the existence of the genes and mutations; it also fails spectacularly to account for sudden changes in those rules or in society's acceptance of them (Rothbard, 1995, p. 66).

However, the existence of a principle of the validation of expectations must be accepted as the other side of the argument in favour of interpretation. There must exist a certain number of elements of ignorance which prevent total success of plans and avoidance of errors. But there must also be both past and present data, correct analysis of which will indicate a possible future, for the work of interpretation to have any meaning at all. If this were not the case, only good luck would allow any entrepreneur to stay in the market, not the most alert. Talking about entrepreneurs' 'competency' and 'efficiency' and not just their 'luck' means their actions are not just a series of gambles.

How can we explain these prediction elements? Rothbard's argument (*The Ethics of Liberty*, 1982) possibly offers some ways forward.

Do Ethics aid the success of plans?

In this somewhat particular book, Rothbard attempts to construct a system of ethics, with no references to 'utilitarianism' or a Hayekian consequentialism. This (to the Austrians) novel reference to a concept of ethics takes place as an ontological demonstration; he founds a norm of law to regulate interpersonal exchange, basing it on a naturalist approach, seen through a rationalist view point.

The Ethics of Liberty is often thought of as being a real rupture with the neo-Austrian tradition and especially with Mises' praxeological thinking. Of course, Mises is totally opposed to any ethical criteria in economic thinking: 'There is no use in arguing about the adequacy of ethical precepts. They are derived from intuition; they are arbitrary and subjective. There is no objective standard available with regard to which they could be judged' (Mises, *Planning for Freedom*, 1962c, p. 131). Rothbard's argument, however, reveals a more subtle reality. The *Ethics of Liberty* cannot be considered a rupture on an epistemological level, as it is the result of thinking started in the 1950s and only reasserts an old desire to reconcile praxeological teachings and epistemological realism. Rothbard does not refute 'the logical implications of the axiom of human action' (1973a, p. 38) incarnated by Praxeology, but tries to convert its formalistic teachings into ontologically meaningful content.[29]

In fact, through his reference to Aristotelian realism, he aims to propose adding a definition of human nature to Mises' simple grammar of action.

Rothbard holds that all phenomena have to be studied from the naturalistic point of view. All the elements of the universe have their own attributes which are their particular expression of their identity. It is therefore possible to classify and group them into different types. This ontological approach allows the definition the nature of things, whether human, animal or vegetable, thus enabling the forming of objective values for each species.

Discovering and respecting ontological values, however, is not the same for humans as for animals, as humans do not instinctively receive commands from nature nor have the means to carry them out.[30] This requires the employment of reason, defined as the objective capacity of 'observation, abstraction, thought' (Rothbard, 1982, p. 30). It is the main instrument of information gathering of natural reality and allows the individual to discover the natural laws which govern his accomplishment as a human being.[31]

Reason, the guide of introspection, shows Man the ontological character of the possession of himself.[32] It clearly establishes that any individual has a Right, in an Ethics sense, over himself. Rothbard extracts from this analysis the idea of legitimacy of the ownership of any reality changed by man; that is to say that any individual who produces anything has the right to full use of it. The definition of liberty flows naturally from this, being the possibility for any individual to control or dispose of his natural property: ('… the full exercise of his natural self-ownership', Rothbard, 1982, p. 45). The frontiers of liberty are easily seen from this as 'absence of molestation of a man's just property' (ibid., p. 43). In Rothbard's view, this ontologically establishes both the definition and the legitimacy of liberty.[33] Natural law then founds the norms of interpersonal exchange, based around the 'rational' foundations of liberty and property. This approach permits the definition of a structure of natural laws concerning the acquisition and transfer of goods, a task which economic analysis as such appears incapable of doing.

Formulating objective norms of natural law has considerable doctrinal consequences: not only does it allow norms of political classical liberalism to flourish but also challenges at the same time the very existence of the state.

The State, whether democratic or dictatorial, minimal or interventionist, according to Rothbard is described by one word, etched into its very way of functioning: violence.[34] The state's needs being met by enforced taxation, this coercion is a disrespect of the principle of voluntary exchange, that is to say it is a violation of natural laws. Whether this is carried out by an individual or in the name of a majority does not really change the basic nature of the act. Rothbard's radical position is a result of this thinking:

> The State is *not*, as most utilitarian free-market economists like to think, a legitimate social institution that tends to be bumbling and inefficient in most of its activities. On the contrary, the State is an inherently illegitimate institution of organized aggression, of organized and regularized crime against the persons and properties of its subjects … from the point of view of justice … the State can own no property, require no obedience, enforce no contracts made with it, and indeed, cannot exist at all (ibid., p. 187).[35]

In fact the market is simply the free exchange of endowments ontologically established by natural laws. It is the only possible expression of the rule of justice organising individual transactions around the principle of free consent; the state then cannot legitimately interfere in interpersonal relations which voluntarily spring up between people. To conclude: 'In a truly free society, a society where individual rights of person and property are maintained, the State then, would necessarily cease to exist' (Rothbard, 1982, p. 171-172). So not only is traditional Austrian political free will replaced by the theory of a rationally-founded doctrinal normativity, but this can only result in a kind of radical libertarianism, anarcho-capitalism.

But similarly, Rothbard's argument in *The Ethics of Liberty* seems to allow the definition of a form of infra-individual normativity for individual values, by widening the application of the scope of rationality. He posits the idea that reason should not only be understood as a process of allocating the proper means to ends but must extend to the ends themselves, through the definition of 'objective' morals, which come, alongside rights from the same source: natural law, which can be defined as the science of real happiness.[36] He establishes this himself: 'political philosophy [that is to say the social sanction of the formulation of laws] is a subdivision of the philosophy of ethics' (1982, p. 391), and 'If it said that moral conduct is rational conduct, what is meant is that it is conduct in accordance with right reason, reason apprehending the objective good for man and dictating the means to its attainment' (Copleston, quoted by Rothbard, 1982, p. 6). If reason can define a principle of justice, it can also define natural values.

The principle of rationality is not only capable of defining inter- but also infra-individual norms, by the intervention of the concept of natural values, to describe an objective structure of the human being. As there is an objective rapport between man and nature, subjective amorality must give way to a rationally discovered ontology.[37] In claiming a principle of 'right reason', which 'dictates to man his proper ends as well as the means for their attainment' (1982, p. 6), Rothbard founds the theory of a normative approach to individual values: 'Every man possesses … The light of reason whereby he can reflect … and promulgate to himself the natural law, which is the totality of the universal precepts or dictates of right reason concerning the good which is to be pursued and the evil which is to be shunned' (Copleston quoted by Rothbard, 1982, p. 8).

The field of rationality appears to be defined differently to Mises' idea of it. In his 'In Defence of Extreme Apriorism', Rothbard already remarked that Mises, following in Hume's traces:

> assumes nothing whatever about the rationality of human action (in fact, Mises does not use the concept at all). He assumes nothing about the wisdom of man's ends or about the correctness of his means. He 'assumes' only that men *act*, that is, that they have *some* ends, and use *some* means to try to attain them (1956, p. 318).

In *The Ethics of Liberty*, Rothbard explicitly seeks to move beyond this amorality and defends 'the idea of a natural law founded on reason and rational inquiry' (Rothbard, 1982, p. 3). He explicitly refutes the idea that reason only can exist within the means-ends category (the process of fitting means to ends) without being able to determine the ends.[38] Quite the opposite, the objectives of action may be judged, following the Thomistic principle of 'Right Reason' as objectively good or bad: 'In natural law philosophy, then, reason is not bound, as it is in modern post-Humean philosophy, to be a mere slave to the passions, confined to cranking out the discovery of the means to arbitrarily chosen end …'man's reason can discover the proper ends for man to follow' (ibid., p. 6; 12).

Asserting this form of rationality has important implications for uncertainty of the future. Doing so interprets the idea of 'moderate uncertainty' (1995, p. 52) that Rothbard thought he could find in Mises and allows the definition of a principle of prediction, springing naturally from the discovery of 'real, true values'.

As O'Driscoll and Rizzo have stressed, it is the indetermination of the formation and transformation of individual values that prevents the definition of a principle of coordination of expectations: 'economists cannot explain the formation of tastes, and hence when these change, the predicted effects of supply shifts may prove entirely wrong' (O'Driscoll and Rizzo, *The Economics of Time and Ignorance*, 1985, p. 24). Rothbard said it himself: the economist 'will have nothing like a perfect score, for he will run aground on the fact of free will altering values and choices, and the consequent impossibility of making exact predictions of the future' (Rothbard, 1973a, p. 43).

Inversely, if we consider human nature to be objective and human reason able to discover its own structure and contents, this indeterminism of the formation and transformation of values simply vanishes. In discovering an objective value structure, which any rational being adopts for their own self-preservation, free choice of values can no longer be considered an essential category of human action. Individual values lose their status of indeterminate, particular and historical data as defined by Lachmann, Hayek and Kirzner. They give way to normative morals, the instrument of 'real happiness', which gains an added dimension due to the positive externality as regards coordination of plans. Once the objective knowledge of values is shared by all, everyone then possesses a principle of prediction. If these values are respected by all, it then becomes possible to formulate expectations of future prices based on knowledge of those of the present.

Of course, knowledge of infra-individual values shared by all would not at all avoid the problem of ignorance; actors' concrete situations are *a priori* unknown and it is these which determine choice and preference. Rationality reveals no *a priori* information to actors concerning others' endowments and particular environments. In the same way as Lachmann and Hayek, Rothbard defends a system of market prices to express agents' preferences and provide a basis for economic calculations.[39]

From this position, coordination has to be seen through a twin dialectic. The first would concern the positive-normative relationship. A positive state of society would take place where the discovery of natural values is still in the future. As long as 'real, true' values are not established, coordinating individual plans would be indeterminate and Rothbard would implicitly be in a traditional Austrian position.

The second level would be the difference between essence and contingency. In the ideal situation of universal discovery and sharing of the 'right values', a zone of temporal ignorance would subsist: the intertemporal structure of revenue distribution is not rigid, even though greatly stabilized; supply, in particular the relation between goods and their characteristics, may change through technological advance or innovating action. These changes may *ex ante* unpredictably affect individuals' choices and related prices. Certain agents may also misinterpret the markets and fail to correctly adjust their activities. These phenomena would badly reduce practical opportunities of strict or full coordination of individual plans.[40] However, because of their contingent character, actors would be able to formulate a principle of expectations based on the present. Failure of expectations would not be the rule. So it is clear that:

> The Misesian praxeological view … is that knowledge of the present, much less of the future, is never perfect, and that the world in general, and the market in particular, are eternally marked by uncertainty. On the other hand, man obtains knowledge, which hopefully increases over time, of natural law, of the laws of cause and effect, which enable him to discover more and better ways of mastering nature and of bringing about his goals ever more effectively (Rothbard, 1995, p. 51).

This type of approach could, moreover, retroactively shed light on some of Mises' own writings. In *The Theory of Money and Credit*, he had already noted

> Prices change slowly because the subjective valuations of human beings change slowly. Human needs, and human opinions as to the suitability for satisfying those needs, are no more liable to frequent and sudden changes than are the stocks of goods available for consumption, or the manner of their social distribution. The

> fact that today's market price is seldom very different from yesterday's is to be explained by the fact that the circumstances that determined yesterday's price have not greatly changed overnight, so that today's price is a resultant of nearly identical factors. If rapid and erratic variations in prices were usually encountered in the market, the conception of objective exchange value would not have attained the significance that it is actually accorded both by consumer and producer. In this sense reference to inertia of prices is unobjectionable, although the errors of earlier economists should warn us of the real danger that the use of terms borrowed from mechanics may lead to a 'mechanical' system, that is, to one that abstracts erroneously from the subjective valuations of individuals (1912, p. 133).

The reference to natural, stable values would seem to provide a logical basis for Rothbard's hostility to Lachmann's thesis of the totally indeterminate success of plans. This success would depend on the exercise of what might be termed 'rational subjectivism'. So the phenomenon of radical ignorance that Lachmann mentions would be removed by a realist style shoring up of the process of values forming. The unpredictable Kaleidic world of Shackle and Lachmann, characterised by disorderly change, would lose its scientific legitimacy. Prediction is indeed possible based on knowledge of natural laws.

Reading between the lines, Rothbard's revisiting of Aristotelian realism may well be the key to understanding the use of rationality, the pivot of praxeology, for solving the problem of individuals' plan success. Rothbard would thus be taking on the mantle of Mises' legacy, in declaring: 'It is not of course, that Mises believes that men will always listen to reason, or follow its dictates; it is simply that, insofar as men act at all, they are capable of following reason, and that pursuing such a course is literally the last best hope for mankind' (1995, p. 64-65).

NOTES

1. O'Driscoll and Rizzo (1985) distinguish between static, or Newtonian time and dynamic, or real time. The first produces no change, or at least no unpredictable change but the second allows changes that we cannot expect.
2. Kirzner seems to mix changes to preference and to resources, which could be described as being endogenous or inside action, with birth, death and illness; he terms them all exogenous change, as in exogenous to the market.
3. This definition of a promoter clearly distinguishes the market entrepreneur from the public and private sector employee; with their security of tenure and wage they have no need to worry about uncertainty of the future in a given period.
4. 'Mises incorporated into his praxeology the useful Knightian distinction between insurable risk (such as lotteries, gambling on roulette) and uninsurable (because heterogeneous, not random, and not replicable uncertainty) which the entrepreneur bears and for which he earns profit or suffers loss' (Rothbard, 1995, p. 51). See also Mises' distinction between case and class probability (*Human Action*, 1966, 107-113).

5. There are two different versions of these interindividual differentiations. It should be possible to establish that all individuals interpret – in certain passages, Mises states that all actors must use elements of appreciation – but most people's interpretations tends to be of the future as a reproduction of today's configurations, not so much in its contents but in its structures; promoters, however, are able to see changes in this structure.

    Another view would be to consider that everyone speculates and interprets but in different time cycles. 'Average man' speculates to near time horizons, where known elements are in the majority compared to elements of ignorance. Entrepreneur-promoters speculate on longer time cycles, where elements of ignorance are strongly in the majority. There are therefore both 'good quality' and 'bad quality' interpretations, respectively by the entrepreneurs and 'average men'.
6. See, among others, the following references to Lachmann's problematic: Grinder, 'In Pursuit of the Subjective Paradigm' (1977); Boehm, 'The Ambiguous Notion of Subjectivism: Comment on Lachmann' (1982); Kirzner (ed.), *Subjectivism, Intelligibility and Economic Understanding, Essays in Honor of Ludwig M. Lachmann on his Eightieth Birthday* (1986), particularly Fehl's contributions, 'Spontaneous Order and the Subjectivity of Expectations: a Contribution to the Lachmann-O'Driscoll Problem' and Hight's, 'Equilibration and Disequilibrium in the Market Process'; Lavoie, 'The Interpretative Turn' (1994); Garrison, 'The Kaleidic World of Ludwig Lachmann' (1987); Vaughn, 'The Problem of Order in Austrian Economics: Kirzner versus Lachmann' (1992); Lewin, 'Time, Change and Complexity: Ludwig M. Lachmann's Contributions to the Theory of Capital' (1996); 'Capital in Disequilibrium: a Reexamination of the Capital Theory of Ludwig M. Lachmann' (1997); Koppl and Mongiovi, 'Subjectivism and Economic Analysis: Essays in Memory of Ludwig M. Lachmann' (1998). Lachmann's theses were keenly enough felt in the Austrian camp to encourage Lavoie, Ebeling, Hight and others to develop a hermeneutical Austrian school. See especially Lavoie (ed), *Economics and Hermeneutics* (1990a).
7. In fact, Lachmann stresses that 'even though changing interpretation need not cause expectation to change while expectation may change without a change in interpretation of the past' (Lachmann, 1986a, p. 57). Interpretation, that is to say perception of past and present events, can change without changing one's expectation of the future. In the same way, agents' expectations can change without changing the way they see the present and the past. However, it appears analytically problematic to conceptualise forming expectations independently of interpretations, although it is legitimate to envisage changing interpretations without changing expectations: 'the formation of anticipations always rests on some interpretation of the past' (ibid, p. 57). Lachmann symmetrically observes that perception's identity does not necessarily influence that of anticipation's: 'Different men's expectations will react differently to the occurrence of the same event' (Lachmann 1969, p. 158). See also Wubben (1995).
8. It could possibly be conceived that time passes without preferences changing. It is impossible, however, regarding the laws of action, that time would pass with no change in interpretations and in reaction, agents' expectations.
9. It is worth noting that agents' interpretations do not need to be identical but simply compatible; this said, there is nothing to guarantee this compatibility.
10. 'On the subject of prediction Professor Shackle's conclusions are quite definite and, in our view, cogent. "Complete prediction would require the predictor to know in complete detail at the moment of making his prediction, first, all 'future' advances of knowledge and inventions, and secondly, all 'future' decisions. To know in advance what an intention will consist of is evidently to make that invention in advance"'(Shackle, p. 103-104, quoted by Lachmann, 1959, p. 88).
11. We already find traces of this 'middle ground' stance in an O'Driscoll article 'Spontaneous Order and the Coordination of Economic Activities' (1978).
12. See for example Hazlitt, 'Review of Competition and Entrepreneurship' (1974); White,

'Entrepreneurship, Imagination and the Question of Equilibrium (1976); Hight, 'Review of 'Perception, Opportunity and Profit' (1980); 'Alertness, Judgment and Entrepreneurship: A Comment on Kirzner' (1982), or even later, Rothbard, 'The Present State of Austrian Economics' (1995).

13. Kirzner validates the role of ignorance as developed by Mises in his approach to entrepreneurship. But he seeks to give it particular foundation by claiming: 'In earlier forays into the field of the Misesian entrepreneur, I developed an interpretation of the entrepreneurial function in which the role of uncertainty, while recognized and certainly not denied, was not emphasized. This failure to emphasize uncertainty was quite deliberate and was indeed explicitly acknowledged. Instead of emphasizing the uncertainty in which entrepreneurial activity is embedded, these earlier treatments stresses the element of alertness to hitherto unperceived opportunities that, I argued, crucial for the Misesian concept of entrepreneurship' (Kirzner, 1985, p. 42). Certainly Mises' extracts on entrepreneurship allow several interpretations. As much as he stresses the roles of uncertainty of the future and the entrepreneurial speculative dimension: 'The driving force of the market process is provided ... by the promoting and speculating entrepreneurs' (Mises, 1966, p. 346), he also, as he does with forecasting, alludes to the element of alertness as to present opportunities. So in the same sentence, he notes that entrepreneurs are 'farther-sighted than other men' and that they are 'quicker of apprehension' (ibid., p. 346).

14. Space imposing its usual constraints, here are just some of the main contributions: Ziegler ('Innovation and the Imitative Entrepreneur', 1985); Loasby (*The Minds and Methods of Economics*, 1989a); O'Driscoll and Rizzo ('Subjectivism, Uncertainty and Rules', 1990); Langlois ('Orders and Organizations: Toward an Austrian Theory of Social Institutions', 1992; 'The Boundaries of the Firm', 1994); Vanberg (*Rules and Choice in Economics*, 1994); Loasby ('Organizationnal Capabilities and Interfirm Relations', 1994); Langlois and Robertson ('Firms, Markets and Economic Changes, a Dynamic Theory of Business Institutions', 1995); Ioannides ('Comments on Israel Kirzner's Notion of Pure Profit', 1993; 'Towards an Austrian Perspective on the Firm', 1999); Langlois and Cosgel ('Frank Knight on Risk, Uncertainty and the Firm: a New Interpretation', 1993); Foss ('The Theory of the Firm: the Austrians as Precursors and Critics of Contemporary Theory', 1994a; 'Austrian and Post-Marshallian Economics: the Bridging Work of George Richardson', 1996b; 'The Alternative Theories of Knight and Coase, and the Modern Theory of the Firm', 1996c; 'Austrian Insights and the Theory of the Firm', 1997); Klein ('Economic Calculation and the Limits of Organization', 1996; 'Entrepreneurship and Corporate Governance', 1999); Yu ('Towards a Praxeological Theory of the Firm', 1999), Garrouste and Langlois ('Cognition, Redundancy and Learning in Organizations', 1997); Lewin ('The Firm, Money and Economic Calculation: Considering the Institutional Nexus of Market Production', 1998; Lewin and Phelan ('Firms, Strategies and Resources: Contributions from Austrian Economics', 1999; 'An Austrian Theory of the Firm', 2000); Witt ('Do Entrepreneurs Need Firms? A Contribution to a Missing Chapter in Austrian Economics', 1999); Dulbecco and Garrouste ('Towards an Austrian Theory of the Firm', 1999); Sautet (*An Entrepreneurial Theory of the Firm*, 2000); for many other useful bibliographical references see the website: http://web.missouri.edu/~kleinp/misc/aus_firm_biblio.html

15. 'The primary function of the Knightian firm is entrepreneurial' (Boudreaux and Holcombe, 1989, p. 147).

16. Hayek's previous remark has some bearing here: 'Mr Keynes obviously arrives at this view by an artificial separation of the function of the entrepreneurs as owners of capital and their function as entrepreneurs in the narrow sense. But these two functions cannot be absolutely separated even in theory, because the essential function of the entrepreneurs, that of assuming risks, necessarily implies the ownership of capital (Hayek, 'Reflections on the Pure Theory of Money of Mr J.M. Keynes', August, 1931, p. 277).

17. The closer people are to each other, the greater their common experience will be, the better the types will be known and the more the field of individual activity will be covered by the

type of predictions. The further apart people are, the less concrete will be the type and the narrower the field of predictions will be; it will however be of higher quality. Seen from this angle, evolutionism would seem to be a process of competition and/or selection of ideal types.

18. 'Thus there exists 'The Primacy of the Abstract' (Hayek, 1969a). This may be seen in the studies on cognitive psychology in *The Sensory Order*.
19. See the very useful works of Caillé 'Pour une critique de la raison libérale critique' (1984); Frydman, 'Individu et totalité dans la pensée libérale: le cas de F. Hayek' (1989) and a little later, Khalil's various contributions: 'Organizations versus Institutions (1995); 'Friedrich Hayek's Darwinian Theory of Evolution of Institutions: Two Problems' (1996); 'Friedrich Hayek's Theory of Spontaneous Order: Two Problems' (1997).
20. 'Though we are not in a position to specify precisely what to expect, or even to list all the possibilities, each observed pattern has meaning in the sense that it limits the possibilities of what else may occur' (Hayek, 'Degrees of Explanation', 1955, p. 18).
21. 'Explanation and prediction of course do not refer to an individual event but always to phenomena of a certain kind or class' (Hayek, 'Degrees of Explanation', 1955, p. 9).
22. The fact that these rules exist in an abstract form, that they physically manifest themselves in action rather than words, explain the lack of knowledge of them and the difficulty of recognising them; this is why the public seems to accept them with difficulty, leading to misunderstandings about the way complex social structures are made.
23. Hayek reflects considerably on the way rules are learned and transmitted (see especially 1973, 1976a, and 1978b). See Paque (1990). Once again, the influence of *The Sensory Order* is perceptible here.
24. There is no need for the rules underlying the spontaneous order to be spontaneous too; their contents may be conscious. There will, however, be an unavoidable difference between the intentions behind these rules and the result of their application, dependant on changing multiple contextual factors. This result, by definition, is clearly spontaneous.
25. These rules 'determine or limit the range of possibilities within which the choice is made consciously. By eliminating certain kinds of action altogether and providing certain routine ways of achieving the object, they merely restrict the alternatives on which a conscious choice is required' (Hayek, 1963a, p. 56). So the rules of just conduct reduce the range of idiosyncrasies and the uncertainly that goes with it. On this point see also Polanyi's 'The Determination of Social Action', 1969, whose intuitions are close to Hayek's.
26. Rothbard ('The Present State of Austrian Economics', 1995); Salerno ('Ludwig von Mises as Social Rationalist', 1990a; 'Commentary: The Concept of Coordination in Austrian Economics', 1991; 'Mises and Hayek Dehomogenized', 1993); Hoppe (*Praxeology and Economic Science*, 1988; *A Theory of Socialism and Capitalism: Economics, Politics and* Ethics, 1989; *The Economics and Ethics of Private Property*, 1993a; 'F.A. Hayek on Government and Social Evolution: A Critique', 1993b); Herbener ('Ludwig von Mises and the Austrian School of Economics', 1991); Hülsmann ('Knowledge, Judgment and The Use of Property', 1997; 'A Realist Approach to Equilibrium Analysis', 2000a).
27. 'The concept of equilibration ... is an *ex ante* concept expressing recognition that entre preneurs responding to the lure of expected monetary profits seek to anticipate and remove the continually emerging maladjustments between means and ends and that their success in doing so would culminate in a state of optimum satisfaction, i.e., no action' (Salerno, 'Mises and Hayek Dehomogenized', 1993, p. 125). Rothbard and his disciples refuse to discount the notion of equilibrium, however. By this, they consider themselves loyal to the Mises thinking, as it uses the method of imaginary constructions to describe economic laws. In the end, this reference to equilibrium shows up the fact that disequilibrium and preference cannot be thought of without conceptualizing the notion of equilibrium and indifference: 'Thus we conceive the category of action by constructing the image of a state in which there is no action (final equilibrium), either because the individual is fully contented and does not feel any easiness or because he does not know any procedure from wh-

ich an improvement in his well being (state of satisfaction) could be expected' (Mises, quoted by Rothbard, 1995, p. 57).

28. For Mises' selection process, see particularly *Human Action*, p. 328-332.
29. Early on, Rothbard took a different line to Mises ('In Defence of Extreme Apriorism') and declared the axiomatic character of human action to be an Aristotelian realism: 'Professor Mises, in the neo-Kantian tradition, considers this axiom a law of thought and therefore a categorical truth a priori to all experience. My own epistemological position rests on Aristotle and St. Thomas rather than Kant, and hence I would interpret the proposition differently. I would consider the axiom a law of reality rather than a law of thought, and hence "empirical" rather than "a priori"' (Rothbard, 1957, p. 314-320).
30. Rothbard, founding himself on Aristotle and St Thomas Aquinas, describes the difference between humans and other living species: 'that is the possession of reason which distinguished man from the animals and which enables him to act deliberately in view of the consciously apprehended end and raises him above the level of purely instinctive behaviour' (Copleston, quoted by Rothbard, 1982, p. 5)
31. '... man's reason [is able] to understand and arrive at the laws, physical and ethical, of the natural order ... There is a systematic order of natural laws open to discovery by man's reason' (Rothbard, 1982, p. 3-4). 'Reason is man's instrument of knowledge and of his very survival; the use and expansion of his mind, the acquisition of knowledge about what is best for him and how he can achieve it, is the uniquely human method of existence and of achievement' (Copleston, quoted by Rothbard, 1982, p. 30)
32. 'The individual man, in introspection of the fact of his own consciousness... discovers the natural fact of his mind's command over his body and its actions: that is, of his natural ownership over his self' (Rothbard, 1982, p. 31).
33. 'The positive theory of liberty then becomes an analysis of what can be considered property rights and therefore what can be considered crimes' (Rothbard, 1982. p. VI).
34. '... there is one crucially important power inherent in the nature of the State apparatus. All other persons and groups in society (except for acknowledged and sporadic criminals such as thieves and bank robbers) obtain their income voluntarily: either by selling goods and services to the consuming public, or by voluntary gift (e.g. membership in a club or association, bequest, or inheritance). Only the State obtains its revenue by coercion, by threatening dire penalty should the income not be forthcoming ... If then, taxation is compulsory, and is therefore indistinguishable from theft, it follows that the State, which subsists on taxation, is a vast criminal organization, far more formidable and successful than any 'private' Mafia in history' (Rothbard, 1982, p. 162; 166).
35. Analogously to *For a New Liberty* (1973b), Rothbard uses economic analysis in *The Ethics of Liberty* (1982) to show that the state is less efficient than private enterprise: 'All of the services commonly thought to require the State – from the coining of money to police protection to the development of law in defence of the rights of person and property – can be and have been supplied far more efficiently, and certainly more morally, by private persons' (Rothbard, 1982, p. 187). From the point of view of efficiency the consumer will always be worse treated by the state than by private enterprise but with *The Ethics of Liberty* the main argument against the state is elsewhere.
36. Natural law 'elucidates what is best for man – what ends man should pursue that are most harmonious with, and best tend to fulfil his nature' (Rothbard, 1982, p. 10). It shows clearly how to move forward to self accomplishment and defines objective ethics: 'goodness or badness can be determined by what fulfils or thwarts what is best for man's nature ... In a significant sense, then, natural law provides man with a 'science of happiness' with the paths which will lead to his real happiness' (ibid., p. 10).
37. '... there is in fact an objective moral order within the range of human intelligence, to which human societies are bound in conscience to conform and upon which the peace and happiness of personal, national and international life depends ... This is the foundation of what we call ethics, or natural law ... Demonstrating that this or that action tends to man's

real happiness, and therefore very justly concluding that the performance of it is a part of the law of nature; or, on the other hand, that this or that action is destruction of man's real happiness, and therefore that the law of nature forbids it' (Kenealy and Blackstone quoted by Rothbard, 1982, p. 11).

38. Bramoullé ('Apriorisme et faillibilisme: en défense de Rothbard contre Popper', 1995) sees in this extension of the scope of rationality a split between an Aristotelian (Rothbard) and a Kantian (Mises) apriorism. The anteriority of the mental categories of causality on the structures of reality opposes the Aristotelian vision of the mind's reproduction of ontological categories, independent of the knowledgeable subject. In the same way, Barry Smith ('Aristotle, Menger, Mises: An Essay in the Metaphysics of Economics', 1990), writes of the difference between an 'impositive' approach (Hume, Kant) and a 'reflexive' (Aristotle) approach to Apriorism. On this same question, see also Selgin (*Praxeology and Understanding: An Understanding of the Controversy in Austrian Economics*, 1982), Cubbedu (*The Philosophy of the Austrian School*, 1993), and Aimar ('Ethique versus coordination? Une controverse autrichienne soulevée par Rothbard', 1999a).

39. The question is if real, true values are respected by all, how exchange can take place and the market emerge (being the expression of a structure of interpersonal exchange). The answer is that preferences expressed by an exchange are not simply a function of differences in natural values but also of inequality of endowments and situations. Uniform values would mean identical individual preferences only with equality of revenue and symmetry of conditions of action.

40. It is only in this restricted way (that each individual's expectations must turn out correctly) that Rothbard strangely assimilates the Hayekian theme of coordination of plans with final, static and fictitious equilibrium.

PART 3

Applications and Debates

Introduction

Having examined the foundations of catallactic theory, we now come to consider a certain number of applications. The neo-Austrians reflected on many aspects of economic and political systems. Distinguishing between information and knowledge opened two debates on the principles of the cognitive organisation of the economy.

The first of these debates concerns Marxist Socialism, the question being the following: in a collectivist regime, can the necessary economic calculation for organising production exist? In other words, is it possible to socially produce information, separately from the market price system? Many socialist authors have tried to answer 'yes' to this question. The neo-Austrian theorists, basing themselves on the teachings of subjectivism, have concluded on the impossibility or at any rate the inefficacy of alternative methods of economic calculation to the market (Chapter 7).

The second debate is on the business cycle in market economy. At the centre of this is the question of information conveyed by money prices. According to authors such as Mises and Hayek, fluctuations in market economy cannot be interpreted through actors' mutual perfect knowledge; this type of hypothesis should be abandoned to be able to understand the way agents' ignorance can result in general breakdown of coordination. This is where money finds its most important role, the Austrians placing the problem of monetary interventionism at the heart of any explanation of the cycle through its influence on the coherence of relative prices and productive activities (Chapter 8).

Finally comes the construction of neo-Austrian welfare economics. This last stage, undoubtedly original to the inheritors of Mises's theories, arrives at the crossroads of the themes of division of knowledge and temporal ignorance. Studying the various steps in its construction and workings will particularly show up its problems with asserting normativity in the Austrian economic problematic (Chapter 9).

7. The Debate on Collectivism

From 1848 to World War 1, the growing success of socialist ideas in public opinion provoked a series of reflections on the theoretical principles of the functioning of a socialist economy. Marx and Engels, paradoxically hardly participated in this debate, their only written references to the socialist project appearing in the *Manifesto of the Communist Party* (1848), *Critique of the Gotha Program* (1875/1890-91) and the *Anti-Dühring* (1878).

Marx and Engels' position can be summed up thus: communist society, the end of History, would mean the end of the State and disappearance of scarcity, but there first needed to be a transitional stage called 'socialism' or 'first phase of communist society'. This would be established by a proletarian revolution to end capitalism and would be centred around three basic economic principles: nationalization of the means of production, thus removing the market of productive factors; planning, the basic socialist method; and lastly that this idea of planning should go hand in hand with the abolition of market value and of monetary calculation.

The abolition of monetary calculation almost immediately raised questions as to the possibility of such a collectivist economy functioning. In one famous passage, Gossen, a precursor of marginalism, considers that: 'the central authority, proposed by the communists, for the distribution of the various tasks and their reward, would very soon find that it had taken on a job the solution of which far surpasses the abilities of individual men' (Gossen, *Entwicklung der Gesetze des Menschlichen* Verkehrs, 1854). Pierson, ('The Problem of Value in the Socialist Society', 1902) in reacting to Kautsky's ideas (*Delft Speech*, 1902), was among the first to carry out a systematic examination of the themes of Marxist socialism. He extends Gossen's analysis in observing that absence of money prices prevents not only economic calculation but also measuring planning results.

Pareto (*Manual of Political Economy,* 1906) and then Barone ('The Ministry of Production in the Collectivist State', 1908) mathematically expressed the size of the problem of consciously building a coherent price system as a guide to production. Barone, taking a Walrasian point of view, claimed that the problem of socialist rationality was of the same type of that of general economic equilibrium. 'The Ministry of Production' would play the role of the auctioneer, solving a system of simultaneous equations and replacing the market system by Walras's system of tatonnement. Equilibrium prices, which

Barone describes as relations of equivalence, would establish themselves through a system of trial and error. Socialism became theoretically possible from this neoclassical viewpoint but the question remained of whether it was possible in practice.

The Russian Bolshevik revolution of 1917 and the risks of its contagion to the rest of Europe revitalised the issue and considerably raised its stakes. A vehement debate broke out between economists for and against socialism which Ludwig von Mises opened with his 1920 'Economic Calculation in the Socialist Commonwealth',[1] a thunderclap; all following controversies on the subject have simply been direct or indirect discussions of its themes.

According to Mises, an economic system requires economic calculation to function concretely, thus needing categories of price and money. As we saw in Chapter 3, these categories require interpersonal exchange to exist, that is, the market. Without this, the necessary economic calculation cannot be made, so a socialist economy in all logic cannot exist. This reflection on the formation and role of money price allowed Mises to establish symmetry between rationality and capitalism on an economic scale. As he summed up later in *Epistemological Problems of Economics*, 'Inasmuch as money prices of the means of production can be determined only in a social order in which they are privately owned, the proof of the impracticability of socialism necessarily follows' (1933, p. 113). Socialism therefore can only result in 'chaos' (1).[2]

The controversy considerably intensified in the 1930s, based on Mises' arguments and returned to in *Socialism* (1922),[3] with the publication of Dickinson's article 'Price Formation in a Socialist Community' (1933a).[4] This important contribution took the debate in a new direction, Dickinson firstly discussing the possibility of finding an alternative to market-based economic calculations and secondly ways of putting it into practice. He was thus asserting the theoretical possibilities of socialism and also strongly suggesting its feasibility.

Other authors took up this debate to variously criticize, extend or reformulate it, particularly around the question of the feasibility of alternative economic calculation to that provided by the market. Hayek ('Nature and History of the Problem', 1935a; 'The Current State of the Argument', 1935b; 'Socialist Calculation, The Competitive Solution', 1940) and Lange's opposing views ('On the Economic Theory of Socialism', 1938) led to questions of quantity and managing the evolution of information. Hayek's main criticism of Dickinson's view concerning the feasibility of socialism is based on the quantity of information that has to be managed by the Plan. Lange's alternative contribution led Hayek to abandon this idea and adopt the thesis of the market's superior capacity over socialism to acquire knowledge and adapt to change (2).

There is another dimension to this debate, through the question of the nature of information and the constraints of its production. Hayek had already presented an argument on the quality of information in various critiques of

Dickinson and Lange and based on certain elements of Mises' from the 1920s, stressing the institutional aspects of economic systems. Knowledge production and its transmission in the price system put the entrepreneur back in the central role of economic efficiency. This reflection, that Lavoie revisited in the 1980s ('A Critique of the Standard Account of the Socialist Calculation Debate', 1981; *National Economic Planning: What is Left?* 1985a; *Rivalry and Central Planning, The Socialist Calculation Debate Reconsidered*, 1985b) put private ownership of the means of production back in the centre of the debate and resulted in a epistemic view of collectivism's problems (3).

The contributions of Rothbard and his followers concerned another argument, around Mises' idea of the impossibility of a collectivist economy. They refused to place knowledge at the heart of the problem and advanced the idea that a collectivist economy cannot work because of the systematic impossibility of centralized information production (4).

1. THE 'IRRATIONALITY' OF COLLECTIVISM

In the aftermath of World War I there reigned a certain consensus in the Soviet and Marxist camps (Bukharin and Preobazhensky, *The ABC of Communism*, 1919; Neurath, *Durch die Kriegwirtschaft zur Naturalwirtschaft*, 1919; Bauer, *Der Weg sum Sozialismus*, 1919; Brutzkus, *Economic Planning in Soviet Russia*, 1921) on establishing the idea that the possibility of monetary calculation was subordinate to the existence of a capitalist structure of society. Bukharin and Preobazhensky (*The ABC of Communism*, 1919) were loyal to Marx and Engels, considering that socialism meant the disappearance of market and money categories. In Neurath's view, categories of value and price could easily be replaced by a calculation in kind. Profit-seeking and interest rates simply meant disorder and crisis. The war economy had shown the possibility of alternative accounting systems, based on *in natura* planning of production, with the objective of satisfying 'physical' needs. In sharp contrast, Mises ('Economic Calculation in the Socialist Commonwealth', 1920) states the possibility that socialist economic organisation is founded on an intellectual mistake.

1.1 Monetary Calculation

Mises agreed with the Marxists when they announced the abolition of money calculation methods along with the disappearance of the market. But most did not understand that this meant stopping any hope of rationally organising production, as price comparisons guided producers in their resources orientation, prices being the tools of economic calculation and the rationale behind the economic system.

As Wieser had already remarked (*Natural Value*, 1889) and Böhm-Bawerk (*Karl Marx and the Close of his System*, 1886; *Positive Theory of Capital*, 1889), not even a slightly developed economic system can manage without categories of economic calculation in order to direct resources.[5] So the techniques of resource allocation in a socialist economy have to be defined.

One possible answer could be the labour theory of value, which Marx passionately defended. But Mises remarked, like Gossen and Pierson[6] before him, that labour is not a value criterion, as it 'is not a uniform and homogeneous quantity'; and besides which, it does not include a relationship with scarcity: 'An article in which more raw material is used can never be reckoned of equal value with one in which less is used' (1920, p. 94; 95).

He consequently rejected the labour theory of value, explaining that price formation is subject to two conditions.

Firstly, an interpersonal comparison of values would seem to require a homogenizing instrument. This is obviously money's role; money calculation enables the valuation by a single good of various individual gains and costs. As this is the necessary instrument of the cardinalization of values, it represents in a modern economic structure,

> a guide through the oppressive plenitude of economic potentialities. It enables us to extend to all goods of a higher order the judgment of value, which is bound up with and clearly evident in, the case of goods ready for consumption, or at best of production-goods of the lowest order. It renders their value capable of computation and thereby gives us the primary basis for all economic operations with goods of a higher order. Without it, all production involving processes stretching well back in time and all the longer roundabout processes of capitalist production would be gropings in the dark (Mises, 1920, p. 101).

Secondly, price formation presupposes the existence of an exchange process. Prices are the result of effective exchange, the reverse to the Walrasian view of it. Through these two elements, Mises was led to identify the notion of economic rationality with the capitalist market.

1.2 The 'Chaos' of Collectivism

Depending on which view his followers adopt, there are different types of socialism. Mises distinguishes in *Socialism* (1922) between state, Christian, military, guild and other types. There may also be, within each one, varying degrees of resource control and distribution. However, any type of socialism is basically defined by the principle of nationalization of the means of production[7] and the fact remains that production, by definition, escapes the process of evaluation by private agents: '... no production-good will ever become the object of exchange, it will be impossible to determine its monetary value.

Money could never fill in a socialist state the role it fills in a competitive society in determining the value of production-goods' (Mises, 1920, p. 92). The absence of the market and therefore of production factor price prevents cost and profit estimations.

Of course, in a socialist system, consumer goods would still be exchanged between individuals, as it is unlikely the planning authority would distribute the types and quantities of goods each individual desires. Agents therefore would spontaneously exchange received goods among themselves and in Mises' view, one particular good would probably appear as a means of exchange,[8] giving birth to prices:

> The administration may know exactly what goods are most urgently needed. But in so doing, it has only found what is, in fact, but one of the two necessary prerequisites for economic calculation. In the nature of the case it must, however, dispense with the other – the valuation of the means of production (ibid., p. 107).

So a socialist economy's resources can be directed to where they make the most gains in satisfaction. However, those allocations must be costed in comparison to the operation's gains, which a planner cannot do. Socialism therefore cannot rationally allocate resources; it logically leads to 'chaos'.[9]

In Mises' view, the technical and economic problems are therefore very different from each other; science can doubtless provide the material means to achieve any given result but where these means are heterogeneous (factor substitutability) and nonspecific,[10] it is important to determine which is the production method bringing lowest costs: 'technical calculation is not enough to realize the "degree of general and teleological expediency" of an event; that it can only grade individual events according to their significance; but that it can never guide us in those judgments which are demanded by the economic complex as a whole' (Mises, 1920, p. 130). At the same time, the problem is not at all one of individual motivation or quality of the socialist manager; the socialist commonwealth may be filled with competent socialists with collective welfare as their primary goal, its problem will still be the absence of a system to rationally indicate the direction of production planning.

The market guarantees the existence of an economic system as it is the condition of economic and monetary calculation; it is actors' only access to a coherent information system. Economic calculation being the rational base of any economic system, Mises concludes logically that any socialist system founded on state control of the means of production is doomed to failure:

> The paradox of 'planning' is that it cannot plan, because of the absence of economic calculation. What is called a planned economy is no economy at all. It is just a system of groping about in the dark. There is no question of a rational choice of means for the best possible attainment of the ultimate ends sought. What is called conscious planning is precisely the elimination of conscious purposive action (1966, p. 700-701).

1.3 A Procedural Conception of Economic Systems

This argument of Mises shows perhaps the most clearly of all his conception of economic problems as being informational. The non-functioning of collectivism is explained by the disappearance of the network of relative price information. The prevalent idea is of a procedural conception of economic systems: the market system's role is to formulate and distribute information. A planned economy would mean the total disappearance of these communications structures.

We can thus easily understand that Mises' thinking was that socialism was completely unfeasible:

> As soon as one gives up the conception of a freely established monetary price for goods of a higher order, rational production becomes completely impossible. Every step that takes us away from private ownership of the means of production and from the use of money also takes us away from rational economics (1920, p. 104).

Mises' argument here shows up the systemic side of the problems of information production, yet it does not clearly show if socialism is impossible because of a technical or an epistemic problem.

If it were technical, there would be no means other than the factor market to make economic calculations (or simply a cardinalist method) to enable organisation of production. So calculation would depend on the private ownership of the means of production.

If an epistemic problem, any alternative price system to that of the market could not, by definition, be linked to individual subjectivities in the same way as to capitalism and so would not benefit from the same heuristic contents. Mises' argument being interpretable in either way, the neo-Austrians participating in the debate were to alternate between both.

2. NEO-AUSTRIAN THEORY VERSUS GENERAL ECONOMIC EQUILIBRIUM

The debate around collectivism was rekindled in the 1930s, a number of authors discussing, criticising or reformulating Mises' but only in the framework that he suggested: the absolute need to determine prices for the factors of production.[11] For Mises, logically, 'Where there is no free market, there is no pricing mechanism; without a pricing mechanism, there is no economic calculation.' (1920, p. 111). Socialist literature had no quarrel with the last part of this equation, but what was contested was the idea of an organic link between the market of production factors and their prices.

This last point was principally argued over by three main protagonists. After Dickinson, Hayek and Lange in turn made their mark on the discussion.

These controversies were to shed light on the specificity of Austrian analyses compared with general economic equilibrium theory and also mark their antagonism to Marxist ideas.[12]

2.1 The Quantity of Information

In Mises' opinion, there was no way of passing from market-based monetary calculation to an alternative accounting system in any kind of developed economy. The factors market

> is the only method available to a society based on the division of labor when it wants to compare the input and the output of its production processes. All attempts on the part of the apologists of socialism to concoct a scheme for 'a socialist economic calculation' must, therefore, necessarily fail (1933, p. 158).

In *Human Action* (1966) he stuck to this viewpoint:

> The system of economic calculation in monetary terms is conditioned by certain social institutions. It can operate only in an institutional setting of the division of labor and private ownership of the means of production in which goods and services of all orders are bought and sold against a generally used medium of exchange, i.e. money (1966, p. 229).

It is Dickinson's contribution ('Price Formation in a Socialist Community', 1933a) which may be considered as the first attempt to counter Mises' idea:[13] 'It is the object of this article to refute the first of Mises' criticisms of socialism and to show that a rational pricing of instrumental goods is at least theoretically possible in a socialistic economy' (1933a, p. 238).

He claimed it was possible to price capital goods based on a free market of consumer goods:[14] 'Consumption goods are sold at a price to consumers by the community, which distributes purchasing power to consumers in ways to be hereafter defined' (ibid., 239).

He had already noted in 'The Economic Basis of Socialism' (1930),

> The device of issuing money to potential consumers and putting a price upon goods high enough to choke off demand in excess of available supply is the best way hitherto discovered of giving everybody the maximum of free choice in consumption. It has the additional advantage of indicating, by high prices, those goods the increased production of which would satisfy most needs or the most insistent needs (1930, p. 562-563).

These consumer goods would be supplied by 'selling agencies' independent of production units. Balancing supplies of stocks and demand would result in a relative price structure of consumer goods, with managers being responsible for proper stock control to meet everyday needs:

> The selling agency will sell on the basis of what the market will bear, raising price when stocks fall short and lowering it when they accumulate. In this way the statistical service of the sales agency will be able to draw up a demand schedule for each type of goods sold (1933a, p. 239-240).

These demand schedules are communicated upstream to the relevant production units, who in turn define their own needs in intermediary goods: 'On the basis of the orders sent back by selling agencies the manufacturing organisations will be able to draw up demand schedules for their products' (ibid., p. 240). Demand for ultimate factors is thus determined at the beginning of the chain.

This is the stage at which the Planning Authority, or as Dickinson called it the SEC (Supreme Economic Council) centralizes information on demand functions of ultimate factors and fits it with information already in its possession about the supply function of these factors. The SEC, according to Dickinson, would then calculate equilibrium prices for ultimate factors based on their supply and demand: 'The quantities of these ultimate factors are known. We will assume provisionally that they are fixed. Then for each factor the SEC will fix prices which, according to the demand schedule, will just ensure its full employment' (ibid., p. 241). Through these prices, the SEC is able to calculate in the same way all the enterprises' cost functions as well as quantities of production factors and their equilibrium prices. From this viewpoint:

> The productive organisations will slow down or stop the production of those goods where demand price is below the cost price and will expand the production of those goods whose demand price is above cost ... Ultimately, by a process of successive approximation, a true economic price for each factor will be established, which can then be used for costing purposes wherever the factor is used. In this way the costs are imputed from the demand for the marginal product and then deputed back to all other products. Also, factors of production will be allotted to different uses so as to bring in equal returns (ibid., p. 241).

Dickinson is aware that the harmonisation process can be complicated by changes in consumer demand. However, his arguments state that this uncertainty is in fact a Knightian-type risk, treatable statistically: 'The socialist community might for a time make use in the same way of the "hunch" or "flair" of the trained manager of industry, but it should in time evolve a statistical treatment of risk based on the frequency distribution of sales and price changes' (ibid., p. 245). He adds

> There is the problem of gains and losses due to unforeseen fluctuations of demand. It would be best to price goods at a small margin above cost and to apply the surplus to an equalisation fund for each undertaking. All surpluses over a certain percentage of annual turnover should revert to the community as a whole (ibid., p. 246).

This type of procedure can lead to the use of a cardinal method to organise production without a factor market. Centralizing all information gathered from production structures in the Plan gives it the data to mathematically fix equilibrium prices. All prices would be fixed by this: 'Selling price must equal the sum of the prices of the factors of production' (ibid., p. 242). All this would allow a rational, socialist, economic structure, as could be described by the system of general economic equilibrium. Dickinson was able to declare 'Under capitalism, demand schedules are apt to exist in the realm of faith rather than in that of works, but within the glass wall of the socialistic economy they would become much easier to draw up' (ibid., p. 240). Economic orthodoxy thus completely respected, as 'The beautiful systems of economic equilibrium described by Böhm-Bawerk, Wieser, Marshall and Cassel are not descriptions of society as it is but prophetic visions of a socialist economy of the future' (ibid., p. 247). He returns to this idea a number of times which would strongly suggest that for him, the socialist economy is the most able, from an informational point of view, to reconcile economic systems' models and practices.

Dickinson's cleverly-made work, which would appear to be along similar lines to some of Barone's, seems to respond well to Mises' argument. One could criticize the fact that with Dickinson, individual agents would not be able to evaluate factors, unlike in the free market and so it would be impossible to subjectively plan gain and cost in planned production. This, however, would not be in line with his own analytical framework, which is the result of a particular reading of Mises. Dickinson's primary goal was to achieve a system of relative production prices which would, independently of the market, ensure coordination of production plans. In the end, it would not matter whether we know if this price system conforms to individual preferences; it is more important to state the socialist system's capacity to construct an indicator for mounting successful production plans.

Hayek understandably does not use the argument of subjectivism to contradict Dickinson[15] in his critical answer 'Nature and History of the Problem' (1935a) and 'The Present State of the Debate' (1935b); on the contrary, he finds the theory of Dickinson's propositions justified. The transfer of information between enterprises to the SEC would lead to the establishment of factor prices, thus enabling production. Hayek was much more critical from a practical point of view, claiming information management systems would be much too unwieldy to work, owing to the amount of demand functions to be processed:

> it must be admitted that this is not an impossibility in the sense that it is logically contradictory. But to argue that a determination of prices by such a procedure being logically conceivable in any way invalidates the contention that it is not a possible solution, only proves that the real nature of the problem has not been perceived. It is only necessary to attempt to visualize what the application of this method would

> imply in practice in order to rule it out as humanly impracticable and impossible (1935b, p. 207-208).

The amount of data needed to rationally plan is too much for a planning centre. Hayek concludes that while socialism is logically conceivable, it is completely impracticable: 'It is probably evident that the mere assembly of these data is a task beyond human capacity. Yet if the centrally run society were to work as efficiently as the competitive society, which as it were decentralizes the task of collecting them, they would have to be present' (ibid., p. 211).

Finally then, Hayek found Mises was right in his view of the impossibility of socialism. However, this is not a theoretical impossibility, as it is possible to construct a coherent relative pricing system for production factors without the market. The problem is essentially a practical one, stemming from the amount of information to be managed. This is the problem that Lange proposed to reduce.

2.2 The Change in Information

Oskar Lange 'On the Economic Theory of Socialism' (1938)[16] was to add to Hayek's thesis of the theoretical possibility of socialism but opposed his idea of its practical impossibility. He questions the amount of equations that Hayek claims the Plan would have to calculate to coordinate production plans; he offers an alternative point of view to Dickinson's model, using Walrasian tatonnement.

Lange follows Dickinson's idea which states that production factor prices can be formed independently of the free market. Adhering to a tradition started by Wicksteed, *The Common Sense of Political Economy* (1910), he sees two price dimensions: exchange relationships and indicators of alternative choice (parametric prices).[17] Only the second criterion is needed to determine prices for production goods guaranteeing the success of production plans:

> The economic problem is a problem of choice between alternatives. To solve the problem three data are needed: 1) a preference scale which guides the acts of choice; 2) knowledge of the 'terms on which alternatives are offered'; and 3) knowledge of the amount of resources available. Those three data being given, the problem of choice is soluble (Lange, 1938, p. 60).

Lange considers these choice indexes to be not only theoretically sound but practicable, thanks to an exchange of information between the socialist enterprise and the planner, called the Central Planning Board.

He starts from the same hypotheses as Mises and Dickinson about freedom of choice in work and free market of consumer goods in socialism; the market provides the central planners with information in consumer preferences.

Productive factor prices are formed in the following way: the Central Planning Board suggests a starting price to the nationalized enterprises, chosen by chance. The enterprise's directors behave just like their capitalist counterparts wishing to maximize profits; they must lower costs as much as possible by the right combination of production factors and fix production volumes following the rule of equalizing the marginal cost to the price. Each firm then sends the Central Planning Board (CP) information concerning the quantities they can produce at the proposed price and the factors they need. CP then compares the quantities offered with demand and sends the enterprises a new series of prices supposed to permit better adjustment. The enterprises recalculate based on the new prices and send the new information back to CP, which in turn – and so on. By this trial and error, or iterative, process of convergence, equilibrium production prices emerge; the CP plays here the role of the 'town crier' from Walras's system.

Lange claims that the tatonnement solution to determination of prices in a collectivist economy allows Central Planning Board to simulate the market, which gives his system its name of market socialism.[18] It is the decentralization of adjustment operations which allows socialism to become possible on a practical and not just a theoretical level. This representation avoids the traps of the mathematical response and its information-heavy treatment by the central authority, as the greatest part of it is decentralized, carried out by the production units.

He considers that apart from the fact that this system avoids the social injustice produced by the market, as any parasitical revenues generated by private ownership of the means of production disappear, it is economically more efficient. Centralized procedures of tatonnement allow quicker coordination than the market. Besides which, in the real world laissez-faire capitalism being some way from a perfect model of competition, rationalizing economic structure based on parametric prices allows the economy to reach Paretian optimum.

In his last specific contribution to the debate, 'Socialist Calculation, The Competitive Solution' (1940), Hayek did not try to contradict Lange on the terrain of the quantity of information, seemingly letting him carry the field. Obviously, he does not question the economic pertinence of the idea of parametric prices, any more than he does in his critique of Dickinson's model, even though it reveals much more of a technical than a subjectivist side to the problem of economic calculation.[19] Where Hayek essentially refuted the economic relevance of Lange's model was in the question concerning dynamics of information.

Lange's proposals for a socialist market led Hayek from the argument of quantity of information to that of managing its evolution. The problem of gathering and treating information is added to by its transformation over time; the continual evolution of individuals' preference structures would oblige the centre to permanently adjust its plans to maintain equilibrium. In

Hayek's eyes, the need for continual adaptation and flexibility would ruin for good any hopes not of the practicability of socialism, but of its efficiency.

In fact Hayek extends and develops many of his ideas from some of Mises' views on the static approach. Mises was already claiming in 1920 that

> The static state can dispense with economic calculation. For here the same events in economic life are ever recurring; and if we assume that the first disposition of the static socialist community follows in the basis of the final state of the competitive economy, we might at all events conceive of a socialist production system which is rationally controlled from an economic point of view. But this is only conceptually possible (1920, p. 109).

In *Socialism* (1922), he was even more precise, declaring:

> Where everything remains unchanged, it is not very difficult to ascertain what becomes used up, and what must therefore be put aside to replace it. Under changing conditions, it is quite otherwise. Here the direction of production and the different processes involved are continually changing. Here it is not enough to replace the used-up plant and the semi-manufactured products consumed in similar qualities and quantities: others – better or at least better corresponding to the new conditions of demand – have to take their place (1922, p. 177-178).[20]

Hayek similarly claims that Lange's construction is fundamentally faulty as it is completely dependent on Walras's static model. The Walras-Lange tatonnement can only lead to convergence if data does not change during the period of tatonnement:

> With given and constant data such a state of equilibrium could indeed be approached by the method of trial and error. But this is far from being the situation in the real world, where constant change is the rule. Whether and how far anything approaching the desirable equilibrium is ever reached depends entirely on the speed with which the adjustments can be made (1940, p. 188).

Real time and consecutive changes to evaluations would prevent the plans from being carried out.

Hayek had already used this type of argument to reinforce his critique in his discussion of Dickinson's propositions. Separately from the question of the quantity of information, the fact that planning 'has to deal with day-to-day changes of every sort' (Hayek, 1935a, p. 22) poses a major problem to collectivism. The system being attached to a consumer goods market, the question of incessant change of individuals' preference structures has to be integrated, which will of course permanently modify the functions of demand, the central planning having to permanently integrate this transformation of data:

> … it is inadmissible to assume that the changes in relative values brought about by the transition from capitalism to socialism would be of a minor order, so permitting the prices of the pre-existing capitalistic system to be used as a starting-point, and making it possible to avoid a complete re-arrangement of the price-system … Almost every change of any single price would make changes of hundreds of other prices necessary and most of these other changes would by no means be proportional but would be affected by the different degrees of elasticity of demand, by the possibilities of substitution and other changes in the method of production (Hayek, 1935b, p. 213-214).

Hayek's argument on the dynamics of information only becomes systemic and forms the core of his critique when he discusses Lange's model. Hayek accepts the idea of the theoretical validity of the socialist economy. He even goes a step further and implicitly accepts Lange's idea of its feasibility. But he asserts its inefficiency compared to capitalism in terms of its dynamic, adaptive possibilities. Hayek is perfectly aware that managing unexpected change is a problem for capitalism too; with the market system, equilibrium is never reached, simply because of the logic of permanent change in human action. Seen from this point of view: 'The practical problem is not whether a particular method would eventually lead to a hypothetical equilibrium' (1940, p. 188).

However, a comparative analysis of the systems must be made, determining the

> method [which] will secure the more rapid and complete adjustment to the daily changing conditions in different places and different industries. How great the difference in this respect would be between a method where prices are currently agreed from above is, of course, a matter of practical judgment. But I find it difficult to believe that anybody would doubt that in this respect the inferiority of the second method would be very great indeed (ibid., p. 188).

So the central economic problem is not finding an impossible general equilibrium but to encourage continuous adjustment of price structures to changes in data, the probabilities of which cannot calculated in advance. So Hayek notes that:

> … the fundamental question is whether it is possible under the complex conditions of a large modern society for such a central authority to carry out the implications of any such scale of values with a reasonable degree of accuracy, with a degree of success equalling or approaching the results of competitive capitalism (1935a, p. 17).

He then remarks

> We should not expect equilibrium to exist unless all external change had ceased. The essential thing about the present economic system is that it does react to some

> extent to all those small changes and differences which would have to be deliberately disregarded under the system we are discussing if the calculations were to be manageable (1935b, p. 212-213).

Walrasian-type tatonnement can only be inferior to a process which immediately integrates incessant changes into price, through the entrepreneurs discovering profit opportunities. Lange's model can only work properly in a statics mode. Because of the much greater technical difficulty of continual adaptation to new information, socialism, practicable though it may be, is shown to be less efficient than capitalism.

The nature of the debate thus turned towards questions of dynamics and this led socialist reflection down new paths. A number of socialist authors, from Sweezy, *Socialism* (1949) to Brus and Laski, *From Marx to the Market: Socialism in Search of an Economic System* (1989) reacted to the challenge of managing unexpected changes in a socialist system of rational and coherent pricing by getting rid of the free consumer goods market which reflects changes in consumer preference structures. It is in fact Dobb (see bibliography) who was the first to question the sovereignty of consumer choice and instead proposed imposing social preferences which would be defined by the Plan. In his own contribution, Lange, echoing his critics, constructed a second version of his model with no consumer freedom or choice of profession.

In this second version, Lange's system no longer connects to a consumer market and therefore unshackles the process of convergence from actors' changing desires. Following Dobb's idea, fickle individual consumer preferences give way to stable collective preferences defined by the Plan. Lange does mention, however that he considers this choice to be second best; like Lerner somewhat earlier in 'Economic Theory and Socialist Economy' (1934), he refuses to recommend this concept for practice, so lacking it is in respect of subjective consumers' desires:

> By demonstrating the economic consistency and workability of a socialist economy with free choice neither in consumption nor in occupation, but directed rather by a preference scale imposed by the bureaucrats in the Central Planning Board, we do not mean, of course, to recommend such a system. Mr Lerner has sufficiently shown the undemocratic character of such a system and its incompatibility with the ideals of the socialist movement (1938, p. 95).

But he took good care to note the exclusively ethical dimension of his critique. He claims that this kind of 'bureaucratic socialism' is in fact practicable, clearly being in this case a form of economic rationalism.

These ideas of 'bureaucratic socialism' emerging in the 1930s are a good illustration of the real nature of the debate taking place at that period between Hayek and the socialist authors. It does not matter whether factor price was linked to individual subjectivities, what does matter is whether factor prices can be calculated, independently of the market, to coordinate production plans. This disappearance of the consumer market does not leave the economic rationale open to question, as the essential problem is to find a coherent price system for the successful organisation of production plans.

Dobb does not consider the idea of subjectivism to be enough of a value to count as data. His concern is to free planning from subjectivism which he sees as an artificial constraint to building a socialist system; he considers that consumer sovereignty implies forming a structure of private information which would counter the Plan's public information and disorient planned resource allocation. It is true that Hayek does not base his own critique of socialism on abandoning these subjectivist variables. It is rather based on the idea that planned economies neglect any factors of change other than agents' values. Of course, 'One of the unpredictable variables would be eliminated and in this way the frequency of the necessary readjustments would be somewhat reduced' (Hayek, 1935b, p. 216), but it would not get rid of planning difficulties:

> The changes in tastes are by no means the only, and perhaps not even the most important, changes that cannot be foreseen. Changes in the weather, changes in the numbers or the state of health of the population, a breakdown of machinery, the discovery or the sudden exhaustion of a mineral deposit, and hundreds or other constant changes will make it no less necessary for him to reconstruct his plans from moment to moment (ibid. p. 217).

2.3 Computing and Mathematics: Linear Programming

The first era of the debate on collectivism closed with Hayek's contribution dating from 1940. His critique of Lange on the question of changes in information should have dashed forever any hopes, not of socialism's feasibility, but of its comparative efficiency. One quick glance at the literature, however, is enough to see this is not the case. Most of the commentators (Schumpeter, *Capitalism, Socialism and Democracy*, 1942; Bergson, *Socialist Economics*, 1948; Ward, *The Socialist Economy: A Study of Organizational Alternatives*, 1967, and so on) believe Lange's market socialism is the scientific demonstration not just of socialism's feasibility but of its efficiency. So Schumpeter, reviewing the debate in 1942 declares: 'Can socialism work? Of course it can. No doubt is possible about that once we assume, first, that the requisite stage of industrial development has been reached and, second, that transitional problems can be successfully resolved' (1942, p. 167).

Once again, this favourable view of the Lange tendency of socialist models is because of a 'technical' approach to the debate. The growing interest in the post-war years in dynamics economics could have meant more interest in Hayek's ideas were it not for the considerable counterweight of computing systems, which went a long way to minimising the cost of gathering and treating information. This progress at first confirmed Schumpeter's prediction of the easier management of a socialist system (see 1942, p. 186). The most striking example of this is linear programming techniques, inspired by Kantorovitch (1959 and 1976), Dantzig and Wolfe (1961) and the school of Soviet mathematicians, notably Nemtchinov and Novojilov.

The aim of this work on optimal planning aided by computers without the help of the markets was to reconcile planning and efficiency[21] in a rationalization of socialist systems. Computers really started to contribute to socialist planning from the 1960s, so much so that many started to consider the traditional Austrian view of socialism's relative inefficiency as obsolete for good.

As Caldwell noted,

> Hayek's arguments about the difficulties of coming up with the necessary data have been challenged by each new generation of socialists, as first input-output analysis, then planometrics, then computable general equilibrium models, then the advent of supercomputers all promised finally to provide an instrument that could replace the market's price adjustment mechanism ('Hayek and Socialism', 1997, p. 1864).

Lange also participated in this thinking with various contributions (*Essays on Economic Planning*, 1960a, *Introduction to Economic Cybernetics*, 1965; 'The Computer and the Market', 1967). In this last article, he noted the problems of calculating equilibrium: 'Were I to rewrite my essay today my task would be much simpler. My answer to Hayek and Robbins would be: so what's the trouble? Let us put the simultaneous equations on an electronic computer and we shall obtain the solution in less than a second' (Lange, 1967, p. 158).

The first attempts rapidly showed the limits to these models' workings. Of course the rudimentary computers of the age were not actually up to the job, quite apart from which, sociological and especially epistemic issues appeared. There was first of all bureaucratic resistance as computers reduced management's discretionary powers (agency problems). There was also particularly another basic problem of the quality of information transmitted by a system of planned prices.

Analysing these problems leads us to a type of argument that both Hayek and Mises make in this debate but which seems to have been somewhat passed over by the literature of their time, which is the role of entrepreneurship and the particular nature of the information contained in prices. The studies carried out in the 1980s concerning the quality of knowledge brought about by prices put these questions centre-stage. This is where subjectivism comes back into the limelight.

3. THE NATURE OF KNOWLEDGE

It was Donald Lavoie who renewed the debate with this view ('A Critique of the Standard Account of the Socialist Calculation Debate', 1981; *National Economic Planning: What is Left?*, 1985a; *Rivalry and Central Planning, the Socialist Calculation Debate Reconsidered,* 1985b).[22] In particular he went into the question of the limits of a socialist system in producing and collectively using singular, tacit individual knowledge. He sheds an original light on some of Hayek's and Mises' ideas on the defence of market institutions. His analysis moves from the idea of a technical problem preventing the good workings of the planned economy to the argument of an epistemic constraint, defining the market as the best form of discovering exchange opportunities.

3.1 Tacit Knowledge

Hayek (1935b) had already realised that knowledge, rather than being unified, breaks down into two distinct parts.

Side by side with objective knowledge couched in and transmissible by whichever language, there is another type, harder to define, presented as know-how. Economically speaking, this part is essential, as '... much of the knowledge that is actually utilized is by no means "in existence" in this ready-made form. Most of it consists in a technique of thought which enables the individual engineer to find new solutions rapidly as soon as he is confronted with new constellations of circumstances' (Hayek, 1935b, p. 210-211).

In Lavoie's view, this epistemic problematic is contained in Hayek's themes dating from the 1950s. These developments, inspired by Polanyi's analyses (*The Logic of Liberty,* 1951; *Personal Knowledge, Towards a Post-Critical Philosophy*, 1962; *The Determinants of Social Action*, 1969) highlight the importance of tacit and non-formulable knowledge in social activities:

> ... much of the knowledge practically necessary for economic production cannot be articulated. Stated more positively, there are in fact two kinds of legitimate knowledge – not only articulate but also what Polanyi calls 'tacit knowledge' ... Such knowledge is dispersed among market participants. It is embedded in their various skills and specialities (1985a, p. 6; 59).

Centralized decision-making efficiency is dependent on authorities' capacity to gather information which is scattered throughout society. As part of this information is tacit, the inevitable question raises its head of central planners' ability to avail themselves of this information and to incorporate it into socialist prices.

Lavoie claims that the problem of the nature and quality of information contained in prices had been neglected too long. The issues at stake in collectivism go beyond any calculation of value of goods and coherence of production plans; they are more to do with the status of information expressed by planned prices. Mises' and Hayek's work should now be viewed under a different light.

3.2 Incentives

Mises had already noted in 'Economic Calculation in the Socialist Commonwealth' (1920) that:

> The motive force disappears with the exclusion of the material interests of private individuals, and if State and municipal enterprises thrive at all, they owe it to the taking over of 'management' from private enterprise, or to the fact that they are ever driven to reforms and innovations by the business men from whom they purchase their instruments of production and raw material (1920, p. 118).

In *Socialism*, he explained that profit cannot be artificially separated from the problem of economic calculation:

> For the motive force of the whole process which gives rise to market prices for the factors of production is the ceaseless search on the part of the capitalists and the entrepreneurs to maximize their profits by serving the consumers wishes. Without the striving of entrepreneurs (including the shareholders) for profit ... the successful functioning of the whole mechanism is not to be thought of. It is only the prospect of profit which directs production into those channels in which the demands of the consumer are best satisfied at least cost. If the prospect of profit disappears the mechanism of the market loses its mainspring, for it is only this prospect which sets it in motion and maintains it in operation. The market is thus the focal point of the capitalist order of society; it is the essence of Capitalism (1922, p. 119).

In *Nation, State and Economy*, he had already criticized the war economy's

> impairment of the initiative of entrepreneurs. Since they shared more heavily in losses than in profits, the incentive to undertake risky ventures was only slight. Many production possibilities remained unused in the second half of the war because entrepreneurs shied away from the risk bound up with new investments and with introducing new production methods (1919, p. 175).

This argument of incentives acquires a particularly interesting dimension when confronted with Lange's models. It is in this way that Hayek returns to Mises' original formulation of the link between economic calculation and private property in 'Socialist Calculation, The Competitive Solution' (1940), in implicitly rehabilitating the entrepreneur's role as a factor of the socialization of tacit knowledge. Although literature mainly ignored it, for Lavoie this rehabilitation was one of Hayek's best angles of attack. On this terrain:

> Although comments by both Hayek and Robbins about computational difficulties of the equation-solving approach were responsible for misleading interpretations of their arguments, in fact their main contributions were fully consistent with Mises' challenge and were similarly unanswered (Lavoie, 1981, p. 46).

In Lange's model, production activity includes an entrepreneurial aspect, as nationalized company directors have to behave in the same way as private sector directors seeking to maximize profits. The socialist managers have to balance production costs with sales prices. In the world of the market, however, only monetary gain motivates the entrepreneur. Competition drives him to discover the available information and to exploit any profit opportunities as fast as possible. He does his job only because he can make a profit at it. Lange, however, never examined the idea of socialist managers' incentive to adopt norms of efficiency, although he was conscious of the problem. He simply considered that 'The discussion of this argument belongs to the field of sociology rather than of economic theory' (Lange, 1938, p. 109), besides which, this could only be examined by comparative analysis with capitalism. He goes on to say that capitalism itself presents more and more bureaucratic, monopolistic and routine dominated tendencies, which call into question capitalist managers' incentives to work efficiently; the problem is thus similar to that of socialist managers. For him, capitalist structures as described by Mises and Hayek are nothing more than myths, and day-to-reality brings them face to face with 'bureaucratization of the economic life' (ibid., p. 109) and to what are today called agency problems.

According to Hayek, in Lavoie's reinterpretation, only competitive processes can unearth this information embedded in individuals' minds and thought patterns; individuals' profit-seeking activities release tacit knowledge into the price system. Put differently, the only way for the tacit knowledge in each mind to be socialized is through the system of bargaining, exchange and price formation. So the market does not only reveal individuals' preferences but their tacit knowledge too. It is obvious then that any change to the system of profit and exchange would be socially costly: if the idea of gain were to be partially affected or even to disappear, society's actors would be less and less motivated to release their tacit knowledge into the price system, thus underusing the community's cognitive capital. Incentives of competition and the will to seize rare resources to promote their own strategies encourage individuals to express their knowledge by their action:[23]

> The question, then, is not whether all problems of production and distribution can be rationally decided by one central authority but whether decisions and responsibility can be successfully left to competing individuals who are not owners or are

> otherwise directly interested in the means of production under their charge (Hayek, 1935b, p. 219).

The essential point, then, is the process of discovering profit opportunities in a capitalist economy, where the entrepreneur plays the crucial role of the individual element under competitive pressure, seeking out all means of maximizing income and lowering production costs. In the socialist system it is all different. Entrepreneurship disappears, linked as it is to profit-seeking. As we have already seen, competition plays a crucial role in Hayek's vision: it motivates the discovery of the best solutions for the community, forcing entrepreneurs to use all their talents and resources to find and use profit opportunities. Lavoie notes thus:

> The money prices he uses in such decentralized calculations embody more information than is consciously possessed by anyone and thus enable him to engage in far more complex production plans than could be designed under a centrally planned system. These prices contain such information because of the rivalrous pressures generated by the competing bids for resources by entrepreneurs (1985, p. 147).

Hayek in fact said as early as 1935 that there could be no competition without private property and that the problem simply was one of defining the decisional element and its relation with responsibility: 'To assume that it is possible to create conditions of full competition without making those who are responsible for the decisions pay for their mistakes seems to be pure illusion' (1935b, p. 237). The idea of competition is only defensible when related to an adequate structure of property in order to make decision-making fully accountable.

In the case of the socialist firm, the idea of a management surveillance committee could be developed but the problem of each manager's tacit, specific knowledge that the committee members, by definition do not have, would remain. How, then, would this committee make sure, from the outside, that this knowledge was being fully used, as the manager does not even know he possesses it? Central Planning would still have the problem of incentives and would still suffer the social cost of moral hazard. Lange's model is not the only one to be concerned by this problem. In the case of linear programming, any gathered information is by necessity decentralized; central planning proposes economic objectives based on the often falsified information of production capacities transmitted by enterprises but which central planning in fact cannot objectively check. The Soviet mathematics school heartily condemned this cheating, but did not suggest any adequate solutions.

3.3 Institutions

We could obviously say that in a socialist system, managers are as motivated as their capitalist counterparts to use their tacit knowledge not only because of the moral dimension of the socialist system but also that they would be eager to display their talents, competency and knowledge in the construction of a high performance socialist economy.[24] The question is not just whether the manager would have the incentive to use his tacit knowledge in a socialist world but whether he in fact would have the freedom to do so. A close examination would seem to show that this freedom would be in fact very limited. In a centrally planned system, prices are the results of calculations which involve the whole economy, so the socialist manager is a 'cost-taker', as opposed to the capitalist entrepreneur able to modify his cost structure.

Whether we use Dickinson's, Lange's or more recent optimal planning systems such as Kantorovitch's, once prices are calculated by central planning, the individual socialist manager has little latitude in modifying its indexes to his level, as they are rigidified data for his activity. If these socialist managers were to follow their own discoveries or changes in their tacit knowledge and question centrally emitted directives on prices, quantities, technology or production direction, then the whole planning system would be in constant disarray with no hope of any coordinating production plans. The system's whole coherency requires a rigidity which offers no possibility of entrepreneurial initiative or use of individual knowledge. Seen from the dynamics point of view, a lack of freedom to modify their activity would probably discourage socialist managers from exploring new ways of improving production efficiency.

Agency problems certainly exist as much in the capitalist world. But in a market economy, the entrepreneur can change his environment and use cheaper production methods. In Lange's system, costs are data for the socialist manager, so he does not have the power, even supposing he had the will, to harness his imagination and talent to redirect his production or his activity. Even on discovering new activities or lower cost structures, that is, new opportunities, he does not have the authority to exploit them. Hayek noted in his comments on Lange:

> … how the S.E.C will insure the actual carrying-out of the principle that prices are equalized to the lowest marginal cost at which the quantity concerned can be produced. The question which arises here is not 'merely' one of the loyalty or capacity of the socialist managers. For the purpose of this argument it may granted that they will be as capable and as anxious to produce cheaply as the average capitalist entrepreneur. The problem arises because one of the most important forces which in a truly competitive economy brings about the reduction of costs to the minimum discoverable will be absent, namely, price competition (1940, p. 196).

It is with this type of argument that he discusses the question of the scope of competition. Competition cannot accomplish its social task inside a system stifled by planned orders: 'Only if competition exists not only between but also within the different industries can we expect it to serve its purpose' (Hayek, 1935b, p. 231). Some would say that planning is the tool of greater justice. But for the moment: 'nobody has yet demonstrated how planning and competition can be rationally combined; and so long as this is not done one is certainly entitled to insist that these two alternatives are kept clearly separate' (ibid., p. 241).

So obviously, reintroducing some competition and responsibility into a planned system, or simply leaving agents some autonomy as to managing their activities would allow the community to benefit from at least some of the same tacit knowledge as a market system. However the cure would possibly be worse than the illness, as it would not be cost-free. Reintroducing some freedom would mean authorizing a private knowledge system to compete with the public, planned price system. This private knowledge would guide central planning to more efficient regulation but it would also continually disorganize production planning structures; therefore 'if competition is to function satisfactorily, it will be necessary to go all the way and not to stop at a partial reintroduction of competition' (Hayek, 1935b, p. 220).

The way socialist systems evolved from the 1960s would seem to bear out this analysis. Many economists opened up their planned economies to certain elements of incentives and freedom of action inspired by market rules. Liberman ('The Plan, Profits and Bonuses', 1962) thus proposed motivating enterprises to the greatest possible production efficiency by directly correlating prices to each one's profitability.[25] Although they could have been called a step in the right direction, these reforms had ruinous and easily predictable consequences as they made an already incoherent system even more so.

In a socialist economy, producers are either not motivated or unable to express their talents by playing on price so the system is deprived of an essential element of economic progress which is agents' tacit knowledge, its interaction and development generating innovation and offering them the opportunity to experiment with yet more efficient production methods.[26]

Knowledge supplied to central planning by definition can only be explicit; opportunities for production and information transmission have to be based on that visible, quantifiable data. In the capitalist system, other forms of tacit, unformalised knowledge are taken into account in the price system through individuals' actions.[27] Central Planning can never construct a conscious economic structure as efficient as the spontaneous market structure; as gains from exchange are not defined by market prices, they are not systematically exploited. The freedom of expression of individuals' subjectivity stemming from exchange means the system transforms more knowledge into information and more information into knowledge. Hayek does not seem to base his various arguments around this question, although he mentions the socialist attempt to organise some sort of pseudo-competition (line 5, 1935b). Yet Lavoie's reformulation of the debate's terms highlights the element's essential characteristic. His approach is a procedural analysis of planning, via the question of cognitive contents of prices; respecting free exchange being the best way to explicit, transmit and exploit knowledge scattered throughout the community.

Examining this cognitive dimension brings us back to the question of institutions and especially to the essential role of private property in the capitalization and the mobilization of knowledge. Freedom of exchange must obviously be based on a structure of private property as it is irrational for the agent to exchange goods if he can not benefit from the gains. Only the individual is able to manage and release the tacit knowledge in his possession, through his activities. Also, only a competitive system allows him to release his knowledge through prices. Private property offers the community the opportunity to benefit from this knowledge embedded in individual practice and know-how, through the market price system. The efficiency of the economic system is reliant on its ability to mobilize, develop and distribute information. The market's role is to integrate all these aspects.

Socialism's epistemological inferiority, as it appears in Lavoie's reformulation of Mises' argument dating from the beginning of the 1920s, results from the impossibility of formulating tacit knowledge. Analysis shows that the basic nature of tacit knowledge and man's cognitive limitations condemns all forms of socialism, particularly Marxist socialism, to be less efficient than capitalism.

Kirzner, in two texts, 'Economic Planning and Knowledge Problem' (1984) and 'The Economic Calculation Debate: Lessons for Austrians' (1988b) was to take the same view as Lavoie's, by pointing out Mises' and Hayek's analytical similarities. Kirzner especially mentions the way this debate set an example as it allowed the Austrians to gather their defining concepts into the same analysis: knowledge, process and competition. This pleasant atmosphere of consensus was, however, to turn sour at the start of the 1990s.

4. AN ALTERNATIVE READING: THE ROTHBARD ARGUMENT

One last opinion should be considered in this debate on collectivism: Rothbard's and his followers'. These authors' very specific reflection does not include any cognitive arguments but is 'arithmetics' based. For them the relevant question is not whether planned prices carry more or less information as Hayek, Lavoie or Kirzner claim is the case (4.1). The point is that in a complex economy there is no other means of calculating other than using market prices (4.2).[28]

4.1 Knowledge and Calculation

'Mises demonstrated that even with perfect information, the central planners in socialism cannot rationally calculate how to combine resources to render efficient production. They can only grope in the dark; as Mises put it, socialism is "planned chaos"' (Herbener, 1991, p. 43).

The authors who support this particular reading of Mises are anxious to show that the economy in general and the entrepreneur in particular should not be seen as a problem of knowledge nor of learning. Rothbard (1991, 1995), Salerno (1990a and b, 1993), Herbener (1991) all contend that production and entrepreneurship are essentially faced with a problem of economic calculation.

The entrepreneur is not concerned with knowledge. Information on present events (or more precisely on data from the immediate past) or even from further back in time are not an essential element. As profits come from future events, the entrepreneur's only task is to anticipate, therefore only the future can possibly interest him in a logic which could be called 'speculative anticipation' (Mises, *Planning for Freedom*, 1962c, p. 126).

Of course the entrepreneur still uses data from the present and the past in this 'speculative' approach. As Mises himself said

> In order to see his way in the unknown and uncertain future man has within his reach only two aids: experiences of past events and his faculty of understanding. Knowledge about past prices is a part of the experience and at the same time the starting point of understanding the future (1966, p. 337).[29]

Obviously a structure of past and present prices is of great help and is a tool of inestimable value. However, it is not the only possible interpretative tool and it could even be said that that it was not indispensible in the formation of expectations of future consumer choice. The entrepreneur just as efficiently uses qualitative as quantitative variables to gauge and calculate the economy. An absence of past and present prices would not prevent entrepreneurs from benefitting from qualitative knowledge used to predict future markets. Indeed, Salerno considers that present (or immediate past) price knowledge is not required to anticipate price structures:

> As one component of experience, past prices are therefore an important, but by no means indispensable, auxiliary for entrepreneurial understanding of the future course of prices … Since it is, in the final analysis, future prices which concern entrepreneurs, Mises concludes that economic calculation and rational allocation of resources could still take place even in the event of a complete obliteration of past prices (1990a, p. 44).

Similarly, learning is not of any decisional help to the entrepreneur. If by learning we mean realising we have made past errors, then learning is certainly not essential data in entrepreneurship; it is the theme of uncertainty of the future which is essential here. If we consider that there is no logical relationship between past and future, realising one's past errors does not help the entrepreneur to adjust better to the future. His eye on present exchange rates teaches him nothing about future exchange rates, as they are by definition unknown:

> In drafting their plans the entrepreneurs look first at the prices of the immediate past which are mistakenly call present prices. Of course, the entrepreneur never makes theses prices enter into their calculations without paying regard to anticipated changes. The prices of the immediate past are for them only the starting point of deliberation leading to forecasts of future prices. The prices of the past do not influence the determination of future prices. It is, on the contrary, the anticipation of future prices of the products that determines the state of prices of the complementary factors of production. The determination of prices has, as far as the mutual exchange ratios between various commodities are concerned, no direct causal relation whatever with the prices of the past ... The prices of the past are for the entrepreneur, the shaper of future production, merely a mental tool (Mises, 1966, p. 336-337).

Learning is not the entrepreneur's essential task; even if, as we saw earlier, it is an effective instrument of opinion-forming and planning, the entrepreneur does not rely on learning to shape his expectations of future exchange structures.

So the entrepreneur essentially never engages in a process of learning or knowledge. His fundamental task is speculation; however he does *ex post* require a price system for consumer goods produced and productive factors used, to be able to calculate possible profit and loss.[30]

Past and present prices therefore bring no relevant knowledge to entrepreneurs of either future consumer or production prices. They are a useful tool for appreciation, *ex ante* any entrepreneurial activity, but for Rothbardians not indispensible. However, *ex post* activity, they are indispensible tools for economic calculation; in this very particular way, according to Mises' statement, 'Monetary calculation is the guiding star of action under the social system of division of labor. It is the compass of the man embarking upon production' (Mises, 1966, p. 228).

This question of monetary calculation is vital to the Rothbardians: 'The Misesian entrepreneur is not a passive, if alert, recipient of "knowledge" provided by the price system. He is a knowledgeable, active, risking, forecasting man using the price system for its indispensable guide to enable him to calculate his costs, and to estimate his future revenues and profits' (Rothbard, 1995, p. 55). According to him, in the totally fictional event of the entrepreneur having advance knowledge of all the consumer choice structures, and therefore of all future prices, it would still not be enough to act on and develop production plans. He would need knowledge of factor prices at the very moment he made his consumer exchanges to be able to properly calculate his activity's profits and costs. The argument is the following: even if the entrepreneur knew everything in agents' minds, he still would not be able to make strategies, as he would still not be able to calculate *ex post* if they had been profitable or not. It is in this very precise balance sheet approach that the relative price system is indispensible data for entrepreneurs.

Economic calculation should not be seen, however, as a tool for achieving planning success. The entrepreneur's problem when forming his plans is not to know future prices. Again, Mises' argument is valuable: 'It is not the task of economic calculation to expand man's information about future conditions. Its task is to adjust his actions as well as possible to his present opinion concerning want-satisfaction in the future' (1966, p. 214).

4.2 The Systemic Impossibility of Centralized Economic Calculation

For Mises, present monetary prices (or rather, prices from the immediate past) form the basis of economic calculations by providing an indication of agents' present choices (again, choices from the immediate past). But this information should never be seen as sufficient, still less essential to entrepreneurial decisions. It simply informs on present consumer strategies and desires. However, producers' activites are future oriented, so what shapes their results is not present but future consumer desires.[31]

The Rothbardians' idea was that if there is no factor price *ex post* activity, there can be neither accounting nor economic calculation. As Mises established himself in *Human Action*, one may imagine that producers might formulate production plans with no present prices, using simple qualitative variables, quantitative data not being indispensible. On the other hand, these *ex post* prices are needed to gauge the results of the activity. The planned economic system is, unfortunately, incapable of proposing these prices. In Salerno's view, 'It is therefore clear that Mises's critique of the possibility of socialism is not about knowledge but about calculation (1990a, p. 45).

Referring to earlier debates, this type of argument is surprising, as there are several concrete propositions for planned price structures, especially Dickinson's and Lange's as well the more recent linear programming. But the article 'The Equations of Mathematical Economics and the Problems of Economic Calculation in a Socialist State' (1938), as well as the two sections from *Human Action* respectively on the themes of 'The quasi-market' (p. 742-747) and 'The differential equations of mathematical economics' (p. 710-715) clearly show that Mises does not see any alternative to market prices in either of these propositions. The Rothbardians' opinions would seem to expand this point of view; several analytical levels can be found in their arguments.

To calculate equilibrium prices (which coordinate agents' activities), the planner needs to know all the data at the same time, which is impossible by its very character. As time passes, it becomes impossible to instantaneously calculate prices which take into account all the available information at any moment. So central planning's prices cannot be equilibrium prices as they do not adjust to supply and demand; plans might not be carried out. Added to this, even if coordination was possible, it would not be permanent, as dynamics would intervene and central planning or consumer agent's evaluations, those at the system's very centre, change constantly in any case.

These arguments concerning ignorance could also be used against the capitalist system, as it is known that market equilibrium prices do not exist; it would therefore seem appropriate to make a comparative analysis of the two systems. If market entrepreneurs are left to use their personal judgement and qualitative knowledge of certain market segments to form their own production prices in a decentralized way, there would certainly be more coherence and success of plans. So planned prices cannot be proper calculation tools as they are not proper prices founded on entrepreneurial judgement and the freedom to buy and sell; which is, in other words, on private property.

The crucial element, however, seems to be elsewhere. Hayek and Lavoie found the fundamental difficulty faced by Marxist socialism to be the following: actors' knowledge cannot be transferred to a planned price system as efficiently as in a market system. There is an unbridgeable gap between knowledge spread through society and knowledge available to Central Planning. But for Rothbard and his followers, the central problem is not whether actors' knowledge can be transferred to Central Planning but rather to determine if any knowledge, hypothetically at least, acquired by Central Planning may be transformed into usable information for managers and other actors in the planned system. Their answer is clear: the planner's centralized knowledge cannot be turned into the kind of prices able to rationally direct production. In other words, the planner cannot transform his qualitative knowledge of data into economic calculation, so it is fundamentally not a question of determining if actors' knowledge can be transferred to central planning, but rather of whether central planning's knowledge can be converted into information for actors' use; in fact restitute centralized knowledge to the economic agents in numerical form is impossible in socialism.

Above and beyond any problem of access to available data is the problem of the treatment of knowledge. Even without the question of central planning's acquisition of actors' knowledge, even with the totally artificial hypothesis that Central Planning possessed all relevant information at all times, it could not distribute it in any usable form to the planned system's various actors. Therefore, large parts of Central Planning's knowledge would not be converted into numerical calculations.[32] Seen from this angle, there can be no centralized production of prices.

Sophisticated information systems do not help the problem; behind central planning there are people with their own minds and therefore the socialist problematic needs to be integrated 'into the system of the theory of human action' (Mises, 1966, p. 701). This particularly constrains Central Planning's management, stopping it from changing data into economic calculation, or put another way, transforming all qualitative and quantitative variables into numerical values. Thus, 'socialism, necessarily devoid of a market in land and capital goods, must lack the ability to calculate and compare goods and services, and therefore any rational allocation of production resources under socialism is indeed impossible' (Rothbard, 1991, p. 65).

Of course, the problem of ignorance is just as prevalent in the market economies but one of their characteristics is that calculation is intrinsically decentralized. Each individual entrepreneur, reacting to his own environment, acts on his contextualised expectations of the state of the market and through bilateral exchanges will form factor prices. It is precisely because price formation is decentralized that it is technically possible. Furthermore, once again the point is not whether these prices are accurate, or entrepreneurs' expectations conform to consumer demand, but simply to know whether factor prices can form independently from privately held factors, which is the one condition of decentralized economic calculation.

The Rothbardian camp's thinking, based on this, is simple: when the exchange of production goods is banned, it is impossible to put a price on them: 'The prerequisite for advanced social production is calculation that allows purposeful action within the framework of the division of labor. Calculation requires money prices and thus, money and free exchange, which requires private property' (Herbener, 1991, p. 43).

This type of argument gives new significance to some of Mises' declarations:

> If no other objections could be raised to the socialist plans than that socialism will lower the standard of living of all or at least of the immense majority, it would be impossible for praxeology to pronounce a final judgment. Men would have to decide the issue between capitalism and socialism on the ground of judgments of value and of judgments of relevance … However, the true state of affairs is entirely different. Man is not in a position to choose between these two systems. Human cooperation under the system of the social division of labor is possible only in the market economy. Socialism is not a realizable system of society's economic organization because it lacks any method of economic calculation (1966, p. 715).

The Austrian argument around collectivism was divided into three steps. After Mises had laid the groundwork, it was agreed that socialism was theoretically feasible, and that it was the question of the quantity and changeability of information that was firstly taken into account in the reflections on planning coordination.

Secondly, the debate moved towards the inferiority of the socialist economy in terms of exploiting exchange opportunities.

This last question engendered the third step of reflecting on modes of knowledge communication. So it emerges that socialism's real problematic is the nature of information expressed by market prices compared with its ability to reproduce similar information either through simulating market processes or improving planning techniques. So without being either theoretically or practically unfeasible, socialism would appear to be faced with such large epistemic obstacles that its ability to mobilize the same level of knowledge as the market is severely limited. Beyond this, centralizing a complex society would mean giving up any hope of maintaining its level of development, which would have been previously ensured by the interaction of various levels of tacit knowledge expressed by capitalist prices. The Austrian argument seems to have influenced Marxist literature. Roemer ('Can There Be Socialism After Communism?', 1993a) even suggests that nationalization of the means of production is not the only way possible to reach socialism's goals.

The most recent contributions, based around Rothbard and his fellows' work, show a more radical reading of Mises' arguments. They claim collectivist socialism is not only inferior, planned prices holding less information than market economy prices, but is actually impossible, being incapable of producing any of the relative factor prices needed in any complex economy to organise production.

Whichever view one takes, however, no-one should let these conclusions put them off the idea of the collectivist economy. The Austrians' clear demonstration that the economic failure of socialism needs to be properly interpreted, for economic science is nothing whatsoever to do with the values and objectives at the root of socialism. Mises, Hayek and the others only managed to demonstrate that collectivism is a less efficient set of treatment processes, knowledge mobilization and economic calculation than capitalism. A lower level of exploitation of knowledge opportunities, or even the disappearance of any complex production economy may be considered as necessary evils to attain the moral and ethical ends of socialism. The consequences must, however, be plain to everyone and Hayek is especially clear on this point:

> There were those who thought that the loss of efficiency, the decline in general wealth which will be the effect of the absence of a means of rational calculation, would not be too high a price for the realization of a more just distribution of this wealth. Of course if this attitude is based on a clear realization of what this choice implies there is no more to be said about it, except that it seems doubtful whether those who maintain it would find many who will agree with their idea (1935a, p. 37).

NOTES

1. This article appeared in German as 'Die Wirtschaftsrechnung im sozialistischen Gemeinwesen' and was only translated into English in 1935.
2. Mises was thus able to write: 'Socialism is the abolition of rational economy' (1920, p. 110).
3. Many of his later writings echoed these themes; see particularly Part 5 of *Human Action* (1966): 'Social Cooperation without a Market'. See also an often neglected text, 'The Equations of Mathematical Economics and the Problem of Economic Calculation in a Socialist State (1938).
4. Dickinson had already shown interest in planned socialism's economic problems in two contributions, 'The Economic Basis of Socialism' (1930) and 'Freedom and Planning, A Reply to Dr Gregory' (1933b). He later published, on the subject, *Economics of Socialism* (1939).
5. Max Weber (*Economy and Society*, 1921) was to develop the same ideas.
6. 'Reality would make mock of an evaluation in hours of work, and would set another in its place. For the value of things does not depend upon the amount of labour they have cost, but on a number of causes, among which the amount of labour plays a part, but not the only part' (Pierson, 1902, p. 77).
7. 'Under socialism all the means of production are the property of the community. It is the community alone which can dispose of them and which determines their use in production' (Mises, 1920, p. 89). Already, in *Nation, State and the Economy* (1919), Mises was saying: 'Socialism means the transfer of the means of production out of the private ownership of individuals into the ownership of society. That alone and nothing else is socialism' (Mises, 1919, p. 172). Finally, in *Human Action*, 'The essential mark of socialism is that one will alone acts. It is immaterial whose will it is. The director may be an anointed king or a dictator, ruling by virtue of his charisma, he may be a Führer or a board of Fürhers appointed by the vote of the people. The main thing is that the employment of all factors of production is directed by one agency only. One will alone chooses, decides, directs, acts, gives orders' (1966, p. 695).
8. In socialism, any use of this good would in fact be limited to the sphere of consumer goods. For Mises, however, this type of good is not really money, as theory defines it as a generalized exchange instrument.
9. 'The choice is between capitalism and chaos ... Socialism is not a realizable system of society's economic organization because it lacks any method of economic calculation ... A society that chooses between capitalism and socialism does not choose between two social systems: it chooses between social cooperation and the disintegration of society' (Mises, 1966, p. 679-680). It is obvious to Mises and the other neo-Austrians who were to examine this problem: the socialist system has long survived to this day; however, this is due to the fact that is founded on a capitalist price system: 'An apparent verification of these errors was seen in the experience of the socialist governments of Soviet Russia and Nazi Germany. People do not realize that these were not isolated socialist systems. They were operating in an environment in which the price system still worked. They could resort to economic calculation on the ground of the prices established abroad. Without the aid of these prices their actions would have been aimless and planless. Only because they were able to refer to these foreign prices were they are able to calculate, to keep books, and to prepare their much talked about plans' (ibid., p. 702-703). From the same viewpoint, see Rothbard ('The End of Socialism and the Calculation Debate Revisited', 1991, p. 73-74). Basing themselves on western prices, the socialist economies were able to introduce some sort of rationality into their activities' organisation. However, for the neo-Austrians, the collapse of socialism became inevitable, as the system became more complex, needs more diversified and, one may add, as it was increasingly affected by Western pricing systems' growing irrationality due to Keynesian policies.

10. It is obvious that if all the production factors were specific, there would be no need for a means of production market. Production would be indicated by levels of consumer needs for the good, expressed by freely formed prices on the consumer goods market.
11. We know that Mises thought labour theory of value was not admissible as a real alternative to market money calculations. He claimed this theory was nullified by the existence of different types of labour at various levels and the realisation of the importance of ultimate factors in production processes. But it is surprising that during the controversy following the articles' publication, no socialist author tried to defend the labour theory of value to counter Mises' ideas. On the contrary, most looked for alternatives to the market based on Mises' analysis. On this point, see Hoff, *Economic Calculation in the Socialist Society* (1949); Vaughn, 'Economic Calculation Under Socialism: The Austrian Contribution' (1980b); Chaloupek, 'The Austrian debate on Economic Calculation in a Socialist Economy' (1990) and Steele, *From Marx to Mises* (1992).
12. Thus Kirzner ('The Economic Calculation Debate: Lessons for Austrians', 1984) defends the idea that this debate was 'a catalyst in the development and articulation of the modern Austrian view of the market as a competitive-entrepreneurial process of discovery' (1992, p. 100).
13. See also an earlier contribution of Dickinson's in this domain, 'The Economic Basis of Socialism' (1930), which in fact skims over the problem of production price determination. Two Americans, Taylor, 'The Guidance of Production in a Socialist State' (1929) and Roper 'The Problem of Pricing in a Socialist State (1929), may be thought of as Dickinson's predecessors; Dickinson refers to Taylor's work as being a 'slightly different solution' to his own (1933a, p. 238).
14. Dickinson also defends freedom of choice of labour, through the idea of 'contracts of service, freely entered into by its citizens' (1933a, p. 239).
15. Robbins (*The Great Depression*, 1934, in the chapter 'Restrictionism and Planning', p. 180-181), had developed an analogous theory to Hayek's; the same ideas appear in *Economic Planning and International Order* (1937)
16. Oskar Lange's article was published in two parts in 1937 and 1938 in *The Review of Economics Studies* (see bibliography). It was then published in a revised form in a collection, edited by Lippincot, also entitled *On the Economic Theory of Socialism* (1938). In it can also be found Taylor's pioneering article, originally published in 1929, 'The Guidance of Production in a Socialist State'. Literature sometimes mentions a Lange-Lerner line because of the similarity between Lange's works and Abba Lerner's (see Kirzner, 1997).
17. This idea of parametric prices is conceived outside of all exchange procedures and can only be viewed through a Walrasian analytical framework. Rather than knowing actors' preferences, it is a question of discovering relations of technical substitution between goods.
18. 'Our study of the determination of equilibrium prices in a socialist economy has shown that the process of price determination is quite analogous to that in a competitive market. The Central Planning performs the functions of the market. It establishes the rules combining factors of production and choosing the scale of output of a plant, for determining the output of an industry, for the allocation of resources, and for the parametric use of prices in accounting' (Lange, 1938, p. 82-83).
19. See Vaughn 'Does It Matter that Costs are Subjective?' (1980a); *Austrian Economics in America: The Migration of a Tradition* (1994, p. 52).
20. In a chapter called 'The Impracticability of Socialism', Mises devotes a whole paragraph to '... the fundamental problems of a socialist community under conditions of change' (see Mises, 1922, p. 186-187).
21. Linear programming was conceived at the end of the 1930s but only published in 1960. Kantorovitch's idea was a mathematical calculation programme which would enable Planning to make a structure of relative prices based on a production programme (dual prices). More exactly, it aims for a solution to a programme of maximisation of a function con-

strained by inequalities. The 'dual' reproduction of this 'primal' problem programme allows the determination of implicit prices corresponding to solutions for this programme, while still respecting its constraints of inequality.

22. See also: 'Computation, Incentives and Discovery: The Cognitive Function of Markets in Market Socialism' (Lavoie, 1990b).
23. Henri Lepage (*Pourquoi la proprieté*) speaks of 'systemic knowledge, which is much more than the sum of the personal knowledge which each of us is able to formulate and transmit. Nobody knows how to consciously reproduce this other than by using the vehicle of competition' (1985, p. 286, our translation).
24. Dickinson ('The Economic Basis of Socialism', 1930), had already discussed the theme of incentives in giving us this reading: 'The Socialist state would have to find some incentive to effort and efficiency other than greed. Public spirit, collective pride, personal ambition, desire for leisure, and fear are possible candidates. Some men will do their best if they feel they are serving the state and their fellow-men. A group of workers can be got to work hard and even to drive its slower and lazier members by appealing to its pride of achievement as a group ...' (1930, p. 566). In 'Price Formation in a Socialist Community' (1933a) he returns to the question simply to mention that it can now be abandoned: 'With the spectacle of collectivist state actually working (even though imperfectly) before our eyes in Soviet Russia, and attempting prodigious feats of economic reconstruction, the incentive argument appears less convincing' (1933a, p. 237).
25. Dickinson ('The Economic Basis of Socialism' 1930), already discussed the possibility of micro-enterprises co-existing, in fairly restricted conditions, side by side with the great mass of nationalized capital industries.
26. Most literature agrees that innovation levels in the ex-Eastern bloc countries were much lower than in market economies.
27. In the capitalist system, the promoter acts on and shapes the structure of his action; in a socialist system, the manager can only react by choosing among a limited series of possibilities, externally defined by central planning.
28. The most important literature is: Rothbard, *Man, Economy and State*, 1962, 'Ludwig von Mises and Economic Calculation Under Socialism', 1976, 'The End of Socialism and the Calculation Debate Revisited', 1991; 'The Present State of Austrian Economics', 1995. By his followers, Herbener ('Ludwig von Mises and the Austrian School of Economics', 1991, 'Economic Calculation and the Question of Arithmetic', 1996); Hoppe (*A Theory of Socialism and Capitalism*, 1989); 'Socialism: a Property or Knowledge Problem?', 1996); Salerno ('Ludwig von Mises as Social Rationalist', 1990a; 'Why a Socialist Economy is Impossible', 1990b; 'Mises and Hayek Dehomogenized', 1993); Hülsmann ('Knowledge, Judgment and the Use of Property', 1997). This sometimes polemical literature caused some tense debate in the neo-Austrian tradition. See particularly the debate between Yeager and Salerno (see bibliography), Kirzner ('Reflections on the Misesian Legacy in Economics', 1996a) and Boettke (*Economic Calculations: The Austrian Contributions to Political Economy*, 1998b)
29. In the same way of thinking, Mises notes that 'The entrepreneurs do not construct afresh every day a radically new structure of prices or allocate anew the factors of production to the various branches of industry. They merely transform what the past has transmitted in better adapting it to the altered conditions. How much of the previous conditions they preserve and how much they change depends on the extent to which the data have changed' (1966, p. 337).
30. In a capitalist economy, consumers do not directly value production factors but the suppliers and demanders of these factors do, through the buying and selling process. Yet the current value of factors is itself dependent on their capacity of making future useful consumer goods, so consumers' preferences in the end are the real yet indirect determining element of factor prices.

31. 'We may admit that in its initial period a socialist regime could to some extent rely upon the experience of the preceding age of capitalism. But what is to be done later, as conditions change more and more? Of what use could the prices of 1900 be for the director in 1949? And what use can the director in 1980 derive from the knowledge of the prices of 1949?' (Mises, 1966, p. 700).
32. This approach seems to conform to Mises' argument, at least in spirit. In *Human Action* he explains his approach: 'We assume that the director has at his disposal all the technological knowledge of his age. Moreover, he has a complete inventory of all the material factors of production available and a roster enumerating all manpower employable. In these respects the crowd of experts and specialists which he assembles in his forces provide him with perfect information and answer correctly all questions he may ask them. Their voluminous reports accumulate in huge piles on his desk. But now he must act. He must choose among an infinite variety of projects in such a way that no want which he himself considers more urgent remains unsatisfied because the factors of production required for its satisfaction are employed for the satisfaction of wants which he considers less urgent' (1966, p. 696).

8. Austrian Theory of the Business Cycle

The Austrian theory of the business cycle fits into a more general context of economic literature's interest between the wars in questions of economic conjuncture which was accentuated by the 1929 crash.[1] From a different angle, the theory is linked to a traditional subject for the Austrians, the mode of integration of money to real phenomena. Although theirs is not the only work in the Austrian theory of the cycle, Mises and Hayek are its two main authors.[2]

Mises initiated a theoretical representation of the channels of influence of money on the real economy in *The Theory of Money and Credit* (1912); it explains economic disturbances as the effects of money creation on the relative prices structure. He developed this analysis between the wars,[3] then in successive editions of *Human Action* (1949, 1963, 1966).

Hayek's first economic research was on trade cycle theory in the middle of the 1920s.[4] He especially developed his ideas during a cycle of four conferences at the London School of Economics, on Lionel Robbins' invitation. They were immediately published under the title *Prices and Production* (1931).

This is undoubtedly the most central of Hayek's theories – and the most stylistic – on the subject. It unleashed a barrage of sometimes violent arguments from such illustrious figures as Keynes, Sraffa and Hicks but even today is the work of reference on Austrian cycle analysis.[5] Hayek returned to some of the ideas of *Prices and Production* to explain and refine them to a limited readership in three later publications: *Monetary Nationalism and International Stability* (1937b), *Profit, Investment and Interest* (1939a)[6] and *The Pure Theory of Capital* (1941).

The important point concerning the cycle is agents' success in their expectations, or in other words, coordination of their plans. Hayek thus concentrates his analysis of modes of interaction between the producers/entrepreneurs and the employees in the shape of consumers/savers, studying procedures of finding compatibility and adjustment between the producer/entrepreneurs' plans and the employees' intertemporal consumer choices. More precisely, crisis is described in theoretical terms as the expression of generalised discoordination between, firstly, entrepreneurs' choices in factor allocation for production of consumer and investment goods and secondly, employees' preferences of directing income to consumption or saving.[7] Hayek considered the problem could only be seen as a break in the information circuit of relative prices.

The young Hayek should be studied with the hindsight of his more mature writings. Chapter 6 shows that in Hayek's view, current prices are not just the expression of a discovery but may also to a certain extent fulfil a function of prediction. Day-to-day transactions are important indications for promoters, offering them the possibility of forming expectations and action plans.

So Hayek seeks the reasons for this destruction of the expectation and calculation systems of relative prices. By which mechanisms do prices spread signals that suddenly lead producers as a whole to form false expectations which will no longer allow their activities to coordinate? Hayek's answer lies in money. *Prices and Production* provides an explanation of the problems of producers' expectations caused by monetary expansion. The goal is to study 'the effects of a change in the amount of money in circulation on production' (1931, p. 97), particularly concentrating on 'what happens if the "natural" movements of prices is disturbed by movements in the supply of money' (ibid., p. 85). So in the end Hayek's cycle theory sets in motion a whole series of reflections on interactions between the real and the monetary economy.

Hayek's analysis rests on a number of theoretical premises which framed his reflection (1). On the basis of these premises, Hayek distinguishes a monetary background to the business cycle, via the consequences of changes in relative prices on production structures (2). The boom is set off by monetary disturbances, which skews the information circuit of market prices, aggravating a natural phenomenon of the non-neutrality of money. Monetary interventionism prevents the success of production plans, forcing their growing incoherence through various cumulative effects. So, coherence is reestablished through a proper policy of stabilizing the money supply (3). Hayek's views on the cycle quickly generated debates, the terms of which illustrate the specificity of the Austrian theory (4).

1. FIRST STEPS OF THE APPROACH

Hayek's business cycle analysis sits at the crossroads of monetary and capital theory (1.1), where notions of interest rates and relative prices emerge. It is here that Hayek firstly formulates the conditions of success of actors' plans and secondly identifies factors of discoordination (1.2).

1.1 Capital as Structure, Roundabout Production Processes

The question of the cycle, a succession of boom and bust periods, should of course be seen in terms of the real economy, through fluctuations of production levels. Hayek on this basis rejects conceptions based simply on variations in industrial production which are 'changes of the willingness of individuals to expand effort' (1931, p. 32) or put 'more unused factors into use' (ibid., p. 93). These two conceptions are meaningless as they suppose that not all of society's productive forces have been previously used; however for Hayek 'The existence of such unused resources is itself a fact which needs explanation' (ibid., p. 34). Why known opportunities remain unexploited is the central question. Then 'we have to start where general economics theory stops; that is to say at a condition of equilibrium when no unused resources exist' (1931, p. 34). Starting from this point, he paid close attention to the method of firms' organisation, especially the question of evolutions in production from the viewpoint of their relationship with the technical structure of firm's activities and particularly

> the increase of output made possible by a transition to more capitalistic methods of production, or, what is the same thing, by organising production so that, at any given moment, the available resources are employed for the satisfaction of the needs of a future more distant than before (1931, p. 35-36).

This increase of capitalistic weight means a lengthening of the production process, or in other words, 'roundaboutness'. Hayek placed this reference, which we already find in Böhm-Bawerk's *Theory of Capital* (1889), at the base of his explanation of crises: 'it is only by an analysis of this phenomenon that in the end we can show how a situation can be created in which it is temporarily impossible to employ all available resources' (ibid., p. 36).

So Hayek adopts a temporal vision of production, based around the notion of production periods or stages, linked by structural relations, demonstrated in Figure 8.1.[8]

The technical production structure is represented by a right-angled triangle with several layers (the number of which Hayek chose haphazardly) related by both technology and time, ranging from original means of production (labour and land, first period), to consumer goods (last period), passing through intermediate periods (intermediate products), which contain a mix of capital and ultimate factors.

An economic or monetary dimension can be added to this technico-temporal description. As the production process advances, production goods logically go up in value to finish their ascension as consumer goods. Each stage in production is accompanied by a value increase, money being exchanged at each step for ultimate, intermediate or consumer goods. Money and goods move in opposite directions on the diagram, each downward movement of goods being matched by an upward movement of money.

The graph had important implications for Hayek; it shows a photograph of coordination, while highlighting roundabout production's role in maintaining this coordination.

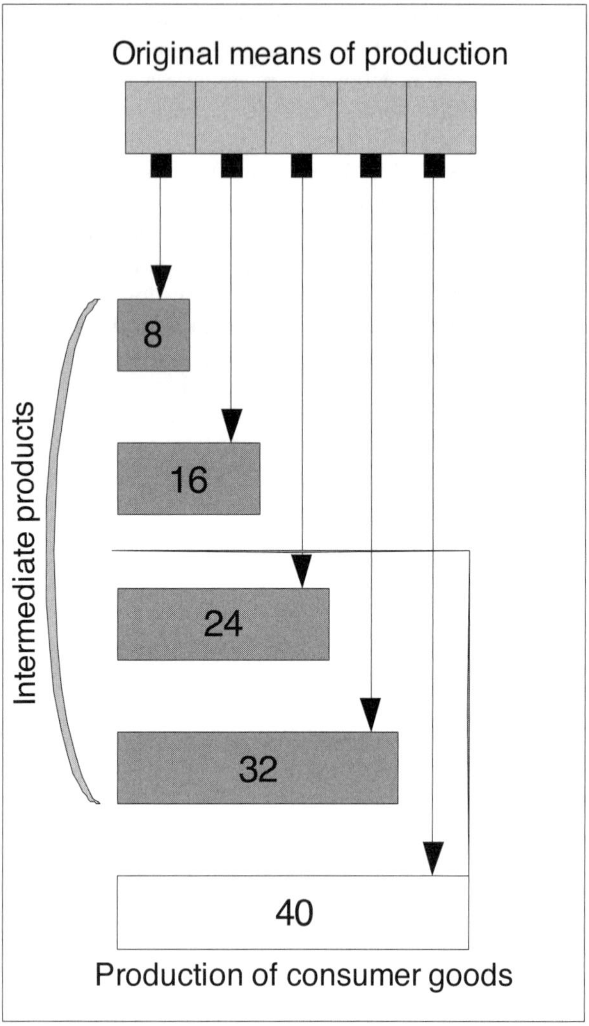

Source: Prices and Production, Hayek, 1931

Figure 8.1 The structure of production

It shows a perfect equilibrium between the consumer goods value and that of earnings of all the factors which make them up. The production system is thus coherent and infinitely reproducible, as agents receive the monetary value created at each stage of production, becoming in their turn consumers. In the end, agents will receive an accumulated value of 40, seen at the bottom of the graph, to resupply the consumer fund. Producers' and consumers' activities are perfectly coordinated and no expectation fails. This is the perfectly fictitious world of the evenly rotating economy.

It may appear surprising to see the sum of production goods values being 80 while consumer goods values stands at 40; however, in Hayek's eyes this corresponds to the very definition of the capitalist economy. Its characteristics imply 'that at any moment a far larger proportion of the available original means of production is employed to provide consumer's goods for some more or less distant future that is used for the satisfaction of immediate needs' (ibid., p. 37). This inequality is an economic strength as it registers the phenomena of productivity gains brought about by roundabout production:

> This way of organising production is, of course, that by lengthening the production process we are able to obtain a greater quantity of consumer's goods out of a given quantity of original means of production … within practical limits we may increase the output of consumers goods from a given quantity of original means of production indefinitely, provided we are willing to wait long enough for the product (ibid., p. 37-38).

The ratio of production goods:consumer goods rises as the roundabout production period lengthens.

But what happens if agents decide to save some of their revenue? In Hayek's figure, savings represent earnings not affected to consumption but to production factors. Creating or increasing savings thus represents a change in inter-temporal consumer choices. So, by definition, 'the proportion of money spent for consumers' goods and money spent for intermediate products is equal to the proportion between the total demand for consumers' goods and the total demand for the intermediate products necessary for their continuous production' (ibid., p. 46). But if some revenue is given over to savings and not consumption, that will surely mean we see a difference between the consumer goods' value and available money for purchasing them? Would this in other words mean the production economy loses its coherence, provoking discoordination? This is where the notion of roundabout production comes into play: it is not just a productivity factor, it is also an adjustment variable in the productive structure. It is the production process length (or size of roundaboutness) which maintains the system's harmony. Indeed, to find a new equilibrium, 'The additional amounts of money available for the purchase of intermediate products must now be so applied that the output of consumer's goods may be sold for the reduced sum now available for that purpose (Hayek, 1931, p. 51). As Figure 8.2 shows, simply lengthening the production process re-establishes the productive structures' coherence. At the process end, more consumer goods are available for purchase, at a lower individual cost.[9]

Raising the resources that employees put at entrepreneurs' service results in hopes of increased gains from production factors (and lower gains from consumer goods production). So a part of the (nonspecific) factors would come from the lower stages and be concentrated to the upper stages.[10] As incorporating these new capital units means, in Hayek's eyes, adding new stages, restructuring production means lengthening the detour. So modifying production structures by lengthening the detour reflects a modification of production goods and consumer goods relative prices: 'the immediate cause of a change in the return obtained from producers' goods of a certain kind used in different stages of production must be a change in the price of the product of the stage of production in question' (ibid., p. 72).

1.2 The Two Interest Rates

Obviously this adjustment is not automatic. Behind this technological presentation of production and its possible transformations there are human decisions with their logic of exploiting profit opportunities; behind the changes in relative prices are subjective variables which express themselves in agents' inter-temporal choices. The notion of interest rates is thus paramount:

> Only in comparatively few cases will the people who have saved money and the people who want to use it in production be identical. In the majority of cases, therefore, the money which is directed to new uses will first have to pass into other hands. The question *who* is going to use the additional funds available for investment in producers' goods will be decided on the loan market. Only at a lower rate of interest than that formerly prevailing will it be possible to lend these funds, and how far the rate of interest will fall will depend upon the amount of the additional funds and the expectation of profits on the part of the entrepreneurs willing to expand their production (ibid., p. 84).

If interest rates were to simply reflect agents' inter-temporal choices, no mechanism of disequilibrium would appear in the production structure: actors' inter-temporal modifications would be 'absorbed' by adjustments in production detours and entrepreneurs would exploit all opportunities known to them.

How can we interpret the phenomenon of cycle and crisis in this analysis? Hayek's answer lies in the analysis of the interest rate mechanisms and their possible duality. As Wicksell had already explained in *Interest and Prices* (1898), interest rates in a monetary production economy can be understood in two ways: the monetary rate, which is the relation between money supply and

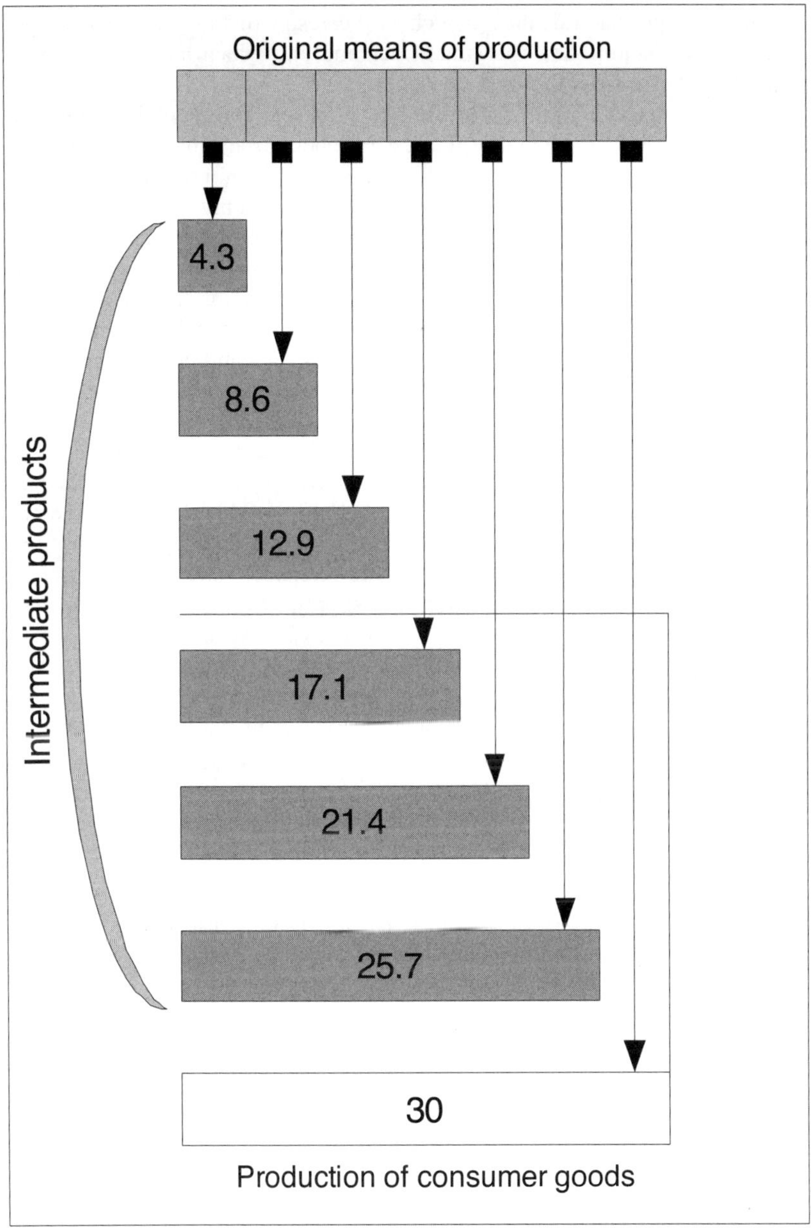

Source: Prices and Production, Hayek, 1931

Figure 8.2 Lengthening of the production process, or roundaboutness

demand, and the natural rate[11] which is the result of the confrontation between savings supply and investment demand and which harmonises entrepreneurs' activities and those of consumer/savers.

So in a monetary economy, Hayek, like Wicksell, considers that coordination is ensured by the monetary interest rate being the same as the equilibrium rate. If the monetary rate is held at the equilibrium rate, the production structure is safe from harm. Hayek thus has it that only if monetary rates move away from the natural rate does discoordination happen. What would the factors of such a gap be? On this subject, the question of money supply is important for the Austrian cycle analysis. The need for liquidity depends above all on individuals' subjective appreciations which are linked to money's purchasing power. As stocks of goods available to the population can only evolve slowly, the demand for money has no cause to make sudden general changes. So if monetary rates were to change in relation to equilibrium rates, the reason would probably be found in the supply of money.

In Mises' view, the creation of means of payment is fundamentally exogenous. In *The Theory of Money and Credit* (1912, p. 220-226), he condemns the authorities' deliberate changes in money values, especially through inflationism, which is simply the result of state monetary interventionism. This ends in political manipulation of monetary supply, which in turn ends in economic catastrophe. This type of analysis was to be expanded in later works (see especially *On the Manipulation of Credit and Money*, 1978a; *Human Action*, 1966; *Money, Method and the Market Process*, 1990). Mises also supported 'the emancipation of monetary value from the influence of government' (1978a, p. 17) as:

> … today credit expansion is exclusively a government practice. As far as private banks and bankers are instrumental in issuing fiduciary media, their role is merely ancillary and concerns only technicalities. The governments alone direct the course of affairs. They have attained full supremacy in all matters concerning the size of circulation credit. While the size of the credit expansion that private banks and bankers are able to engineer on an unhampered market is strictly limited, the governments aim at the greatest possible amount of credit expansion (1966, p. 794).

Hayek offered a more fine-tuned analysis. In *Monetary Theory and Trade Cycle* (1928b), he explains that the expansion of currency in circulation was due to 'the credit creation of the commercial banks' (1928b, p. 150). In *Prices and Production*, he takes a wide view of money supply, refusing to separate money, in its narrower sense, from monetary substitutes or any form of credit in its widest sense, as long as they allow agents' purchasing power to rise without reducing means of payment to others:

> When, in the course of analysis, I speak of changes in the quantity of money, this is always meant to include that total of all kinds of media of exchange (including all so-called 'substitutes' for money) [as] any increase or decrease of these money

> substitutes will have exactly the same effects as an increase or decrease of the quantity proper, and should therefore, for the purposes of theoretical analysis, be counted as money. In particular, it is necessary to take account of certain forms of credit not connected with banks which help, as it commonly said, to economise money, or to do the work for which, if they did not exit, money in the narrower sense of the word, would be required (Hayek, 1931, p. 109; 113-114).

Hayek sees the credit structure as being a multi-layered pyramid, its internal organisation being difficult to directly regulate. Even if the quantities of central bank money are stable, other parts of the structure may decide to increase credit supply through mechanisms which escape the authorities' control. So money supply in its wider sense can be increased outside central banks' expansionist policies.

However the money supply is defined, for both Hayek and Mises its expansion is at the root of disturbances. One point must be underlined which widened the gap between the Austrians and Wicksell's representation of crises: these disturbances are nothing to do with any effects of money supply on general price levels. Only implications for relative prices, that is to say relations of exchange between real goods should be taken into account. Hayek considers that Wicksell 'erred' in promoting 'a rigid connection between the rate of interest and the changes in the general price level' (1931, p. 23) and he notes two points on the subject.

Firstly, he considers that Wicksell's theory is contradictory; it is meant to ensure general price level stability by maintaining equality between monetary and natural rates. But this supposes that credit levels are always equal to agents' savings supply. So if, for example, the savings supply changes to X degrees, so must the amount of credit; if credit supply changes, then price stability goals cannot be achieved and must be scrapped. Conversely, if the priority is to maintain the general price level, if savings supply or investment demand were to change, a gap between monetary rates and natural rates would have to be accepted, opening the door to disequilibrium in Wicksell's model:

> Save a society in which there were no additions to the supply of savings, i.e., a stationary society, to keep the money rate of interest at the level of the equilibrium rate would mean that in times of expansion of production the price level would fall. To keep the general price level steady would mean, in similar circumstances, that the loan rate of interest would have to be lowered below the equilibrium rate (Hayek, 1931, p. 27).

So Hayek's contention was that in a dynamic world, the goals of general price level stability and those of natural and monetary rates equality are incompatible.

Hayek's second point is that Wicksell's idea does not work because it implies that disturbances are a result of variations in general price level, whereas Hayek claims these variations do not themselves explain production fluctuations:

> We have to give up the generally received opinion that if the general price level remains the same, the tendencies towards economic equilibrium are not disturbed by monetary influences, and that disturbing influences from the side of money cannot make themselves felt otherwise than by causing a change of the general price level … it seems obvious as soon as one once begins to think about it that almost any change in the amount of money, whether it does influence the price level or not, must always influence relative prices. And, as there can be no doubt that it is relative prices which determine the amount and the direction of production, almost any change in the amount of money must necessarily also influence production (ibid., p. 28).

To understand the cycle, production changes have to be explained; these are the consequence of other changes in the relative prices structure. An 'across the board' modification of all prices would not lead to any restructuring of production.[12]

Here, Hayek is simply reproducing Mises' thinking. In *The Theory of Money and Credit* (1912), Mises, although he supported the existence of both monetary and natural interest rates, had already questioned Wicksell's analysis. In Mises' eyes, price rises are never simultaneous and would develop following the various industries' proximity to the banking sector. Following a tradition started by Cantillon, Mises conceptualised the temporal process of money circulation. Variations in the internal purchasing power of money lead to a sequential price modification of various goods. During the expansion process, relative price changes bring about modifications both in distribution of revenue and in the structure of incentives to produce one or the other category of goods.

Once he had established all these positions, Hayek concentrated on analysing the processes which lead the productive economy from credit expansion into crisis.

2. THE MONETARY LOGIC OF THE CYCLE

Increased money, in the form of extra credit from the banks, will either be distributed to consumers or producers and thus throughout the economy; Hayek finds there to be no difference between the two monetary spending channels as their effects are in the end the same. Consumer credit directly increasing agents' income, production credit is shown by an increase in earnings of production factors and so in higher agents' income. The impact on consumer income being the same, he thus concentrated in *Prices and Production* on 'the case most frequently in practice' (1931, p. 54), production credit.

2.1 A Monetary Mirage: The Boom

Increasing production credit is done through lowering monetary interest rates. Of course, lowering monetary rates (without lowering equilibrium rates) will make investment in factors more attractive in an uneven way, depending on the sector; the higher the sectors' capitalization, the more attractive investment will be: '... the fall in the rate will also change the relative profitableness of the different factors of production for the existing concerns, it will be seen to be quite natural that it should give a relative advantage to those concerns which use proportionately more capital' (Hayek, 1931, p. 86). In the graph, the highest placed will then be the ones most concerned, according to Hayek, as the most upstream industries have proportionately the highest fixed capital, by the very nature of their production.

As Hayek starts from a base of equilibrium, where all known resources are exploited, higher demand for production goods will immediately be met by a rise in their prices. Seen differently, only by bidding upwards, auction-wise, will the managers in the most capitalized sectors be able to get hold of necessary production factors (provided they are nonspecific), acting, of course, to the detriment of other, lower capitalized sectors such as consumer goods. So resources will undergo a general transfer to production goods sectors away from consumer goods sectors.

If this happens, consumer goods production will logically be reduced. Through the action of supply and demand, if the value of the sum of produced goods must correspond to the sum of available revenue to buy them (which at this stage has not moved up or down), the goods' unit price will rise. A phenomenon of forced savings would then be undergone by consumers, or in other words 'they get less goods for their money income' (Hayek, 1931, p. 57).

These mechanisms can be diagrammatically illustrated; if we base the reasoning on Figure 8.2, we see, in Figure 8.3, that the transfer of factors towards the higher stages results in a deepening, or a lengthening of production structures. The phenomenon is simply a reflection of higher degrees of roundaboutness.

Of course, the same process could start with spontaneous changes in agents' intertemporal choices, towards savings and away from consumption, or in other words by a change in equilibrium rates. Savings growth would thus result in a lowering of monetary rates, changing relative profitability in various production sectors. The same transfer of factors as just seen would take place towards the most capitalized sectors so consumer goods production would be reduced. The only difference would be that this lowering of consumer production would be concomitant with lowering revenue available for consumption, freely desired by consumers; there would be no discord and production changes would correspond to consumer/saver preferences. The technical aspects would reflect the subjective.

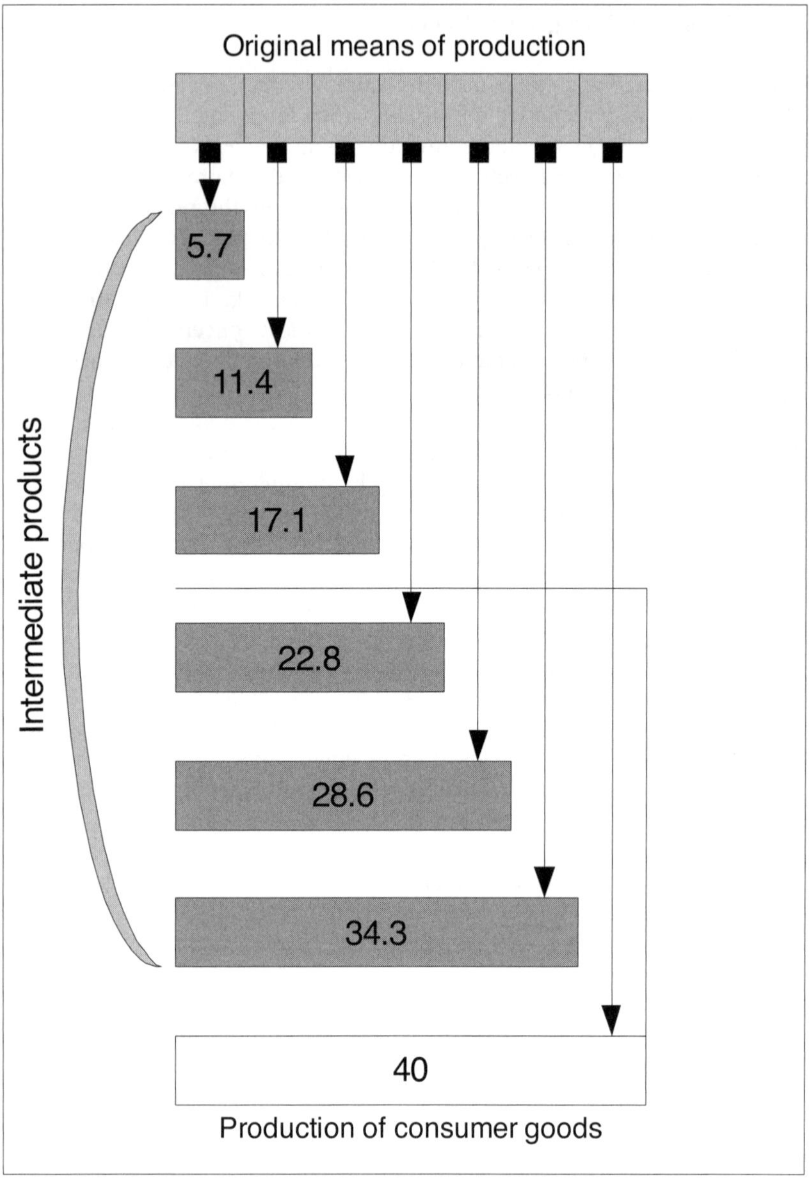

Source: Prices and Production, Hayek, 1931

Figure 8.3 The Boom

But the situation would be very different with a gap between monetary and equilibrium rates, as the process would not be triggered by consumer/savers but would be imposed on them, denying them their capacity to decide the form of production structures. Firms' producers/promoters would be the victims of a monetary 'misunderstanding'; as Ioannides puts it: '... the portion of income which is transferred via the credit market from consumers to producers can be thought of as a signal from the former to the latter, informing them about the time they are prepared to wait for the acquisition of consumer goods' (Ioannides, 1992, p. 119). But here it is not the case; producers/entrepreneurs register erroneous signals from the relative price structure, which is what conditions their expectations about consumer preferences. The process might be seen as beneficial if the production detour allowed consumer goods production to increase, in turn increasing consumers' real income levels. The only difficulty is that this process would not be completed before the underlying discord between agents' subjective, intertemporal preferences and entrepreneurs' technological and production choices would be revealed. This would mean the end of the boom and the beginning of the crisis.

2.2 The Constraint of Subjectivism: The Crisis

In fact it is the almost mechanical aspect to the process that sets off the crisis. Artificial scarcity of consumer goods created by evolution in production structures means their higher unit prices, which would contribute to higher profits from their production. This process will then move in the opposite direction from the one before. Continually auctioneering still unvarying quantities of production goods (the processes described above, not having gone far enough, according to Hayek, to increase their production), the owners of consumer goods sectors will have the incentive and the means to capture for themselves non-specific factors, thus depriving the more capitalized sectors, which had initially concentrated them in the first phase. Their situation will then rapidly deteriorate, contaminating upstream sectors as well:

> The first effect on these processes will be that the producers' goods of a more specific character, which have become relatively abundant by reason of the withdrawal of the complementary non-specific goods, will fall in price. The fall of the prices of these goods will make their production unprofitable; it will in consequence be discontinued (Hayek, 1931, p. 92).

The difficulties will then spread to all sectors of factor production.

At the same time, this degradation would be aggravated by consumer purchasing power growth in the boom's first stages. Employees would possess additional money in the form of wage rises as a result of the inter-sector competition for non-specific production factors: 'they [the producers] have spent the additional money which put them in a position to increase their demand for producers' goods and in consequence it has become consumers' income' (ibid., p. 60). This phenomenon of increased revenue will see inevitable consumption increases, all the stronger as a result of consumer frustration with the forced savings period of before.[13] As consumers catch up, increasing the consumer production sector's profitability and its capacity to capture non-specific factors, the more highly-capitalized sectors' problems are aggravated. By a phenomenon which later came to be called the Ricardo effect, 'in conditions of full employment, an increase in the demand for consumer goods will produce a decrease of investment, and vice-versa' (Hayek, 'Three Elucidations of the Ricardo Effect', 1969b, p. 165-166).

One last element should be mentioned: the demand for money will become ever more urgent because of sectors' increasing economic difficulties. If new money is not injected,[14] monetary rates will climb to match equilibrium rates. Borrowing enterprises during the boom would find it more difficult to pay interest, and their investments would be less profitable. Entrepreneurs would therefore not achieve their expectations, which they would have been able to had it been agents' subjective motivations which had set off the investment movement.

The congruence of these three factors pushes a production economy from a boom phase (exploited opportunities are greater than real opportunities) to a crisis (exploited opportunities are lower that known opportunities). The gap between monetary and equilibrium rates, created by the expansion of credit would result in capitalization of monetary, imaginary savings nothing to do with real, voluntary agents' savings. Monetary creation cannot increase the quantity of capital goods. The situation results in entrepreneurs' faulty forecasting; they thus start to invest wrongly as regarding consumer/saver desires. The difference between real and monetary supply of capital would not be sustainable in the long term and there would have to be an adjustment. Evolutions in the economy would give a dominant position back to individuals' subjective preferences; producer-imposed structures of production would thus be faced with change to less capitalized models to match individuals' free choice (Figure 8.4). The shortening of production structures would destroy some capital value, or more exactly would result in the realisation that, subjectively speaking, the capital accumulated in the previous period did not actually exist. Restructuration would be socially costly, involving as it does, redundancy and lower income.

Hayek, however, finds it important not to interfere with processes of adjustment; on the contrary: 'the thing which is needed to secure healthy conditions is the most speedy and complete adaptation possible of the structure of production to the proportion between the demand for consumer's goods and the demand for producers' goods as determined by voluntary saving and spending' (Hayek, 1931, p. 98). He condemns the raising of false hopes, especially calls for increased consumer credit in crisis periods, a 'desperado'

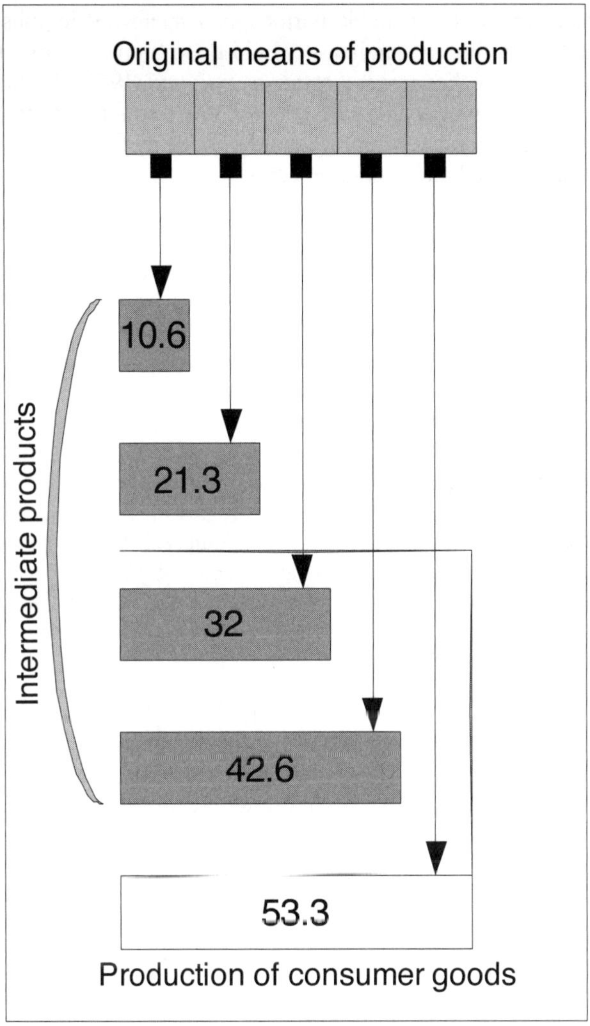

Source: Prices and Production, Hayek, 1931

Figure 8.4 The Crisis

policy, already unhealthy in stable periods as it means difficulties similar to those created by production credits. It would be to 'pull a tiger by the tail' (*A Tiger by the Tail, The Keynesian Legacy of Inflation*, 1972). In the middle of a crisis, this policy would increase problems even more. In boosting consumer against production demand, it would only delay the adjustment process and aggravate its social and economic costs.

3. MONETARY STABILITY, A DEFAULT SOLUTION

A cure to economic cycles can only be brought about by stability in money creation, even if this will never ensure the complete neutrality of money (3.1). Hayek and other neo-Austrian authors thus examined the institutional conditions meant to guarantee this stability.

3.1 Monetary Neutrality and its Limits

> Any currency policy which seeks to arbitrarily influence the 'value of money' will prevent the establishment of that natural structure of prices through time corresponding to the intertemporal exchange relations originating from barter, and alone able to ensure undisturbed self-reproduction in a monetary economy as well (Hayek, 1928a, p. 95).

Hayek considers that the tools to encourage healthy economies and prevent crises do exist and that stability requires proper money management. *Prices and Production* is meant to show that economic difficulties stemmed from the differences between saving and investment levels due to monetary expansion. Therefore maintaining equality is important as it is the only guarantor of coordination. Stability in monetary circulation improves coherency in the relative price structure and favours achievement of production plans.

So aiming for monetary neutrality and setting up conditions to prevent state interference is desirable. However, moving towards money neutralisation does not in fact mean there is any hope of being able to actually reach it.

Firstly, money supply in its widest sense is outside central banks' complete control, which means its general circulation is difficult to stabilize and regulate. Certainly, if one credit segment's variations could be perfectly and instantly matched by another segment's movements in the other direction, the total quantity of money would indeed be stabilised. This is never the case in practice, however.

Secondly and more fundamentally, a stable monetary mass is never neutral, quite the opposite; several cases come to mind. When changes occur in firms' organisation that nobody anticipates or controls, for example vertical integration or disintegration of production, 'changes in the proportion between the total flow of goods to that part of it which is effected by money'

(Hayek, 1931, p. 121) may be noted. They may require lowering or raising the quantity of money if 'money is to remain neutral towards the price system and the structure of production' (ibid., p. 121). It is also a question of responding not only to general needs in money but of affecting greater or fewer supplies of money to agents or sectors concerned. From a concrete point of view, 'it should be clear that only to satisfy the legitimate demand for money in this sense, and otherwise to leave the amount of the circulation unchanged, can never be a practical maxim of currency policy' (ibid., p. 124). Another case would be of changes in the speed of money circulation which may require changes to its supply on the market: 'any change in the velocity of circulation would have to be compensated by a reciprocal change in the amount of money in circulation if money is to remain neutral towards prices' (ibid., p. 124).

So finally there are many difficulties 'which makes this concept of the total quantity of the circulating medium somewhat vague, and which makes the possibility of ever actually fixing its magnitude highly questionable' (Hayek, 1931, p. 113). In addition to this, associating neutral money and constant money supply is an error of theory:

> Hence the only practical maxim for monetary policy to be derived from our considerations is probably the negative one that the simple fact of an increase of production and trade forms no justification for an expansion of credit, and that – save in an acute crisis – bankers need not be afraid to harm production by overcaution. Under existing conditions, to go beyond this is out of question … It is probably an illusion to suppose that we shall ever be able entirely to eliminate industrial fluctuations by means of monetary policy (ibid., p. 125).

Hayek saw neutral money similarly to equilibrium; they are simply conceptual markings, completely divorced from economic reality. On analysis, neutral money is shown to be an inaccessible ideal, even if trying to approach neutrality is, in practice, desirable.

3.2 From Gold Standard to Private Currencies

Even if completely neutral money is an unattainable goal, the main factor in reality leading to 'monetary deneutrality' is still governmental expansionist policy. This led Hayek (1928b, 1931, 1932, 1937b) to preach a return to the impersonal constraints of the gold standard in order to reduce arbitrary political intervention.

> So long as we do not see more clearly about the most fundamental problems of monetary theory and so long as no agreement is reached on the essential theoretical questions, we are also not yet in a position drastically to reconstruct our monetary system, in particular to replace the semi-automatic gold standard by a more or less arbitrarily managed currency (Hayek, 1931, p. 127).

The gold standard limits monetary creation to gold reserves, and with it the state's ability to arbitrarily raise the money supply.

Hayek's thoughts on this matter have evolved interestingly. Experience taught him that for the gold standard to work properly, the state was required to strictly adhere to the rules. All governments needed to behave in a disciplined way, which they started to be more and more reluctant to do between the wars, as they tried to gather or keep electoral majorities to stay in power.[15] They showed a growing tendency to raise state spending to satisfy the demands of various pressure groups. As they were not keen to finance these either with unpopular taxes or by borrowing, which sooner or later would need to be repaid, they resorted directly to monetary creation.

This reflection led Hayek (*Denationalisation of Money, An Analysis of the Theory and Practice of Concurrent Currencies*, 1976b; *Denationalisation of Money – the Argument Refined. An Analysis of the Theory and Practice of Concurrent Currencies*, 1978c)[16] to support the idea of money privatisation which would deny the state the monopoly of minting money. His idea, which followed Benjamin Klein's initial model ('The Competitive Supply of Money', 1974), was that money is not a public good and it should not be monopolistically produced by just one supplier. In Hayek's eyes any bank should be allowed to produce its own money (deposit and cash) in a decentralised way. There would then be as many units of account as money brands; agents would have a whole range of competing currencies that they could choose from at will.

Each of these currency's values would be based on an exchange rate fixed to a commodity basket which would measure the stability of each currency's purchasing power. Hayek believed, however, that these would have to be inconvertible either into gold or goods. But the currencies could be exchanged against each other, according to agents' subjective desires, the value of each fluctuating following a variable rate, depending on the stability of their power of purchase.

The banking system therefore would only be made up of paper currencies, with one unit of account for each bank. The fear would be that the best of them would be forced out of the system by the worst but in Hayek's view, Gresham's law ('bad money drives out good') only applies to currencies in a legal monopoly. So it is not a theoretical law, it is limited by specific institutional constraints. In a world of competing currencies, Gresham's law is reversed: competing banks would need to either supply safe currencies or see them disappear from use; this is obviously not the case for legal tender, protected from competition. Good money would therefore drive out the bad.

This system would guarantee limits to currency creation. If any of them were issued in too great a quantity they would lose value; that is, purchasing power, by the laws of supply and demand. Individuals would change to other currencies enabling them to buy more for their money. The bank emitting this money in such a lax way would lose the public's confidence and go to the wall as demand for its product fell. This system would be a certain guarantee of stability and avoid general crises.

Many commentators have tried to find what continuity of ideas there is between Hayek's solutions to privatised money and those to the gold standard from the 1930s. Based on White (1999), we should probably consider these as extensions of the virtues of competition in the field of money, or a process of discovery applied to the monetary system. There are several elements which point to this.

The first is that the propositions in favour of competitive money would solve the paradoxical refusal to accept the theory of monetary quantitativism ('the point of view from which it springs is a positive hindrance to further progress', Hayek, 1931, p. 62) while supporting, whether by pragmatism or opportunism, monetary policies based on this same quantitativism ('one of the worst things which would befall us if the general public should ever again cease to believe in the elementary propositions of the quantity theory', ibid., p. 3). Quantitativism in fact does not properly describe the relationship between money, prices and production; however, basing monetary policies on its principles does give results tending towards coordination. Privatizing money would reconcile theory and practice, setting up principles of healthy monetary regulation without basing these on faulty reasoning about money's general value.

The second element is that even if historically, metallic money has shown its practical usefulness, Hayek finds that things are not so simple, analytically speaking:

> not only is a metallic money also exposed to the risks of fraud by government; even at its best it would never be as good a money as one issued by an agency whose whole business rested on its success in providing a money the public preferred to other kinds (1978c, p. 83).

The last and most important element, apart from political concerns, is the fact that monetary competition is one solution to a cognitive problem with major practical implications. Indeed, efficiency in centralised monetary policy is based on finding the best possible means of stabilizing exchange rates between goods and money, but to do this, the central bank must not only know what demand there is for currency, which is a challenge, but also control it. This is nearly impossible, so scattered is demand, coming as it does from the disparate population of actors. This unavoidable ignorance on the part of the central institutions charged with stabilizing prices is a severe brake on the scope and efficiency of their mission.

By decentralizing and privatizing the supply of money, ignorance about its global demand loses all its grip; supply no longer adapts to unknown levels of demand. It is demand which regulates supply, through buying and selling currency in competition with others. So it is through the competition process (individuals' desire to possess strong currencies) that the most suitable quantities of money will be discovered.

Hayek would appear to oppose the idea that a competitive process can deliver adequate money supply in a system with only one reserve currency (gold). Commercial banks always seem to over-produce cash. In his very first writings, he considers that a merchandise-based currency puts price stability at risk, although less so than arbitrary governmental interference would. A 100% reserve forced on the banks to limit currency creation would not solve the problem but Hayek still did not think a banking system based on fractional reserves would be desirable. He saw it as being unstable as it would cause cash flow problems in the banks.

All the neo-Austrians agreed on principles of monetary noninterventionism, claiming to be the inheritors of the spirit if not the letter of Mises' teachings on the subject. They in fact were not united, as each author interpreted Mises differently. Thus Hayek's writings on the subject inspire a variety of reactions, including several critiques.

Some commentators, like White, Selgin or Garrison,[17] while not questioning the core of his argument, do not agree with the techniques employed. Freedom to issue is certainly one element of efficiency but the idea of inconvertibility of currencies must be opposed, as it only encourages banks to increase currency creation. 'A "free banking" regime with competing issuers of redeemable notes and deposits is quite distinct from an Hayekian regime of "competing fiat monies"' (Selgin and White, 1996, p. 86). In claiming Mises' inheritance, they are supporting the idea of fractional reserves.

But certain critiques go beyond the technical aspects of Hayek's propositions. On the strictly economics front, some very strong oppositions have arisen. Percy Greaves in the preface to *On the Manipulation of Credit and Money* (1978a), emits strong doubts that Mises would have agreed with Hayek's proposal. In a very similar way, Rothbard ('The Case of Genuine Gold Standard', 1986; 'The Myth of Free Banking in Scotland', 1988; 'Aurophobia: or Free Banking on What Standard', 1992; 'The Present State of Austrian Economics', 1995) is convinced that Hayek's vision is nothing to do with Mises'. Rothbard does agree with Hayek on the abolition of centrally emitted currency, claiming each establishment should be free to issue money but – in a departure from Hayek – under the control of the legal system rather than some easily by-passed administrative set of rules. He also claimed the law should enforce the following: banks must hold 100% of gold reserves for every penny of cash and credit emitted; any printing of money above the gold or any other real goods reserve limit would simply be counterfeit. He claimed Mises would have condemned the destructive effects of a banking system not based on that principle. Money must be purely metallic or else based on a real counterpart. Hayek does not propose the abolition of counterfeit, he proposes generalizing and privatizing it.

So Rothbard[18] and his followers criticize not only Hayek but all the other neo-Austrian authors who consider that a fractional reserve system could be an efficient solution. Their contrary claim is that all crises stem from this system:

> without fractional reserve banking, there will be no more booms and busts, no more terrible malinvestments, distorsions, and shocks of euphoria and distress brought about by business cycles. Investment will be limited to voluntary savings, and therefore there will be no periodic outbreaks of unsound investments that will have to be liquidated by recession. The world oecumene will at last be secured by the money required for freedom: a metallic money, produced by the market and the value of which is decided totally by the market and not at all by government (Rothbard, 1995, p. 81).

4. THE GREAT DEBATES

The publication of *Prices and Production* gave rise to a series of debates in which several major authors crossed pens with Hayek to challenge his version of the cycle. Revisiting some of these debates shows three points which would appear central to understanding the Austrian problematic: firstly, the respective positions of the theories of capital and money in the theory of the cycle (4.1); secondly, the status of the notion of equilibrium in Hayek's explanation of fluctuations (4.2); and lastly the ability of real economy analytical tools to examine the workings of a monetary economy, based on the notions of value and price (4.3).

4.1 Savings, Investment and Money: the Hayek-Keynes Collision

The Hayek-Keynes debate[19] is one of the best starting points, historically and analytically speaking, to examine these controversies; it represents the clash of two totally different personalities and worlds of theory.

Oddly enough, it was Hayek who started off the debate with a revue of Keynes's *A Treatise on Money* (1930-31).[20] In fact, a comparison of *Treatise* and *Prices and Production* show that the two authors agree on at least one central point: the concepts of savings, investment and money must constitute the three central points of any cycle theory.[21] However the causal relationship between these elements in triggering crisis seems to be reversed in the two analyses. We have seen that Hayek considers that growth of money supply results in artificial capitalization, in excess of agents' voluntary savings, which sets off the cycle and therefore inevitably crisis. For Keynes in *Treatise*, however, excess savings on investment is the root of problems. So the role of monetary expansion is to allow investment to catch up. Agents' savings therefore do not automatically end up in investment.

Hayek immediately shows his difficulty in understanding Keynes's position, asking for more details on this 'theoretically stimulating', work but apparently in 'an unfinished state' (Hayek, August, 1931, p. 271). Hayek sees ambiguities and contradictions in Keynes's thinking as the result of its insufficient grounding in a theory of capital and production processes. He claims Keynes cannot then properly understand Wicksell's theory, the bearing of which is difficult to grasp if it is separated from Böhm-Bawerk's analysis: 'Mr Keynes ignores completely the general theoretical basis of Wicksell's theory' (ibid., p. 279). Hayek in particular does not see how it is possible to conceive of a gap between savings and investment without introducing a hypothesis of the evolution of the quantity of money.

The problem for Hayek is that these weaknesses prevent the understanding of the formation of profits. He claims that according to Keynes, profits are necessarily the result of an excess of investment on savings. Following the logic of the *Treatise* this excess cannot exist without increasing the money supply. So profit, which is the expression of economic dynamics, can only stem from monetary expansion. Seen from Hayek's point of view, this profit must bring on crisis, as monetary expansion destroys production processes, with increasingly disastrous implications as one continues down the same route: 'Any attempt to combat the crisis by credit expansion will therefore, not only be merely the treatment of symptoms as causes, but may also prolong the depression by delaying the inevitable real adjustments' (Hayek, February, 1932, p. 44).

Keynes's own contributions to the controversy somewhat increased the misunderstandings and divergences between the two authors. He does not agree with Hayek's views on *Treatise*. He particularly does not agree with the idea of a relation between monetary expansion and profit, firstly because the difference between investment and savings can be conceived as being brought about independently of the banking system,

> merely as a result of the public changing their rate of saving or the entrepreneurs changing their rate of investment, [so] there being no automatic mechanism in the economic system (as Dr Hayek's view would imply there must be) to keep the two rates equal, provided that the effective quantity of money is unchanged (Keynes, November, 1931, p. 251)

and secondly because monetary expansion does not necessarily affect profits. The injection of money can 'meet losses' (ibid., p. 248). More generally, when agents sell stocks to a bank which then uses them to increase its deposits, 'the quantity of money is changed without anything having happened either to saving or to investment' (ibid., p. 248). Keynes discovered this wrong interpretation of the *Treatise* in the method and theory of *Prices and Production*, the critique of which was to constitute a large part of his argument.[22]

Of course, Keynes willingly accepts that a theory of capital is somewhat absent from *Treatise*, but not that it is necessary to construct a monetary theory of the cycle (see Keynes, November, 1931, p. 252-253).

In the second half of his commentary, Hayek points to this absence to explain the oddities in Keynes's arguments. He notes the

> little use he finally makes of the effects of a monetary dis-equilibrium on *real* investment ... What he is really interested in is merely the shifts in the money streams and the consequent changes in price levels. It seems never to have occurred to him that the artificial stimulus to investment, which makes it exceed current saving, may cause a dis-equilibrium in the real structure of production which, sooner or later, must lead to a reaction. Like so many others who hold a purely monetary theory of the trade cycle (as, for example, Mr. R. G. Hawtrey in this country and Dr. L. A. Hahn in Germany), he seems to believe that, if the existing monetary organisation did not make it impossible, the boom could be perpetuated by indefinite inflation (February, 1932, p. 40).

Hayek claims the fact that Keynes sees no contradiction in the idea of a difference between savings and investment with no modification in the real quantity of money is a demonstration of his incapacity to see the effects of the variations in interest rates on the structure of capital. This prevents him from understanding the meaning and effect of a distinction between voluntary and forced savings, which he himself allows in his response (see November, 1931, p. 251-252) and later correspondence (p. 257-261). This question of capital and real economy mechanisms is behind the debates on the role of equilibrium in *Prices and Production*.

4.2 'Equilibrium' and 'Equilibriums': Hicks's Critique

Examining Hicks's reflections on *Prices and Production* is the best way to approach Hayek's use of equilibrium. In 'The Hayek Story' (1967), he offers a neoclassical reading of Hayek's thinking, on the basis of which he questions the logic of Hayek's cycle theory. He concentrates on the static aspect of the idea of equilibrium and thus seems to refute the idea that economic adjustment vectors other than prices might exist in Hayek's reasoning. When prices are free to move, money stays neutral as it cannot influence quantities. So if the hypothesis of perfect flexibility is accepted, lowering the monetary rate in relation to natural rates would affect prices but not real production variables; monetary rates would thus follow natural rates: 'In Wicksell, the "Cumulative Process" is a matter of prices. When the "market rate" of interest is reduced below the natural rate, prices rise. Nothing is said about the movement of quantities (inputs and outputs)' (Hicks, 1967, p. 205).

Certainly, Wicksell's model can be read in several ways. Following the way that Hicks seems to note certain hypotheses in *Prices and Production*, especially on perfect price flexibility, Hayek's ideas on triggering a boom appear to be erroneous:

> When the market rate is reduced below the natural rate, what will happen to the quantities of inputs and outputs? The correct answer, on these assumptions, is very simple: the effect will be nil. Prices will rise uniformly; and that is that. When the Wicksell model is taken strictly (as it was being taken strictly), it is in Neutral equilibrium ... Thus there is no room for a prolonged discrepancy between market rate and natural rate if there is instantaneous adjustment of prices. Money prices will simply rise uniformly; and that is that (Hicks, 1967, p. 206).

No real process arising from any kind of time lag between production and consumer prices is actually therefore triggered. Factor price rises must immediately be followed by wage rises, which

> must be followed, nearly at once ... by a rise in the demand for consumption goods. Then, in view of the full employment assumption, the prices of consumption must also rise. And there can be no equilibrium of supply and demand, over the whole system, until they have risen enough to withdraw the incentive for the rise in real investment (ibid., p. 208).

In spite of Hayek's claims, the Ricardo effect, that is a rise in production goods prices, with its corollary of lowering in consumer goods prices, cannot work.

There are several points to make about Hicks's argument. Firstly, his surprising claim that the flexibility argument in *Prices and Production* is so central, when Hayek himself mentions the: 'notorious rigidity of wages' (1931, p. 106). Furthermore, at the end of the book (p. 127-128), he explains that the largest part of the crisis of the moment was not due to monetary factors but to state intervention. *Prices and Production* does propose a monetary explanation of the cycle but the depth of the depression stemmed, rather than from monetary causes, from the institutions and the rigidity associated with their growing interventionism.[23] Hayek claims that this rigidity, reinforcing the consequences of monetary expansion, leads to mechanisms which deform production structures. This is perhaps why he noted in *Monetary Theory and the Trade Cycle* '... there is no necessary reason why the initiating change, the original disturbance eliciting a cyclical fluctuation in a stationary economy, should be of monetary origin' (1928b, p. 182). In the same way, in his answer to Hicks ('Three Elucidations of the Ricardo Effect', 1969b), he was to write, on the central argument of *Prices and Production* that 'This theory never claimed to do more than account for the upper turning point of the typical nineteenth-century business cycle' (1969b, p. 174).

A second point concerns the idea of equilibrium as such. Literature has no doubt over-stressed the static dimension of equilibrium described by Hayek, much discussion taking place over the fact that the starting point of his thinking on the subject implicitly adheres to Walras' static reasoning. So in spite of there being no explicit data on expectations, Hicks considers 'We shall hardly go wrong if we take it [Hayek's model] to be the simplest possible assumption: the 'static' assumption. The same prices as rule today (whatever they are) are expected to continue to rule in the future' (1967, p. 206). However, there are a few remarks to be made about Hicks's argument, notably that the static dimension has to be thought of as a convenient springboard to reflection, a '... methodologically valuable fiction ... by which time is abstracted from' (Hayek, 1928a, p. 71). It is more of a logic or teaching tool to better show up the concept of disequilibrium by contrast with the entirely imaginary concept of equilibrium. This idea is close to some of Mises' notions of an evenly-rotating economy[24] and/or the stationary economy being imaginary but necessary departure points of reasoning. It is the contrary of the idea of general economic equilibrium, which is an arrival point: '... it is possible to apply the concept of equilibrium, and the static mode of analysis adopted in doing so, only to an economy which is presumed to be without time' (Hayek, 1928a, p. 74). Hayek does mention that 'All economic activity is carried out through time' (ibid., p. 71). The notion of static equilibrium is therefore not supposed to realistically represent an economic state at all.

Another remark about Hicks's argument would be that contemporary economies are monetary. Hayek from his first writings posits the mutual exclusion of the static state and the monetary economy, within which agents' real choices are never totally expressed by the relative price structure, especially where saving and consumption are concerned. He had already established this position in 'Intertemporal Price Equilibrium and Movements in Money Value':

> we must finally give up all thoughts of completely eliminating monetary influences by restricting money to the role of a passive mediator, so that the economy proceeds as if money were not employed in it ... The principles derived for an economy with money can be applied to an economy with money only with substantial qualifications (1928a, p. 103).

Money is an essential component in a production economy; seeing the economy as primarily monetary prevents thinking in static terms.

Behind this refusal to envisage an equilibrium economy with neutral money is a temporal and structural vision of production where money has no effect on relative prices. This is what leads Hayek's thinking a long way from Walras' equilibrium structure and his 'numerary', starting with his first writings through to *Prices and Production* and then much later, following the same idea, he answers Hicks ('Three Elucidations of the Ricardo Effect'):

> Sir John Hicks is right to the extent that the relationships determined by the real data only must assert themselves sooner or later. But this does not happen as instantaneously as he assumes. There may be a prolonged period during which the re-

lations corresponding to the 'real equilibrium' are greatly distorted by monetary changes. It still seems to me that this has much to do with the phenomenon of industrial fluctuations (1969b, p. 178).

4.3 Real Economies versus Monetary Economies: The Hayek-Sraffa Debate

Hicks questioned the triggering itself of the cycle, but Sraffa ('Dr. Hayek on Money and Capital', March, 1932) chose to concentrate on Hayek's logic of the change of boom into crisis. Sraffa's analysis came after Keynes's and it could be seen as an illustration of a certain number of ideas running through Keynes's work.[25]

This is how Sraffa's question on the conservation of capital had already been asked by Keynes in his correspondence with Hayek (see Keynes, January, 1932, p. 261). Sraffa turned Hayek's own reasoning on him, considering that during the intermediate, boom phase, the quantity of consumer goods has physically risen but not their monetary value (the value of the consumer goods block stays the same). This would therefore mean that money growth had been accompanied by a unit price drop of consumer goods. This would wipe out both the phenomenon of forced savings and consumer desire to return to levels of consumption that had been prevented by rising factor prices. Consumers would replace bankers in financing extra investment, preventing decapitalization. The main cause of depression would be removed, claimed Sraffa, as the crisis would not be triggered: 'One class has, for a time, robbed anther class of a part of their incomes; and has saved the plunder. When the robbery comes to an end, it is clear that the victims cannot possibly consume the capital which is now well out of their reach' (March, 1932, p. 48).

So what we see here is a disagreement on the order of events which Hicks expressed in terms of prices and Sraffa in terms of quantities. There is only one source of these disagreements, putting aside the importance of time in the production processes. Against Sraffa's argument is the fact that consumer goods cannot increase in quantity during this intermediate phase. Only at the end of the period of extra capitalization can consumer goods increase; however, in Hayek's scheme the extra investment is unfinished, which is why capital loses value in spite of being physically augmented. Also, during this process of extra capitalization, extra income coming from payment for factors is distributed to the agents.

In his response, 'Money and Capital: A Reply' (June, 1932), Hayek considered this is where Sraffa's analytical weakness lay:

> would he really deny that, by a sudden relative increase in the demand for consumers' goods, capital may be destroyed against the will of its owners? Surely the case which we are discussing is just the same: as incomes rise in consequence of the preceding credit expansion and the mass of consumers, who under our assumption spend all their income on consumption goods, increase their expenditure accord-

> ingly, while the money available for investment in capital goods does not increase any longer, the value of some capital goods produced under the inducement of a relatively stronger demand for such goods will fall below their cost of production ... The fact is simply this, that any increase of incomes used for consumptive purposes relatively to the sums available for productive purposes, will tend to decrease the 'purchasing power' of these sums (i.e. the purchasing power of money-capital); and that, whereas in the former case, where the relative rise of incomes follows only a preceding relative rise in the demand for capital goods, only part of the capital created by the inflation is destroyed again, in the latter case, the destruction of capital is not offset by any preceding gain (June, 1932, p. 244).

Without actually refuting it, Sraffa received this argument with some scepticism in his last, brief contribution to the debate, 'Money and Capital: A Rejoinder' (June, 1932).

Sraffa also questioned the idea of equilibrium in the real economy. Keynes had noted, in his debate with Hayek that a monetary economy observing neutrality can still be disequilibriated, as the decision to invest is independent from the supplies of savings. So in the case of more investment being decided upon, resources will flow to factor production, depriving consumer production and thus triggering forced savings. This phenomenon led Keynes to doubt the relevance of distinguishing between forced and voluntary savings, as the former may be caused by the system's own evolution. He thus questioned the inherent stability of a monetary economy of production; it would be possible to have a difference between savings and investment without changing the quantity of money.

Sraffa went further than Keynes on this, or one could possibly say he went right to the bottom of the argument. He claimed it was no longer simply the equilibrium of a monetary economy of production which was being questioned but the equilibrium of the real economy, that is, without money. Saffra claimed that Hayek was mistaken in automatically postulating the equilibrium of the real economy:

> An essential confusion, which appears clearly from this statement, is the belief that the divergence of rates is a characteristic of a money economy ... The 'arbitrary' action of the banks is by no means a necessary condition of the divergence; if loans were made in wheat and farmers (or for that matter the weather) 'arbitrarily changed' the quantity of wheat produced, the actual rate of interest on loans in terms of wheat would diverge from the rate on other commodities and there would be no single equilibrium rate (March, 1932, p. 49).

In the real economy, where lending is made in the form of real goods, there would by definition be as many interest rates as goods.

Hayek shows he did not understand the nature of that critique by his answer to it. He easily allows Sraffa the idea of multiple interest rates in relation to the real goods involved, but they are not apparently a problem: 'there might, at any moment, be as many "natural" rates of interest as there are commodities, *all* of which will be equilibrium rates' (Hayek, June, 1932, p. 145). Sraffa's position seems to utterly surprise Hayek, which for him expresses 'an extreme theoretical nihilism which denies that existing theories of equilibrium provide any useful description of the non-monetary forces at work (ibid., p. 238).

Hayek's answer in fact gives weight to Keynes's preceding argument that an equilibriated monetary economy of production is impossible, even in the case of neutral money. If we allow, as does Hayek, that in the real economy – where the borrowing market operates through quantities of goods – there would be differing equilibrium rates, it would be impossible to support the idea that one lone monetary rate would be compatible with these various interest rates. Sraffa clearly points this out in this brief comment on Hayek's response, incidentally insisting that it is impossible to reason in terms of average natural rates, as Hayek himself refuses to do in *Prices and Production*:

> … neither aggregates nor averages do act upon one another, and it will never be possible to establish necessary connections of cause and effect between them as we can between individual phenomena, individual prices, etc. I would even go so far as to assert that from the very nature of economic theory, averages can ever form a link in its reasoning (1931, p. 4-5).

Several arguments, however, can be opposed to that line of thinking.

A first level of argument would be a reminder that Hayek himself has always pointed out that reasoning in a monetary economy is not at all the same thing as reasoning in the real economy. In a monetary economy, savings and investment take monetary form and there is no other interest rate in practice than the monetary rate. So parity between the monetary and equilibrium rates expresses the fact that the monetary rate reflects agents' subjective preferences between savings and consumption. There is no need to refer to the barter economy, which by definition cannot coexist with a monetary economy as they exclude each other. Hayek, in his response to Sraffa, develops an argument which implicitly takes this problem into account:

> I have been assuming that the body of existing pure economic theory demonstrates that, so long as we neglect monetary factors, there is an inherent tendency towards an equilibrium of the economic system; and what I tried to do in *Prices and Production*, and in certain earlier publications, was to show that monetary factors may bring about a kind of disequilibrium in the economic system – which could not be explained without recourse to these monetary factors (Hayek, June, 1932, p. 228).

A second level of argument is that Hayek had noted quite clearly in *Prices and Production* that money can never be totally neutral, so there will at all times be disequilibria. Sraffa's mentioning situations where equilibrium cannot exist in spite of money supply stability is rather an obvious point. The real meaning of Hayek's message is a negative one, which is that any monetary expansion can only increase the amount and intensity of disequilibria, making money even less neutral. So the least bad solution is to keep to objectives of stability in the amount of money in circulation.

There is one final argument, corresponding to dynamics: the idea of a tendency towards equilibrium of natural rates. Both Sraffa's and Hayek's hypotheses of multiple natural rates would only work in a static world. As soon as there are differences, profit opportunities arise which of course entrepreneurs will exploit. Of course, dynamic conditions being what they are (changes in technology, agents interacting, etc), this process is never-ending. But the idea could be floated of the natural rates' tendency towards equilibrium among themselves, which would make the transformation process of the various natural rates into one single rate much easier. Hayek's initial reference to stationary equilibrium is simply used as an illustrative thought experiment; he is perfectly clear that introducing money into the economic model prevents thinking in the statics mode and of achieving general equilibrium.

NOTES

1. Hawtrey, Aftalion and Rist are obvious examples of this. See Tinbergen's review of literature from the era ('Annual Survey: Suggestions on Quantitative Business Cycle Theory', 1935).
2. Either at the same time or after Mises and Hayek, other authors occupied the terrain with their own contributions. Haberler ('Some Reflections on the Present Situation of Business Cycle Theory', 1936; *Prosperity and Depression: A Theoretical Analysis of Cyclical Movements*, 1937), Lachmann ('Uncertainty and Liquidity-Preference' 1937; 'On Crisis and Adjustment', 1939); *Capital and Its Structure*, 1956), Machlup (*The Stock Market, Credit and Capital Formation*, 1940), Rothbard (*America's Great Depression*, 1975), Garret and Rothbard (*The Great Depression and New Deal Monetary Policy*, 1978), Kirzner (*An Essay on Capital,* 1966; *Essays on Capital and Interest*, 1996b). However, their analyses are either not specific enough or too close to Mises' and Hayek's to be thought of as real alternatives.
3. See the collection *The Manipulation of Credit and Money* (1978a) and the section of *Money, Method and the Market Process* (1990) on monetary questions (p. 55-109).
4. One of Hayek's first posts was as Director of the Austrian Institute for Business Cycle Research, which he got through Mises' support. Before this, he had made a study trip to the USA (1923-1924), writing several articles on his return on the problems of fluctuations in the market economy (1925-1929), the most important of which were translated into English and were published in a 1985 collection, together with later texts, entitled *Money, Capital and Fluctuations, Early Essays*. Hayek's first full-length book, in a similar vein, was entitled *Monetary Theory and Trade Cycle* (1928b). For some biographical elements from this period, see Lepage's 'Demain le libéralisme', 1980, p. 410-413; Kresge and Wenar, *Hayek by Hayek, An Autobiographical Dialogue*, 1994; Dostaler, *Le libéralisme de Hayek,* 2001; Ebenstein, *Friedrich Hayek: A Biography* 2001.

5. This theory of the cycle that had been long sidelined by post-war economic thinking won Hayek the 1974 Nobel Prize. The best contemporary versions of his view are no doubt Garrison (*Time and Money: The Universals of Macroeconomic Theorizing*, 1987; 'The Austrian Theory of the Business Cycle in the Light of Modern Macroeconomics', 1989; Austrian Theory of Business Cycles, 1997; *Time and Money,* 2001)*;* see also Wainhouse ('Empirical Evidence for Hayek's Theory of Economic Fluctuations', 1984), Bellante and Garrison ('Phillips Curve and Hayekian Triangles: Two Perspectives on Monetary Dynamics', 1988), Skousen (*The Structure of Production*, 1990; 'The Great Depression', 1994), Hugues ('The Recession of 1990: an Austrian Explanation', 1997), Keeler ('Empirical Evidence on the Austrian Business Cycle Theory', 2001), Carilli and Dempster ('Expectations in Austrian Business Cycle Theory: An Application of the Prisoner's Dilemma', 2001).
6. The work is a collection of articles published 1929 and 1937, except the first part which is an original representation of the cycle mechanisms.
7. 'The existence of equilibrium implies that the plans of consumers and those of producers are mutually compatible, so that the portion of their income which consumers wish to save is exactly equal to the volume of investment which producers wish to undertake' (Ioannides, 1992, p. 119).
8. In a footnote on p. 38, Hayek explains that he is the author of the graphs in *Prices and Production* but admits that he later noticed that Jevons (*Theory of Political Economy*, 1871) and Wicksell (*Lectures of Political Economy*, 1901) had previously used similar items in their works.
9. We should not mistake consumer goods' reduced value for a reduction of quantities produced. Quite the opposite, the advantage of lengthening the production process is to raise production quantities, or rather to allow the same quantity to be produced for lower cost. In the same way, lowering factor unit cost does not mean fewer factors are used in the intermediary stages, as in fact their quantity is increased.
10. It should be remembered that at the start of this reasoning, all known resources have supposedly been utilised. Technologically speaking, it is impossible to raise production levels in one sector without taking factors being used for other sectors.
11. Hayek (1931, p. 80) prefers to call this the 'equilibrium rate'.
12. This is the way that the vision of the cycle as a real phenomenon logically needs to refer to changes in relative prices and not in the general price level: 'Now everybody agrees that a change of prices would be of no consequence whatever if all prices in the widest sense of the term were affected equally and simultaneously' (Hayek, 1931, p. 5). And also: 'The interesting problems are those of the effect of monetary changes on particular prices, and about these, index numbers or changes of general price levels tell us nothing' (Hayek, 1978a, p. 6-7).
13. 'The forced saving of consumers can only be a temporary phenomenon, since, as the costs of means of production increase, so do the incomes of those who own them. Consequently, consumers begin to obtain a share of the money which producers had originally acquired' (Ioannides, 1992, p. 124).
14. Raising capital goods prices along with wages logically reduces the perspectives of investment profitability. For them to become profitable, a continual raise of the money in circulation would be necessary to lower the interest rates proportionate to the future, lower profitability: 'Thus the deeper structure of production can only be maintained if the banking system continues to increase the supply of credit money, thereby progressively lowering the lending rate, as it is only in this way that producers can overcome the increasing cost of the new investment projects' (Ioannnides, 1992, p. 124).
15. For an analysis of the similarities of Public Choice with the neo-Austrians' point of view, see in particular DiLorenzo ('Competition and Political Entrepreneurship: Austrian Insights into Public Choice Theory', 1986); Baird ('James Buchanan and the Austrians: The

Common Ground', 1989). A special edition of *The Review of Austrian Economics* (vol. 15, n° 2-3, June 2002) was devoted to relations between Austrian analysis and Public Choice's views, notably with contributions from Buchanan and Vanberg, Holcombe, Foldvary, Sutter and Lopez (see bibliography).

16. Barry (*Hayek's Social and Economic Philosophy*, 1979, p. 177) rightly remarks this means abandoning the idea of monetary policy. In principle the idea was already latent in the 1930s, which would have meant Hayek losing influence as a result of the seductions of *The General Theory* (see on this point Machlup, *Essays on Hayek*, 1976, p. 26). Among the great mass of literature on the subject of private money, impossible to list here, see particularly Garrison ('The Cost of a Gold Standard', 1986); Dowd (*The Experience of Free Banking*, 1992; *Free Banking*, 1994; *Laissez-faire Banking*, 1996); Selgin (*The Theory of Free Banking,* 1988); White (*Free Banking in Britain: Theory, Experience and Debate, 1800-1845*, 1984); Klausinger, *From Neutral Money to Competing Currencies: Hayek on Monetary Policy*, 1997).
17. White ('Competition and Currency: Essays on Free Banking and Money', 1989; 'Mises on Free Banking and Fractional Reserves', 1992; 'Hayek's Monetary Theory and Policy: A Critical Reconstruction', 1999); Selgin and White ('In Defence of Fiduciary Media – or, We Are Not Devolutionnists, We Are Misesians', 1996); Garrison ('Central Banking, Free Banking and Financial Crisis', 1996).
18. The idea of fractional reserves supported by Selgin and White was vigorously attacked by some of Rothbard's followers. See Block ('Fractional-Reserve Banking: An Interdisplinary Perspective', 1988a); Hoppe ('How is Fiat Money Possible? – or The Devolution of Money and Credit', 1993c); Salerno ('Ludwig von Mises's Monetary Theory in Light of Modern Monetary Thought', 1994a); de Soto ('A critical Analysis of Central Banks and Fractional-Reserve Free Banking from the Austrian Perspective', 1995; 'New Light on the Prehistory of the Theory of Banking and the School of Salamanca', 1996; 'A Critical Note on Fractional-Reserve Free Banking', 1998); Block and Garschina ('Hayek, Business Cycles and Fractional Reserve Banking: Continuing the De-Homogenization Process', 1996); Hülsmann ('Free Banking and the Free Bankers', 1996; 'Banks Cannot Create Money', 2000b); Hoppe, Hülsmann and Block ('Against Fiduciary Media', 1998). For a counter argument, see Horwitz ('Misreading the 'Myth': Rothbard on the Theory and History of Free Banking', 1988).
19. See particularly Cochran and Glahe ('The Keynes-Hayek Debate: Lessons for Contemporary Business Cycle Theorists', 1994), Steele (*Keynes and Hayek, The Money Economy*, 2001).
20. Hayek's critique was a long two-part argument on 'A Treatise on Money'; 'Reflections on the Pure Theory of Money of Mr. J.M. Keynes' (August, 1931; February, 1932). Keynes replied to the first part on publication with 'The Pure Theory of Money, a Reply to Dr Hayek' (November, 1931) which in turn provoked Hayek's, 'A Rejoinder to Mr Keynes' (November, 1931). On Keynes's suggestion, the two engaged in a parallel correspondence throughout December, 1931 and January, 1932 (see bibliography).
21. In *Treatise on Money* (see vol. 1 p. 178), Keynes, specifically mentioning Hayek and Mises suggests similarities with his own ideas. Hayek notes, on *A Treatise on Money* that 'The new approach, which Mr Keynes has adopted, which makes the rate of interest and its relation to saving and investing the central problem of monetary theory … directs the attention to what is really essential' (Hayek, August, 1931, p. 270). Similarly, Hansen, referring to *Prices and Production*, notes that 'The present volume is, it seems to me, the only book of recent years which at all approaches Keynes's *A Treatise of Money* in the impetus it has given to renewed interest and discussion of business-cycle theory' (Hansen, June 1933, p. 332)
22. In his rejoinder, Hayek admits that his analysis of *Treatise* is more the result of his interpretation than of its letter. But he also admits he can find no argument other than that of

seeing an exclusively monetary origin in profits, 'I have been compelled to do so because I have been unable, and indeed still am unable, to detect in his *Treatise* or his subsequent elucidations any other tenable explanation of this phenomenon' (November, 1931, p. 399-400). Hayek is also surprised by Keynes's idea of a possible difference between savings and investment with no relation to money: 'Mr. Keynes' assertion that there is no automatic mechanism in the economic system to keep the rate of saving and the rate of investing equal (p. 393 above) might with equal justification be extended to the more general contention that there is no automatic mechanism in the economic system to adapt production to any other shift in demand. I begin to wonder whether Mr. Keynes has ever reflected upon the function of the rate of interest in a society where there is no banking system' (ibid., p. 401).

23. On the damage wrought by interventionism, see also Mises *A Critique of Interventionism* (1929); *On the Manipulation of Money and Credit* (1978a); *Human Action* (1966).
24. To see the difference between Mises' definitions of the evenly-rotating economy and stationary economy: *Human Action* (1966, p. 244-256). Some references can also be found in *Planning for Freedom* (1962c, p. 123 and 147-148).
25. A small anecdote sheds light on Keynes and Sraffa's relationship: when Hayek ('Money and Capital: A Reply'), accused Sraffa of having 'understood Mr. Keynes' theory even less than he has my own', Keynes cheekily inserted the following footnote (he was the review editor) in Hayek's article itself, '[With Prof. Hayek's permission I should like to say that, to the best of my comprehension, Mr. Sraffa has understood my theory accurately. – J.M. KEYNES.]' (Hayek, June, 1932, p. 249). For a review of the 'Hayek-Sraffa duel' see Lachmann, 1986b.

9. Welfare Economics: Workable Definitions

> ... a business deal is always advantageous for both parties. If both the buyer and the seller were not to consider the transaction as their most advantageous action they could choose under the prevailing conditions, they would not enter into the deal (Mises, *The Ultimate Foundations of Economic Science*, 1962a, p. 90).

Myrdal (*The Political Element in the Development of Economic Theory,* 1953) was right to claim, 'The Austrians were preoccupied with value theory and never elaborated a detailed theory of welfare economics' (1953, p. 128). This was rapidly corrected, however, as if in reply by Rothbard ('Toward a Reconstruction of Utility and Welfare Economics', 1956), which was the start of an abundance of Austrian literature on the question of welfare.

This writing should not be confused with traditional welfare economics, various versions of which are riddled with theoretical weaknesses that the Austrians have continually condemned. The subjectivist paradigm obviously prevents interpersonal comparisons of utility between agents and so excludes any use of utilitarist criteria as valueless.[1] Pareto's version, which avoids this kind of comparison, is faced with the impossibility of *a priori* knowledge of agents' indifference curves and therefore of considering it as data for the theorist.

More contemporary approaches, notably Coase's ('Social Cost', 1960) are based on a criterion of welfare centred on reducing transaction costs. But the mistake of believing in a fictitious 'Nirvana' (Kirzner, *Competition and Entrepreneurship*, 1973) where transaction costs would be eliminated, is obvious. Moreover, this situation would in any case not be the optimal one of all available opportunities being known and exploited; the basic problem is not one of eliminating transaction costs but acquiring knowledge:

> To take advantage of available opportunities one must first *perceive* them. To 'learn' free information, one must perceive the opportunity to do so. To complete a mutually profitable transaction one must not merely have free access to the requisite information, but must perceive its availability (and thus the possibility of the profitable transaction) (Kirzner, 1973, p. 227).

The traditional approach to welfare has been generally based on the idea of having a situation of perfect knowledge of agents' ends and available means; however, these cannot be thought of as theoretical data of which the observer would have *a priori* knowledge. It is precisely the entrepreneur's role to transform information into knowledge and spread it throughout society by his activities. So a dynamic, real-world market approach is needed to replace the static, fictitious one, where the problem of knowing which resources should be allocated to which ends has already been solved.

This is what neo-Austrian theories of welfare economics have been based on.

Interestingly, although Mises' followers agree that it is possible to found an Austrian analysis of welfare, they disagree on its characteristics and normative consequences: they all refer to a common method (individualism and subjectivism), but they break down into several often opposing conceptions of welfare.

Some of these neo-Austrian authors use welfare economics to support normative positions favouring classical liberalism yet others do not see this attempt as being well-founded: there are in fact disagreements among all neo-Austrian welfare economists about the possibility of founding a free market normativity grounded in economic analysis.

The Austrian welfare economy was framed within a procedural approach to welfare and based on the concept of demonstrated preference.[2] The idea of procedure allowed the analytical scope to be reduced to market exchange and to establish a certain symmetry between the market and satisfaction (1). The second notion, 'demonstrated preference', threw up a debate on whether it was possible to define free market normativity. Some Austrians considered it was impossible to define normative welfare economics, continuing to express their respect for the neutrality of values; others supported an opposing view (2). So must all hope be abandoned of agreeing on establishing a normative Austrian economy? Some of Hayek's contributions, especially in his last work, *The Fatal Conceit* (1988), in fact appear to open a few doors of fruitful inquiry (3).

1. THE MARKET AND SATISFACTION: A PROCEDURAL APPROACH TO WELFARE

There are today three schools of Austrian analysis of welfare economics, based mainly around three authors: Rothbard, Kirzner and Cordato. They all of course operate firmly within the subjectivist frame, common to the whole Austrian tradition. This frame imposes two constraints: it prevents any thought of agents' common preference, disallowing any substantive definition of welfare; it also prevents any interpersonal comparison of gain and cost. Beyond this common ground, the concepts of 'social utility' (1.1), of 'coordination' (1.2) and of 'catallactic efficiency' (1.3) intermingle to create a rainbow of different theories.

1.1 Exchange Producing 'Social Utility'

It was Rothbard who was first among Mises' followers to publish on Austrian welfare economics, with his 'Toward a Reconstruction of Utility and Welfare Economics' (1956).

Rothbard's and Pareto's concepts of welfare paradoxically hold in common the principle of unanimity. Austrian subjectivity excludes any interpersonal comparison of individual gains and costs, so an Austrian welfare economy must be based on the principle of unanimity; the need then is to define an economic landscape in accordance with this requirement. In Rothbard's eyes, the field of market exchange is the very expression of unanimity:

> Let us now consider exchanges on the free market. Such an exchange is voluntarily undertaken by both parties. Therefore, the very fact that an exchange takes place demonstrates that both parties benefit (or more strictly, expect to benefit) from the exchange. The fact that both parties chose the exchange demonstrates that they both benefit. The free market is the name for the array of all the voluntary exchanges that take place in the world. Since every exchange demonstrates a unanimity of benefit for both parties concerned, we must conclude that the free market benefits all its participants. In others words, welfare economics can make the statement that the free market increases social utility, while still keeping to the framework of the Unanimity Rule (1956, p. 28-29).

In addition, any utility generated by monetary exchange is not dependent on particularities of the participants' aims. The market benefits all its participants, whatever their reasons for exchanging. So, based on this, it should be possible to construct an Austrian welfare economy simply out of the virtues of bilateral exchange.

Rothbard also considers that this principle of unanimity allows him to establish that state intervention in exchange has no scientific connection with the production of welfare; when it is not opposing free exchange, state intervention imposes transactions, for example in taxing individuals in exchange for 'public goods'.[3] The state cannot then produce satisfaction without violating the principle of unanimity as 'State action obviously and demonstrably benefits one group and injures another, thus violating the Unanimity Rule' (1956, p. 251), with indetermined and unknowable results in terms of net creation of satisfaction:

> If therefore, free market exchanges always increase social utility, while no coerced exchange or interference can increase social utility, we may conclude that the maintenance of a free and voluntary market 'maximizes' social utility (provided we

> do not interpret 'maximize' in a cardinal sense) … The free market always increases social utility and no act of government can ever increase social utility. These two propositions are the pillars of the reconstructed welfare economics (Rothbard, 1956, p. 252-253).

So, according to Rothbard, simply defining rules of voluntary exchange opens the door to constructing an Austrian welfare economy based on market activities. This thinking runs into difficulties which Rothbard is perfectly aware of, that is, the question of the twin principles of voluntary exchange and real production of satisfaction. Mises' praxeological model (1933, 1957, 1962, 1966) tells us that the notion of uncertainty of the future is a theorem of action, as its result is in the unknowable future. Market exchange being one category of action, it cannot guarantee satisfaction in advance. Indeed, voluntary exchange, which expresses one form of coordination of individual action, does not necessarily achieve success of expectations. The time gap between prediction forming and exchange can induce expectations to fail.[4] Rothbard had to adjust his idea, announcing that people who expect exchange will provide satisfaction, but in fact there is no guarantee that it will be the case. This constraint would lead him, in 'Praxeology, Value Judgements and Public Policy' (1976b) to finely distinguish between *ex ante* and *ex post* utility.[5] His idea is that voluntary exchange is associated with an expected gain in satisfaction but not necessarily to an achieved gain. The analysis being considerably weakened by this, Rothbard himself admitted that the principle defining welfare economy is 'restricted' (1976b, p. 98); referring to hoped-for utility, it leaves the question of effective success of expectations unanswered. This possibly explains Rothbard's later contributions aiming to reduce the field of uncertainty of the future (see Chapter 6).

1.2 The Kirzner Alternative: Coordination as Process

Kirzner takes on the subject of Austrian welfare economics in his 'Welfare Economics: A Modern Austrian Perspective' (1988a). Although published as part of a collection in honour of Rothbard (*Man, Economy and Liberty: Essays in Honor of Murray Rothbard*, 1988), Kirzner's analysis is quite different to Rothbard's, being founded on the idea of coordination as process. Kirzner claims that in a dynamic world, coordination must not so much be seen as a state of mutual satisfaction (Rothbard's *ex post* utility), as a procedure able to 'to detect and to move towards correcting situations in which activities have until now been discoordinated' (1988a, p. 87).

This vision of coordination as process, which Kirzner accurately described as one of the foundations of Austrian analysis, neatly gets him round the delicate question of the difference between *ex ante* and *ex post* utility by concentrating much more on the idea of a tendency towards producing satisfaction than the absolute achievement of it:

> We shall be interested in the economic well-being of society not merely in terms of its level of economic well-being (however defined), but also in regard to the ability of its institutions to stimulate and support those economic processes upon which the attainment of economic well-being depends (1988a, p. 78).

This indirect approach means favouring the economic conditions that encourage opportunities of welfare rather than guaranteeing satisfaction through exchange. Kirzner considers that the market is the best way to increase knowledge; when its mechanisms are free to act, agents find more opportunities of evacuating error, creating a tendency towards equilibrium so that 'initially clashing, discoordinated activities, are somehow being hammered out in a manner such as to approach a more smoothly dovetailing with one another' (ibid., p. 87). He considers this to be the one proper way of linking market and welfare.

He without a doubt considerably widens the theoretical scope of Austrian welfare economics with the notion of process, but at first glance it would seem that by doing so, he weakens its heuristic aspect. There are two points to this.

Firstly, in subjective terms it is difficult to separate the ideas of individual welfare and actual success of plans. So it is hard to see in his argument how the market as process might be seen as a factor of economic welfare, here totally undefined. Of course it could be imagined that, compared to centralized processes, the market is more capable of approaching a state of plan success because of the inevitably dispersed nature of knowledge. But more or less approaching it does not guarantee the idea of producing welfare if it is not reached. Kirzner runs into the same obstacle as Rothbard: uncertainty of the future, etched into the laws of praxeology, with logical implications found in catallaxy. This is what had forced Rothbard to take refuge in the concept of *ex ante* rather than *ex post* utility.

Secondly, Kirzner's approach runs into other difficulties, as Cordato indicated (*Welfare Economics and Externalities in an Open Ended Universe: A Modern Austrian Perspective*, 1992). He noticed that Mises and Rothbard dealt only briefly with externalities,[6] as simply a question – which Coase ('The Problem of Social Cost', 1960) treated – of an insufficient definition of property rights. State intervention, for these two, is illegitimate as it attempts to correct so-called market failures, where these 'failures' in fact are due to a lack of property rights.

However, even if this analysis is correct, Cordato claims Austrian theory must go further. He notices a certain type of negative externality relative to discovering opportunities, which neither Kirzner nor Rothbard do:

> For Kirzner, improvements in knowledge are synonymous with increased plan coordination among market participants. As the market process brings new coordination to light, the plans of market participants become more closely coordinated and social efficiency is improved. He argues that, '... [the] learning process ... nudges

individual plans into closer and closer coordination' (Kirzner, 1963, pp. 218-219) (Cordato, 1992, p. 47).

There is no foundation, however, to the idea of any link between knowledge improvement and progression towards coordination: acquiring knowledge allows agents to rapidly redirect their activities, yet will inevitably cause the defeat of some plans; so the process does not necessarily favour coordination as a whole. Cordato agrees with Hight ('Equilibrium and Disequilibrium in the Market Process', 1986) when he notes the possibility of plan failure due to knowledge improvement. From a dynamic point of view, any improvement in knowledge counters initially compatible plans:

> … where Professor Kirzner sees coordination as synonymous with improvements in information, I suggest that the knowledge improvement process often leads to disruptions in previously formulated plans and, at least temporarily, some 'discoordination'... Contrary to Kirzner's conclusions, I do not argue that these exchange facilitating acts are always coordinating (Cordato, 1992, p. 70).

Obviously the Kirznerian entrepreneur's equilibrating role is questioned here; he is supposed to be a factor of welfare as he rids the market of errors. In fact it could be argued that by his activities, he disturbs any equilibrating process or even makes it obsolete.[7] So the process of knowledge diffusion could be seen either as facilitating a tendency towards equilibrium or, just as well, as inducing permanent endogenous disequilibrium. Kirzner's cognitive criterion is therefore not reflected in the idea of improvement of individual satisfactions.

Kirzner, as we have seen in Chapter 6, indirectly answers these critiques. On the first point, the entrepreneur's creative ability is what ensures some sort of link between the imagined and the real future. As for the entrepreneur's disequilibrium-oriented activities, Kirzner was quite clear on the subject at the beginning of the 1990s: the entrepreneur is not a factor of disequilibrium but on the contrary one of equilibrium, facilitating the adjustment of action by responding to essentially external change.

He continues this train of thought in 'Coordination as a Criterion for Economic "Goodness"', without denying the inevitable cognitive collateral damage wrought by entrepreneurial activity:

> The innovator competitor who, entering the industry and pushing out the older firms, disrupting the earlier plans, is replacing a less coordinated set of market activities, by a better coordination set. In the 'dynamic' sense of the term 'coordination' … this brash, aggressive competition is coordinative. The disruption it causes in earlier plans of the inefficient producers is the evidence for and manifestation of the earlier state of discoordinatedness which has generated the changes (of which this disruption is part). The apparent earlier calm which, as a result of the aggressive new competition, has been followed by sudden disruption, was in fact utterly misleading. This calm was a fact expressing the presence of as yet undis-

> covered (but very real) discoordinatedness; dynamic competition shattered that calm, replacing the earlier uncoordinated sets of activities by a better-coordinated set (1998, p. 297).

From this point of view, entrepreneurial activity is simply a response to a perceived gap between existing activity and available information. Leaving the market free to act would let activities rapidly adjust to available opportunities, discovered sooner or later through the laws of human action. Kirzner knows that any reduction of disequilibrium will result in other, new disequilibrium, as new information and opportunities are created. His argument, however, seems to be this: interference with the catallactic process only increases the gap between available and known opportunities and therefore raises the level of discoordination.

This reasoning is obviously correct; however this progression towards an ever narrower and more abstract definition of market coordination tendencies, leading us from Rothbard to Kirzner, has the negative effect of blurring the relation with the idea of welfare. Kirzner says it himself, surprisingly enough in the light of his initial objective: 'In fact, well-being is not referred to in the coordination criterion at all' (ibid., p. 297).

1.3 Private Property as a Condition of Forming Plans: 'Catallactic Efficiency'

Cordato's contribution in *Welfare Economics and Externalities in an Open Ended Universe: A Modern Austrian Perspective* (1992),[8] manages to be at once critical and constructive. On the constructive side his approach refers to Kirzner's, which he judges 'the most well developed and thought out conception of welfare economics in modern Austrian economics' (1992, p. 45).

On the critical side, as has just been seen, he distances himself from the link Kirzner makes between market and tendency towards equilibrium, as in his eyes it does not take into account the problem of the negative externalities caused by the division of knowledge. Therefore, the catallactic foundations of a welfare economy have to be looked for elsewhere.

So Cordato gave up on the theme of success of individual plans to concentrate on the question of the condition of forming these plans. This is where the theme of property came back into favour. He rightly remarks that the Austrian welfare economy, however it is defined, was constructed on the distinction between voluntary and forced exchange and therefore on an implicit reference to a system of property rights, this notion being essential for him to any reflection on the formation of individual plans. Whatever meaning the market/welfare link takes, it is impossible to avoid a reference to property rights: 'Any discussion of markets or catallactics assumes the right to trade' (1992, p. 84).[9]

In Cordato's opinion, private property does not ensure the success of plans but is required for their formation, as 'No meaningful means ends framework is even possible without the ability to access and control physical resources' (1992, p. 65). Catallactic competition for scarce resources requires the existence of individuals' property rights. Another point is, as ends constantly change, so must resources; indeed, 'an act of exchange is an act of giving up less appropriate means for more appropriate means' (ibid., p. 63); being able to acquire new ones becomes paramount. Similarly, as individuals may make errors in their choice of resources, they must be able to make corrections by substituting one for the other. The market, of course, encourages this. Its role, through the price process, is 'to disseminate as much information concerning appropriate exchange opportunities as possible' (ibid., p. 65). The legitimacy of legal endowments of resources extends to that of the product of interpersonal exchange.

Cordato formed the concept of catallactic efficiency expressing the two complementary ideas of control over resources and the possibility of procuring new ones out of the respect of individual property rights and freedom of market exchange, so linking property and knowledge. An appropriate institutional framework called Institutional Ideal Setting (IIS) allows these two elements their full expression.

Cordato's positions may at first glance seem to be a further retreat from the Austrian front of welfare economics. After the theme of plans' hoped-for success, then that of the tendency towards plans' success, comes the condition of formation of plans. The main point is, however, elsewhere: the theory of catallactic efficiency is above all faced with internal contradictions.

Certainly, as Gordon remarks ('Toward a Deconstruction of Utility and Welfare Economics', 1993), any growth of actors' knowledge of opportunities to appropriate new resources is beneficial. But it can also damage the existence of profit stemming from information and/or devalue stocks of resources. It may become impossible for actors to exploit opportunities left by others actors' ignorance if the latter increase their knowledge level. So the spread of knowledge may threaten individual interests and Cordato's critique of Kirzner could well turn on his own argument.

Another point is that plan formation does not in fact require private property but simply a situation where resources are readily available. Plan forming is a fact of the world of business, families and the state, without their actors necessarily legally owning the resources they use. Private property is not then indispensible to plan forming but can be seen as the best condition for a maximum of plans to be formed. However, it may be thought that this would indirectly lead to utilitarist reasoning.

So, Austrian welfare economics does not in fact stand up well to critique. Its various developments do not hide the weaknesses of its various positions; from Rothbard to Cordato via Kirzner, successive stages of its literature display a steady thinning of its heuristic contents. Commentators reacting to this

(Cowen, 'What a Non-Paretian Welfare Economics Would Have to Look Like', 1991; 'Austrian Welfare Economics', 1994; Hamlin, 'On the Possibility of Austrian Welfare Economics', 1992; Sugden, 'Austrian Prescriptive Economics', 1992; Aimar, 'L'économie autrichienne du bien-être: quelle définition possible?', 1998, etc) openly state their disillusion, distancing themselves from these arguments.

Cowen even speaks of a crisis of Austrian welfare economics; its representatives may well share the same critique of traditional welfare approaches, 'there has been no agreement upon an operational or even coherent alternative' (Cowen, 1994, p. 307). Not only are its authors divided on its characteristics, but divisions as to its doctrinal implications appear as well.

2. NEO-AUSTRIAN WELFARE ECONOMICS AND NORMATIVITY

In spite of holding in common a procedural conception of welfare, the Austrians did not manage to reach analytical consensus on the characteristics and functioning of these procedures. Similarly, in spite of their shared respect for the principle of 'demonstrated preference' (2.1), they were not able to reach doctrinal agreement. Strong oppositions appeared between Kirzner and Cortado on the one hand (2.2) and Rothbard on the other (2.3) on the possibility of deducing free market normativity from a procedural approach (2.4).

2.1 The Argument of 'Demonstrated Preference'

Austrian welfare economics has always quite deliberately ignored the psychological approach to welfare. Rothbard supported this restricted analysis based on the principle of demonstrated preference, which Mises claimed as a praxeological theorem. It displays the traditional Austrian separation between praxeology and psychology. It means that only action reveals agents' preference at the moment they make a choice. Rothbard knows, as did Mises, that individuals who do not move on from their initial endowments may not be neutral as regards others' exchanges, possibly developing feelings of envy, or even aversion to capitalism. The market would then create negative psychological externalities in those who do not exchange. This element would counter the essential reference to the principle of unanimity which considers that actors' *ex ante* production of utility has no negative effects on other actors. So it is impossible to assume that every exchange only produces satisfaction on a social level. 'Consideration of the welfare implications of envy, for example, makes it impossible even to say that welfare will be increased by everyone having more of every commodity' (Reder quoted by Rothbard, 1956, p. 249).

Rothbard thus establishes on this basis that the theorist's appreciation of the level of social utility can never refer to these psychological values:

> How do we know that this hypothetical envious one loses in utility because of the exchanges of others? Consulting his verbal opinions does not suffice, for his proclaimed envy might be a joke or a literary game or a deliberate lie... we are not interested in his opinions about the exchanges made by others, since his preferences are not demonstrated through action and are therefore irrelevant (1956, p. 250).

Rothbard's approach offered the framework for all later contributions on the subject. Kirzner and Cordato, both unwavering in this approach, recognised the impossibility of knowing individuals' preferences outside of action: 'Economic analysis has nothing to say about sensations' (Kirzner, 1988a, p. 79).

The issue is to define an economy of welfare, not a psychology of it, which in praxeological terms is unknowable. So their approach, like Rothbard's, logically prevents any accounting for behaviour of envy of and aversion to the market. Kirzner's and Cordato's positions would appear to be more satisfactory than Rothbard's if the criterion is no longer 'social utility'.[10] Substituting the concept of coordination or of catallactic efficiency for social utility as a concept of welfare more officially limits the problem to indirect exchange; yet this restriction was already implicitly present in Rothbard's reasoning.

So the Austrians agreed on the epistemological implications of demonstrated preference and the need to free the analysis of welfare from any psychological dimension. However, they reached very different conclusions among themselves as to associating a normative dimension to Austrian welfare economics.

2.2 From Wertfreiheit to Free Market Normativity

In Kirzner's eyes (1988a), the Austrian welfare economy is, in the end, simply associated with the increase of opportunities of eliminating errors through the market; his attachment to classical liberalism comes about through the concept of tendency towards coordination. The concept of welfare takes into account only the ends pursued through market exchange. So logically it is associated with normativity promoting 'the institutional environment in terms of its potential to inspire genuine discovery (of opportunities previously overlooked as a result of utter ignorance)' (1988a, p. 88).

This argument can be viewed in relation to one of Kirzner's analyses from 12 years earlier: 'Philosophical and Ethical Implications of Austrian Economics' (1976). Although it is not directly linked with welfare economics it is important in that he shoulders responsibility for a rupture with his thinking on the question of norms. Until then, he supported the traditional Austrian idea that respecting Wertfreiheit (the principle of the theorist's neutrality to actor's values) prevented the formation of norms favouring market economy. He now changed directions, seeking to 'reconcile Mises's strong normative position in economics with his declared insistence on Wertfreiheit' (1976, p. 80).

It is in fact surprising to find Mises writing in defence of Wertfreiheit at the same time as pleading in favour of political classical liberalism. Kirzner, based on the concept of demonstrated preference, attempts an explanation. If the logic of the world of catallaxy is retained, where market prices are formed, improvement in cognition encouraged by the free market will benefit all the market actors, whatever their particular objectives. So Mises' repeated positions in favour of the market do not at all contradict the principles of Wertfreiheit.[11] In Kirzner's mind, it is possible to state normative criteria, while respecting neutrality regarding agents' values. He has not wavered on this subject since. He considers that 'Economic science is thus, through the notion of coordination, able, we shall maintain, to provide an objective criterion in terms of which the economic goodness and badness of economic situations or economic policies, may be judged' ('Coordination as a Criterion for Economic "Goodness"', 1998, p. 292).

In *Discovery, Capitalism and Distributive Justice* (1989), Kirzner was already defending the principle of ethics in capitalism, through his 'finders-keepers' theory. The promoter can rightfully keep profits, as they have been generated through his own discovery; it is as if he created his own revenue. This legitimization of profit is not however a normative position in the way that Kirzner was to develop it in 'Coordination as a Criterion for Economic "Goodness"' (1998). It simply tried to illustrate the following: although most people see capitalism as a violation of the fundamental rules of justice, on closer analysis it can be seen that the market economy is established on the same ethical principles that are generally accepted by most people as fair. Kirzner stops there; it is not his intention with his finders-keepers' theory to present the profit system as a rationally occurring norm to which everyone has to adhere.[12]

Similarly to Kirzner, Cordato (1992) attempted to associate the concept of catallactic efficiency to free market normativity. The improvement of knowledge itself certainly does produce negative externalities which prevent coordination by changing situations and spoiling certain expectations; Cordato expressed doubt, seen above, on the possibility of associating coordination to market processes. However, in Cordato's eyes, the doctrinal dimension of catallactic efficiency is not related to the theme of coordination; it refers simply to the ability of institutions to help or hinder the formation of individuals' plans. It is limited to respecting private property rights, without inquiring as to the origin of the rights. He is very explicit on this point: 'Catallactic efficiency can provide a normative justification, in a general sense, for the establishment and maintenance of private property rights, but economics must remain agnostic from a normative perspective with respect to the question of how the institutions meant to establish and maintain those rights are initially created' (Cordato, 1992, p. 85-86).

So for Cordato, normativity is not linked to a result (Rothbard), nor to a process (Kirzner) but a legal framework which facilitates individuals' ability to form plans, which is to say, capitalism.

Kirzner and Cordato attempted to form a liberal doctrine through their analysis of welfare. For both authors, examining the advantages of the free market allows the establishment of normativity in its favour, whatever the nature of its agents' ends. According to Kirzner, the market is the best system to facilitate the discovery of available information of benefit to all the individuals in it; Cordato holds that the market respects individual property rights which themselves are a condition of plan formation. It allows the creation of a normative economy and the definition of free market institutions as the 'ideal institutional setting' (Cordato, 1992, p. 64).

2.3 The Pre-eminence of Value Judgements

The differences in terminology between Rothbard and the Kirzner-Cordato duo does not mean a shift of fields. Rothbard may well use the term 'social utility' but in his analysis he only refer to the catallactic field as forming welfare, like Kirzner and Cordato. Like these two, he respects the principle of Wertfreiheit where creating welfare is independent from the particular character of ends pursued by market actors.

Rothbard claims, however that constructing an Austrian welfare economy does not permit the establishment of market normativity. He explains this position, which literature has often ignored, as early as 1956:

> It must not be thought that we have, in our discussion of welfare economics, been attempting to set any ethical or political program. On the contrary, the proposed welfare economics has been put forward without inserting ethical judgments. Economics by itself and standing alone cannot establish an ethical system and we must grant this regardless of what philosophy of ethics we hold. The fact that the free market maximized social utility, or that State action cannot be considered voluntary … in itself implies no plea for laissez-faire or for any other social system (1956, p. 41).

Rothbard's position can be explained and supported by three elements.

The first of these takes to the difference between praxeology and psychology. The scope of analysis of welfare creation is reduced to the question of the market: because of the principle of demonstrated preference, only actors present in the market will have their preferences taken into account. The Austrian theory of welfare does not, however, take into account some individuals' feelings of envy; some, not advancing from their initial endowments, may not be neutral concerning others' exchanges, or they may develop an aversion for the processes of catallaxy. Mises himself noticed in *Planning for Freedom* that: 'Envy is a common weakness of men. People are loath to acknowledge the fact that they themselves could have earned profits if they had displayed the same foresight and judgment the successful businessman did. Their resentment is the more violent, the more they are subconsciously aware of this fact' (1962c, p. 122). The market might then cause negative psychological externalities in those who do not exchange well. Market actors' gains may cause subjective costs to the agents 'out of the market'. This would cause the violation of the principle of unanimity. Society being larger than the market, it is impossible to guarantee that exchange brings global gains in satisfaction, or that the respect of individual property laws is beneficial for all. Defining and imposing market normativity on all in society (and not just in the catallactic world) is therefore scientifically unacceptable.

The second element is very well known to the authors on welfare: that is that the reference to utility is already a value judgement. Rothbard claims that Austrian welfare economics is neutral as regards agents' values but the attempt to apply norms of welfare is the result of a particular value judgement.[13]

The last obstacle is the principle of unanimity itself: '... many of the strictures against the unanimity principle apply here too; for example should we really be eager to preserve the utility of the slaveholder against loss?' (1976b, p. 100). Rothbard claims, contrary to Kirzner and Cordato that unanimity is required to found the Austrian welfare economy but he refuses to consider it as a criterion for forming normativity.

In later years, Rothbard (*The Ethics of Liberty*, 1982) was to consider the question of norms in support of the free market as the centre of his reflection, yet based on other, ontological criteria the goal of which was precisely to establish norms.[14] Objective examination of his contributions, however, does not allow the confusion of the question of justice with welfare. While the definition of an ethical principle aims at establishing the justice of individual property distribution rights, Rothbardian welfare economics examines the question of knowing if social organisation of activities based on the market provide gains in satisfaction. So, whether legal endowments are founded or not on ethical principles, is of no importance whatsoever. The question is simply to decide if market processes bring satisfaction to catallactic agents.

This being said, it might in fact be possible to enlarge the field of welfare economics by referring to ethics. We have already seen (Chapter 6) that the definition of 'natural values' can ease the change from *ex ante* to *ex post* utility, creating a twin principle of market exchange and creation of satisfaction. Agents' knowledge and respect of these natural values permits the founding of a principle of success of expectations, based on relative price structures. Even the question of negative externalities of market exchange is dealt with, as reason, says Rothbard, is able to foresee the unwanted results of individual acts.

In addition, the definition of an ethical principle is linked with the idea of ontological production of satisfaction, of which the market is finally only the logical superstructure. If we refer to natural values, then agents cannot be envious or have feelings of aversion for the market. In this case, the principle of unanimity would be enlarged beyond the sphere of market exchange, to a universally respected unanimity as the principle of the natural justice of endowments. So utility would not be a value judgement, but instead a criterion of rationality defined by human nature.

All this is exact. But still, the definition of norms and the principle of Wertfreiheit are mutually exclusive; the formulation of ethics is the result of discovering natural, normative values, incompatible with the idea of value neutrality; yet Rothbard is determined to build welfare economy on Wertfreiheit, whereas the normativity he defends is precisely brought about by willingly abandoning 'the hobgoblins of Wertfreiheit' (Rothbard, 1982, p. 26).

Another point must be mentioned: from an economic viewpoint, it can be considered that the absence of reference to natural values makes the Austrian model of welfare economics undetermined; however, from a normative viewpoint, the reference to ethics overdetermines it. Even if the market's activities led to economic crisis, it would still have to be respected, based as it is on natural law, expressing ontological values. So the utility of the market processes is 'derived' from that achieved by the workings of natural laws which underpin its exercise and not from their ability to independently produce economic welfare. Norms can be declared with no reference at all to a welfare economy; as a result, the construction of a welfare economy is neither a condition of, nor sufficient to found normativity.

The theory of demonstrated preference can allow the exclusion of feelings of envy and aversion in the analysis of welfare creation by the market. But it can never allow the question of welfare to be reduced to the catallactic domain. It is therefore illegitimate to establish a normative position favourable to the free market on that basis.

This is the reason that Rothbard chose a different route (*The Ethics of Liberty*, 1982). He had introduced a normative dimension into the Austrian problematic through a philosophical approach based on natural law. Until then, the neo-Austrian thinking had been ruled by the Wertfreiheit principle of moral neutrality, preventing the proper transformation of doctrine into political norms. Rothbard attempted, contrary to all the other Austrians, to free the Austrian analysis from the rule of Wertfreiheit. By defining a rational ethic of human behaviour reflecting the ontological character of property and individual liberty, he raises a normative defence of the free market, independent from the question of economic efficiency. For him, liberty and property rights of the individual being natural laws, the market rationally must be respected when it is made up of voluntary transactions of ontologically founded endowments. In the end, it is an expression of 'the full exercise of his natural self-ownership' (1982, p. 45). But his normative approach had a disadvantage: abandoning any reference to the economic analysis of catallaxy.

So some Austrian authors' attempt to infer market normativity from their own procedural approach to welfare is countered by the reduction of the analytical scope to the market field. This means a normative Austrian economy does not exist. Is that the end of it? Some of Hayek's work suggests it is not and pushes us to reflect a little further on the matter.

3. AN OPEN QUESTION: THE ARGUMENT OF SURVIVAL

It is not at all easy to see any evidence of normative thinking in Hayek, contrary to many commentators' opinions. He certainly did support the idea of laissez-faire market mechanisms and principles but none of his writings show any direct link between his liberal ideas and normative propositions. Kirzner rightly states 'While both Mises and Hayek provocatively challenged the possibility of efficiency under socialism, they too emphasized the wertfrei character of their economics. Both writers would see their free market stance at the policy level as related to, but not central to, their Austrianism' (*The Meaning of Market Process*, 1992, p. 68).

We will, however be examining the possibility of certain of Hayek's reflections providing the base for a normative Austrian economy. Hayek mentions the notion of survival several times in his last work, *The Fatal Conceit*. We will firstly be looking at how this reference can be viewed as an empirical criterion of coordination (3.1). We will then see how and to what extent this survival argument might constitute an economic criterion of normativity (3.2). Lastly, if we agree with the analyses, we will attempt to identify the meaning of such a normativity from the point of view of the actors' interests (3.3).

3.1 Survival and Coordination

According to the above literature, Austrian theory was not able to identify proper empirical criteria of coordination. The main obstacle to this, undoubtedly, was subjectivism, which forced the recognition of a wide diversity of individual values. This obliged the Austrians to take refuge in a procedural dimension of coordination, via the logic of change of information into knowledge. But this did not allow the formulation of empirical criteria which would differentiate between situations of coordination and discoordination.

This is no small question from Hayek's point of view. In 'Economics and Knowledge' (1937a), he explains that the social sciences and particularly economics cannot avoid the empirical dimension. The *a priori* tool is not enough to make propositions relative to learning in society. So it is important to find complementary epistemological foundations to those of Mises. Popper's work shows that it is possible but only on condition of establishing a link between an 'explanation' of the phenomena in question and an empirical reference, through which the theory can be tested. From Popper's viewpoint, from which Hayek apparently did not waver starting with 'Economics and Knowledge',[15] a theory only has meaning if it is associated with empirical criteria able to corroborate or refute its conclusions through testing. Hayek's attempt to found a market theory required the definition of an empirical reference which would go through falsification procedures.

The explanation could in fact be thought of as the abstract rules of just conduct and Hayek would seem to find the notion of tendency towards equilibrium to be the best qualified to be the empirical reference: 'It is only by this assertion that such a tendency exists that economics ceases to be an exercise in pure logic and becomes an empirical science; and it is to economics as an empirical science that we must now turn' (Hayek, 1937a, p. 44). Without empirical criteria, economic analysis can never attain the status of a science. So Hayek adds, referring to 'The Logic of Scientific Discovery' (Popper):

> In short, I shall contend that the empirical element in economic theory – the only part which is concerned not merely with implications but with causes and effects and which leads therefore to conclusions which, at any rate in principle, are capable of verification (or rather falsification, see K.R. Popper, *Logik der Forschung* [Vienna, 1953], *passim*) – consists of propositions about the acquisition of knowledge (1937a, p. 33).

This being said, the notion of tendency towards equilibrium requires empirical contents to be used as tests of falsification. At the time of 'Economics and Knowledge', Hayek gives no clues on this subject.[16] How then is it possible to test for the existence of tendency towards equilibrium? To what can this notion be empirically linked?

The Fatal Conceit (1988), although often neglected or criticized by literature was in fact the natural continuation of Hayek's work and would appear to address the above questions. It would seem to offer empirical criteria of coordination, corroborating the explanation provided by the rules of just conduct. In the chapter on 'The Extended Order and Population Growth', he gathers many elements previously scattered through previous works, particularly in *Law, Legislation and Liberty*. He addresses themes of population, of the division of labour and especially of survival. Based on empirical experience, he identifies the relation between the capitalist societies (the Great Society) and the capacity of survival of their ever-increasing populations.

Hayek seemed to be saying that the idea of survival allowed an empirical, general criterion to be formed which appears to corroborate his conjectural theory of the rules of just conduct, which he views through an evolutionist prism. Societies founded on the market and the rules of just conduct have been able to spread and flourish, through a system of selection, competition and imitation:

> Yet if the market economy did indeed prevail over other types of order because it enabled those groups that adopt its basic rules the better to multiply, the calculation in market values is a calculation in terms of lives: individuals guided by this calculation did what most helped to increase their numbers, although this could hardly have been their intention (1988, p. 132).[17]

It could be objected of course that population increase would represent an objective cost, reducing chances of survival as competition increases for available goods; Hayek claims the opposite. The labour factor is associated with increasing output: the division of knowledge and talent together with population growth and the interaction of individual subjectivities associated with a richer and ever more widely diversified human capital, the intensification of the processes of knowledge acquisition all increase the opportunities of discovery. This explains that 'step by step, momentary impediments to further population increase are penetrated, increases of population provide a foundation for further ones, and so on' (ibid., p. 127).

Hayek received many critiques after *The Fatal Conceit* for having analysed not in terms of individuals but of the group, thus using holistic concepts.[18] Hayek does concentrate on one central point which is that the social order is moved towards seeking out and selecting rules favouring the survival of the greatest number.

Yet this type of reference is not a real change in direction for Hayek. In *The Sensory Order* he referred to learning processes acquired during the 'development of the species' (1952a, p. 73); some time later in the *The Constitution of Liberty* he was more precise when he noted, 'in social evolution, the decisive factor is not the selection of the physical and inheritable properties of the individuals but the selection by imitation of successful institutions and habits ... this operates also through the success of individuals and groups' (Hayek, 1960, p. 59); finally in *Law, Legislation and Liberty*, he often mentions the criterion of survival of the group. For example: '... such rules come to be generally accepted because in fact they give the group in which they are practised superior strength' (Hayek, 1973, p. 19).

More importantly, all the attacks completely ignore the epistemological constraints to the grasping of extended, which is to say complex, social orders. Hayek states on this subject:

> 'Explanation' and 'prediction' of course do not refer to an individual event but always to phenomena of a certain kind or class' because '... the more we move into the realm of the very complex, the more our knowledge is likely to be of the principle only, of the significant outline rather than of the detail. Especially where we have to deal with the extreme complexity of human affairs, the hope of ever achieving specific predictions of particulars seems vain (1955, p. 9; 20).

As 'the extended order [is] probably the most complex structure in the universe' (Hayek, 1988, p.127), individual situations cannot be appreciated at this analytical level.

He explains that to define complex structures one has to use 'The minimum number of elements of which an instance of the pattern must consist in order to exhibit all the characteristic attributes of the class of patterns in question' ('The Theory of Complex Phenomena', 1964, p. 25). The idea of tendency towards equilibrium must express a structure of coordinated expectations. Of course, the complexity of social phenomena means that not all particular forms of coordination or of particular groups of actors can be taken into account. The objective is to simply treat the general coordination type, the common characteristics of social coordination.

The reflection in *The Fatal Conceit* on the argument of survival, would seem to be an empirical definition of this type of coordination: firstly, survival is definitely one of the common characteristics of coordination, when, whatever they may be, for the plans to succeed, the agents must in fact stay alive. This objective element is transversal to all the subjective concepts of coordination imaginable. Secondly and especially, in the situation of the division of labour, the survival of growing populations is proof of the exercise of coordinating forces. If individual activities were not coordinated, there could be no specialisation or production levels of goods in sufficient quantities to supply these growing populations: 'If we ask what men most owe to the moral practices of those who are called capitalists the answer is: their very lives' (1988, p. 130).

It could obviously be thought that the proposed theory's level of falsifiability is low. There are many circumstances to condition the survival, the preservation and the development of the human race. Hayek remarked very early on, however:

> ... our difficulty is precisely that we are unable to ascertain by observation the presence and specific arrangement of the multiplicity of factors which form the starting point of our deductive reasoning. Neither the assumption that factors of the kind assumed are present, nor of course the validity of the deductive reasoning, need, therefore, be regarded as disproved if the conclusions at which we arrived are not borne out by observation. But though observation of such complex situations cannot decide whether our conditional ('if then') statement is true, it will help us to decide whether to accept it as an explanation of the facts which we observe (1955, p. 10).

The twin references to the ideas of social tests and predictions requires demonstrating, if not of the field of study's stability, at least the existence of certain regularities. So, for Hayek in *Studies*, the researcher must look for recurrent structures, although regularities are not easy to study directly, by the very nature of the social sphere. However, constructing a social science becomes possible by the existence of structures of abstract regularities, the starting point of research being their recognition. So it is from this point of view, as Hayek states in *Studies*, that one should start off by examining 'partial regularities', visible on the level of classes of phenomena, somewhat in an algebraic form; then continuing by offering an explanation of principle of the existence of this recurring abstract structure, which is to say a description of its general lines and an interpretation of the conditions of its emerging.

Hayek states that the explanation of principle can be coupled with a dimension of predictability. In fact 'degrees of prediction' may correspond to 'degrees of explanation', which themselves are permitted by the reference to abstract or partial regularities:

> ... it may be taken for granted that prediction and explanation are merely two aspects of the same process where in the first instance, known rules are used to derive from the known facts what will follow upon them, while in the second instance these rules are used to derive from the known facts what preceded them (Hayek, 1955, p. 9).

The 'explanations of structures' thus lead to 'pattern predictions', which enable testing of the theory being studied. Because of the generic dimension of explanations of principle which 'will always state only some and never all the properties of any particular phenomenon to which they refer' (1955, p. 9), the level of falsifiability will always correspond to the levels of predictions that it will be supposed to reach, that is to say, weak.[19] However, in Hayek's eyes, the character of testability, associated with abstract orders is still workable as

> it is also not only predictions of individual events which can be empirically tested. We are equally interested in the recurrence of abstract patterns as such; and the prediction that a pattern of a certain kind will appear in defined circumstances is a falsifiable (and therefore empirical) statement (1964, p. 28).[20]

He is thus able to consolidate his representation of the capitalist social order through the correspondence between empirical criteria of coordination, via the notion of survival and the explanation of principle, around the notion of abstract rules of just conduct. *The Fatal Conceit* seems to have closed a line of thinking he started with 'Economics and Knowledge', the question now being whether it is possible to use this whole construction to find a criterion of normativity founded on economic analysis.

3.2 A Praxeological View of the Survival-Normativity Relation

Greater population survival and growth corresponds both to the empirical and general description of coordination. The rules of the Great Society represent the explanation of principle (the theory). The relationship which Hayek established in *The Fatal Conceit* between the notion of coordination and the theme of survival may allow the foundation of an Austrian economic normativity.

We have seen that the many Austrian attempts to establish a symmetry of coordination and normativity have all shown their limits, essentially because of the constraints of the subjectivist paradigm, which prevent the substantive-type definition of a common-interest zone between individuals.

The criterion of survival can, however, be used to overcome these difficulties. By expressing an objective element of coordination, which itself corresponds to a value shared by all agents, present on the market or not, it offers a criterion of normativity founded on economic analysis.

Kirzner examined at length the question of material goods and subsistence in *The Economic Point of View*, two subjects which long dominated economic thinking, particularly while analysing most of the classics but also the institutionalists such as Veblen (*The Theory of the Leisure Class*, 1899; *The Place of Science in Modern Civilization and Other Essays*, 1919).

In the chapter 'The Science of Wealth and Welfare', he disapproves of the fact 'that many writers of this opinion still further narrowed down the concept of wealth to the idea of material wealth, and many of those stressing welfare of mankind' (Kirzner, 1960, p. 21). As a result of this, he refutes 'the view that saw economics as essentially concerned with the goods necessary to ensure the physical subsistence of mankind' (ibid., p. 33).

He rightly opposes the faults and scope of these concepts, considering that the criterion of materiality would not be able to define the frontiers of an economic science distinct from other social disciplines. Neither can this criterion define the economic principle's nature or essence, which must come out of the rules of human action. Man freely chooses his ends, which are heterogeneous and there is no question of limiting them to 'biological survival' (ibid., p. 36). Kirzner sees a legacy of scientism in these physiological criteria which seeks to apply the methods of the natural sciences to the social sciences.[21]

From our point of view, nevertheless, the reference to materiality and subsistence can be very useful, based on precisely the Misesian praxeological rules, not by limiting the frontiers of economic science but in the formulation of the terms of a welfare economy and the normativity which would emerge from it.

Shearmur, in *Hayek and After*,[22] was the first to explore the relation between the theme of survival and of normativity:

> The biologically based is not a bad starting-point. We can, indeed, talk about gains in well-being in terms of people's not being frustrated in their biologically based desires; or, if they wish not to eat, drink, live in decent conditions and so on, of this being a matter of their choice, rather than something that is forced upon them by their circumstances (1996, p. 174).

He considers, nevertheless, that this reference carries analytical restrictions which have major implications:

> I should stress, in view of my earlier emphasis upon the biological, that I do not mean to limit what we can say about well-being to the biologically based' (ibid., p. 174) because 'as part of this theory, the insights of subjectivism should be recognized: it is important that individuals may prefer to choose not to eat or to copulate, and may even, in some circumstances, prefer to die (ibid., p. 175).

In stressing this point, Shearmur puts the cat among the Austrian pigeons of normativity, as the way he presents the problem prevents the establishment of a lexicographical order of the biological or subjective elements; nothing obliges each individual to consider his survival as the number one priority among all other ends. So any assertion of normativity based on the notion of biological survival is necessarily unfounded. In the end, Shearmur seems to see this biological reference as just one element among others, or a second best solution filling the vacancy of a 'proper' Austrian economic normativity.

Seen on this level, the survival argument certainly cannot be defined as a 'proper' norm. The door that Shearmur opened, however, would appear to at least lead down the road to a solution to the problem of a normative Austrian economy; although prolonging this argument requires returning to the roots of the neo-Austrian analysis, which is to say Mises' praxeology.

As Mises defines it, praxeology is the 'a theoretical science of human action, i.e., a science that aims at the ascertainment of universally valid laws of human conduct' (*Epistemological Problems of Economics*, 1933, p. 68). Action is the fundamental axiom of the whole construction of economic theory. It is the 'ultimate given' of knowledge about society as the human mind is unable to move back beyond it.

We already know that in all his epistemological writings (1933, 1957, 1962, 1966) he stressed the apodictic character of the praxeological teachings, which is that they are applicable and valid outside of time and place. Similarly, he had always supported the idea of a praxeological subjectivism, establishing that its theorems 'are valid for every human action without regard to its underlying motives, causes, and goals' (*Human Action*, 1966, p. 21).

Can we then define a logical relation between the praxeological structure and the notion of survival? Praxeology's teachings are by definition aimed at actors, individuals in an ends/means structure. It is precisely at this level that the notion of survival is praxeologically legitimate; the objective of action of course not being conservation of life, as, 'to live is for man the outcome of a choice, of a judgment of value' (Mises, 1966, p. 20). Life is, however an inevitable condition of action; the ends/means relation that action expresses requires the use of life, which can be defined as a non-substitutable means of production for all action; therefore there does exist a logical correlation between action and valuing resources allowing life to be preserved until the plan is achieved. This does not imply any hypothesis concerning agents' subjective ends, nor does it require at all that the goal of action be the preservation of life.[23]

So we speak of apodictic values when they exist outside time and place; yet the term 'praxeological values' would seem to be more appropriate as the existence of these values in each actor is established by human action whatever the nature of the ends, monetary or not. Recognising the existence of praxeological values does not at all imply any reduction of the sphere of subjectivism or abandoning the principle of Wertfreiheit. Each individual is still considered as a singular being with contingent (praxeologically undetermined), evolving objectives.[24]

The Austrian analysis of welfare as it has developed until today is limited in two areas: firstly, subjectivism prevents welfare from acquiring a common meaning for all individuals; authors therefore reduce the view of welfare to a procedure which takes place through free market exchange. Secondly, the attempt to find any identity between market value and the effective creation of utility in society has in fact failed. The idea of preference is shown in interpersonal exchange, yet the market's *ex post* production of utility for all is not, as some less alert or entrepreneurial agents will be disappointed in their plans.

The reference to praxeological values would appear to overcome both difficulties. In the first case, praxeological values, whose contents are apodictic, offer a universal criterion of welfare, whether the actors are present on the market or not, so there is no need to limit the analysis to an arbitrarily chosen field. In the second case, the problem of effective creation of utility, the correct welfare criterion is not procedural but substantive. It refers to the existence of 'praxeological goods', that is, to the resources which shape all action processes and thus satisfy the praxeological values. The term 'praxeological goods' may be precisely defined, as it simply stems from the satisfaction of physiological needs. A welfare index would seem to be measurable in principle, although open to discussion on the technical front; it would correspond to the level of production of praxeological goods.

This approach might appear to be very close to Rawls's in *A Theory of Justice* (1971) in terms of primary goods.[25] But although it has the same advantages from the viewpoint of founding normativity, it does not face the same difficulties. Our formulation escapes the logical problems found in two often-criticized elements in Rawls's theory. The first of these is the heterogeneity of all primary goods as he defines them, which leads him into logical contradictions in his presentation of the theorems of justice (see Boudon, *Effets pervers et ordre social*, 1977), whereas our 'praxeological goods' refers to a homogenous sub-group of material goods. The second element is that many authors (Roemer, 'A Pragmatic Theory of Responsibility for the Egalitarian Planner', 1993b; Sen, 'Ethical Measurement of Inequality: Some Difficulties', 1978, *Commodities and Capabilities*, 1985) raised the question of individuals' capacity of using (that is deriving psychological income from) these Rawlsian primary goods. If we take into account individuals' asymmetries in their abilities of consuming these goods then the principles of justice are affected and Rawls's equity rule loses in quality. This critique, however, vanishes in our praxeological approach; individuals are certainly able to get satisfaction from use of these praxeological goods as they are valued by each actor in an apodictic way. They are the preconditions of any type of action.

So the reference to Mises' structure of human action founds a universal acceptation of the praxeological value of survival. Derived from this, all individuals, whether in the market or not, have to value not only 'praxeological goods' but also the institutions of the socio-economic state which highly favours their production; this socio-economic state, Hayek's Great Society (*The Extended Order*), is thus logically what enables the highest increase of its constituent individuals' hopes for survival.

This type of analysis incidentally calls to mind Menger's argument which constantly refers to 'the common good' while defining the scope of the economy as being 'the precautionary activity of humans directed toward covering their material needs' (Menger, 1883, p. 63). Menger also referred to the plight of the 'weak and the poor' (see Boehm, 1985). This approach is rightly considered to be too reductive in comparison with the wider conception of 'the economic point of view' (Kirzner, 1960). It is, however the key to understanding a universal definition of welfare, established on Mises' praxeological scheme of things.

The definition of Austrian normativity, founded on the idea of survival, takes into account a zone of agents' common valorization of it. Is it therefore possible to rationally consider that each individual will prefer a system leading to their satisfaction, in this case market economy and the spontaneous order? The answer is no. The existence of a zone of common values does not always mean a rational obligation for agents to prefer the socio-economic states most suited to these values.

3.3 Unprescribed Normativity

Austrian normativity does not mean that a rational individual must express a doctrinal preference[26] for the market system, as the formation of such a preference depends on each agent's situation, so this normativity cannot be defined as prescriptive.

The distinction marked out between prescription and normativity corresponds to the difference between 'judgements' and 'interests'. Of course, all individuals put lexicographical value on praxeological goods, because of the laws of human action, so their judgements could be considered to be identical. But their differences of situations (in particular of budgetary constraints) might produce different 'interests'. Some, with small amounts of praxeological goods, might consider increasing production of material resources to be a priority; others might have enough to be able to prefer other subjective goods not necessarily produced by the market and even possibly contradictory to it, for example, 'social justice'. It would therefore be in these individuals' interests to encourage a reduction of praxeological goods' production, to allocate society's scarce resources to other types of objectives.

So these two categories of actors have similar judgements but their doctrinal preferences would be different: the first category would favour the market but the second would prefer other socio-economic systems, so an individual's doctrinal preferences do not depend on his judgements but on his interests, which in our example depend on his initial endowments and praxeological goods.

Other cases come to mind, for example an actor being ignorant of his initial endowments of praxeological goods and/or their subjective values, but knowing his own talents. So while he is conscious of the free market's greater ability to produce praxeological goods and he wishes to accumulate as many as possible, he might still prefer a more centrally-controlled, redistributive economy if he believes he is capable of directing it towards his interests and acquire a greater quantity of these goods than on the free market.

It is now possible to define precisely what Austrian normativity might be. It would be established on a condition of impartiality which Rawls defines as the ideal observer position:

> A rational and impartial sympathetic spectator is a person who takes up a general perspective: he assumes a position where his own interests are not at stake and he possesses all the requisite information and powers of reasoning. So situated he is equally responsive and sympathetic to the desires and satisfactions of everyone affected by the social system (1971, p. 186).[27]

This position of impartiality is itself a theory originating in the axiom of the original position characterised by the 'veil of ignorance'. The definition of Austrian normativity is similar in that it refers to individuals knowing the lexicographical nature of their values but not knowing their endowments, their idiosyncrasies (values other than praxeological) and their particular talents. That normativity would be thus based on an impartial judgement, leaving their own interests to one side.

To continue the parallel with Rawls, the normativity criterion that we have just defined is an Austrian equivalent of the maximin.[28] The Austrian version is however different from Rawls's in two distinct ways.

Firstly it expresses infra-individual and not inter-individual criteria as described in *A Theory of Justice*. In Rawls's version, the maximin implies a classification of social alternatives based on the least favoured individual's situation. Seen from an Austrian point of view, it is simply the fact that the satisfaction of praxeological needs (minimal or primary conditions of action) is characterised by a lexicographical priority over other sorts of needs. Socio-economic states should therefore be classified to promote them according to their ability to best promote the minimal or prior conditions for any action.

Secondly, Rawls's version of the maximin principle corresponds to a theorem of justice rooted in the 'original position'. This principle is axiomatic in the Austrian framework, because it reflects praxeological reality.

A normative Austrian economy, as is defined today, is faced with significant conceptual constraints such as subjectivism and demonstrated preference. A re-examination of Hayek would seem to offer new perspectives; he asserts the coordinating function of the spontaneous institutions in *The Fatal Conceit* (1988), based on the experience of their ability to support growing populations. It is this reference to survival reinterpreted through the terms of Mises' praxeology that leads to an Austrian normative economy free of the critiques levelled at its previous versions.

NOTES

1. 'unless one is prepared to make interpersonal comparisons of utility, it is not at all clear what one is to mean by the notion of a ranking of the importance to society of alternative production possibilities' (Kirzner, 1985, p. 153).
2. Rothbard uses the notion of 'demonstrated preference' to differentiate it from Samuelson's concept of 'revealed preference', which he judges to be wrong: 'the critical difference is this: Samuelson assumes the existence of an underlyng preference scale that forms the basis of a man's action, and that remains constant in the course of his actions over time ... There is no reason whatever for making any such assumption. All we can say is that an action, at a specific point of time, reveals part of a man's preference scale *at that time*. There is no warrant for assuming that it remains constant from one point of time to another' (Rothbard, 1956, p. 228-229).
3. Rothbard refused the notion of 'public goods', necessarily produced only by the state. Apart from the fact that most goods produced by modern states do not conform to the rules of non-exclusion and non-rivality the theory does not bear out the concept: if goods are not produced by the market, how to tell the value consumers place on them? (see Rothbard 'Public Goods and External Benefits', 1962b for more details). Rothbard developed an entire reflection to show that the State is a non-voluntary institution, which explains his opposition to Arrow's theories (*Social Choice and Individual Values*, 1951) of social choice.
4. For example, the industrialist who decides to make cars on 1 January which will roll off the production lines on 31 December, aiming for a certain income, might see his expectations fail if consumers do not to turn up to buy. The failure of a plan does not necessarily mean, however, there is no exchange; the industrialist who cannot turn a profit on his cars will sell them cheaper than expected, to cut his losses. Exchange does mean that activities are coordinated, but there will be no heuristic aspect to the coordination. The important thing is to make sure that plans are subjectively fulfilled. Armentano expresses a somewhat narrow conception of achieving expectations when he considers that the 'act of (price) agreement is explicit evidence of social cooperation and plan coordination' (Armentano, foreword to 'Property Rights, Efficiency and Social Welfare', 1992, p. XIII).

5. '… praxeology maintains that when a person acts, his utility, or at least his *ex ante* utility, increases' (Rothbard, 1976b, p. 98).
6. Hayek also examined the theme of externalities, notably in *Law, Legislation and Liberty* (1979). However Cordato claims that Hayek's approach, which may legitimize public action, is erroneous, appearing to be 'inconsistent with much of his own general framework of analysis in other areas' (1992, p. 24).
7. Mises himself had already visited this in *Human Action*: 'Within a world organized on the basis of the division of labor, every change must in one way or another affect the short-run interests of many groups' (Mises, 1966, p. 82).
8. Certain of the work's analytical elements are an extension of an argument Cordato developed previously in 'The Austrian Theory of Efficience and the Role of Government' (1980).
9. Therefore: 'A pollution externality is a social problem because the pollution interferes with the use of property by its "legitimate" owner, i.e., it represents a coerced exchange' (Cordato, 1992, p. 42).
10. Cordato clearly rejects the criterion of 'social utility' as Rothbard formulates it. Society not being solely constructed on market exchange, it is impossible to definitely state that any market exchange is socially useful, even when preferences are not demonstrated: 'Rothbard's approach does not eliminate this problem, but simply ignores it' (1992, p. 43).
11. It is worth remembering that the principle of Wertfreiheit takes the principles of praxeology to be valid whatever individuals' ends might be. So if the catallactic model derived from praxeology can be associated with the idea of better opportunities of improving agents' knowledge, thus favouring the achievement of market actors' ends, Kirzner claims it is rational to support normative classical liberalism.
12. In his response to Burczak ('A critique of Kirzner's Finders-Keepers Defense of Profit', 2002), Kirzner is explicit on this subject, saying his theory must be seen 'as an argument that should convince those who, for their own philosophical or other reasons, happen to accept the finders-keepers ethic' (Kirzner, 2002, p. 91).
13. 'What welfare economics does is to present these conclusions to the framer of ethical judgments as part of the data for his ethical system. To the person who scorns social utility or admires coercion, our analysis might furnish powerful arguments for a policy of thoroughgoing Statism' (Rothbard 1956, p. 262). Value judgments are always unavoidable in the economist (see Rothbard, 1976b; Egger, 'Efficiency Is Not a Substitute for Ethics', 1979).
14. 'Ethics is the discipline, or what is called in classical philosophy the 'science', of what goals should or should not pursue. All men have values and place positive or negative value judgments on goods, people and events. Ethics is the discipline that provides standards for a moral critique of these value judgments. In the final analysis, either such a discipline exists and a rational or objective system of ethics is possible, or else each individual's value judgments are ultimately arbitrary and solely a creature of individual whim. It is not my province to try to settle one of the great questions of philosophy here. But even if we believe, as I do, that an objective science of ethics exists, and even if we believe still further that ethical judgments are within the province of the historian or social scientist, one thing is certain: praxeology, economic theory, cannot itself establish ethical judgments' (Rothbard, 1976b, p. 89).
15. Hayek's later works show that the references to Popper's works are not for show. The problematic of *Studies in Philosophy, Politics and Economics* (1967b), gathering Hayek's texts from the 1950s and 1960s are concerned with Popperian themes, whether on the level of principles of demarcation or corroboration. A little later, in his Nobel Memorial Lecture, 'The Pretence of Knowledge', he was to say 'We cannot be grateful enough to such modern philosophers of science as Sir Karl Popper for giving us a test by which we can distinguish between what we may accept as scientific and what not … I am anxious to repeat, we still achieve predictions which can be falsified and which therefore are of empirical significance' (1974-1975 p. 31).

16. The obvious 'common sense' (Selgin, *Praxeology and Understanding: An Analysis of the Controversy in Austrian Economics*, 1982) of the tendency towards equilibrium must have aroused many a doubt in the Austrian commentator. Loasby (*Economics and Dispersed and Incomplete Information,* 1982); Langlois ('Knowledge and Rationality in the Austrian School: An Analytical Survey', 1985); Hight ('Equilibration and Disequilibrium in the Market Process', 1986) and also Lachmann (*The Market as an Economic Process*, 1986a) all questioned the 'tendency towards equilibrium' in both theory and practice. Caldwell ('Hayek's Transformation', 1983) also discussed the nature of Hayek's insistence on this theme. He presents it as originating in the Austro-Marxist debates on collectivism and Hayek's rejection of any form of economic interventionism.
17. Hayek had noted already in 'Notes on the Evolution of Systems of Rules of Conduct': 'The individual may have no idea what this overall order is that results from his observing such rules as those concerning kinship and inter-marriage, or the succession to property, or which function this overall order serves. Yet all individuals of the species which exist will behave in that manner because groups of individuals which have thus behaved have displaced those which did not do so' (Hayek, 1963a, p. 70). See also Zywicki (2000).
18. A counter-argument can be seen in Vromen, *Economic Evolution, an Inquiry into the Foundations of New Institutional Economics* (1995) and Aimar, 'Coordination, Survival and Normativity: A Hayekian Perspective Revisited' (1999).
19. 'The peculiar thing about these kinds of models is that, because we have to draw deductions from what we know about some factors contributing to the phenomenon and know nothing about others, our conclusions and predictions will also refer only to some properties of the resulting phenomenon, in other words, to a kind of phenomenon rather than to a particular event' (Hayek, 1955, p. 15).
20. The scope of predictive capacities concerning this type of structure would seem to relate to the limits that Popper himself underlined of the predictive power of his theory: '... because the following passage of my *Logic of Scientific Discovery* has been interpreted – or rather misinterpreted – as showing that I was using corroboration as an index of the *future* performance of a theory: "Instead of discussing the 'probability' of a hypothesis we should try to assess what tests, what trials, it has withstood; that is, we should try to assess how far it has been able to prove its fitness to survive by standing up to tests. In brief, we should try to assess how far it has been 'corroborated'" (L.Sc. D., p. 251). Some people thought that the phrase "prove its fitness to survive" shows that I had here intended to speak of a fitness to survive in the *future*, to stand up to future tests. I am sorry if I have misled anybody, but I can only say that it was not I who mixed the Darwinian metaphor. Nobody expects that a species which has survived in the past will therefore survive in the future: all the species which ever failed to survive some period of time *t* have survived up to that time *t*. It would be absurd to suggest that Darwinian survival involves, somehow, an expectation that every species that has so far survived will continue to survive' (*Objective Knowledge*, 1972, p. 19). In Hayek's opinion, this 'solution of the problem of induction' (Popper, ibid., p. 29) would extend the boundaries of scientific knowledge, 'while it is certainly desirable to make our theories as falsifiable as possible, we must also push forward into fields where, as we advance, the degree of falsifiability necessarily decreases. This is the price we have to pay for an advance into the field of complex phenomena' ('The Theory of Complex Phenomena', 1964, p. 29).
21. 'The fitness that survives, according to the biological notion of evolution, is an unforeseen fitness, an adjustment wrought out in consequence of the struggle. But psychical activities are essentially purposeful; the fitness that survives in social adjustments is prearranged. Sociologists are guilty of un-scientific procedure when they group the phenomena of economic adjustments together with those of unexplained and fortuitous biological change' (Kirzner, 1960, p. 153-154).
22. This work partially constitutes the development of an earlier article 'From Menger to Hayek: Biology, Subjectivism and Welfare' (1990).

23. Most ends pursued by agents do however require them to stay alive: 'Notwithstanding all declarations to the contrary, the immense majority of men aim first of all at an improvement of the material conditions of well-being. They want more and better food, better homes and clothes, and a thousand other amenities. They strive after abundance and health' (Mises, 1966, p. 96). This insight is not, however, praxeological; the aim of action may be to suppress life: 'The impulse to live, to preserve one's own life and to take advantage of every opportunity of strengthening one's vital force is a primal feature of life, present in every living being. However, to yield to this impulse is not – for man – an inextricable necessity ... He can give up his life when the conditions under which alone he could preserve it seem intolerable; Man is capable of dying for a cause or of committing suicide. To live is for man the outcome of a choice, of a judgment of value' (Mises, 'The Treatment of Irrationality in the Social Sciences', 1944a, p. 25). However, what is praxeologically certain is that any actor does not necessarily value life as an end but always as a means. Curious as it as may seem, an individual attempting suicide is still in this vision: between the moment of decision and action, the individual will value all the resources he needs to accomplish his act and therefore, perhaps paradoxically, life itself.
24. Rothbard (*The Ethics of Liberty*, 1982) defines life as being an objective value but his naturalist approach leads him to establish the irrationality of certain individual objectives: 'If Crusoe had eaten the mushrooms without learning of their poisonous effects, then his decision would have been incorrect – a possibly tragic error based on the fact that man is hardly automatically determined to make correct decisions at all times. Hence his lack of omniscience and his liability to error. If Crusoe, on the other hand, had known of the poison and eaten the mushrooms anyway – perhaps for "kicks" or from a very high-time preference – this decision would have been objectively immoral, an act deliberately set against his life and health' (Rothbard, 1982, p. 32). He refers to the idea of human nature to establish an ethics system of objective values; but praxeology shows it is not necessary to refer to any form of naturalism or abandon the Austrian principle of Wertfreiheit to establish the existence of common, permanent values in actor/individuals.
25. Rawls (*A Theory of Justice*, 1971) tries to establish criteria of justice to evaluate socioeconomic states. To do this, he developed an axiom by referring the 'original position'. This axiom showed up agents' common preferences, which corresponded to 'primary goods'. Based on this axiom of the original position, he deduced theorems of social justice which correspond to a rational criterion of endowment sharing.
26. By doctrinal preference we mean the socio-economic situation procuring the highest degree of satisfaction for the individual concerned out of a range of given opportunities. It is of no importance for our analysis whether this preference is expressed electorally or not.
27. Hayek (*Law, Legislation and Liberty*) meaningfully expresses his interest in Rawls's approach. Thus, 'In one instance the feeling that I ought to justify my position vis-à-vis a major recent work has also contributed to delay the completion of this volume. But after careful consideration I have come to the conclusion that what I might have to say about John Rawls's *A Theory of Justice* (1972) would not assist in the pursuit of my immediate object because the differences between us seemed more verbal than substantial' (Hayek, 1976a, p. XVII).
28. In '*A Theory of Justice*', Rawls carefully distinguishes the 'difference principle' from the economic criterion of maximin. This has no bearing at all on our analysis.

Appendix: Schumpeter and the Austrian Tradition

Complex relations

It is difficult to avoid the dominant figure of Joseph Schumpeter when examining the theory of entrepreneurship; quite apart from the central position this question occupies in his work (*The Theory of Economic Development*, 1912; *Capitalism, Socialism and Democracy*, 1942) the fact that this economist was born and educated in Austria would seem to gain him at least some attention in the present book. However, he at no point claimed he followed the line of thought started by Menger or even less of his contemporary, Mises. It is true he was, with Mises, a member of Böhm-Bawerk's seminar and he does name Carl Menger as one of the *Ten Great Economists* (1952), again paying homage to his 'genius' in his famous *History of Economic Analysis* (1954). Yet a few lines later he proclaims,

> Walras is in my opinion the greatest of all economists. His system of economic equilibrium, uniting, as it does, the quality of 'revolutionary' creativeness with the quality of classic synthesis, is the only work by an economist that will stand comparison with the achievements of theoretical physics. Compared with it, most of the theoretical writings of that period, – and beyond – however valuable in themselves and however original subjectively, look like boats beside a liner, like inadequate attempts to catch some particular aspect of Walrasian truth (1954, p. 827).

As a result, Menger's heirs' view was unequivocal:

> Because Austrian economics is a theory of human action, Schumpeter does not belong to the Austrian school. In his first book he significantly related himself to Wieser and Walras, but not to Menger and Böhm-Bawerk. Economics, to him, is a theory of 'economic quantities', and not of human action. Schumpeter's *Theory of Economic Development* is a typical product of the equilibrium theory (Mises, *Notes and Recollections*, 1978, p. 36-37).

And Hayek tended to agree:

> … though he had been trained at the University of Vienna and had been a leading member of the famous seminar of Eugen von Böhm-Bawerk, he had also absorbed the teaching of Léon Walras, who had received little notice by the Austrians and

> had adopted the positivist approach to science expounded by the Austrian physicist Ernst Mach. In the course of time he moved further away from the characteristic tents of the Austrian school so it became increasingly doubtful later whether he could still be counted as a member of that group ('Joseph Schumpeter', 1980, p. 160).[1]

Lastly, according to Lachmann, Schumpeter considered 'that economics is not concerned with men and their actions but solely with relationships between measurable quantities' ('Ludwig von Mises and the Extension of Subjectivism', 1982, p. 34). '... though well acquainted with subjectivism, [he] pointedly ignores the achievements of Austrian subjectivism' (Lachmann, *The Market as an Economic Process*, 1986, p. 144).

So Schumpeter would appear to be well on the outside of both the Austrian and neo-Austrian traditions and he ought to have been completely excluded from this book. On closer examination of the literature, however, it appeared that Schumpeter's reflections can to some degree be seen as being close to Mises' problematic from certain angles and especially from that of dynamic economics. Yet the origins, nature and above all the reality of that proximity have raised controversial debate within the Austrian tradition. The mere existence of this debate must move us to make a more profound examination of Schumpeterian ideas.

In his *The Theory of Economic Development*, Schumpeter defines the state of equilibrium as the 'circular flow of economic life', presenting it as an intellectual construction, analogously to Mises' 'evenly rotating economy' with real time as having no analytical dimension. Only Newtonian or mechanical time can exist in equilibrium, producing no nonpredicted or nonpredictable changes.

In Schumpeter's eyes, the essence of economic development is in the disturbance of that circular flow. The economic problem is not the way that capitalism administers existing structures but how it creates and destroys them. Entrepreneurship, here defined in its relation to innovation, is at the heart of this process of rupture:

> ... the function of entrepreneurs is to reform or revolutionize the pattern of production by exploiting an invention or, more generally, an untried technological possibility for producing a new commodity or producing an old one in a new way, by opening up a new source of supply of materials or a new outlet for products, by reorganizing an industry and so on (1942, p. 132).

The Schumpeterian entrepreneur ensures economic development by rupturing the production process in a phenomenon called creative destruction.[2]

Convergences and divergences

It is certainly Kirzner among all Mises' inheritors who has written the most on Schumpeter, for reasons linked to his own theories on entrepreneurship.

In his early work (*Competition and Entrepreneurship*, 1973), Kirzner recognises certain convergences between his own analyses and Schumpeter's:

> In many respects the picture of the entrepreneur which I have sought to delineate shows much resemblance to that elaborated by Schumpeter. The Schumpeterian innovator is, after all, the decision-maker whose alertness to unnoticed opportunities has enabled him to depart from the routine, repetitive working of widely known opportunities. The distinction which Schumpeter draws at length between the way men would act in 'the accustomed circular flow' on the one hand and when 'confronted by a new task' on the other is closely parallel to my own distinction between 'Robbinsian' decision-making and entrepreneurial activity (1973, p. 79- 80).

Kirzner, like Schumpeter, refuses certain conceptions of entrepreneurial profit; he neither sees the entrepreneur as a factor of production and therefore his revenue as not being a marginal productivity return, nor are his gains the fruit of luck as

> they are deliberately created by the entrepreneur's 'new combination' ... Schumpeter leaves no room for any suggestion that profits so won should be seen as the reward for risk-bearing. It is strictly the capitalist who bears the risk of any entrepreneurial venture. Entrepreneurial profits are won in the course of innovating new productive combinations ... Uncertainty has nothing to do with the matter (1989, p. 60-61).

These points of convergence show a certain common view between Schumpeter and neo-Austrian authors; however, Kirzner is careful to draw a line between his theory and Schumpeter's. He raises the following two major points, somewhat based on his Austrian predecessors.

Firstly, he considers that progress, in Schumpeter's sense, does not systematically come from discovery. Many Schumpeterian innovations are based on existing, known opportunities, so the entrepreneur's characteristic is not capacity to discover opportunities but his will to exploit them. Only the entrepreneur has the strength of character and the boldness to do this:

> No doubt that Schumpeter did not see profit as being that which the entrepreneur has discovered. This emerges very clearly from his discussion of the qualities required for leadership – in which he sees the essence of entrepreneurship. Schumpeter emphasizes that the difficulty involved in leadership activity, and the circumstance that makes leadership a scarce commodity is not that of discovering opportunities, but that of actually grasping them once they have been perceived. It is, Schumpeter remarks, no part of the function of leadership, 'to 'find' or 'to create' new possibilities. They are always present, abundantly accumulated by all sorts of people. Often, they are also generally known and being discussed by scientific and literary writers. In other cases there is nothing to discover about them, because they are quite obvious'. The difficulty of leadership in general, and of 'economic leadership' (that is, entrepreneurship) in particular, is that of breaking away from estab-

> lished, familiar ways of activity. What is needed is not so much superior vision as superior will (Kirzner, 1989, p. 61-62).

The Schumpeterian entrepreneur thus is characterised by his impulse to change the course of events rather than his perception of new opportunities; he is more a leader of men than an explorer alert to discovery.

It is incidentally quite logical that the Schumpeterian entrepreneur does not make his profits from any discovery. In Schumpeter's world, the entrepreneur starts his activities from a situation where there is nothing to discover: equilibrium. His role is to disrupt the economy from its circular flow to push it towards a process of creative destruction. Kirzner says this is the central point of understanding the difference between Schumpeter and the neo-Austrian tradition: the Schumpeterian creates disequilibrium, pulling the economy out of its circular flow, whereas the Misesian entrepreneur starts from disequilibrium to create a movement towards equilibrium:

> What entrepreneurship achieves within the Schumpeterian system is the disruption of the circular flow, the creation of disequilibrium out of equilibrium. For me, on the contrary, the entrepreneurial role, although of course the source of movement within the system, has an equilibrating influence; it is entrepreneurial alertness to unnoticed opportunities which creates the tendency toward the even circular flow of equilibrium. For Schumpeter, entrepreneurship is important primarily in sparking economic development; for me it is important primarily in enabling the market process to work itself out in all contexts (Kirzner, 1973, p. 81).

Based on this, in Schumpeter's work only the first one to reach the discovery can be called an entrepreneur, those who follow being mere imitators. For Kirzner, in the end, the entrepreneur realises and corrects his mistakes, which means that even imitators are entrepreneurs.

The second major point is where Kirzner draws attention to the insufficient relevant reflection on the institutional conditions of entrepreneurship in Schumpeter's reasoning; he considers it thus becomes also applicable outside of the market economy: 'The notion of circular flow and the possibility of its disturbance through creative spontaneous decisions are in principle entirely relevant to the nonmarket economy' (1979, p. 119).

He considers that Schumpeter especially does not sufficiently stress the nature and cognitive aspects of entrepreneurial incentives; for there to be innovation, the mere opportunity to innovate is not enough:

> ... a social mechanism is needed to ensure that possibilities are perceived and embraced. Schumpeter fails to show how the nonmarket economy can grapple with this central problem ... Instead of seeing how the entrepreneur has disturbed the placid status quo, we must see how the status quo is nothing but a seething mass of unexploited maladjustments crying for their correction. Instead of seeing entrepreneurship as jerking the system out of equilibrium, we must see it as fulfilling the tendencies toward equilibrium. My belief is that only such a theoretical scheme can

> be helpful in the great policy questions that face the developing countries of the world (Kirzner, 1979, p. 119).[3]

It is known, of course, that Schumpeter developed a pessimistic vision of the future of market societies by precisely introducing an institutional dimension. The Schumpeterian entrepreneur is at the source of creativity and the economic dynamic. He considers that endogenous change to the capitalist firm's structure inevitably leads to the 'the obsolescence of the entrepreneurial function' and the gradual disappearance of the innovative entrepreneur that dogs the advance of any managerial activity:

> Technological progress is increasingly becoming the business of teams of trained specialists, who turn out what is required and make it work in predictable ways. The romance of earlier commercial adventure is rapidly wearing away, because so many more things can be strictly calculated that had of old to be visualized in a flash of genius (Schumpeter, *Capitalism, Socialism and Democracy*, 1942, p. 132).

The entrepreneur disappears in the wake of growing routine; profit margins shrink as a result and so the market system cannot flourish. The logical result of this encroaching bureaucracy in entrepreneurship is that a market economy gradually transfers to a socialist system.

Mises and Hayek were developing a pessimistic view of the markets' fate at the same time as Schumpeter, based, however, on diametrically opposite premises. While Schumpeter held that socialism was the result of the progressive shrinking of entrepreneurship, Hayek's view was that socialism was the cause of it. He condemns the fatal damage that growing interventionism was causing to market opportunities while encouraging rent-seeking:

> ... the policies which are now followed everywhere, which hand out the privilege of security, now to this group and now to that, are nevertheless rapidly creating conditions in which the striving for security tends to become stronger than the love of freedom. The reason for this is that with every grant of complete security to one group the insecurity of the rest necessarily increases. If you guarantee to some a fixed part of a variable cake, the share left to the rest is bound to fluctuate proportionally more than the size of the whole. And the essential element of security which the competitive system offers, the great variety of opportunities, is more and more reduced (1944, p. 153).

The disturbance of activities, the flip side of price manipulation, brings the authorities to intervene more and more, increasingly reducing market opportunities and lowering the amount of entrepreneurial activity. Mises in the same way repeatedly emphasises the drawbacks of bureaucracy and interventionism (*Liberalism: In the Classical Tradition*, 1927; A *Critique of Interventionism*, 1929; *Bureaucracy*, 1946).

Kirzner's view is that Schumpeter's erroneous and underdeveloped institutional dimension of entrepreneurship led him to mistake the nature of the entrepreneur's role within multi-period time: 'The primary consequence of Schumpeter's entrepreneurship was the long-run economic development of the capitalist system' (Kirzner, 1999, p. 7).

But the logic of entrepreneurial movement must be seen on a much shorter time-scale, where Schumpeter's idea of development does not necessarily fit. It is this short term which is responsible for market agitation.[4] So Kirzner regrets that in Schumpeter's eyes, entrepreneurship is not exercised at the price level, which is an expression of daily market activity but at a level of products and technology, where the analysis has to be on a longer time-scale. Yet paradoxically, it is only when short-term entrepreneurial activity is grasped that his longer term role can be understood: 'In other words, the way to permit long-run entrepreneurial growth processes to take off is to recognize and encourage the kinds of entrepreneurial discoveries that make up the short-run processes' (Kirzner, 1985, p. 69).[5]

Towards 'reconciliation'

Most of the Austrian writers perceived a strong difference between the views of Schumpeter and Mises' followers. Authors such as Loasby ('The Entrepreneur in Economic Theory', 1989b) and Boehm ('The Austrian Tradition: Schumpeter and Mises', 1990[6]) underlined points of divergence. This has been questioned as opinions have started to comment on the relevance of such a gap. Hébert and Link ('The Entrepreneur, Mainstream Views and Radical Critiques', 1982), or Boudreaux ('Schumpeter and Kirzner on Competition and Equilibrium', 1994) think of this opposition as exaggerated or superficial. According to these authors, the two types of theories can be seen as complementary, while others go further: Choi ('The Entrepreneur: Schumpeter versus Kirzner', 1995) and Yu ('Entrepreneurial Alertness and Discovery', 2001) list the many advantages of considering Kirzner's and Schumpeter's visions as being globally similar.

For them, Kirzner was further from the letter than the spirit of Schumpeter's theory. They consider that innovation could indeed be thought of as a form of discovery, if it is thought of as the result of the perception of new possible productive combinations. Early on, Kirzner himself recognised that

> much of Schumpeter's notion of entrepreneurship-as-leadership could fairly easily be translated into the idea of entrepreneurship-as-vision-and-discovery. Presumably one's intensity of will in pursuing what appears to be a profitable opportunity is an expression of the clarity with which one 'sees' that opportunity. So that the central ingredient in Schumpeter's economic leadership need not be identified exclusively as the determination to pursue possibilities that are visible to all; it can, altogether equivalently, be identified as the superior vision to see as profitably attainable that which others see only as an abstract possibility. But the point is that Schumpeter, as

> we have seen, was explicit in insisting that innovation, not discovery, is the essential contribution and indentifying feature of the entrepreneur (1989, p. 62).

It is quite possible to come to the same conclusions as Kirzner on discovery by using the role of innovation. Yu ('Entrepreneurial Alertness and Discovery', 2001) holds the view that taking a new look at Schumpeterian innovation in terms of alertness was important, as the opposing of the two views would simply reduce the Kirznerian entrepreneur to the role of an imitator. Kirzner's promoter must also have the will to apply his discoveries if he hopes to make a profit.

It appears that Kirzner felt the need to refine his position seeing the growing amount of literature on the subject, the utility of a large part of which he recognises. He comes out in favour of a simultaneous acceptation of the two versions ('Creativity and/or Alertness: A Reconsideration of the Schumpetarian Entrepreneur', 1999). He does not question the difference between his own position and Schumpeter's, but seeks a form of reconciliation, by demonstrating 'how each of these apparently conflicting views can be seen as plausible and realistic; and how each can usefully advance economic understanding (of respectively different aspects of the capitalist economy' (1999, p. 5).

He firmly maintains that the Schumpeterian process of creative destruction should in fact be considered as equilibrating. What Schumpeter seems to see as a state of equilibrium, Kirzner sees as underlying disequilibria between information and knowledge. The entrepreneur's activity is a reaction to these disequilibria and he aims to match the organisation of his activities with the structure of existing and available opportunities, even if, because of their mis-knowledge of these available opportunities, some individuals and their plans will be inevitably affected by entrepreneurial discovery. So to use Kirzner's example, the horse-drawn carriage industry was obviously affected by the advent of the car. This changes nothing in the equilibriating nature of entrepreneurial activity in whatever case or era; therefore: 'while understanding how Schumpeter can focus on the creative destruction which this successful and dramatic entrepreurial innovation has wrought, I maintain that we must, at the same time, recognize the coordinative quality of this innovation' (Kirzner, 1999, p. 14).

Kirzner softens his opposition to Schumpeter's positions in the field of entrepreneurial characteristics and qualities when he returns to the difference between statics (single period time) and dynamics (multi-period time). Consistent with his earlier analyses, he persists in the idea that to conceptualise entrepreneurial activity there is no need to be in a multi-period world; even in the static world there is room for alertness, as ignorance is not only created by real time, it is also created by knowledge division, in which case the entrepreneur is not essentially an innovator as Schumpeter saw him.

But Kirzner admits that when looking at the real, multi-period world, where the future is always uncertain, there is a place for entrepreneurial qualities described by Schumpeter such as self-confidence, boldness and leadership. In a dynamic world, the imagined future has to fit with the real one, which means possessing qualities of imagination and self-confidence. So Schumpeter correctly described in this context the extra qualities added to alertness to express entrepreneurship. Kirzner thus recognised

> how the multi-period world requires its entrepreneurs to display the Schumpeterian qualities, while still maintaining that it does not require me to surrender one iota of my earlier view of the entrepreneurial role as one of pure, alert, discovery of hitherto overlooked, exogenously created, changes ... My 'obstinacy' consists in my continuing to insist that what is important for analytical purposes is not the leadership qualities in themselves, but the pure 'alertness' which these qualities express and sustain (1999, p. 13).

So if we include real time in the analysis, there is indeed a place for Schumpeter's entrepreneurial qualities; but Kirzner kept to his position: there is no need for dynamics in order to recognise the entrepreneur's essential quality in a market economy: alertness.

NOTES

1. As early as 'The Use of Knowledge in Society' (1945), Hayek had criticized Schumpeter on the implications and hypotheses that it brought up on knowledge. See also Kirzner's *Perception, Opportunity and Profit* (1979, p. 68-69).
2. 'The opening up of new markets, foreign or domestic, and the organizational development from the craft shop and factory to such concerns as U.S. Steel illustrate the same process of industrial mutation – if I may use that biological term – that incessantly revolutionizes the economic structure from within, incessantly destroying the old one, incessantly creating a new one. This process of Creative Destruction is the essential fact about capitalism' (Schumpeter, 1942, p. 83).
3. Witt similarly remarked that 'While Schumpeterian evolution deals with novelty diffusing, in the form of innovations, through the given institutional framework of the economy, Hayek goes beyond this to focus on the evolution of the institutional framework itself' (1995, p. 90).
4. See Kirzner, 1973, p. 128; 'The Theory of Entrepreneurship in Economic Growth' (1982c); Kirzner (1985) p. 68-69.
5. See also Steele, *Entrepreneurship and the Economics of Growth* (1998).
6. See also Kirzner's comments, 1990, following Boehm's article.

General Conclusion

We are in Ignorance of Far More Than We Know.

This may appear a little brief as a conclusion to such a study, yet they seem appropriate to a stormy era of fast-moving events.

The history of thought has recorded many attempts to master economic events, definitive answers to the great problems of the times being trumpeted from the highest monuments and institutions; the broader history of humankind has recorded many attempts to control the lives of others in the name of the pretence of knowledge, bringing unavoidable disaster.

Certainties and over-simplified thinking do not encourage the free development of ideas; internal quarrels and ideological biases can only weaken the support and strength of any tradition of thought. The opportunities for Austrians for inspiring new ideas and exploring rich, new territories are obvious and immense, as is clearly shown in some of the more recent Austrian initiatives.

One of these is the forming of 'New Comparative Economics' (Boettke et al. 2005), which shines a bright light on the nature of transition processes in the old planned economies in Eastern Europe. More broadly, this new approach recounts the constraints to the field of development by revealing cultural and institutional elements in the coordination process. Different institutional arrangements are distinguished inside capitalism itself and the way these alternatives determine economic performance is examined. It contains an original application of a number of tools and concepts on a societal level that are normally used in the economy of organisations (Coase, Williamson, etc).

Another is the appearance of a spatial and urban Austrian economy, notably around the works of Desrochers (1998, 2001), Ikeda (2004, 2007) and Holcombe (2004). The notion of space in economics is far removed from the idea of general economic equilibrium. Mises and Hayek were to distance themselves very early from the latter, yet oddly enough hardly mention the notion of space in their works. But the developments of spatial and urban Austrian economics show that the notions of territory and distance must be interpreted in not only physical but also in cognitive and evolutionary terms. Space thus finds itself in a field of study that the Austrians, out of all the contemporary economists, are the best equipped to deal with.

One final example of this renewal is in the recent use made of Hayek's psychological theories. The first edition of *The Sensory Order* was in 1952, but overall studies of the sources of subjectivity and ignorance found in it were strangely enough not started until very much later. The 'rediscovery' of the work contributes to the widening of the Austrian paradigm by showing the actor is not just ignorant of others but of also of himself (Aimar, 2008a, 2008b); the exploration of psychosensory decision-making processes would encourage researchers towards the development of an Austrian neuroeconomy. Exciting new vistas would be opened by experimental studies to improve understanding of ignorance in decision-making processes and the psychological roots of entrepreneurial behaviour. These approaches would quite possibly be parallel to the areas opened by the works of Kahneman, Tverski and Vernon Smith.

So the Austrian school is still alive and kicking; all these examples show not only the importance of the ignorance paradigm but of the need to free it from a certain number of now clichéd critiques. So the school must be allowed to continue to grow as it has always has: as a heterodoxy, resisting and questioning the dominant ideas and certainties of the moment, whatever their source and nature, becoming more and more involved in the great theoretical debates of the day yet staying well away from any damaging partisanship. While remaining solidly anchored to its fundamentals, the multiple, constantly evolving, glittering facets of this complex system of thought will greatly contribute to preventing it from being petrified into some sort of dull totem.

It is in the pursuit of all these ambitions that the present work has strived to contribute to better understanding of the Austrian tradition and to encourage greater respect for its ideas.

Bibliography

Abramovitz, Moses (ed) *The Allocation of Economic Resources,* Stanford, USA: Stanford University Press.

Addleson, M. (1984), 'Robbins's Essay in Retrospect: On Subjectivism and an "Economics of Choice"' *Rivista Internazionale di Scienze Economiche e Commerciali*, 31 (6), 506-523.

Addleson, Mark (1994), 'Competition' in Boettke, Peter (ed), *The Elgar Companion to Austrian Economics*, Aldershot, UK and Brookfield, USA: Edward Elgar, 96-102.

Aimar, Thierry (1996), 'Money and Uncertainty in the Economic Thought of Carl Menger' in Schmidt, Christian (ed) (1996) *Uncertainty in Economic Thought*, Cheltenham, UK and Brookfield, USA: Edward Elgar.

Aimar, T. (1998), 'L'économie autrichienne du bien-être: quelle définition possible?' *Revue d'Economie Politique,* September-October, n°5, 691-709.

Aimar, T. (1999a), 'Ethique versus coordination ? Une controverse autrichienne soulevée par Rothbard', *Revue Economique*, March, vol. 50, n° 2, 301-321.

Aimar, T. (1999b), 'Time, Coordination and Ignorance: A Comparison Between Hayek and Lachmann', *History of Economic Ideas*, VII/1999/1-2 June 1999, 139-167.

Aimar, Thierry (2001a), 'Coordination, Survival and Normativity: A Hayekian Perspective Revisited' in Aimar, Thierry, Jack Birner and Pierre Garrouste (eds) (2001b), *Hayek as a Political Economist*, New York, USA; London, UK: Routledge.

Aimar, Thierry, Jack Birner and Pierre Garrouste (eds) (2001b), *Hayek as a Political Economist*, New York, USA; London, UK: Routledge.

Aimar, T. (2008a), 'Self-Ignorance: Toward an Extension of Austrian Paradigm', *The Review of Austrian Economics*, 21, n°1, 23-43.

Aimar, T. (2008b), 'Economie et psychologie, une réflexion autrichienne sur l'organisation de l'esprit', *Revue Française d'Economie*, XXII, 189-222.

Alchian, A.A. and H. Demsetz (1972), 'Production, Information Costs and Economic Organization', *The American Economic Review*, 62, 777-795.

Alter, Max (1990), *Carl Menger and the Origins of Austrian Economics*, Chicago, USA: Westview Press.

Antonelli, E. (1953), 'Léon Walras et Carl Menger à travers leur correspondance', *Economie appliquée*, 6, 269-287.

Arena, R. (1997), *A propos de l'origine autrichienne de l'économie des coûts de transaction*, Congrès annuel de l'AFSE, Carré des Sciences, working paper.

Arena, R. (1999), 'Hayek et l'équilibre économique: une autre interprétation', *Revue d'économie politique*, n°6, November-December, 847-859.

Armentano, D. T. (1992), 'Property Rights, Efficiency and Social Welfare', Foreword to Cordato, Roy, *Welfare Economics and Externalities in an Open-Ended Universe: A Modern Austrian Perspective*, Boston, USA: Kluwer Academic Publishers, 1992, IX-XV.

Arrow, Kenneth (1951), *Social Choice and Individual Values*, New York, USA: Wiley.

Arrow, Kenneth (1959), 'Toward a Theory of Price Adjustment', in Abramovitz, Moses (ed), *The Allocation of Economic Resources*, Stanford, USA: Stanford University Press.

Atlantic Economic Journal (1978), 'Carl Menger and Austrian Economics', VI, n°3, September.

Augier, M. (1999), 'Some Notes on Alfred Schütz and the Austrian School of Economics: Review of Alfred Schütz's Collected Papers', *The Review of Austrian Economics*, vol. 11, 145-162.

Baird, C.W. (1989), 'James Buchanan and the Austrians: The Common Ground', *Cato Journal*, vol. 9, n°1, Spring/Summer, 201-230.

Bardhan, Pranhab K. and John E Roemer (1993), *Market Socialism*, New York, USA and Oxford, UK: Oxford University Press.

Barone, Enrico (1908), 'The Ministry of Production in the Collectivist State' in Hayek, Friedrich (ed) (1935c), *Collectivist Economic Planning*, Clifton, USA: Augustus Kelly.

Barry, Norman (1979), *Hayek's Social and Economic Philosophy*, London, UK: MacMillan.

Barry, Norman (1987), *On Classical Liberalism and Libertarianism*, New York, USA: Saint-Martin's Press.

Bauer, Otto (1919), *Der Weg zum Sozialismus,* Vienna, Austria: Wiener Volksbuchhandlung Ignaz Brand.

Baumgarth W. P. (1978), 'Hayek and Political Order: The Rule of Law', *The Journal of Libertarian Studies*, 2, n°1, Winter, 11-28.

Bay, C. (1971), 'Hayek's Liberalism: The Constitution of Perpetual Privilege, *Political Science Review*, 1, Fall, 93-124.

Bellante, D. and R. Garrison (1988), 'Phillips Curve and Hayekian Triangles: Two Perspectives on Monetary Dynamics', *History of Political Economy*, 20 (2), Summer, 207-234.

Bergson, Abram (1948), 'Socialist Economics', in Ellis Howard (ed) (1948), *A Survey of Contemporary Economics*, Philadelphia, USA: Blackiston, 412-448.

Birner, Jack (1990), 'A Roundabout Solution to a Fundamental Problem in Menger's Methodology and Beyond', *Carl Menger and his Legacy in Economics*, Durham, USA; London, UK: Duke University Press, 241-263.

Birner, J. (1997), *Human Knowledge and Social Institutions: Popper and Hayek on Evolution,* working paper.

Birner, Jack (1999), 'The Surprising Place of Cognitive Psychology in the Work of F.A. Hayek', *History of Economic Ideas*, 7 (1-2), 43-84.

Black, R.D. Collison, Alfred W. Coats and Craufurd D.W. Goodwin (eds) (1973), *The Marginalist Revolution in Economics*, Durham, USA: Duke University Press.

Blaug, Mark (1980), *The Methodology of Economics: Or How Economists Explain*, Cambridge, UK: Cambridge University Press.

Blaug, Mark (1990), 'Comment on O'Brian's Briar Patch' in Bruce J. Caldwell (ed) (1990), *Carl Menger and his Legacy in Economics*, Durham, USA; London, UK: Duke University Press, 185-188.

Blaug, Mark (1992) (ed), *Carl Menger (1840-1921)*, Cambridge, UK: Cambridge University Press.

Block, Walter (1988a), 'Fractional-Reserve Banking: An Interdisplinary Perspective' in Block, Walter and Llewellyn H. Rockwell (eds) (1988), *Man, Economy and Liberty: Essays in Honor of Murray Rothbard*, Auburn, USA: The Ludwig von Mises Institute, Auburn University, 24-31.

Block, Walter and Llewellyn H. Rockwell (eds) (1988b), *Man, Economy and Liberty: Essays in Honor of Murray Rothbard*, Auburn, USA: The Ludwig von Mises Institute, Auburn University.

Block, W. and Garschina K. M. (1996), 'Hayek, Business Cycles and Fractional Reserve Banking: Continuing the De-Homogenization Process', *The Review of Austrian Economics*, vol. 9, n°1, 77-94.

Boehm, Stephan (1982) 'The Ambiguous Notion of Subjectivism: Comment on Lachmann', in Kirzner, Israel (ed), (1982), *Method, Process and Austrian Economics: Essays in Honour of Ludwig v. Mises*, Lexington, USA: Lexington Books, 41-52.

Boehm, Stephan (1985), 'The Political Economy of the Austrian School' in Roggi, Piero (ed), *Gli economisti e la politica economica*, Naples: Edizione Scientifiche Italiane.

Boehm, Stephan (1990), 'The Austrian Tradition: Schumpeter and Mises', in Hennings, Klaus and Warren J. Samuels (1990), *Neoclassical Economic Theory, 1870-1930*, Boston, USA; Dordrecht, Netherlands; London, UK: Kluwer, 201-241.

Boehm, Stephan and Bruce Caldwell (eds) (1992), *Austrian Economics: Tensions and New Directions,* Boston, USA: Kluwer.

Boettke, P. (1990), 'Interpretative Reasoning and the Study of Social Life', Methodus, 2 (2), 35-45.

Boettke, Peter and David L. Prychitko (1994) (eds), *The Market Process, Essays in Contemporary Austrian Economics*, Aldershot, UK and Brookfield, USA: Edward Elgar.

Boettke, Peter (ed) (1994), *The Elgar Companion to Austrian Economics*, Aldershot, UK and Brookfield, USA: Edward Elgar.

Boettke, Peter and Mario Rizzo (eds) (1995), *Advances in Austrian Economics*, vol. 2, Part A, Greenwich, USA; London, UK: JAI Press.

Boettke, Peter and David L. Prychitko (eds) (1996), *Advances in Austrian Economics*, vol. 3, Greenwich, USA: JAI Press.

Boettke, Peter (1998a), 'Rational Choice and Human Agency in Economics and Sociology: Exploring the Weber-Austrian Connection' in Giersch, Herbert (ed) (1998), *Merits and Limits of Markets*, Berlin, Germany: Springer.

Boettke, Peter (1998b, 'Economic Calculation: The Austrian Contribution to Political Economy' in Boettke, Peter (2001), *Calculation and Coordination, Essays on Socialism and Transitional Political Economy*, London, UK and New York, USA: Routledge, 29-46.

Boettke, Peter (2001), *Calculation and Coordination, Essays on Socialism and Transitional Political Economy*, London, UK; New York, USA: Routledge.

Boettke, P. and R. Koppl (2001), 'Introduction to the Special Issue on Alfred Schütz's Centennial', *The Review of Austrian Economics*, vol. 14, n°2/3, September, 211-217.

Boettke, P. (2002), 'Information and Knowledge: Austrian Economics in Search of its Uniqueness', *The Review of Austrian Economics*, vol. 14, n°4, 263-274.

Boettke, P.J., C.J. Coyne, P.T. Leeson and F. Sautet (2005), 'The New Comparative Political Economy', *The Review of Austrian Economics*, 18, n°3/4, 281-304.

Böhm-Bawerk, Eugen, von (1886), *Karl Marx and the Close of his System*, New York, USA: Augustus M. Kelley.

Böhm-Bawerk, Eugen, von (1889), 'Positive Theory of Capital', in *Capital and Interest*, 3 volumes, South Holland, USA: Libertarian Press.

Bostaph, S. (1978), 'The Methodological Debate Between Carl Menger and the German Historicists', *Atlantic Economic Journal*, VI, n°3, September, 3-16.

Boudon, Raymond (1977), *Effets pervers et ordre social*, Paris, France: P.U.F, Quadrige.

Boudreaux, D. and Holcombe R. (1989) 'The Coasian and Knightian Theories of the Firm', *Managerial and Decision Economics,* 10, 147-154.

Boudreaux, D. (1994), 'Schumpeter and Kirzner on Competition and Equilibrium', in Boettke, Peter and David Prychitko (eds), *The Market Process, Essays in Contemporary Austrian Economics*, Aldershot, UK and Brookfield, USA: Edward Elgar, 52-61.

Bramoullé, G. (1995), 'Apriorisme et faillibilisme: en défense de Rothbard contre Popper', *Journal des économistes et des études humaines*, 6 (1), March, 91-104.

Brus, Wlodzimierz and Kazimierz Laski (1989), '*From Marx to the Market: Socialism in Search of an Economic System*', Oxford, UK: Clarendon.

Brutzkus, Boris (1921), '*Economic Planning in Soviet Russia*', London, UK: Routledge and Sons, 1935.

Buchanan, J. M. and V. Vanberg (2002), 'Constitutional Implications of Radical Subjectivism', *The Review of Austrian Economics*, vol. 15, n°2/3, 121-128.

Bukharin, Nikolai and Evgenie Preobazhensky (1919), *The ABC of Communism*, Ann Arbor: University of Michigan Press.

Burczak, T. (2002), 'A Critique of Kirzner's Finders-Keepers Defense of Profit', *The Review of Austrian Economics*, vol. 15, n°1, 75-90.

Butler, Eamonn (1983), *Hayek: His Contribution to the Political and Economic Thought of our Time*, Worcester, UK: Billing and Sons Ltd.

Butler, Eamonn (1988), *Ludwig von Mises: Fountainhead of the Modern Microeconomics Revolution*, Brookfield, USA: Gower.

Butler, E. (1991), 'Hayek on the Evolution of Morality', *Journal of Income and Distribution*, vol. 1, n°2, 199.

Caillé, A. (1984), 'Pour une critique de la raison libérale critique', *Bulletin du Mauss*, n°9, 1er trimestre 1984, 43-78 and n°10, 2ème semestre, 97-129.

Caldwell, B. (1988), 'Hayek's Transformation', *History of Political Economy*, 20: (4), 513-541.

Caldwell, Bruce (ed) (1990), *Carl Menger and his Legacy in Economics*, Durham, USA and London, UK: Duke University Press.

Caldwell, B. (1997), 'Hayek and Socialism, *Journal of Economic Literature* vol. XXXV (December), 1856-1890.

Caldwell, B. (2000), 'The Emergence of Hayek's Ideas on Cultural Evolution', *The Review of Austrian Economics*, vol. 13, n°1, 5-22.

Caldwell, Bruce (2004), *Hayek's Challenge, an Intellectual Biography of F.A. Hayek*, Chicago and London; University of Chicago Press.

Carilli, A.M. and G.M. Dempster (2001), 'Expectations in Austrian Business Cycle Theory: An Application of the Prisoner's Dilemma', *The Review of Austrian Economics*, vol. 14, n°4, 319-330.

Chaloupek, G.K. (1990), 'The Austrian Debate on Economic Calculation in a Socialist Economy', *History of Political Economy*, 22 (4), 659-675.

Choi, Young Back (1995), 'The Entrepreneur: Schumpeter versus Kirzner', in Boettke, Peter and Mario Rizzo (eds), *Advances in Austrian Economics*, vol. 2, Part A, Greenwich, USA; London, UK: JAI Press, 55-66.

Coase, R. (1937), 'The Nature of the Firm', *Economica*, vol. 4, n°16, 386-405.

Coase, R. (1960), 'The Problem of Social Cost', *Journal of Law and Economics*, v. 3, n°1, 1-44.

Cochran, J.P. and F. Glahe (1994), 'The Keynes-Hayek Debate: Lessons for Contemporary Business Cycle Theorists', *History of Political Economy*, vol. 26, n°1, 69-94.

Commetti, Jean-Pierre and Kevin Mulligan (eds) (2001), *La philosophie autrichienne de Bolzano à Musil*, Histoire et actualité, Paris, France: Vrin.

Cordato, R. (1980), 'The Austrian Theory of Efficiency and the Role of Government', *The Journal of Libertarian Studies*, vol. 4, n°4, 393-404.

Cordato, Roy (1992), *Welfare Economics and Externalities in an Open-Ended Universe: A Modern Austrian Perspective*, Boston, USA: Kluwer Academic Publishers.

Cowen, Tyler (1991) 'What a Non-Paretian Welfare Economics Would Have to Look Like', in Lavoie, Don (ed) (1991), *Economics and Hermeneutics*, London, UK; New York, USA: Routledge and Kegan, 285-299.

Cowen, T. (1994), 'Austrian Welfare Economics', in Boettke, Peter (ed) (1994), *The Elgar Companion to Austrian Economics*, Aldershot, UK; Brookfield, USA: Edward Elgar, 304-308.

Craver, E. (1986), 'The Emigration of the Austrian Economics', *History of Political Economy*, vol. 18, n°1, 1-32.

Cubbedu, Raimondo (1993), *The Philosophy of the Austrian School*, London, UK and New York, USA: Routledge and Kegan.

Damasio, Antonio R. (1999), *The Feeling of What Happens: Body and Emotion in the Making of Consciousness*, New York, USA: Harcourt Brace.

Dantzig, G.B. and P. Wolfe (1961), 'The Decomposition Algorithm for Linear Programs', *Econometrica,* vol. 29, n°4, 767-778.

Desrochers, P. (1998), "Geographical Proximity and the Transmission of Tacit Knowledge", *The Review of Austrian Economics,* 14, n° 1, 25-46.

Desrochers, P. (2001), "A Geographical Perspective on Austrian Economics", *The Quaterly Journal of Austrian Economics* 1 (2), 63-83.

Dickinson, H.D. (1930), 'The Economic Basis of Socialism', *The Political Quarterly*, vol XL, September-December, 561-572.

Dickinson, H.D. (1933a), 'Price Formation in a Socialist Community', *Economic Journal*, 43, 588-598.

Dickinson, H.D. (1933b), 'Freedom and Planning, a Reply to Dr Gregory', *Manchester School*, vol. IV, 82-89.

Dickinson, H.D. (1939), *Economics of Socialism*, London, UK: Oxford University Press.

DiLorenzo, T. (1986), 'Competition and Political Entrepreneurship: Austrian Insights into Public Choice Theory', *The Review of Austrian Economics,* vol. 1, 59-71.

Dobb, M (1933), 'Economic Theory of a Socialist Economy', *Economic Journal*, June, 43 (170), 237-250.

Dobb, M. (1935a), 'Economic Theory and the Problems of a Socialist Economy', *Economic Journal*, 588-598.

Dobb, M. (1935b), 'Economic Theory and Socialist Economy, a Reply', *The Review of Economics Studies*, vol. II, n°1, 144-151.
Dobb, M. (1935c), 'Review of Brutzkus 1935 and Hayek 1935', *Economic Journal*, 45, n° 179, September.
Dobb, Maurice (1937), *Political Economy and Capitalism*, London, UK: Routledge.
Dobb, Maurice (1948), *Soviet Economic Development since 1917*, London, UK: Routledge.
Dobb, Maurice (1955), *On Economic Theory and Socialism: Collected Papers*, London, UK: Routledge.
Dobb, Maurice (1969), *Welfare Economics and the Economics of Socialism: Towards a Commonsense Critique*, London, UK: Cambridge University Press.
Dobb, Maurice (1970), *Socialist Planning: Some Problems*, London, UK: Lawrence and Wishart.
Dolan, Edwin G. (ed) (1976), *The Foundations of Modern Austrian Economics*, Kansas City, USA: Sheed and Ward.
Dosi, G. and G. Fagiolo (1997), 'Explaining the Unknown on Entrepreneurship, Coordination and Innovation Driven Growth', *International Institute for Applied System Analysis Report*, IR-97-077, October.
Dostaler, Gilles (2001), *Le libéralisme de Hayek*, Paris, France: Repères, La Découverte.
Dowd, Kenneth (1992), *The Experience of Free-Banking*, London, UK: Routledge.
Dowd, Kenneth (1994), 'Free-Banking' in Boettke, Peter (ed), *The Elgar Companion to Austrian Economics*, Aldershot, UK and Brookfield, USA: Edward Elgar, 408-413.
Dowd, Kenneth (1996), *Laissez-Faire Banking*, London, UK: Routledge.
Dulbecco, P. and P. Garrouste (1999), 'Towards an Austrian Theory of the Firm' in *The Review of Austrian Economics*, vol. 12, n°1, 43-64.
Dupuy, Jean-Pierre (2002), *The Mechanization of the Mind: On the Origins of Cognitive Science*, Princeton, USA: Princeton University Press.
Ebeling, Richard (1986), 'Toward a Hermeneutical Economics: Expectations, Prices and the Role of Interpretation in a Theory of the Market Process', in Kirzner, Israel (ed), *Subjectivism, Intelligibility and Economic Understanding*, London, UK: MacMillan, 39-55.
Ebeling, R. (1987), 'Cooperation in Anonymity', *Critical Review*, 1, 50-59.
Ebeling, Richard (ed) (1991), *Austrian Economics*, Hillsdale, USA: Hillsdale College Press.
Ebeling, Richard (1995), 'Austrian Subjectivism and Phenomenological Foundations' in Boettke, Peter and Mario Rizzo (eds), *Advances in Austrian Economics*, vol. 2, Part A, Greenwich, USA; London, UK: JAI Press, 39-54.

Ebenstein, Alan (2001), *Friedrich Hayek: A Biography*, Basingstoke, UK; New York, USA: Palgrave Macmillan.

Edelman, Gerald M. (1987), *Neural Darwinism: The Theory of Neuronal Group Selection*, New York, USA: Basic Books.

Edelman, Gerald M. (1988), *Topobiology*, New York, USA: Basic Books.

Edelman, Gerald M. (1989), *The Remembered Present: A Biological Theory of Consciousness*, New York, USA: Basic Books.

Edelman, Gerald M. (1992), *Bright Air, Brilliant Fire: on the Matter of Mind*, London, UK: Allen Lane, The Penguin Press.

Edelman, Gerald M. and Tononi, Giulio (2000), *A Universe of Consciousness, How Matter Becomes Imagination*, New York, USA: Basic Books.

Edelman, Gerald M. (2004), *Wider than the Sky, a Revolutionary View of Consciousness*, New Haven, USA: Yale University Press.

Egger, John (1979), 'Efficiency is Not a Substitute for Ethics', in Rizzo, Mario (ed) (1979), *Time, Uncertainty and Disequilibrium, Exploration of Austrian Themes*, Lexington, USA: Lexington Books, D.C. Heath and Company, 117-125.

Ellis, Howard S. (ed) (1949), *A Survey of Contemporary Economics*, Philadelphia, USA: Blackiston.

Engels, Friedrich (1878), *Anti-Dühring*, London: Lawrence and Wishart (Moscow: Foreign Languages Publishing House).

Fehl, Ulrich (1986), 'Spontaneous Order and the Subjectivity of Expectations: a Contribution to the Lachmann-O'Driscoll Problem', in Kirzner, Israel (ed), *Subjectivism, Intelligibility and Economic Understanding*, London, UK: MacMillan, 72-86.

Feinstein, Charles H. (ed) (1967), *Socialism, Capitalism and Economic Growth: Essays presented to Maurice Dobb*, Cambridge, UK: Cambridge University Press.

Foldvary, F.E. (2002), 'Small Group, Multi-Level Democracy: Implications of Austrian Public Choice for Governance Structure', in *The Review of Austrian Economics*, vol. 15, n°2/3, 161-174.

Foss, N. (1993), 'Theories of the Firm: Contractual and Competence Perspective', *Journal of Evolutionary Economics*, 3, 127-44.

Foss, N. (1994a), 'The Theory of the Firm: the Austrians as Precursors and Critics of Contemporary Theory', *The Review of Austrian Economics* (7), 31-64.

Foss, N. (1994b), 'The Two Coasian Traditions' *Review of Political Economy*, 6 (1), 37-61.

Foss, N. (1994c), 'More on "Hayek's Transformation"', *History of Political Economy*, 27, 2, 345-364.

Foss, N. (1996a), 'Spontaneous Social Order: Economics and Schützian Sociology', *American Journal of Sociology*, 92, 1-26.

Foss, Nicolai (1996b), 'Austrian and Post-Marshallian Economics: the Bridging Work of Georges Richardson', in Foss, Nicolai and Brian Loasby (eds) (1998), *Capabilities and Coordination: Essays in Honor of G.B. Richardson*, London, UK: Routledge.

Foss, N. (1996c), 'The Alternative Theories of Knight and Coase, and the Modern Theory of the Firm', *Journal of the History of Economic Thought*, 18 (1), 76-95.

Foss, N. (1997), 'Austrian Insights and the Theory of the Firm', *Advances in Austrian Economics*, 4, 175-198.

Foss, Nicolai and Brian Loasby (eds) (1998), *Economic Organization, Capabilities and Coordination: Essays in Honour of G.B. Richardson*, London, UK: Routledge.

Frowen, Stephen (ed) (1997), *Hayek, the Economist and Social Philosopher, a Critical Retrospect*, New York, USA: St Martin's Press; London, UK: MacMillan.

Frydman, R. (1989), 'Individu et totalité dans la pensée libérale: le cas de F. Hayek' *Cahiers d'Economie Politique,* n° 16/17, 91-127.

Garrett, Garet and Murray Rothbard (1978), *The Great Depression and New Deal Monetary Policy*, San Francisco: Cato Institute, Cato Paper, n°13.

Garrison, Roger (1982), 'Austrian Economics as the Middle Ground: Comment on Loasby', in Kirzner, Israel (ed) (1982), *Method, Process and Austrian Economics: Essays in Honour of Ludwig v. Mises*, Lexington, USA: Lexington Books, 131-138.

Garrison, R.W. (1984), 'Time and Money: The Universals of Macroeconomic Theorizing', *Journal of Macroeconomics*, 6, 197-213.

Garrison, Roger W. (1986), 'The Cost of a Gold Standard', in Rockwell, L.H. Jr. (ed) (1986), *The Gold Standard. An Austrian Perspective*, Lexington, USA: Lexington Books, 61-81.

Garrison, R.W. (1987), 'The Kaleidic World of Ludwig Lachmann', *Critical Review*, Summer, 77-89.

Garrison, R.W. (1989), 'The Austrian Theory of the Business Cycle in the Light of Modern Macroeconomics', *The Review of Austrian Economics*, 3-29.

Garrison, R.W. (1996), 'Central Banking, Free Banking and Financial Crises', *The Review of Austrian Economics*, vol. 9, n°2, 109-127.

Garrison, Roger W. (1997), 'Austrian Theory of Business Cycles' in Glasner, David (ed), *Business Cycles and Depressions: an Encyclopedia*, New York, USA; London, UK: Garland Publishing, 23-27.

Garrison, Roger W. (2001) *Time and Money, The Macroeconomics of Capital Structure*, London, UK and New York, USA: Routledge.

Garrouste, P. (1994), 'Léon Walras et Carl Menger à propos de l'utilisation des mathématiques en économie politique', *Economies et Sociétés*, Série Oeconomia, Histoire de la pensée économique, P.E., n°20-21, 10 November, 11-27.

Garrouste, P. and R.N. Langlois (1997), 'Cognition, Redundancy and Learning in Organizations', *Economics of Innovation and New Technology*, 4, 287-299.

Giersch, Herbert (1998) (ed), *Merits and Limits of Markets*, Berlin, Germany: Springer.

Glasner, David (ed) (1997), *Business Cycles and Depressions: an Encyclopedia*, New York, USA and London, UK: Garland Publishing.

Gordon, David (1988), *Ludwig von Mises: An Annotated Bibliography*, Auburn, USA: Ludwig von Mises Institute.

Gordon, D. (1993), 'Toward a Deconstruction of Utility and Welfare Economics', *The Review of Austrian Economics*, vol. 6, N° 2, 99-112.

Gordon, D. (1994), 'The Philosophical Contributions of Ludwig von Mises', *The Review of Austrian Economics*, 7 (1), 95-106.

Gossen, Hermann (1854), *The Laws of Human Relations, and the Rules of Human Action Derived Therefrom*, Cambridge, USA: MIT Press.

Grassl, Wolfgang and Barry Smith (eds) (1986), *Austrian Economics: Historical and Philosophical Background*, London, UK: Croom Helm.

Gray, John (1984), *Hayek on Liberty*, New York, USA: Basil Blackwell.

Grinder, Walter E. (1977), 'In Pursuit of the Subjective Paradigm', in Lachmann, Ludwig M. (1977), *Capital, Expectations and the Market Process: Essays on the Theory of the Market Economy*, Kansas City, USA: Sheed Andrews and MacMeel, 3-25.

Haberler, G. (1936), 'Some Reflections on the Present Situation of Business Cycle Theory', *Review of Economic Statistics*, February, 1966-1967.

Haberler, Gottfried (1937), *Prosperity and Depression*, Geneva: League of Nations.

Hamlin, Alan P. (1992), 'On the Possibility of Austrian Welfare Economics', in Boehm, Stephan and Bruce Caldwell (eds) (1992), *Austrian Economics: Tensions and New Directions*, Boston, USA: Kluwer, 193-206.

Hamowy, R. (1978), 'Law and The Liberal Society: F.A. Hayek's Constitution of Liberty', *Journal of Libertarian Studies*, 2 (4), 287-297.

Hamowy, R. (1982), 'The Hayekian Model of Government in an Open Society', *Journal of Libertarian Studies*, 6 (2), 137-143.

Hansen, A. (June, 1933), 'Review of "Prices and Production"', *American Economic Review*, n°23, 334.

Harper, David A. (1998), 'Institutional Conditions for Entrepreneurship', in Ikeda, Sanford and Peter J. Boettke (eds), *Advances in Austrian Economics*, 5, 241-275.

Hayek, F.A. (1928a), 'Intertemporal Price Equilibrium and Movements in the Value of Money' in McCloughry, Roy (ed), *Money, Capital and Fluctuations, Early Essays*', London, UK, Melbourne, Australia and Henley, UK: Routledge and Kegan Paul, 1984, 71-117.

Hayek, Friedrich August (1928b), *Monetary Theory and the Trade Cycle,* London, UK: Jonathan Cape.

Hayek, Friedrich August (1931), *Prices and Production*, London, UK: George Routledge and Sons Ltd.

Hayek, F.A. (1931), 'Reflections on the Pure Theory of Money of Mr J.M. Keynes', first part, *Economica*, vol. XI, n°33, August, 270-245.

Hayek, F.A. (1931), 'A Rejoinder to Mr Keynes', *Economica*, Vol. XI, n° 34, November, 398-403.

Hayek, F.A. (1932), 'Money and Capital: A Reply', *Economic Journal*, Vol. XLII, n° 166, June, 237-249.

Hayek, F.A. (1932), 'L'étalon-or; son évolution', *Revue d'Economie Politique*, n°6, November-December, 1966, 1091-1117.

Hayek, F.A. (1932), 'Reflections on the Pure Theory of Money of Mr J.M. Keynes', second part, *Economica*, vol. XII, February, 22-44.

Hayek, Friedrich August (1935a), 'The Nature and History of the Problem', in Hayek, Friedrich August (ed), *Collectivist Economic Planning* (1935c), London, UK: Routledge and Kegan Paul Ltd, 1-40.

Hayek, Friedrich August (1935b), 'The Present State of the Debate', in Hayek, Friedrich August (ed) (1935c), *Collectivist Economic Planning* (1935c), London, UK: Routledge and Kegan Paul Ltd, 201-243.

Hayek, Friedrich August (ed) (1935c), *Collectivist Economic Planning* (1935c), London, UK: Routledge and Kegan Paul Ltd.

Hayek, F.A. (1937a), 'Economics and Knowledge' in Hayek, Friedrich August (ed) (1948a), *Individualism and Economic Order,* Chicago: The University of Chicago Press 33-56.

Hayek, Friedrich August (1937b), *Monetary Nationalism and International Stability*, New York, USA. Augustus M. Kelley.

Hayek, Friedrich August (1939a), *Profits, Interest and Investment, and Other Essays on the Theory of Industrial Fluctuations*, New York, USA: Augustus M. Kelley.

Hayek, Friedrich August (1939b) 'The Economic Condition of Interstate Federalism' in Hayek, Friedrich August (ed) (1948a), *Individualism and Economic Order*, Chicago, USA: University of Chicago Press, 255-272.

Hayek, Friedrich August (1940), 'Socialist Calculation, the Competitive Solution', *Economica* 7, 125-149.

Hayek, Friedrich August (1941), *The Pure Theory of Capital*, Chicago, USA: University of Chicago Press.

Hayek, Friedrich August (1942), 'The Facts of the Social Sciences' in Hayek, Friedrich August (ed) (1948a), *Individualism and Economic Order,* Chicago, USA: University of Chicago Press, 57-76.

Hayek, Friedrich August (1944), *The Road to Serfdom*, Chicago, USA: University of Chicago Press.

Hayek, F.A. (1945), 'The Use of Knowledge in Society', in Hayek, Friedrich August (1948a), *Individualism and Economic Order*, Chicago: University of Chicago Press, 77-91.

Hayek, Friedrich August (1948a), *Individualism and Economic Order*, Chicago, USA: University of Chicago Press.

Hayek, Friedrich August (1948b), 'The Meaning of Competition', in Hayek, Friedrich August (1948a), *Individualism and Economic Order*, Chicago, USA: University of Chicago Press, 92-106.

Hayek, Friedrich August (1952a), *The Sensory Order, an Inquiry into the Foundations of Theoretical Psychology*, Chicago, USA: University of Chicago Press.

Hayek, Friedrich August (1952b), *The Counter-Revolution of Science*, Glencoe, USA: The Free Press.

Hayek, F.A. (1955), 'Degrees of Explanation', in Hayek, Friedrich August (1967b), *Studies in Philosophy, Politics and Economics*, Chicago, USA: University of Chicago Press, 3-21.

Hayek, Friedrich August (1960), *The Constitution of Liberty,* Chicago, USA: University of Chicago Press.

Hayek, Friedrich August (1963a), 'Rules, Perception and Intelligibility', in Hayek, Friedrich August (1967b), *Studies in Philosophy, Politics and Economics*, Chicago, USA: University of Chicago Press, 43-66.

Hayek, Friedrich August (1963b), 'Notes on the Evolution of Systems of Rules of Conduct', in Hayek, Friedrich August (1967b), *Studies in Philosophy, Politics and Economics*, Chicago, USA: University of Chicago Press, 66-81.

Hayek, Friedrich August (1964), 'The Theory of Complex Phenomena', in Hayek, Friedrich August (1967b), *Studies in Philosophy, Politics and* Economics, Chicago, USA: University of Chicago Press, 22-43.

Hayek, Friedrich August (1965), 'Kinds of Rationalism', in Hayek, Friedrich August (1967b), *Studies in Philosophy, Politics and Economics*, Chicago, USA: University of Chicago Press, 82-95.

Hayek, Friedrich August (1967a), 'The Results of Human Action but Not of Human Design' Hayek, Friedrich August (1967b), *Studies in Philosophy, Politics and Economics*, Chicago, USA: University of Chicago Press, 96-105.

Hayek, Friedrich August (1967b), *Studies in Philosophy, Politics and Economics*, Chicago, USA: University of Chicago Press.

Hayek, Friedrich August (1968), 'Competition as a Discovery Procedure' in Hayek, Friedrich August (1978b), *New Studies in Philosophy, Politics, Economy and the History of Ideas*, London, UK: Routledge and Kegan, 179-190.

Hayek, Friedrich August (1969a), 'The Primacy of the Abstract' in Hayek, Friedrich August (1978b), *New Studies in Philosophy, Politics, Economics and the History of Ideas*, London, UK: Routledge and Kegan, 35-50.

Hayek, Friedrich August (1969b), 'Three Elucidations of the Ricardo Effect' in Hayek, Friedrich August (1978b), *New Studies in Philosophy, Poli-*

tics, Economics and the History of Ideas, London, UK: Routledge and Kegan, 165-178.

Hayek, Friedrich August (1972), *A Tiger by the Tail, the Keynesian Legacy of Inflation*, Norfolk, UK: Institute of Economics Affairs, Hobart Paperback 4.

Hayek, Friedrich August (1973, 1976a, 1979), *Law, Legislation and Liberty*, London, UK: Routledge and Kegan.

Hayek, Friedrich August (1976b), *Denationalisation of Money, an Analysis of the Theory and Practice of Concurrent Currencies*, London, UK: The Institute of Economic Affairs.

Hayek, F.A. (1978a), 'Coping with Ignorance' *Imprimis,* vol. 7, n°7, 1-6.

Hayek, Friedrich August (1978b), *New Studies in Philosophy, Politics, Economy and the History of Ideas*, London, UK: Routledge and Kegan.

Hayek, Friedrich August (1978c), *Denationalisation of Money - The Argument Refined. an Analysis of the Theory and Practice of Concurrent Currencies*, London, UK: Institute of Economic Affairs, Hobart Special Paper 70.

Hayek, Friedrich August (1980), 'Joseph Schumpeter', preface to 'Methodological Individualism' (translation of an extract from 'Das Wesen und der Hauptinhalt der Theoretischen Nationalökonomie', Schumpeter, 1908), in Klein, P. (1992), *The Collected Works of F.A. Hayek, the Fortunes of Liberalism,* 4, Chicago, USA: University of Chicago Press, 160-165.

Hayek, Friedrich August (1984), *Money, Capital and Fluctuations, Early Essays*, London and Henley, UK and Melbourne, Australia: Routledge and Kegan.

Hayek, Friedrich August (1988), *The Fatal Conceit: The Errors of Socialism,* Chicago: The University of Chicago Press.

Hazlitt, H. (1974) 'Review of "Competition and Entrepreneurship"' *Freeman* 24, December, 1974, 759.

Hebb, Donald (1949), *The Organisation of Behavior: a Neuropsychological Theory*, New York and London: John Wiley.

Hébert, Robert and Albert Link (1982), *The Entrepreneur, Mainstream Views and Radical Critiques*, New York, USA: Praeger.

Helling, I.K. (1984), 'A. Schütz and F. Kaufmann: Sociology between Science and Interpretation', *Human Studies*, 7 (2), 141-161.

Hennings, Klaus and Warren J. Samuels (1990), *Neoclassical Economic Theory, 1870-1930*, Boston, USA; Dordrech, Netherlands; London, UK: Kluwer Academic Publishers.

Herbener, J. (1991), 'Ludwig von Mises and the Austrian School of Economics', *The Review of Austrian Economics*, 5, n°2, 33-50.

Herbener, Jeffrey (ed) (1993), *The Meaning of Ludwig von Mises*, Boston, USA: Kluwer Academic Publishers.

Herbener, J. (1996), 'Economic Calculation and the Question of Arithmetic', *Review of Austrian Economics*, 9, n°1, 151-162.

Hicks, John Richard (1939), *Value and Capital*, Oxford, UK: Clarendon Press.

Hicks, John Richard (1967), 'The Hayek Story', in *Critical Essays in Monetary Theory*, Oxford, UK: Oxford University Press, 203-215.

Hicks, John Richard and Wilhelm Weber (eds) (1973), *Carl Menger and the Austrian School of Economics*, Oxford, UK: Clarendon Press.

Hight, J. (1980), 'Review of "Perception, Opportunity and Profit"', *Austrian Economics*, Newsletter 2, 3, 14.

Hight, Jack (1982), 'Alertness, Judgment and Entrepreneurship: A Comment on Kirzner' in Kirzner, Israel (ed) (1982), *Method, Process and Austrian Economics: Essays in Honour of Ludwig v. Mises*, Lexington, USA: Lexington Books, 161-168.

Hight, Jack (1986), 'Equilibration and Disequilibrium in the Market Process', in Kirzner, Israel (1986) (ed), *Subjectivism, Intelligibility and Economic Understanding*, London, UK: MacMillan, 111-121.

Hodgson, Geoffrey M. (1993), *Economics and Evolution, Bringing Life Back into Economics*, Cambridge, UK: Polity Press.

Hoff, Trygve J.B. (1949), *Economic Calculation in the Socialist Society*, London, Edinburgh and Glasgow, UK: William Hodge and Company Limited.

Holcombe, R.G. (2002) 'Political Entrepreneurship and the Democratic Allocation of Economic Resources', *The Review of Austrian Economics*, vol. 15, n°2/3, 143-159.

Holcombe, R.G. (2004), 'The New Urbanism versus the Market Process', *The Review of Austrian Economics*, 17, n°2/3/, 285-300.

Hoppe, Hans-Hermann (1988), *Praxeology and Economic Science*, Auburn, USA: Ludwig von Mises Institute.

Hoppe, Hans-Hermann (1989), *A Theory of Socialism and Capitalism: Economics, Politics and Ethics*, Boston, USA: Kluwer Academic Publishers.

Hoppe, Hans-Hermann (1993a), *The Economics and Ethics of Private Property*, Auburn, USA: Ludwig von Mises Institute and Boston, USA; Dordrecht, Netherlands; London, UK: Kluwer.

Hoppe, H-H. (1993b), 'F.A. Hayek on Government and Social Evolution: A Critique', *The Review of Austrian Economics,* 7, n°1, 67-93.

Hoppe, H-H. (1993c), 'How is Fiat Money Possible? – or The Devolution of Money and Credit', *The Review of Austrian Economics*, 7 (2), 49-74.

Hoppe, H-H. (1996), 'Socialism: A Property or Knowledge Problem?', *Review of Austrian Economics*, 9, n°1, 143-149.

Hoppe, H-H., J.G. Hülsmann and W. Block (1998), 'Against Fiduciary Media', *The Quarterly Journal of Austrian Economics*, vol. 1, (1), 19-50.

Horwitz, Steven (1988), 'Misreading the "Myth": Rothbard on the Theory and History of Free Banking', in Boettke, Peter and David Prychitko (ed) (1994), *The Market Process, Essays in Contemporary Austrian Economics*, Cheltenham, UK and Northampton, USA: Edward Elgar, 166-176.

Horwitz, S. (2000), 'From The Sensory Order to the Liberal Order: Hayek's Non-Rationalist Liberalism', *The Review of Austrian Economics*, vol. 13, n°1, 23-40.

Hugues, A.M. (1997), 'The Recession of 1990: An Austrian Explanation' *The Review of Austrian Economics*, vol. 10, n°1, 23-40.

Hülsmann, J.G. (1996), 'Free Banking and the Free Bankers', *The Review of Austrian Economics*, vol. 9, n°1, 3-53.

Hülsmann, J.G. (1997), 'Knowledge, Judgment and the Use of Property', *Review of Austrian Economics*, 10, n°1, 23-48.

Hülsmann, J.G. (2000a), 'A Realist Approch to Equilibrium Analysis', *The Quarterly Journal of Austrian Economics*, vol. 3, n°4, Winter, 3-51.

Hülsmann, J.G. (2000b), 'Banks Cannot Create Money', *The Independent Review*, vol. 5, n°1, Summer, 101-110.

Hülsmann, J.G. (2007), *Mises, the Last Knight of Liberalism*, Auburn, USA: Ludwig von Mises Institute.

Hutchison, Terence W. (1981), *The Politics and Philosophy of Economics: Marxists, Keynesians and Austrians*, Oxford, UK: Blackwell.

Ikeda, Sanford (1997), *Dynamics of the Mixed Economy: Towards a Theory of Interventionism*, London, UK: Routledge.

Ikeda, Sanford and Peter Boettke (1998) (eds), *Advances in Austrian Economics*, Stamford, USA and London, UK: JAI Press.

Ikeda, S. (2004), 'Urban Interventionism and Local Knowledge', *The Review of Austrian* Economics, 17, n°2/3, 247-264.

Ikeda, S. (2007), Urbanizing Economics, *The Review of Austrian Economics,* 20, n°4, 213-220.

Ioannides, Stavros (1992), *The Market, Competition and Democracy: a Critique of Neo-Austrian Economics*, Cheltenham, UK and Northampton, USA: Edward Elgar.

Ioannides, S. (1993), 'Comments on Israel Kirzner's Notion of Pure Profit', *Journal des Economistes des Etudes Humaines*, (4), 329-333.

Ioannides, S. (1999), 'Towards an Austrian Perspective on the Firm', *The Review of Austrian Economics*, 11, n°1/2, 77-97.

Ioannides, S. (2003), 'Orders and Organizations: Hayekian Insights for a Theory of Economic Organization', *The American Journal of Sociology*, July, vol. 62, n°3, 533-566.

Jaffe, W. (1976), 'Menger, Jevons and Walras De-Homogenized', *Economic Inquiry*, 14, December, 511-524.

Jevons, Stanley (1871), *The Theory of Political Economy*, New York, USA: Kelley and Millman.

Johnston, William (1972), *The Austrian Mind: An Intellectual and Social History 1848-1938*, Berkeley, USA: University of California Press.

Jones, R. (1976), 'The Origin and Development of Media of Exchange', *Journal of Political Economy*, 84, 757-775.

Kantorovitch, Leonid (1959), *The Best Use of Economic Resources*, Oxford and London, UK: Pergamon Press.

Kantorovitch, Leonid (1976), *Essays in Optimal Planning*, New York, USA: J. Smolinsky and Wiley.

Kauder, E. (1953), 'The Retarded Acceptance of Marginal Utility Theory', *Quarterly Journal of Economics*, 67, 564-575.

Kautsky, Karl (1902), *Delft Speech*, published as *The Social Revolution and on the Morrow of the Social Revolution*, London, UK: Twentieth Century Press, 1907.

Keeler, J.P. (2001) 'Empirical Evidence on the Austrian Business Cycle Theory', *The Review of Austrian Economics*, vol. 14, n°4, 331-351.

Keynes, John Maynard (1930/1931), *A Treatise on Money*, volumes 1-2, in Keynes, John Maynard (1971), *Collected Writings*, Cambridge, UK: Cambridge University Press, vol. V-VI.

Keynes, J.M. (November, 1931), 'The Pure Theory of Money: A Reply to Dr Hayek', *Economica*, vol. XII, n°34, 387-397.

Keynes, John Maynard (December, 1931-January, 1932), 'Correspondence Hayek-Keynes', in Keynes, John Maynard (1971), *Collected Writings*, Cambridge, UK: Cambridge University Press, vol. XIII, 257- 264.

Keynes, John Maynard (1971), *Collected Writings*, Cambridge, UK: Cambridge University Press, vol. V-VI.

Khalil, E.L. (1995), 'Organizations versus Institutions', *Journal of Institutional and Theoretical Economics*, 151 (3), 445-466.

Khalil, E.L. (1996), 'Friedrich Hayek's Darwinian Theory of Evolution of Institutions: Two Problems', *Australian Economic Papers*, 35, 183-201.

Khalil, E.L. (1997), 'Friedrich Hayek's Theory of Spontaneous Order: Two Problems', *Constitutional Political Economy*, 8, 301-317.

Kirzner, Israel (1960), *The Economic Point of View*, Kansas City, USA: Sheed and Ward, Inc.

Kirzner, Israel (1963), *Market Theory and the Price System*, New York, USA; London, UK; Toronto, Canada: D. Van Nostrand Company.

Kirzner, Israel (1966), *An Essay on Capital*, New York, USA: Augustus M. Kelley.

Kirzner, Israel (1973), *Competition and Entrepreneurship*, Chicago, USA: University of Chicago Press.

Kirzner, Israel (1976), 'Philosophical and Ethical Implications of Austrian Economics', in Dolan, Edwin G. (ed) (1976), *The Foundations of Modern Austrian Economics*, Kansas City, USA: Sheed and Ward, 75-88.

Kirzner, Israel (1979), *Perception, Opportunity and Profit: Studies in the Theory of Entrepreneurship*, Chicago, USA: University of Chicago Press.

Kirzner, Israel (ed) (1982a), *Method, Process and Austrian Economics: Essays in Honor of Ludwig v. Mises*, Lexington, USA: Lexington Books.

Kirzner, Israel (1982b), 'Uncertainty, Discovery and Human Action: A Study of the Entrepreneurial Profile in the Misesian System', in Kirzner, Israel (ed) (1982a), *Method, Process and Austrian Economics: Essays in Honour of Ludwig v. Mises*, Lexington, USA: Lexington Books, 139-160.

Kirzner, Israel (1982c), 'The Theory of Entrepreneurship in Economic Growth' in C.A. Kent, Donald L. Sexton, and Karl H. Vesper (eds), *Encyclopedia of Entrepreneurship*, Englewood Cliffs, USA: Prentice-Hall.

Kirzner, Israel (1984), 'Economic Planning and Knowledge Problem' in Kirzner, Israel (1992), *The Meaning of Market Process: Essays in the Development of Modern Austrian Economics*, London, UK and New York, USA: Routledge, 152-162.

Kirzner, Israel (1985), *Discovery and the Capitalist Process*, Chicago, USA and London, UK: University of Chicago Press.

Kirzner, Israel (1986) (ed), *Subjectivism, Intelligibility and Economic Understanding, Essays in Honour of Ludwig M. Lachmann on his Eightieth Birthday*, London, UK: MacMillan.

Kirzner, Israel (1988a), 'Welfare Economics: A Modern Austrian Perspective', in Block, Walter and Llewellyn H. Rockwell (eds) (1988), *Man, Economy and Liberty: Essays in Honor of Murray Rothbard*, Auburn, USA: The Ludwig von Mises Institute, Auburn University, 77-89.

Kirzner, Israel (1988b), 'The Economic Calculation Debate: Lessons for Austrians' in Kirzner, Israel (1992a), *The Meaning of Market Process: Essays in the Development of Modern Austrian Economics*, London, UK and New York, USA: Routledge, 100-118.

Kirzner, Israel (1989), *Discovery, Capitalism and Distributive Justice*, New York, USA; Oxford, UK: Basil Blackwell.

Kirzner, Israel (1990), 'Commentary on Boehm, Stephan, 'The Austrian Tradition: Schumpeter and Mises', in Hennings, Klaus and Warren J. Samuels (1990), *Neoclassical Economic Theory, 1870-1930*, Boston USA; Dordrecht, Netherlands and London, UK: Kluwer, 242-249.

Kirzner, Israel (1992a), *The Meaning of Market Process: Essays in the Development of Modern Austrian Economics*, London, UK and New York, USA: Routledge.

Kirzner, Israel (1992b), 'Commentary: Entrepreneurship, Uncertainty and Austrian Economics', in Boehm, Stephan, and Bruce Caldwell (eds) (1992), *Austrian Economics: Tensions and New Directions*, Boston, USA: Kluwer, 85-102.

Kirzner, I. (1996a), 'Reflections on the Misesian Legacy in Economics', *Review of Austrian Economics*, 9 (2), 143-154.

Kirzner, Israel (1996b), *Essays on Capital and Interest, an Austrian Perspective*, Cheltenham, UK and Brookfield, US: Edward Elgar.

Kirzner, I. (March 1997), 'Entrepreneurial Discovery and the Competitive Market Process', *Journal of Economic Literature*, vol. XXXV, 60-85.

Kirzner, I. (1998), 'Coordination as a Criterion for Economic "Goodness"', *Constitutional Political Economy*, 9: 289-301.

Kirzner, I. (1999), 'Creativity and/or Alertness: A Reconsideration of the Schumpeterian Entrepreneur' *Review of Austrian Economics*, 11, n°1/2, 5-19.

Kirzner, Israel (2001), *Ludwig von Mises, the Man and his Economics*, Wilmington Delaware, USA: ISI Books

Kirzner, I. (2002), 'Comment on "A Critique of Kirzner's Finders-Keepers Defense of Profit"', *The Review of Austrian Economics*, vol. 15, n°1, 91-94.

Klausinger, Hansjorg, (1997), 'From Neutral Money to Competing Currencies: Hayek on Monetary Policy' in Frowen, Stephen (ed) (1997), *Hayek, the Economist and Social Philosopher, a Critical Retrospect*, New York: St Martin's Press; London: MacMillan, 195-214.

Klein, B. (1974), 'The Competitive Supply of Money', *Journal of Money, Credit and Banking*, VI, n°4, November, 1974, 423-454.

Klein, Peter (ed) (1992), *The Fortunes of Liberalism* in *The Collected Works of F.A. Hayek*, vol. 4, Chicago, USA: University of Chicago Press, 126-159.

Klein, Peter (1996), 'Calculation and the Limits of Organization', *Review of Austrian Economics,* 9 (2), 3-28.

Klein, Peter (1999), 'Entrepreneurship and Corporate Governance', *The Quarterly Journal of Austrian Economics*, 2, 19-42.

Klein, Peter and George Selgin (2000), 'Menger's Theory of Money: Some Experimental Evidence', in Smithin, John (ed) *What is Money?*, London, UK: Routledge and Kegan, 217-234.

Knight, Frank (1921), *Risk, Uncertainty, and Profit*, Chicago, USA: University of Chicago Press.

Koppl, R. (1992), 'Schütz and Shackle: Two Views of Choice', *Review of Austrian Economics*, 2001, 14 (2/3): 181-191.

Koppl, R. (1994), 'Lachmann on Schütz and Shackle', in *Advances in Austrian Economics*, 1, 289-302.

Koppl, R. (1997), 'Mises and Schütz on Ideal Types', *Cultural Dynamics*, 9 (1), 63-79.

Koppl, Roger and Gary Mongiovi (ed) (1998), *Subjectivism and Economic Analysis: Essays in Memory of Ludwig M. Lachmann*, New York, USA; London, UK: Routledge.

Koppl, Roger (2002), *Big Players and the Economic Theory of Expectations*, New York, USA: Palgrave, MacMillan.

Kresge, Stephen and Leif Wenar (eds), (1994), *Hayek on Hayek, An Autobiographical Dialogue*, Chicago, USA: The University of Chicago Press, The Bartley Institute.

Kurrild-Klitgaard, P. (2001), 'On Rationality, Ideal-Types and Economics: Alfred Schütz and the Austrian School', *The Review of Austrian Economics*, September, vol. 14, n°2/3, p. 119-143.

Lachmann, Ludwig M. (1937), 'Uncertainty and Liquidity-Preference', in Lavoie, Don (ed) (1994), *Expectations and the Meaning of Institutions*, London, UK and New York, USA: Routledge, 29-41.

Lachmann, Ludwig M. (1939), 'On Crisis and Adjustment', in Lavoie, Don (ed) (1994), *Expectations and the Meaning of Institutions*, London, UK: Routledge, 76-91.

Lachmann, Ludwig M. (1943), 'The Role of Expectations in Economics as a Social Science' in Lachmann, Ludwig M. (1977), *Capital, Expectations and the Market Process: Essays on the Theory of the Market Economy*, Kansas City, USA: Sheed Andrews and MacMeel, 65-80.

Lachmann, Ludwig M. (1951), 'The Science of Human Action' in Lachmann, Ludwig M. (1977), *Capital, Expectations and the Market Process: Essays on the Theory of the Market Economy*, Kansas City, USA: Sheed Andrews and MacMeel, 94-111.

Lachmann, Ludwig M. (1956), *Capital and its Structure*, Kansas City, USA: Sheed Andrews and Mc Meel.

Lachmann, L.M. (1959), 'Professor Shackle and the Economic Significance of Time', *Metroeconomica*, 11, 64-73.

Lachmann, Ludwig, M. (1967), 'Causes and Consequences of the Inflations of Our Time' in Lachmann, Ludwig M. (ed) (1977), *Capital, Expectations and the Market Process: Essays on the Theory of the Market Economy*, Kansas City, USA: Sheed Andrews and MacMeel, 289-307.

Lachmann, Ludwig, M. (1969), Methodological Individualism and the Market Economy' in Lachmann, Ludwig M. (ed) (1977), *Capital, Expectations and the Market Process: Essays on the Theory of the Market Economy*, Kansas City, USA: Sheed Andrews and MacMeel, 149-165.

Lachmann, Ludwig M. (1971a), *The Legacy of Max Weber*, Berkeley, USA: The Glendary Press.

Lachmann, Ludwig M. (1971b), 'Ludwig von Mises and the Market Process', in Lachmann, Ludwig M. (1977), *Capital, Expectations and the Market Process: Essays on the Theory of the Market Economy*, Kansas City, USA: Sheed Andrews and MacMeel (1977), 181-197.

Lachmann, Ludwig M. (1976a), 'On the Central Concept of Austrian Economics: Market Process', in Dolan, Edwin G. (ed) (1976), *The Foundations of Modern Austrian Economics*, Kansas City, USA: Sheed and Ward, 126-132.

Lachmann, Ludwig M. (1976b), 'From Mises to Shackle: An Essay on Austrian Economics and the Kaleidic Society' in Lavoie, Don (ed) (1994),

Expectations and the Meaning of Institutions, London, UK and New York, USA: Routledge, 229-240.

Lachmann, Ludwig M. (1977), *Capital, Expectations and the Market Process: Essays on the Theory of the Market Economy*, Kansas City, USA: Sheed Andrews and MacMeel.

Lachmann, Ludwig M. (1982), 'Ludwig von Mises and the Extension of Subjectivism' in Kirzner, Israel (ed) (1982), *Method, Process and Austrian Economics: Essays in Honour of Ludwig v. Mises*, Lexington, USA: Lexington Books, 31-40.

Lachmann, Ludwig M. (1986a), *The Market as an Economic Process*, Oxford, UK: Blackwell.

Lachmann, Ludwig M. (1986b), 'Austrian Economics under Fire: The Hayek-Sraffa Duel', in Grassl, Wolfgang and Barry Smith (eds) (1986), *Austrian Economics: Historical and Philosophical Background*, London, UK: Croom Helm, 225-243.

Lange, O. (1936), 'On the Economic Theory of Socialism', Part 1, *The Review of Economics Studies*, 53-71.

Lange, O. (1937), 'On the Economic Theory of Socialism', Part 2, *The Review of Economics Studies*, 123-142.

Lange, Oskar (1936-7/1938), 'On the Economic Theory of Socialism', in Lippincott, Benjamin E. (ed) (1938), *On the Economic Theory of Socialism*, New York, USA: McGraw-Hill, 55-129.

Lange, Oskar (1960a), *Essays on Economic Planning*, Calcutta, India: Indian Statistical Institute.

Lange, Oskar (1965), *Introduction to Economic Cybernetics*, Oxford; London, UK: Pergamon Press.

Lange, Oskar (1967), 'The Computer and the Market', in Feinstein, Charles H. (ed) (1967), *Socialism, Capitalism and Economic Growth: Essays presented to Maurice Dobb*, Cambridge, UK: Cambridge University Press, 158-161.

Langlois, R.N. (1985), 'Knowledge and Rationality in the Austrian School: an Analytical Survey', *Eastern Economic Journal*, 9:4, 309-330.

Langlois, Richard N. (1992), 'Orders and Organizations: Toward an Austrian Theory of Social Institutions', in Boehm, Stephan and Bruce Caldwell (eds) (1992), *Austrian Economics: Tensions and New Directions*, Boston, USA: Kluwer, 165-183.

Langlois, R.N. and M. Cosgel (1993), 'Frank Knight on Risk, Uncertainty and the Firm: a New Interpretation', *Economic Inquiry*, 31, 456-465.

Langlois, Richard N. (1994), 'The Boundaries of the Firm', in Boettke, Peter (ed) (1994), *The Elgar Companion to Austrian Economics*, Aldershot, UK and Brookfield, USA: Edward Elgar, 173-178.

Langlois, R. N. (1995), 'Do Firms Plan?' in *Constitutional Political Economy* vol.6, 3, 247-261.

Langlois, Richard N. and Paul L. Robertson (1995), *Firms, Markets and Economic Changes, a Dynamic Theory of Business Institutions*, London, UK: Routledge.

Latzer, Michael and Stephan W. Schmitz (eds) (2002), *Carl Menger and the Evolution of Payments Systems*, Cheltenham, UK and Northampton, USA: Edward Elgar.

Lavoie, D. (1981), 'A Critique of the Standard Account of the Socialist Calculation Debate', *Journal of Libertarian Studies*, 5, 41-87.

Lavoie, Don (1985a), *National Economic Planning: What is Left?*, Cambridge, UK: Ballinger Publishing Company.

Lavoie, Don (1985b), *Rivalry and Central Planning, the Socialist Calculation Debate Reconsidered*, Cambridge, UK: Cambridge University Press.

Lavoie, Don (ed) (1990a), *Economics and Hermeneutics*, London, UK; New York, USA: Routledge and Kegan.

Lavoie, D. (1990b), 'Computation, Incentives and Discovery: The Cognitive Function of Markets in Market Socialism' (1990), *Annual American Academic Political Social Sciences*, 507, 72-79.

Lavoie, Don (1994), 'The Interpretative Turn' in Boettke, Peter (ed), *The Elgar Companion to Austrian Economics*, Aldershot, UK and Brookfield, USA: Edward Elgar, 54-62.

Lepage, Henri (1980), *Demain le libéralisme*, Paris, France: Pluriel.

Lepage, Henri (1985), *Pourquoi la propriété*, Paris, France: Pluriel.

Lerner, A.P. (1934), 'Economic Theory and Socialist Economy', *The Review of Economics Studies*, 2, 51-61

Lewin, Peter (1996), 'Time, Change and Complexity: Ludwig M. Lachman's Contributions to the Theory of Capital', in Boettke, Peter and David L. Prychitko (eds) (1996), *Advances in Austrian Economics*, vol. 3, Greenwich, USA: JAI Press, 107-168.

Lewin, P. (1997), 'Capital in Disequilibrium: a Reexamination of the Capital Theory of Ludwig M. Lachmann', *History of Political Economy*, vol. 29, 3, 523-548.

Lewin, P. (1998), 'The Firm, Money and Economic Calculation: Considering the Institutional Nexus of Market Production', *The American Journal of Economics and Sociology*, vol. 57, n°4, 499-512.

Lewin, P. and S.E. Phelan (1999), 'Firms, Strategies and Resources: Contributions from Austrian Economics', *The Quarterly Journal of Austrian Economics*, vol. 2, n°2, 3-18.

Lewin, P. and S.E. Phelan (2000), 'An Austrian Theory of the Firm', *The Review of Austrian Economics*, vol. 13, n°1, 59-79.

Liberman, Evsei (1962), 'The Plan, Profits and Bonuses' in Nove, Alec and Dominico Mario Nuti (eds) (1972), *Socialist Economics*, London, UK: Penguin Books.

Lippincot, Benjamin E. (ed) (1938) *On the Economic Theory of Socialism*, New York, USA: McGraw-Hill.

Littlechild, Stephen C. (1978), *The Fallacy of the Mixed Economy: An Austrian Critique of Economic Thinking and Policy*, London, UK: Institute of Economic Affairs.

Littlechild, Stephen C. (1982), 'Equilibrium and the Market Process', in Kirzner, Israel (ed) (1982), *Method, Process and Austrian Economics: Essays in Honor of Ludwig v. Mises*, Lexington, USA: Lexington Books.

Littlechild, Stephen C. (ed) (1990), *The Austrian Economics*, vol. 1, 2, 3, Aldershot, UK and Brookfield, US: Edward Elgar.

Loasby, Brian (1976), *Choice, Complexity and Ignorance*, Cambridge, UK: Cambridge University Press.

Loasby, Brian (1982), 'Economics and Dispersed and Incomplete Information', in Kirzner, Israel (ed) (1982), *Method, Process and Austrian Economics: Essays in Honor of Ludwig von Mises*, Lexington, USA: D.C. Heath, 111-130.

Loasby, Brian (1989a), *The Minds and Methods of Economics*, Cambridge, UK: Cambridge University Press.

Loasby, B. (1989b), 'Entrepreneurship in Economic Theory', *Scottish Journal of Political Economy*, 29.

Loasby, B. (1994), 'Organizational Capabilities and Interfirm Relations', *Metroeconomica*, 45, 3, 248-265.

Lopez, E.J. (2002), 'The Legislator as Political Entrepreneur: Investment in Political Capital', *The Review of Austrian Economics*, vol. 15, n°s 2/3, 211-228.

Machlup, Fritz (1940), *The Stock Market, Credit and Capital Formation*, New York, USA: Macmillan.

Machlup, Fritz (1952), *The Economics of Sellers' Competition*, Baltimore, USA: John Hopkins University Press.

Machlup, Fritz (ed) (1976), *Essays on Hayek*, New York, USA: New York University Press.

Maki, Uskali (1990), 'Mengerian Economics in Realist Perspective', in Caldwell, Bruce (ed) (1990), *Carl Menger and his Legacy in Economics*, Durham, USA; London, UK: Duke University Press.

Manin, B. (1983), 'Le libéralisme radical de Friedrich-August Hayek', *Commentaire,* Summer, 15-22.

Marx, Karl (1848), 'Manifesto of the Communist Party', 1969, vol. 1, 98-137.

Marx, Karl (1875/1890-91), Critique of the Gotha Program, in *Marx and Engels Selected Works*, Moscow: Progress Publishers, 1970, vol. 3, 13-30.

McCann, C.R. Jr. (2002), 'F.A. Hayek: The Liberal as Communitarian', *The Review of Austrian Economics*, vol. 15, n°1, 5-31.

Meijer, Gerrit (ed) (1995), *New Perspectives on Austrian Economics*, London, UK; New York, USA: Routledge and Kegan.
Menger, Carl (1871), *Principles of Economics*, New York, USA; London, UK: New York University Press.
Menger, Carl (1883), *Investigations into the Method in Social Sciences, with Special Reference to Economics*, New York, USA and London, UK: New York University Press.
Menger, Karl (1973), *Austrian Marginalism and Mathematical Economics*, in Hicks, John Richard and Wilhelm Weber (eds) (1973), *Carl Menger and the Austrian School of Economics*, Oxford, UK: Clarendon Press, 38-60.
Milford, Karl (1990), 'Menger's Methodology', in Caldwell, Bruce (ed) (1990), *Carl Menger and his Legacy in Economics*, Durham, USA; London, UK: Duke University Press, 215-239.
Minsky, Marvin (1986), *The Society of Mind*, New York, USA: Simon and Schuster.
Mises, Ludwig von (1912), *The Theory of Money and Credit*, New Haven, USA: Yale University Press.
Mises, Ludwig von (1919), *Nation, State and Economy: Contributions to the Politics and History of Our Time*, New York, USA; London, UK: New York University Press.
Mises, Ludwig von (1920), 'Economic Calculation in the Socialist Commonwealth', in Hayek, Friedrich (ed) (1935c), *Collectivist Economic Planning*, London, UK: Routledge and Kegan Paul Ltd, 87-130.
Mises, L. von (1922), *Socialism,* Indianapolis, USA: Liberty
Mises, Ludwig von (1927), *Liberalism in the Classical Tradition*, Irvington-on-Hudson, New York, USA: Foundation for Economic Education.
Mises, Ludwig von (1929), *A Critique of Interventionism*, New Rochelle, USA: Arlington House.
Mises, Ludwig von (1933), *Epistemological Problems of Economics*, New York, USA and London, UK, New York University Press.
Mises, L. von (1938), 'The Equations of Mathematical Economics and the Problem of Economic Calculation in a Socialist State', *The Quarterly Journal of Austrian Economics*, Spring, 2000, vol. 3, n°1, 27 -32.
Mises, Ludwig von (1940), *Nationalökonomie: Theorie des Handelns und Wirtschaftens*, Geneva, Switzerland: Editions Union.
Mises, Ludwig von (1942), 'Social Science and Natural Sciences', *Money, Method and the Market Process,* Norwell, USA; Dordrecht, Netherlands: Kluwer Academic Publishers (1990), 3-15.
Mises, Ludwig von (1944a), ' The Treatment of Irrationality in the Social Sciences' in Mises, Ludwig von (1990), *Money, Method and the Market Process*, Norwell, USA; Dordrecht, Netherlands: Kluwer Academic Publishers, 16-36.
Mises, Ludwig von (1944b), *Omnipotent Government: The Rise of the Total State and Total War*, New Haven, USA: Yale University Press.

Mises, Ludwig von (1946), *Bureaucracy*, New Haven, USA: Yale University Press.

Mises, Ludwig von (1947), *Planned Chaos*, Irvington-on-Hudson, USA: Foundation for Economic Education.

Mises, Ludwig von (1957), *Theory and History*, Auburn, USA: The Ludwig von Mises Institute.

Mises, Ludwig von (1962a), *The Ultimate Foundation of Economic Science*, Sheed Andrews and MacMeel.

Mises, Ludwig von (1962b), 'Epistemological Relativism in the Sciences of Human Action' in Mises, Ludwig von (1990) *Money, Method and the Market Process*, Norwell, USA; Dordrecht, Netherlands: Kluwer Academic Publishers (1990), 37-51.

Mises, Ludwig von (1962c), *Planning for Freedom, and Other Essays and Addresses*, South Holland, USA: Libertarian Press.

Mises, Ludwig von (1966) (third revised edition), *Human Action, a Treatise on Economics*, New Haven, USA: Yale University Press.

Mises, Ludwig von (1969), *The Historical Setting of the Austrian School of Economics*, New Rochelle, USA: Arlington House.

Mises, Ludwig von (1978a), *On the Manipulation of Money and Credit*, New York, USA: Free Market Books,

Mises, Ludwig von (1978b), *Notes and Recollections*, South Holland, USA: Libertarian Press.

Mises, Ludwig von (1990), *Money, Method and the Market Process,* Norwell, MA, USA; Dordrecht, Netherlands: Kluwer Academic Publishers.

Mises, Margit von (1984), *My Years with Ludwig von Mises*, Cedar Falls, USA: Center for Future Education.

Moss, Laurence S. (ed) (1976), *The Economics of Ludwig von Mises, Toward a Critical Appraisal*, Kansas City, USA: Sheed and Ward.

Myrdal, Gunnar (1953), *The Political Element in the Development of Economic Theory*, Cambridge, USA: Harvard University Press.

Nadeau, R (2001), 'Friedrich Hayek la théorie de l'esprit', in Commetti, Jean-Pierre and Kevin Mulligan (eds) (2001), *La philosophie autrichienne de Bolzano à Musil*, Histoire et actualité, Paris, France: Vrin, 209-227.

Nelson, Richard and Sidney G. Winter (1982), *An Evolutionary Theory of Economic Change*, Cambridge, USA: Belknap Press.

Nemo, Philippe (1988), *La société de droit selon F.A. Hayek*, Paris, France: Presses Universitaires de France, Libre-Echange.

Neurath, Otto (1919), *Durch die Kriegwirtschaft zur Naturalwirtschaft*, Munich: Callwey.

Nove, Alec and Dominico Mario Nuti (eds) (1972), *Socialist Economics*, London, UK: Penguin Books.

O'Brien, D.P. (1990), 'Lionel Robbins and the Austrian Connection (1990) in Caldwell, Bruce (ed) (1990), *Carl Menger and his Legacy in Economics*, Durham, USA and London, UK: Duke University Press, 155-184.

O'Driscoll, Gerald P. (1978), 'Spontaneous Order and the Coordination of Economics Activities' in Spadero, L.M. (ed.) (1978), *New Directions in Austrian Economics*, Kansas City, USA: Sheed Andrews, MacMeel, 111-142.

O'Driscoll, Gerald P. (1982), 'Monopoly in Theory and Practice' in Kirzner, Israel (ed) (1982), *Method, Process and Austrian Economics: Essays in Honor of Ludwig v. Mises*, Lexington, USA: Lexington Books.

O'Driscoll, Gerald P. and Mario Rizzo (1985), *The Economics of Time and Ignorance,* Oxford, UK; New York, USA: Basil Blackwell.

O'Driscoll, P. (1986), 'Money: Menger's Evolutionary Theory', *History of Political Economy*, 18:4, 601-617.

O'Driscoll, Gerald P. and Mario Rizzo (1990), 'Subjectivism, Uncertainty and Rules', in Littlechild, Stephen C. (ed) (1999), *Austrian Economics*, vol.1, Aldershot, UK and Brookfield, USA: Edward Elgar.

Paque, K-H (1990), 'Pattern Predictions in Economics: Hayek's Methodology of the Social Sciences Revisited', *History of Political Economy*, 22, n°2, 281-294.

Pareto, Vilfredo (1906), *Manual of Political Economy,* New York, USA: Augustus M. Kelley.

Penrose, Edith (1959), *The Theory of the Growth of the Firm*, Oxford, UK: Oxford University Press.

Pierson, Nicholas G. (1902), 'The Problem of Value in the Socialist Community', in Hayek, Friedrich August (ed) (1935c), *Collectivist Economic Planning*, London, UK: George Routledge and Sons, 41-85.

Polanyi, Michael (1951), *The Logic of Liberty*, London: Routledge and Kegan Paul, 1951; Chicago: University of Chicago Press.

Polanyi, Michael (1962), *Personal Knowledge: Towards a Post-Critical Philosophy*, Chicago, USA: University of Chicago Press.

Polanyi, Michael (1969), 'The Determinants of Social Action', *Roads to Freedom: Essays in honour of Friedrich A. von Hayek,* London, UK: Routledge and Kegan, 165-179.

Popper, Karl (1934), *The Logic of Scientific Discovery*, London, UK: Hutchinson.

Popper, Karl (1963), *Conjectures and Refutations*, London, UK: Routledge and Kegan.

Popper, Karl (1972), *Objective Knowledge*, Oxford, UK: Clarendon Press.

Prendergast, C. (1986), 'A. Schütz and the Austrian School of Economics', *American Journal of Sociology*, 92, 1-26.

Prendergast, Christopher (1993), 'Rationality, Optimality and Choice', *Rationality and Society*, 47-57.

Prychitko, D.L. (1987), 'Ludwig Lachmann and the Farther Reaches of Austrian Economics', *Critical Review*, Summer, 63-76.

Prychitko, D.L. (1993), 'Formalism in Austrian School Welfare Economics: Another Pretense of Knowledge?', *Critical Review*, Fall, 7 (4), 567-592.

Prychitko, David L. (2002), *Markets, Planning and Democracy*, Cheltenham, UK and Northampton: Edward Elgar.

Rawls, John (1971), *A Theory of Justice*, Oxford: Oxford University Press.

Richardson, G.B. (1972), 'The Organization of Industry', *The Economic Journal*, 82, 883-896.

Rizzello, Salvatore (2003), *Cognitive Developments in Economics*, London, UK; New York, USA: Routledge and Kegan.

Rizzo, Mario J. (1978), 'Praxeology and Econometrics: A Critique of Positivist Economics' in Spadero, Louis M. (ed.) (1978), *New Directions in Austrian Economics*, Kansas City, USA: Sheed Andrews, MacMeel.

Rizzo, Mario J. (ed) (1979), *Time, Uncertainty and Disequilibrium, Exploration of Austrian Themes*, Lexington, USA: Lexington Books, DC Heath and Company.

Robbins, John W. and Mark Spangler (eds) (1992), *A Man of Principle: Essays in Honor of Hans F. Sennholz*, Grove City, USA, Grove City College Press.

Robbins, Lionel (1932), *An Essay on the Nature and Significance of Economic Science*, London, UK: Macmillan.

Robbins, Lionel (1934), *The Great Depression*, London, UK: Macmillan.

Robbins, Lionel (1937), *Economic Planning and International Order*, London: Macmillan.

Rockwell, Llewellyn H. Jr. (ed.) (1986), *The Gold Standard: an Austrian Perspective*, Lexington, USA: Lexington Books.

Roemer, John E. (1993a), 'Can There Be Socialism after Communism?' in Bardhan Pranhab K. and John E. Roemer (eds) (1993), *Market Socialism*, New York, USA; Oxford, Oxford University Press.

Roemer, J.E. (1993b), 'A Pragmatic Theory of Responsibility for the Egalitarian Planner', *Philosophy and Public Affairs*, 22, 146-166.

Roper, Willet (1929), *The Problem of Pricing in a Socialist State*, Cambridge, USA, Harvard University Press.

Rosier, M. (1989), 'Critique épistémologique de la défense hayekienne du libéralisme' *Cahiers d'Economie politique*, 179-189.

Rosier, M. (2003), *On Smith's Bargaining Process: Learning by Talking*, working paper.

Rothbard, M. (1956), 'Toward a Reconstruction of Utility and Welfare Economics', in Sennholz, Mary (ed) (1956), *On Freedom and Free Enterprise, Essays in Honor of Ludwig von Mises*, Princeton, USA: D. Van Nostrand Company, 224- 262.

Rothbard, M. (1957), 'In Defense of Extreme A Priorism', *Southern Economic Journal*, January, 314-320.

Rothbard, Murray (1960), 'The Mantle of Science', in Rothbard, Murray, (1979), *Individualism and the Philosophy of Social Sciences*, San Francisco, USA: Cato Institute, 1-27.

Rothbard, Murray (1962), *Man, Economy and State: A Treatise on Economic Principles*, vols. 1 and 2, Princeton and New York, USA; Toronto, Canada; London, UK: D. Van Nostrand Company.

Rothbard, Murray (1973a), Praxeology as the Method of the Social Sciences, in *Individualism and the Philosophy of Social* Sciences, San Francisco, USA: Cato Institute, 1979, 29-61.

Rothbard, Murray (1973b), *For a New Liberty: The Libertarian Manifesto*, New York, USA: MacMillan.

Rothbard, Murray (1975), *America's Great Depression*, Kansas City, USA: Sheed and Ward.

Rothbard, Murray (1976a), 'Ludwig von Mises and Economic Calculation under Socialism', in Moss, Laurence S. (ed) (1976), *The Economics of Ludwig von Mises*, Kansas City, USA: Sheed and Ward, 67-77.

Rothbard, Murray (1976b), 'Praxeology, Value Judgements and Public Policy', in Dolan, Edwin (ed) *The Foundations of Modern Austrian Economics*, Kansas City, USA: Sheed and Ward, 89-111.

Rothbard, Murray (1981), 'The Laissez-Faire Radical: A Quest for the Historical Mises', *The Journal of Libertarian Studies*, vol. V, n°3, 237-253.

Rothbard, Murray (1982), *The Ethics of Liberty*, Atlantic Highlands, New Jersey, USA: Humanities Press.

Rothbard, Murray (1986), 'The Case of Genuine Gold Standard', Rockwell, Llewellyn H. Jr. (ed) (1988), *The Gold Standard: An Austrian Perspective*, Lexington, USA: Lexington Books, 1-17.

Rothbard, M. (1988), 'Rothbard, the Myth of Free Banking in Scotland', *The Review of Austrian Economics*, vol. 2, n°1, 229-246.

Rothbard, M. (1991), 'The End of Socialism and the Calculation Debate Revisited', *The Review of Austrian Economics*, 5 (2), 51-76.

Rothbard, M. (1992), 'Aurophobia: Or, Free Banking on What Standard?', *The Review of Austrian Economics*, vol. 6, n°1, 97-108.

Rothbard, M. (1995), 'The Present State of Austrian Economics', *Journal des Economistes et des études humaines,* 6 (1) March, 43-89.

Salerno, J. (1990a), 'Ludwig von Mises as Social Rationalist', *The Review of Austrian Economics*, 4, 26-54.

Salerno, J. (1990b), 'Why a Socialist Economy is Impossible', post-script to Ludwig von Mises, 'Economic Calculation in the Socialist Commonwealth', Auburn, AL, USA, Ludwig von Mises Institute, 51-71.

Salerno, J. (1991), 'Commentary: The Concept of Coordination in Austrian Economics' in Ebeling, Richard (ed) (1991), *Austrian Economics*, Hillsdale, USA: Hillsdale College Press, 325-343.

Salerno, J. (1993), 'Mises and Hayek Dehomogenized', *The Review of Austrian Economics*, vol. 6, n°2, p. 113-146.

Salerno, J. (1994a) 'Ludwig von Mises's Monetary Theory in Light of Modern Monetary Thought', *The Review of Austrian Economics*, vol. 8, n°1, 71-115.

Salerno, J. (1994b), 'Reply to Leland Yeager', *The Review of Austrian Economics*, 7, n°2, 111-125.

Salerno, J. (1996), 'A Final Word: Calculation, Knowledge and Appraisement', *The Review of Austrian Economics*, 9, n°1, 141-142.

Samuelson, Paul (1947), *Foundations of Economic Analysis*, Cambridge, USA: Harvard University Press.

Sautet, Frédéric (2000), *An Entrepreneurial Theory of the Firm*, London, UK; New York, USA: Routledge and Kegan.

Schmidt, C. and D. Versailles (1999), 'Une théorie hayekienne de la connaissance économique?' *Revue d'Economie Politique*, n°6, November-December, 817-833.

Schmitz, Stephan W. (2002), 'Carl Menger's 'Money' and the Current Neoclassical Models of Money', in Latzer, Michael and Stephan W. Schmitz, (eds) (2002), *Carl Menger and the Evolution of Payments Systems*, Cheltenham, UK and Northampton, USA: Edward Elgar, 111-132.

Schumpeter, Joseph (1912), *The Theory of Economic Development*, Edison, USA: Transaction Publishers

Schumpeter, Joseph (1942), *Capitalism, Socialism and Democracy*, London, UK: George Allen and Unwin Ltd.

Schumpeter, Joseph (1952), 'Carl Menger, 1840-1921', *Ten Great Economists: from Marx to Keynes*, New York, USA and Oxford, UK: Oxford University Press, 80-90.

Schumpeter, Joseph (1954), *History of Economic Analysis*, London: George Allen and Unwin Ltd.

Schütz, Alfred (1932), *The Phenomenology of the Social World*, Evanston, USA: Northwestern University Press, 1967.

Schütz, Alfred (1935), 'Political Economy: Human Conduct in Social Life', in Wagner, Helmut R., George Psathas and Fred Kersten (1996) (eds), *Alfred Schütz, Collected Papers*, vol. IV, 93-105, Dordrech, Netherlands: Kluwer Academic Publishers, 1996.

Schütz, Alfred (1953), 'Common-Sense and Scientific Interpretation of Human Action', in Schütz, Alfred (1962), *Collected Papers*, vol. 1, The Hague, Netherlands: Martinus Nijhoff.

Seager, H.R. (1893), 'Economics at Berlin and Vienna', *Journal of Political Economy*, vol. 1, March, 236-62.

Seigel, Barry (1984) (ed), *Money in Crisis*, San Francisco, USA: Pacific Institute for Public Policy Research.

Selgin, George A. (1982), *Praxeology and Understanding: An Analysis of the Controversy in Austrian Economics*, Auburn, USA: The Ludwig von Mises Institute.

Selgin, George A. (1988), *The Theory of Free Banking*, Totowa, USA: Rowman and Littlefield and the Cato Institute.

Selgin, G.A. and L.H. White (1996), 'In Defense of Fiduciary Media – or, We are Not Devolutionnists, We are Misesians', *The Review of Austrian Economics*, vol. 9, n°2, 83-107.

Sen, Armatya, K (1978), 'Ethical Measurement of Inequality: Some Difficulties', in *Choice, Welfare and Measurement*, Oxford: Basil Blackwell, 1982, 416-431.

Sen, Armatya, K (1985), *Commodities and Capabilities*, Amsterdam, North Holland; Elsevier.

Sennholz, Mary (ed) (1956), *On Freedom and Free Enterprise, Essays in Honor of Ludwig von Mises*, Princeton, USA: D. Van Nostrand Company.

Shackle, George L.S. (1949), *Expectation in Economics,* Cambridge, UK: Cambridge University Press.

Shackle, George L.S., (1955), *Uncertainty in Economics and Other Reflexions*, Cambridge, UK: Cambridge University Press.

Shackle, George L.S. (1958), *Time in Economics,* Amsterdam, The Netherlands: North-Holland Publishing Company.

Shackle, George L.S., (1961), *Decision, Order and Time in Human Affairs,* London, UK: Cambridge University Press.

Shackle, George L.S., (1972), *Epistemics and Economics*, London, UK: Cambridge University Press, 1972,

Shand, Alexander H. (1981), *Subjectivist Economics, the New Austrian School*, The Pica Press.

Shand, Alexander H. (1984), *The Capitalist Alternative, an Introduction to Neo-Austrian Economics*, Brighton, UK: Wheatsheaf.

Shearmur, Jeremy (1990), 'From Menger to Hayek: Biology, Subjectivism and Welfare', in *Carl Menger and his Legacy in Economics*, Durham, USA and London, UK: Duke University Press.

Shearmur, Jeremy (1996), *Hayek and After*, London, UK and New York, USA: Routledge.

Skousen, Mark (1990), *The Structure of Production*, New York, USA: New York University Press.

Skousen, Mark (1994), 'The Great Depression' in Boettke, Peter (ed), *The Elgar Companion to Austrian Economics*, Aldershot, UK and Brookfield USA: Edward Elgar, 431-439.

Smith, Barry (1986), 'Austrian Economics from Menger to Hayek', Grassl, Wolfgang and Barry Smith (eds) (1986), *Austrian Economics: Historical and Philosophical Background*, London, UK: Croom Helm, VII-X.

Smith, Barry (1990), 'Aristotle, Menger, Mises: An Essay in the Metaphysics of Economics' in Caldwell, Bruce (ed) (1990), *Carl Menger and his Legacy in Economics*, Durham, USA and London, UK: Duke University Press, 263-288.

Smith, Barry (1997), 'The Connectionnist Mind: A Study of Hayekian Psychology', in Frowen, Stephen F. (ed) (1997), *Hayek, Economist and Social Philosopher, a Critical Retrospect*, London, UK: MacMillan, 9-29.

Smithin, John (ed), *What is Money*? London, UK: Routledge and Kegan.

Soto, de J.H. (1995), 'A Critical Analysis of Central Banks and Fractional-Reserve Free-Banking from the Austrian Perspective', *The Review of Austrian Economics*, 8 (2), 25-38.

Soto, J.H. de (1996), 'New Light on the Prehistory of the Theory of Banking and the School of Salamanca' *The Review of Austrian Economics*, vol. 9, n°2, 59-81.

Soto, J.H. de (1998), 'A Critical Note on Fractional-Reserve Free Banking', *The Quarterly Journal of Austrian Economics*, vol. 1, n°4, 25-50.

Spadero, Louis M. (ed.) (1978), *New Directions in Austrian Economics*, Kansas City, USA: Sheed Andrews and McMeel.

Sraffa, P. (March, 1932), 'Doctor Hayek on Money and Capital', *Economic Journal*, vol. XLII, n°165, 42-53.

Sraffa, P. (June, 1932), 'Money and Capital: A Rejoinder', *Economic Journal*, vol. XII, n° 166, 249-251.

Steele, C.N. (1998), 'Entrepreneurship and the Economics of Growth', in Ikeda, Sanford and Peter Boettke (1998) (eds), *Advances in Austrian Economics*, Greenwich, USA and London, UK: JAI Press, 51-84.

Steele, D. R. (1987), 'Hayek's Theory of Cultural Group Selection', *Journal of Libertarian Studies*, 8, 2, 171-195.

Steele, David Ramsay (1992), *From Marx to Mises, Post Capitalist Society and The Challenge of Economic Calculation*, La Salle, USA: Open Court.

Steele, Gerry (2001), *Keynes and Hayek, the Money Economy*, London, UK and New York, USA: Routledge.

Stigler, G. (1937), 'The Economics of Carl Menger', *Journal of Political Economy*, April, 229-250.

Streissler, Erich (1973), 'To What Extent Was the Austrian School Marginalist?', in Black, R.D. Collison, Coats, Alfred W. and Craufurd, D.W. Goodwin (eds) (1973), *The Marginalist Revolution in Economics*, Durham, USA: Duke University Press, 160-175.

Sugden, Robert (1992), 'Austrian Prescriptive Economics', comment by Alan Hamlin, in Boehm, Stephen and Bruce Caldwell (eds) (1992), *Austrian Economics: Tensions and New Directions*, Boston, USA: Kluwer, 207-214.

Sutter, D. (2002), 'The Democratic Efficiency Debate and Definitions of Political Equilibrium', *The Review of Austrian Economics*, vol. 15, n°2/3, 199-209.

Sweezy, Paul (1949), *Socialism*, New York, USA: McGraw-Hill.

Tarde, Gabriel (1902), *Psychologie économique*, Paris, France: Felix Alcan.

Taylor, Fred (1929), 'The Guidance of Production in a Socialist State', in Lippincot, Benjamin E. (ed) (1938), *On the Economic Theory of Socialism*, New York, USA: McGraw-Hill, 41-54.

Thomsen, Esteban (1992), *Prices and Knowledge – A Market-Process Perspective*, London, UK and New York, USA: Routledge.

Tinbergen, J. (1935), 'Annual Survey: Suggestions on Quantitative Business Cycle Theory', *Econometrica*, January, vol. 3, 241-308.

Tuerck, D.G. (1995), 'Economics as Mechanism: The Mind as Machine in Hayek's Sensory Order', *Constitutional Political Economy*, 1995, 281-292.

Vanberg, V. (1986), 'Spontaneous Market Order and Social Rules: A Critical Examination of F.A. Hayek's Theory of Cultural Evolution', in *Economics and Philosophy*, 2, 75-100.

Vanberg, Victor (1994), *Rules and Choice in Economics*, London, UK: Routledge.

Varela, Francesco J., Evan Thomson and Eleanor Rosch (1991), *The Embodied Mind: Cognitive and Human Experience*, Cambridge, USA: The MIT Press.

Varela, F. J. and J. Shear (1999), 'The View from Within: First-Person Approaches to the Study of Consciousness', *Journal of Consciousness Studies*, 6 (2-3).

Vaughn, K. (1980a), 'Does It Matter that Costs are Subjective?', *Southern Economic Journal*, 46, 702-715.

Vaughn, K. (1980b), 'Economic Calculation under Socialism: The Austrian Contribution', *Economic Inquiry*, 18, 535-554.

Vaughn, K. (1992), 'The Problem of Order in Austrian Economics: Kirzner versus Lachmann', *Review of Political Economy* 4, 251-274.

Vaughn, Karen (1994), *Austrian Economics in America: The Migration of a Tradition*, New York, USA and Melbourne, Australia: Cambridge University Press.

Vaughn, K. (1999b), 'Hayek's Implicit Economics: Rules and the Problem Order', *The Review of Austrian Economics*, vol. 11, n°1-2, 129-144.

Veblen, Thorstein (1899), *The Theory of the Leisure Class*, London, UK: Penguin Classics.

Veblen, Thorstein (1919), *The Place of Science in Modern Civilization and Other Essays*, New York, USA: B.W. Huebsch.

Vromen, Jack, (1995), *Economic Evolution: An Enquiry into the Foundations of New Institutional Economics*, New York, USA and London, UK: Routledge.

Wagner, Helmut R., George Psathas and Fred Kersten (1996) (eds), *Alfred Schütz, Collected Papers*, vol. IV, Dordrech, Netherlands: Kluwer Academic Publishers.

Wainhouse, Charles (1984), 'Empirical Evidence for Hayek's Theory of Economic Fluctuations' in Seigel, Barry (1984) (ed) *Money in Crisis*, San Francisco, USA: Pacific Institute for Public Policy Research, 37-71.

Walras, Léon (1874-1877), *Eléments d'économie politique pure*, OEC, vol. VIII, Paris, France: Economica, 1988.

Walras, Léon (1883), *Théorie mathématique de la richesse sociale*, OEC, vol. IX, Paris, France: Economica, 1993.

Ward, Benjamin (1967), *The Socialist Economy: A Study of Organizational Alternatives*, New York, USA: Random House.

Weber, Max, *Economy and Society: An Outline of Interpretive Sociology*, (1921), New York, USA: Bedminster Press.

Weimer, Walter B. (1982), 'Hayek's Approach to the Problems of Complex Phenomena: An Introduction to the Theoretical Psychology of the Sensory Order', in Weimer, Walter B. and Palermo, David S. (eds) (1982), *Cognition and the Symbolic Processes*, vol. 2, Hillsdale, USA: Lawrence Erlbaum Associates Publishers, 241-285.

Weimer, Walter B. and Palermo, David S. (eds) (1982), *Cognition and the Symbolic Processes*, vol. 2, Hillsdale, USA: Lawrence Erlbaum Associates Publishers,

White, Larry (1976), 'Entrepreneurship, Imagination and the Question of Equilibrium', in Littlechild, Stephen (ed) (1990), *The Austrian Economics*, vol. III, Aldershot, UK and Brookfield, USA: Edward Elgar, 87-104.

White, Larry (1977), *The Methodology of the Austrian School of Economics*, Auburn, USA: The Ludwig von Mises Institute, Auburn University.

White, Larry (1984), *Free Banking in Britain: Theory, Experience and Debate, 1800-1845*, New York, USA: Cambridge University Press.

White, Larry (1989), *Competition and Currency: Essays on Free Banking and Money*, New York, USA: New York University Press.

White, Larry (1992), 'Mises on Free-Banking and Fractional Reserves', in Robbins, John W. and Mark Spangler (eds), *A Man of Principle: Essays in Honor of Hans F. Sennholz*, Grove City: Grove City College Press.

White, L. (1999), 'Hayek's Monetary Theory and Policy: A Critical Reconstruction', *Journal of Money, Credit and Banking*, vol. 31, n°1, 109-120.

Wicksell, Knut (1898), *Interest and Prices*, New York, USA: Augustus M. Kelley.

Wicksell, Knut (1901), *Lectures of Political Economy* (1 and 2), London, UK: Routledge and Kegan.

Wicksteed, Philip (1910), *The Common Sense of Political Economy*, London, UK: Routledge and Kegan.

Wiener, Norbert (1948a), *Cybernetics*, New York, USA: John Wiley.

Wiener, Norbert (1948b), 'Time, Communications and the Nervous System', in Frank, L.K. (ed) (1948), *Annals of the New York Academy of Sciences*, 50, 197-278.

Wieser, Friedrich von, (1889), *Natural Value*, New York, USA: Augustus M. Kelley.

Wieser, Friedrich von (1914), *Social Economics*, New York, USA: Augustus M. Kelley.

Wieser, F. von (1927) 'Geld', *Handworterbuch der Staats Wissenschaften*, 121-162.

Williamson, Oliver E. (1975), *Markets and Hierarchies*, New York, USA: Free Press.

Williamson, O.E. (1981), 'The Modern Corporation: Origins, Evolution, Attributes', *Journal of Economic Literature*, XIX, 1537-1568.

Williamson, Oliver E. (1985), *The Economic Institutions of Capitalism*, New York, USA: Free Press.

Wiseman, J. (1985), 'Lionel Robbins, the Austrian School and the LSE Tradition', *Research in the History of Economic Thought and Methodology*, 3, 147-159.

Witt, Ulrich (1992), 'Turning Austrian Economics into Evolutionary Theory' in Boehm, Stephen and Bruce Caldwell (eds) (1992), *Austrian Economics: Tensions and New Directions*, Boston, USA: Kluwer Academic Publishers, 215-236.

Witt, Ulrich (1995), 'Schumpeter versus Hayek: Two Approaches to Evolutionary Economics', in Meijer, Gerrit (ed) (1995), *New Perspectives on Austrian Economics*, London, UK; New York, USA: Routledge and Kegan, 81-101.

Witt, U. (1999), 'Do Entrepreneurs Need Firms? A Contribution to a Missing Chapter in Austrian Economics', *The Review of Austrian Economics*, vol. 11, n°1/2, 99-109.

Wubben, E. (1995), 'Austrian Economics and Uncertainty: on a Non-Deterministic but Non-Haphazard Future', in Meijer, Gerrit (ed) (1995), *New Perspectives on Austrian Economics,* London, UK; New York, USA: Routledge and Kegan, 106-145.

Yeager, Leland B. (1984), *Hayek on the Psychology of Socialism and Freedom*, The AEI Economist, November, 1-5.

Yeager, L.B. (1994a) 'Mises and Hayek on Calculation and Knowledge, *The Review of Austrian Economics*, 7, n°2, 93-109.

Yeager, L.B. (1994b) 'Salerno on "Calculation, Knowledge and Appraisement": A Rejoinder', *The Review of Austrian Economics*, 9, n°1, 137-139.

Yeager, Leland B. (2001), *Ethics as Social Science, The Moral Philosophy of Social Cooperation*, Cheltenham, UK and Northampton, USA: Edward Elgar.

Yu, T.F.-L (1999), 'Towards a Praxeological Theory of the Firm', *The Review of Austrian Economics*, vol. 12 (1), 25-41.

Yu, T.F.-L (March, 2001), 'Entrepreneurial Alertness and Discovery', *The Review of Austrian Economics*, 14:1, 47-63.

Ziegler, C.A. (1985), 'Innovation and the Imitative Entrepreneur', *Journal of Economic Behaviour and Organization*, 103-121.

Zywicki, T. (2000), 'Was Hayek Right About Group Selection After All? Review Essay of Unto Others: The Evolution and Psychology of Unselfish Behaviour by Elliot Solber and David Sloan Wilson', *The Review of Austrian Economics*, vol. 13 (1), 81-95.

Analytical Index

Index of Names

Identities

*Starred equations are valid only in Cartesian coordinates.

$$(1)\quad (\boldsymbol{A}\times\boldsymbol{B})\cdot\boldsymbol{C}=\boldsymbol{A}\cdot(\boldsymbol{B}\times\boldsymbol{C})$$

$$(2)\quad \boldsymbol{A}\times(\boldsymbol{B}\times\boldsymbol{C})=\boldsymbol{B}(\boldsymbol{A}\cdot\boldsymbol{C})-\boldsymbol{C}(\boldsymbol{A}\cdot\boldsymbol{B})$$

$$(3)\quad \boldsymbol{\nabla}(fg)=f\boldsymbol{\nabla}g+g\boldsymbol{\nabla}f$$

$$(4)\quad \boldsymbol{\nabla}(a/b)=(1/b)\boldsymbol{\nabla}a-\left(a/b^2\right)\boldsymbol{\nabla}b$$

$$(5)*\quad \boldsymbol{\nabla}(\boldsymbol{A}\cdot\boldsymbol{B})=(\boldsymbol{B}\cdot\boldsymbol{\nabla})\boldsymbol{A}+(\boldsymbol{A}\cdot\boldsymbol{\nabla})\boldsymbol{B}+\boldsymbol{B}\times(\boldsymbol{\nabla}\times\boldsymbol{A})+\boldsymbol{A}\times(\boldsymbol{\nabla}\times\boldsymbol{B})$$

$$(6)\quad \boldsymbol{\nabla}\cdot(f\boldsymbol{A})=(\boldsymbol{\nabla}f)\cdot\boldsymbol{A}+f(\boldsymbol{\nabla}\cdot\boldsymbol{A})$$

$$(7)\quad \boldsymbol{\nabla}\cdot(\boldsymbol{A}\times\boldsymbol{B})=\boldsymbol{B}\cdot(\boldsymbol{\nabla}\times\boldsymbol{A})-\boldsymbol{A}\cdot(\boldsymbol{\nabla}\times\boldsymbol{B})$$

$$(8)\quad (\boldsymbol{\nabla}\cdot\boldsymbol{\nabla})f=\boldsymbol{\nabla}^2f$$

$$(9)\quad \boldsymbol{\nabla}\times(\boldsymbol{\nabla}f)=\boldsymbol{0}$$

$$(10)\quad \boldsymbol{\nabla}\cdot(\boldsymbol{\nabla}\times\boldsymbol{A})=0$$

$$(11)\quad \boldsymbol{\nabla}\times(f\boldsymbol{A})=(\boldsymbol{\nabla}f)\times\boldsymbol{A}+f(\boldsymbol{\nabla}\times\boldsymbol{A})$$

$$(12)*\quad \boldsymbol{\nabla}\times(\boldsymbol{A}\times\boldsymbol{B})=(\boldsymbol{B}\cdot\boldsymbol{\nabla})\boldsymbol{A}-(\boldsymbol{A}\cdot\boldsymbol{\nabla})\boldsymbol{B}+(\boldsymbol{\nabla}\cdot\boldsymbol{B})\boldsymbol{A}-(\boldsymbol{\nabla}\cdot\boldsymbol{A})\boldsymbol{B}$$

$$(13)\quad \boldsymbol{\nabla}\times(\boldsymbol{\nabla}\times\boldsymbol{A})=\boldsymbol{\nabla}(\boldsymbol{\nabla}\cdot\boldsymbol{A})-\boldsymbol{\nabla}^2\boldsymbol{A}$$

The above equation defines the Laplacian of a vector in other than Cartesian coordinates.

$$\begin{aligned}(14)\quad (\boldsymbol{A}\cdot\boldsymbol{\nabla})\boldsymbol{B}=&\left(A_x\frac{\partial B_x}{\partial x}+A_y\frac{\partial B_x}{\partial y}+A_z\frac{\partial B_x}{\partial z}\right)\hat{\boldsymbol{x}}\\&+\left(A_x\frac{\partial B_y}{\partial x}+A_y\frac{\partial B_y}{\partial y}+A_z\frac{\partial B_y}{\partial z}\right)\hat{\boldsymbol{y}}\\&+\left(A_x\frac{\partial B_z}{\partial x}+A_y\frac{\partial B_z}{\partial y}+A_z\frac{\partial B_z}{\partial z}\right)\hat{\boldsymbol{z}}\end{aligned}$$

Theorems

The *divergence theorem*:

$$\int_{\mathcal{A}}\boldsymbol{A}\cdot\boldsymbol{d\mathcal{A}}=\int_v\boldsymbol{\nabla}\cdot\boldsymbol{A}\,dv\,,$$

where $\mathcal{A}$ is the area of the closed surface that bounds the volume v.

Stokes's theorem:

$$\oint_C\boldsymbol{A}\cdot\boldsymbol{dl}=\int_{\mathcal{A}}(\boldsymbol{\nabla}\times\boldsymbol{A})\cdot\boldsymbol{d\mathcal{A}}\,,$$

where $\mathcal{A}$ is the open surface bounded by the closed curve C.